BLAKE'S HAYLEY
The Life, Works, and Friendships of William Hayley

If the writer of this memorial could be disposed to delineate at full length all the personal and mental characteristics of Hayley, this would be the place to insert such a description: but he is rather inclined to leave so delicate a task to a future memorialist. . . .

He resigns the pen, therefore, in a pleasing persuasion, that the person who devoted so much of his time and labour to render all the justice in his power to the talents and the virtues of several among the most deserving of his contemporaries, will, in due time, find another honest chronicler who may be . . . qualified to estimate the extent of all his merits, and of all his defects; and to form, from a judicious contemplation of them, useful literary, and moral lessons for the amusement and instruction of such readers as peculiarly delight in the history of authors; a branch of literature perhaps inferior to none in its attractions, and also in its utility!

Memoirs of William Hayley (Book X, Cap. II), by William Hayley.

BLAKE'S HAYLEY

The Life, Works, and Friendships of William Hayley

by

MORCHARD BISHOP

Biography Index Reprint Series

BOOKS FOR LIBRARIES PRESS
FREEPORT, NEW YORK

Copyright 1951 by Morchard Bishop

Reprinted 1972 by arrangement.

Library of Congress Cataloging in Publication Data

Stonor, Oliver, 1903-
   Blake's Hayley; the life, works, and friendships
of William Hayley.

   (Biography index reprint series)
   Bibliography: p.
   1. Hayley, William, 1745-1820. 2. Blake, William,
1757-1827. I. Title.
[PR3506.H9S8 1972]   821'.6   72-5490
ISBN 0-8369-8133-2

PRINTED IN THE UNITED STATES OF AMERICA

TO
MARGARET PENN

TABLE OF DATES

(Dates before 1752 converted to New Style)

1724	Mrs. Unwin born	died	1796
1731	William Cowper born, November 26	,,	1800, April 25
1733	Lady Hesketh born	,,	1807
1734	Joseph Wright of Derby born	,,	1797
	George Romney born, December 26, married 1756	,,	1802, November 15
1735	Jeremiah Meyer born	,,	1789
1736	John Warner born	,,	1800
1737	Edward Gibbon born, May 8	,,	1794, January 16
1743	Frances Page born	,,	1807
1745	WILLIAM HAYLEY born, November 9, married Elizabeth Ball, October 23, 1769, separated 1789, left a widower 1797, married Mary Welford, March 28, 1809, separated 1812	,,	1820, November 12
1746	Mme. de Genlis born	,,	1830
1747	Anna Seward born	,,	1809
	Henrietta Poole born	,,	1827
1749	Charlotte Turner (Mrs. Charlotte Smith) born, married 1765	,,	1806
1750	Elizabeth Ball (Mrs. Hayley I) born	,,	1797, November 8
	John Sargent, the elder, born	,,	1831
1755	John Flaxman born, July 6, married 1782	,,	1826, December 7
1757	William Blake born, November 28, married 1782	,,	1827, August 12
1763	James Hurdis born	,,	1801
1767	Samuel Rose born	,,	1804
1769	John Johnson born	,,	1833
	Amelia Alderson (Mrs. Opie) born, married 1798, widowed 1807	,,	1853
1770	William Huskisson born	,,	1830
1772	Henry Francis Cary born	,,	1844
1777	Thomas Sockett born	,,	1859
1780	THOMAS ALPHONSO HAYLEY born, October 5	,,	1800, May 2
1781	Mary Welford (Mrs. Hayley II) born	,,	1848, September 19
1786	William Hersee born	,,	1854

PREFACE

WILLIAM HAYLEY DIED in 1820, and no full-length biography of him has been written. Fortunately, however, he wrote his autobiography, or *Memoirs*, as he called them, which were edited after his death by John Johnson, LL.D., Rector of Yaxham with Welborne, in Norfolk (better known as Cowper's "Johnny of Norfolk"), and published by Henry Colburn in 1823.

Since these two massive volumes are, with a few not very important exceptions (which are duly referred to in the *List of Sources* hereafter), the only substantial published record that we have of the events of Hayley's life, I have drawn upon them copiously, and would here like to make two observations upon them. The first is this: an autobiography is by no means necessarily the best source from which to obtain the true facts of a man's career; and I have consequently been at some pains to check, wherever I could, the record as it is given by Hayley himself, with such other independent sources of information as exist. I think it is only fair to add that in no case have I found his version of a given fact at variance with that of the independent record; and this has led me to believe him to be a reliable witness—with one very important proviso: namely, that he was a past-master in the art of suppression. And there, I am afraid, he now has the laugh of us. Where I have been able to fill from other sources the gaps caused by his suppressions, I have naturally done so; but where I have failed to find such other sources, I have had no alternative but to take his record, incomplete and partial as it may be, and make the best of it.

By far the most fruitful of these secondary sources are the *Letters of Anna Seward*, at one time his friend and admirer, though later in her life quite otherwise. Though her later comments are spiced with malice, I have, on the whole, found her also a fundamentally trustworthy witness on matters of fact.

The second thing I have to say about Hayley's *Memoirs* is this: they are, for the most part, written in an inflated and grotesque style which I, personally, have often found very amusing. When, therefore, it has seemed to me that I could best bring out Hayley's mind and character by using his own words, I have done so; and in some of these cases I have not used quotation marks. I have also provided no Notes to these passages, since the process would have been one laborious to reader and writer alike. The same proviso applies to Hayley's other writings, and especially to his biographies of Cowper and Romney; upon which I have drawn heavily.

In other cases, however, where material has come from what may be described as independent sources, I have duly annotated the source. Furthermore, where I have abbreviated quotations from original sources, I have indicated by dots . . . where passages have been omitted, and must take full responsibility for such omissions, which have been rendered necessary by considerations of space. Where, inside quoted material, I have interpolated any explanatory matter of my own, I have enclosed it within square brackets [ ].

Some explanation may also be needed for the fact that this book contains a considerable amount of Hayley's own verse, either in complete poems, or in excerpts. The reason for this is, that his poems are now extremely hard to come by, and I have therefore thought it desirable, since they throw a good deal of light both upon his character and his career, to incorporate some portions of them in my text. I hope that a few of them may be regarded as not without a certain merit of their own.

I have the following acknowledgements to make to those whose generous help and kindness have rendered my task far easier than it would otherwise have been: To the National Central Library, which procured for me every book I required for my investigations, and especially to Mr. E. J. Coombe, F.L.A., the Devon County Librarian, and his staff; also to Mr. H. K. Gordon Bearman, F.L.A., the County Librarian in Hayley's own city of Chichester. To the late Sir William Bird, the former owner of Eartham House, and his secretary, Miss Watt; to The Rt. Revd. Bishop D. A. Thompson and Mrs. Thompson, the present occupiers of Turret House, Felpham; and to Mr. Howell, the occupier of Blake's cottage, in the same village: all of whom most kindly let me look over their houses, though I arrived, in each case, without previous introduction. To Miss Jane Norton, the Gibbon authority, for a valuable piece of information about Edward Gibbon's Will; to Mr. F. H. A. Engleheart, for two rare plates for the illustrations; to Mr. Geoffrey Keynes, for suggesting to me the most appropriate portrait of Blake; to my friend, Charles Branchini, for sundry notes made in the Library of the Royal Institution; and to the authorities at the British Museum, the National Portrait Gallery, the Fitzwilliam Museum at Cambridge, and the Manchester City Art Gallery, all of whom gave me every possible assistance, and to the Director of the last of which, Mr. David Baxandall, I am particularly indebted, since it was he who introduced me to Mr. Kenneth Povey of Liverpool, who is in a class by himself, so far as Hayleian matters are concerned, in this country at any rate. I cannot say too much of the great kindness and good counsel which I received from him. He constantly saved me from falling into ignorance and error; and if there are still, as I fear there must be, ignorances and errors in this book, he is the very last man that can be held responsible for them. Both I, and this book, stand quite immeasurably in his debt.

My grateful thanks must also be given to the following publishers, editors and authors who kindly allowed me to use material from certain under-noted books or periodicals, that are more fully described in the *List of Sources*: Messrs. J. M. Dent & Sons Ltd. (Gilchrist's *Life of Blake*); Messrs. Hutchinson & Co. Ltd. and Messrs. A. P. Watt & Son (*The Farington Diary*); The Oxford University Press (*Horace Walpole's Letters*); The Editors of *The Cornhill Magazine*, and of *Notes & Queries*; Mr. Geoffrey Keynes (The Nonesuch *Blake*); Miss Jacobine Menzies-Wilson & Miss Helen Lloyd (*Amelia*); Mr. Wilfred Partington (*Scott's Letter-Books;* and *Scott's Post-Bag*); Mr. Kenneth Povey (articles in the *Sussex County Magazine*); and Miss Mona Wilson (*Life of William Blake*).

CONTENTS

CHAP.		PAGE
Preface		7

I. Introduction 17
   The Man—The Indictment—The Age of Sensibility.

II. Early Life (1745–1769) 24
   Ancestry—Thomas Hayley—Mary Hayley—Childhood—Eton—Fanny Page—Cambridge—Scottish Journey—Courtship and Marriage.

III. Life in London (1769–1774) 43
   First Assault on the Muses—"Retirement"; and the Death of Mary Hayley.

IV. Eartham (1774–1780) 51
   Eartham to-day—"A seat of social and poetical pleasure"—George Romney—The Bard of Sussex—Miss Betts.

V. Eliza: and Anna Seward (1780–1782) . . . 62
   The "pitiable Eliza"—Mrs. Hayley at Bath—1781: to Lichfield—Anna Seward—"The state of our exchequer . . ."—Miss Seward at Eartham.

VI. Friendships: and the Drama (1782–1785) . . . 78
   Flaxman—Gibbon—Sargent and Charlotte Smith—Guy, Sadleir and Joseph Warton—The Amanuensis—The Successful Playwright—The *Essay on Old Maids*.

VII. "The Calamitous Pressure of Connubial Infelicity" (1786–1787) 91
   "No *human friend* could relieve me . . ."—Thomas Alphonso—Hayley as Pedagogue—Hayley as Medical Man—Romney and Lady Hamilton—"Our Magical Opera."

CHAP.		PAGE
VIII.	SEPARATION: AND THE REFUSAL OF THE LAUREATESHIP (1786–1790)	104
	Dr. Warner—Gibbon once more—A History Reading—Eliza's Banishment—Anna Seward at forty-two—*The Young Widow*; and the Archbishop—"The most cheaply-supported pair of hermits in the country"—Drury Lane and Covent Garden—The Rejected Laurel.	
IX.	THE WORKS TO DATE (1778–1790)	121
	Mock-heroics and Didacticism—Hayley's Epitaphs—Dante and Ercilla—The Sportive Muse—The Plays—*The Triumphs of Temper*—The *Old Maids*—An Old Maid's Library.	
X.	THE PARIS VISIT: PRELUDE TO COWPER (1790–1792) .	136
	Paris; and the Governess—Huskisson—1791—The Letter to Cowper.	
XI.	WILLAM THE FIRST AND WILLAM THE SECOND (1792) .	146
	Cowper in 1792—"The red-breast of Eartham and the sky-lark of Weston"—The first visit to Weston Underwood—The Electrical Machine; and The Pension—"A delightful and innocent project"—Lord Thurlow—Preparations for a Journey—Cowper at Eartham—The Return.	
XII.	THE PENSION (1792–1794)	168
	Mr. Huskisson's Machinations—The Year 1793—Second visit to Weston—"Mr. Hayley presents his respects to Mr. Pitt . . ."—The Prince Regent's Librarian—"A Hermit deceived by a Prime Minister."	
XIII.	INTERIM: THE GIBBON PAPERS (1793–1794) . .	182
	The Death of Gibbon—"A period of complicated calamity"—Mrs. Hayley returns to the Metropolis—The Gibbon Papers.	
XIV.	THE YOUNG SCULPTOR (1794–1797) . . .	191
	Tom's Apprenticeship—More Poems—The Final Breach with Eliza—Tom in London—The Spring of 1796—Tom's first Illness—Mr. Udney's Pictures; and the Revd. John Romney—Architectural and Benevolent—"You live upon your feelings"—The start of the Marine Turret—"My infinitely dear Invalid . . ."	

CHAP.		PAGE
XV.	THE HEAVENLY VISION (1797–1798) . . .	217
	The Plot—The Response—"A single Letter such as I used to receive. . . ."	
XVI.	THE END OF TOM (1797–1800)	226
	The two sick artists—The Death of Eliza—Tom at Felpham—The Muse of Todgers's—The Afflicted Mrs. Lushington—The Wayward Parent—"The interesting cripple"—London again—The Winter of 1799—The Deaths of Cowper and Tom—Thomas Alphonso Hayley.	
XVII.	THE BIOGRAPHER: AND WILLIAM BLAKE (1800)	250
	Bereavement and Biography—The End of Eartham—Felpham, and The Turret—William Hayley and William Blake—"Away to Sweet Felpham, for Heaven is there."	
XVIII.	BLAKE AT FELPHAM (1800–1802)	264
	The first Winter—The Trials of a Biographer—"Time flies faster than in London"—The second Winter: Harriet Poole—"In all He does . . . a penetrating eye will discover true Genius"—"The Visions were angry with me at Felpham."	
XIX.	SUCCESS (1802–1804)	284
	The *Life of Cowper*—Tom's Monument: Edward, the Bard of Oxford—Private Schofield's Complaint—The Acquittal of William Blake—Alone in the Turret—The Correspondence with Blake—"Can I be angry with Felpham's old mill?"	
XX.	THE SOLITARY HERMIT (1804–1809) . . .	311
	Years of decline—Second Thoughts on Matrimony—William Hersee—Second Marriage—Hersee continued.	
XXI.	WILLIAM AND MARIA OF THE TURRET (1809–1817) .	323
	"As happy for a . . . time as any mortals could expect to be"—After the second Separation—Mrs. Amelia Opie—"Johnny of Norfolk"—Hersee concluded.	
XXII.	"THE LAND UNKNOWN" (1817–1820) . . .	343
	Claudite jam rivos—The End.	

CHAP.		PAGE
XXIII. THE AFTER-RECORD	. . . . . .	348

The Memoirs and their Reception—John Romney's Opportunity—The Emptied Stage—Gilchrist, Swinburne and their Successors.

LIST OF THE PRINCIPAL SOURCES 357

NOTES 361

INDEX 365

ILLUSTRATIONS
(*Between pp. 160–161*)

WILLIAM HAYLEY.
> From a mezzotint (1779) by Johann Jacobé, after a painting by George Romney. (*British Museum photograph.*)

GEORGE ROMNEY, 1782.
> From an unfinished self-portrait. *By permission of the Trustees of the National Portrait Gallery.*

EDWARD GIBBON AT LAUSANNE.
> From a painting by J.-L. Piot. *By courtesy of the Musée des Beaux-Arts, Lausanne.*

LADY HAMILTON AS SENSIBILITY, 1786.
> From an engraving by Richard Earlom, after a painting by George Romney. (*British Museum photograph.*)

ANNA SEWARD, 1786.
> From a painting by George Romney. *By courtesy of the Knoedler Galleries. Formerly in a private collection, New York.*

JEREMIAH MEYER, R.A.
> From a photograph by Linda Moller, B.A., A.R.P.S., of his monument, after a design by George Dance, in Kew Church, Surrey.

WILLIAM COWPER, 1792.
> From a pastel by George Romney, painted at Eartham. *By permission of the Trustees of the National Portrait Gallery.*

JOHN FLAXMAN MODELLING THE BUST OF HAYLEY, 1795.
> From a painting by George Romney. *By courtesy of the Rt. Hon. the Countess of Lichfield, daughter of the late Henry Dawson-Greene, in whose family the picture has been for many years.* (*Photograph by permission of Messrs. Christie, Manson and Woods.*)

THOMAS ALPHONSO HAYLEY AS ROBIN GOODFELLOW, 1791.
> From a painting by George Romney. *By permission of the Trustees of the National Gallery, London.*

EARTHAM.
> From an engraving after Stebbing Shaw in *The Topographer*, Vol. 4, No. 25 (April, 1791) at page 232. (*British Museum photograph.*)

THE TURRET, FELPHAM.
> From a pencil drawing (*c.* 1810) by George Engleheart. *By courtesy of F. H. A. Engleheart, Esq.*

WILLIAM HAYLEY, THOMAS HAYLEY AND WILLIAM MEYER, 1796.
> From an engraving by Caroline Watson, after a painting by George Romney, reproduced as frontispiece to Vol. II of the *Memoirs of William Hayley*. (*British Museum photograph.*)

THOMAS ALPHONSO HAYLEY.
> From a tempera painting done by William Blake for the Library of The Turret, Felpham. *By permission of the Trustees of the Manchester City Art Gallery.*

WILLIAM BLAKE.
> From a pencil drawing (*c.* 1803) by John Flaxman, R.A. *By courtesy of His Grace the Duke of Hamilton.* (*Oxford University Press electrotype.*)

BLAKE'S COTTAGE AND GARDEN AT FELPHAM.
> From *Milton*, Plate 36. (*British Museum photograph.*)

THE HORSE.
> From Hayley's *Ballads*, 1805, from an original engraving by William Blake. (*British Museum photograph.*)

THE DOG.
> Frontispiece to Hayley's *Ballads*, 1805, from an original engraving by William Blake. (*British Museum photograph.*)

AMELIA OPIE, 1807.
> From a painting by her husband, John Opie, R.A. *By permission of the Trustees of the National Portrait Gallery.*

WILLIAM HAYLEY IN LATER LIFE.
> From a drawing (*c.* 1810) by George Engleheart. *By courtesy of F. H. A. Engleheart, Esq.*

HAYLEY'S "MARINE VILLA" AT FELPHAM, NOW TURRET HOUSE.

BLAKE'S COTTAGE AT FELPHAM.

EARTHAM HOUSE, AS REMODELLED BY SIR EDWIN LUTYENS AND OTHERS.
> From photographs by the Author, 1949.

CHAPTER I

INTRODUCTION

I

SAFE BENEATH THEIR marble tablets, lapped in stifling folds of mortuary verse, the minor poets of the eighteenth century lie complacently awaiting the Last Trumpet. Nothing less will wake them now. As the dust gathers more thickly upon such copies as remain of their once eagerly demanded works, the shades of Messrs. Glover and Mason, of Jephson and Darwin and Pye, of even such more respected practitioners as Akenside and Young, may well console themselves with the thought that they had their day, and that it was not one of insignificant proportions. Indeed, by the standards of our time, it was not—such a work, for example, as the *Night Thoughts* commencing its run under the eyes of Pope and Johnson, and continuing it merrily until at least as late as 1857, when George Eliot, training upon it the impressive batteries of her intellect, proclaimed·it: "a Juggernaut made of gold and jewels, at once magnificent and repulsive".

Among this shadowy host there is one who, as to his works, seems even less substantial than the rest; whose poems are virtually unprocurable, of whose entire output but one line remains enshrined in the most inclusive dictionary of quotations. And this poet, who, had he wished it, might have been the Laureate, this poet whose most popular work ran, during his lifetime, into some fourteen editions, has suffered a fate much more peculiar, certainly much less endurable, than that of his colleagues whose deeds are now permitted to moulder in a decent obscurity. For he is far from dead; for, in fact, he lives, uncomfortably yet abundantly, in the references, almost universally disparaging, of other men, his contemporaries, and his superiors. His name is one that is for ever cropping up in the reading of anybody who takes the slightest interest in the period in which he flourished; and, though hardly anyone living, we hazard, can cite a line of his verse, or profess the least knowledge of his numerous poems, almost everyone is familiar with his name, and has a general impression of him as a ludicrous and futile personage. In short, there is no end of life in him, poor Felpham Billy, the Bard of Sussex, the Hermit of Eartham: that William Hayley who was once the friend of Gibbon and of Flaxman, the friend and biographer of Cowper and of Romney, and, above all, the friend, or the enemy, and the erstwhile patron, of that devastating man of genius, William Blake.

So, whether we like it or not, it is apparent that William Hayley is a figure not to be dislodged from English literature so long as that literature lasts; and, as this is so, it seems as well to try to get him into true perspective. The thing has never been done. In 1823, his *Memoirs* were posthumously published, a couple of vast volumes, so foolish, so formidable that no one has had the courage or inclination since then to unearth the man that lies beneath them. It is a pity, for, as I hope to show, Hayley was a remarkable creature, with any number of good qualities, of heart if not of intellect; and he lived a long and various life, which it is highly entertaining to contemplate. Furthermore, in two instances at least, he performed services to English literature for which we should do well to be grateful, since they are of a value beyond calculation. First, it was he who, in his *Life of Cowper* (1803), collected together for the first time the inimitable letters of that poet; second, it was he who was responsible for the conveyance of William Blake to Felpham for his "three years' slumber on the banks of the Ocean". Either of these activities alone would entitle Hayley to a place in our regard. Taken together, they render him a figure worthy of more intensive investigation than he has yet received. Such an investigation the present writer has endeavoured to carry out: with results that he hopes may be found instructive.

2

It will be as well, in order to clear the air, to approach the figure of Hayley by way of those references to him that are most likely to strike the eye of the casual reader. Most people come to him to begin with, as I did, by way of the epigrams which Blake wrote about him; and though these, which are extremely uncomplimentary, are well known, it is, for this very reason, best to start with them. The commentary shall come later. Here they are:

Of Hayley's Birth
Of Hayley's birth this was the happy lot:
His mother on his father him begot.

On Hayley
To forgive enemies Hayley does pretend,
Who never in his life forgave a friend,
And when he could not act upon my wife
Hired a villain to bereave my life.

To Hayley
Thy friendship oft has made my heart to ache:
Do be my enemy—for friendship's sake.

On Hayley's Friendship

When Hayley finds out what you cannot do,
That is the very thing he'll set you to;
If you break not your neck, 'tis not his fault;
But pecks of poison are not pecks of salt.

On Hayley the Pickthank

I write the rascal thanks, till he and I
With thanks and compliments are quite drawn dry.

There is more, but that is enough to be going on with; and, on the face of it, it is a damning indictment. Moreover, one has only to dig a little deeper to find, in the *English Bards and Scotch Reviewers* of 1808, some further well-known lines in which the scornful spirit of Lord Byron administers what appears to be the *coup de grâce*:

Behold!—ye tarts! one moment spare the text,
Hayley's last work, and worst—until his next;
Whether he spin poor couplets into plays,
Or damn the dead with purgatorial praise,
His style in youth or age is still the same,
For ever feeble and for ever tame.
Triumphant first see *Temper's Triumphs* shine!
At least I'm sure they triumph'd over mine.
Of *Music's Triumphs*, all who read may swear
That luckless music never triumph'd there.

It is but too easy to swell the chorus of ridicule. Gilchrist in his *Life of Blake*, Swinburne in his critical essay on the same, almost every writer up to the present time who has thought it necessary to mention Hayley's name, have taken their cue from the foregoing references; and the picture given is one of a fussy, pompous, pretentious, moneyed little dilettante. And indeed, so far as Hayley the poet is concerned, it is idle to deny that his cause is a lost one. Later on, when we come to discuss his works, it will have to be conceded straightway that, with the exception of an occasional epitaph or scrap of verse, the enormous total output of the Bard of Sussex is of little value. The interesting question is, however, whether Hayley as a man was as valueless as his work; and in this connection a curious doubt arises. I think the best way in which I can explain what it is, is to describe the fashion in which the problem presented itself to me. Familiar as I was with the foregoing observations of Blake and Byron, I came across, some years since, a copy of that very engaging work, Hayley's *Life of Cowper*, from the reading of which I derived two impressions. The first was that Hayley had been, at least, a gentleman and a scholar; the second, that Cowper had valued his friendship very highly. It was, I confess, this last revelation which pulled me up, since Cowper was a man not greatly given to expending his affection upon fools and triflers. I went deeper, and found that, in the same way, Gibbon, Romney, Flaxman and a number of other persons only less eminent, had also had a great regard for Hayley; and the wonder grew. Was it possible, I reflected, that perhaps after all the last word on him had not been said by Byron and Blake? I investigated the circumstances in which the epigrams of the latter had been written, and a light began to break. I inspected the correspondence of Gibbon, and the light broadened. Finally I came across, in a letter written by Southey to Coleridge in 1802, a remark which seemed to me to sum up admirably the suspicions I was beginning to entertain. Coleridge, in his usual lavish style, had been proposing that he should edit a critical edition of the living poets, and Southey was endeavouring to dissuade him from doing so, because of the invidious nature of the transaction. Consider such a writer as Hayley, he said, in effect; how can you hurt his feelings by saying what you really think of his works? "Everything," wrote Southey[1]*—and this was the sentence that seemed to provide the key I was looking for—"everything about that man is good except his poetry."

A dire summing-up, no doubt, for a man who aspired to the name of poet; but there was something in it that chimed with the way in which I was beginning to see Hayley. I still think, now that I have travelled a good deal further in his company, that it is the fairest verdict ever passed upon him.

3

In September 1826, Lady Louisa Stuart wrote a letter to Sir Walter Scott[2] which raises the very interesting question of "the alterations of Taste produced by time". She told Scott how, on a book being required to read aloud from, the company chose *The Man of Feeling*, by Henry Mackenzie, "though some apprehended it would prove too affecting". The reading began; Lady Louisa had not seen the book for several years; her company had never seen it before. "I am afraid," she wrote, "I perceived a sad change in it, or myself. . . . Nobody cried, and at some of the passages, the touches that I used to think so exquisite—Oh Dear! They laughed. . . . Yet," she continued, "I remember so well its first publication [in 1771], my mother and sisters crying over it, dwelling upon it with rapture! And when I read it, as I was a girl of fourteen not yet versed in sentiment, *I had a secret dread I should not cry enough to gain the credit of proper sensibility.*"

How revealing is the passage which I have italicized, to anyone at all familiar with the mood of polite society during the last quarter of the eighteenth century! And how revealing too, since Mackenzie's

*For numbered references throughout, see pp. 361–3.

book first appeared when William Hayley had attained the impressionable age of twenty-six, is it to the comprehension of the character with which we are here concerned. In an age of sensibility that may be said to have originated with Rousseau and his *Nouvelle Héloïse*, Hayley, to the very end of his long life, was always filled with a secret dread that he should *not cry enough*. It is, indeed, the keynote of his character and his work; and it is the reason why his work is forgotten, and why his character, obscured as it is beneath excessive layers of frantic feeling, bears to us, to-day, an appearance of extreme insincerity. That both were rather less insincere than they seem, it is my purpose to demonstrate; and, in order to do this, it is necessary to examine in some small detail the extraordinary convention within which he elected to pass his life.

The cult of sensibility, as I have said, derived from Rousseau, than whom no greater blackguard, one supposes, ever influenced the history of thought. Times have changed amazingly since that evening in April 1798 when William Hazlitt was able to devour the *New Eloise* at the inn at Llangollen, together with "a bottle of sherry and a cold chicken". This book, together with the *Sorrows of Werter*, and *Ossian*, and a good deal else which, at the time, was eagerly wept over, is now so unreadable as to render it almost inexplicable that it should ever have been read. Yet it was, and widely too; and no one who thinks of the eighteenth century exclusively in terms of that rational Tory, Dr. Johnson, will ever even begin to understand what it must have felt like to be a Whig and a democrat and an apostle of sensibility in the years which preceded the outbreak of the French Revolution. For the younger men, for Southey and Wordsworth and Coleridge, that outbreak was an awakening indeed; but for the older ones, of whom Hayley is an example, the habit of a lifetime had grown too strong and even the Revolution itself failed to provide a shock sufficiently great: they went to their graves unconverted, exponents to the last of that same doctrine which had caused Maximilien Robespierre to keep beneath his pillow, throughout the raging of the Terror, that affecting compendium of Gothic feeling, the *Night Thoughts* of Dr. Young.

There is no understanding Hayley without an equal comprehension of this over-riding influence, which, together with its belief in the virtue of feeling for its own sake, came out also extremely strong in favour of liberty, fraternity, romantic scenery, and, generally speaking, the whole range of the more Spartan virtues; of which by no means the least was the concept that the wise man was he who early retired from the corruption of Courts, to enjoy the peaceful pleasures of a cultivated, unambitious rural existence. Though, as will I hope be shown, Hayley was possessed of at least some of the admirable qualities of his contemporary, James Boswell, there can hardly be a greater contrast than between his career and that of

Boswell's idol, of whom Hayley could never be persuaded, I am sorry to say, to speak without disparagement; and who had his revenge by scarcely ever speaking of Hayley at all.

It is necessary to stress this, since, because of Boswell's genius, there is, I think, a tendency for the latter half of the eighteenth century to take upon itself the colours of existence which are revealed in his wonderful book. Here the other side of the picture is displayed; a side which, oddly enough, was to be familiar to one, at least, of the Johnson circle, after her fall from grace—I mean the charming if rather light-headed Mrs. Piozzi. For the Della Cruscan absurdities into which she fell in her later years, it is fair to say that the foundations had been laid by Hayley and his friends, Anna Seward and Dr. Darwin. It is idle to pretend that the activities of these people had merits which have lasted on to our own time; yet it is also true that their activities, however oddly they may strike us now, have in them still a great deal that is capable both of amusing and instructing us. Cowper's strain of evangelicalism saved him from their excesses; and so did Coleridge's genius. But the tradition was carried on, in a slightly different form, by Southey and by Moore; and, though it was a bad tradition, it is not an uninteresting one, since all movements of the human mind, however alien, must have their interest for the student of human behaviour. What is, moreover, extremely piquant is the fact that we should be in a position to see, so fully documented, the effect of this particular aberration upon the mind of a natural genius such as Blake.

Hayley, when all is said, will remain most important because of his connection with the fiery little engraver whom the strangest trick of fate caused him to patronize for more than three years; but this is not quite the same thing as saying that he is not also, in his own right, a figure. He spanned with amiable loquacity the immeasurable intellectual gulf which lies between Gibbon and Mrs. Opie; he knew and helped and was respected by a great many people whom the world still chooses to honour; unlike Charles II, he almost always said the foolish thing, and almost always did the kindly one; he is, in the last analysis, a man whom it is nearly impossible to dislike, and one whom it is not intolerably difficult to respect. The circle returns on itself, and we come back to the words we have quoted from Southey: "Everything about the man was good—except his poetry."

It is not a bad epitaph. For Hayley, for all his superficial pomposity, was that rarest of literary phenomena, a modest man; he knew and, in the end, accepted his limitations; he recognized his superiors when he met them, and he was quite singularly free from both jealousy and envy. He spent his days, often ridiculously, it is true, in trying to help his fellow-men and his fellow-artists. He was a man who revered and endeavoured to foster the arts; and, though it was his misfortune that he should seem always to do so in a manner more than a little bizarre, he was also a man truly acquainted with sorrow. With a genius for friendship, almost all his friends predeceased him: he wrote their epitaphs; then he wrote biographies of the more notable of them. He passed a great part of his life endeavouring to serve others; and it is high time that, for all the occasional incoherence of his proceedings, it were realized that there is a good deal more to be said for him than is contained in the lethal epigrams of William Blake.

It is now my task to say this, always remembering that the figure I am trying to resuscitate is not that of William Hayley, the discredited poet, but that of William Hayley, the friend and, according to his own often peculiar lights, the patron of genius. Even more, perhaps, it is William Hayley, the character, the eccentric, the cultivated eighteenth century Whig country gentleman; the Man of Feeling made perfect.

CHAPTER II

EARLY LIFE (1745-1769)

I

NOT MUCH IS KNOWN about the ancestors of William Hayley, and what is can soon be told.

Hayley's cousin claimed that the family originally came from Ireland, in which case it is likely that they were, in their beginnings, members of the still numerous tribe of the Healeys. It is, however, safer not to look back quite so far, but, fortified by the knowledge that, both in Gloucestershire and Herefordshire, Hayley exists as a place-name, to assume for the family a West Midlands origin, and to start the story with that William Hayley of Bridgnorth in Shropshire who, about the year 1660, married Catherine Bach of Cleobury Mortimer, in the same county, and later went to live in his wife's native town.[1]

This William Hayley has two claims to distinction: he had many children, and he was able to number among them two single and separate Deans, both of Chichester, in the persons of William, his eldest son, and Thomas, his youngest. It is with Dean William that the family first appears to rise to eminence, since it was he who procured for them a patent of arms, which, for those who are interested in such matters, may be thus described: *Or*, on a cross *Azure*, a cinquefoil between four pierced (or voided) lozenges *Or*. To this impressive display must be added a crest: On a Crescent *Argent*, a cross patée *Gules*, and a motto: *Cruce Coelum*; and these last items are interesting because they have direct relation to the early career of Dean William, who started his clerical life as domestic chaplain to Sir William Trumbal, the British Ambassador in Constantinople. The silver crescent of the crest is a pleasing allusion to he whom William Hayley, the poet, in one of his "sportive" letters to Cowper, calls "my Turkish namesake Hali, the son-in-law of Mahomet";[2] and the bloody cross, and the motto accompanying it, are no doubt symbolical of the Christianization of this infidel emblem by the activities in Constantinople of the future Dean.

This William Hayley, who became Dean of Chichester before the end of the seventeenth century, was the great-uncle of the poet, who was named after him.

As for Dean Thomas, the youngest brother and successor of Dean William, and the grandfather of Poet William, a handsome monumental slab in the cathedral of Chichester tells us all we need to know of him. He died in August 1739, aged fifty-nine; and he married Sarah, the daughter of Thomas Harlowe of Bromley in Middlesex (sic), who predeceased him. It was this Dean (I regret the plurality of Deans which renders clarity difficult), it was this Dean who was the father of Thomas Hayley, who, in his turn, was the father of our William Hayley.

Thomas Hayley, the son of Dean Thomas, was twice married, and another handsome tablet in Chichester Cathedral tells you what happened to his first wife, Penelope Baker, who died June 15, 1740, in the twenty-fourth year of her age. This lady was the heiress to a considerable property, and thus the Hayley monopoly of the Deanery was broken, and her young widower was able to settle down as a gentleman of no occupation. In this capacity he wooed and won the hand of Mary Yates, the daughter of Colonel Thomas Yates, the Member for Chichester, whom he married in the same year as he lost his first wife. His first marriage had been without issue; but by his second wife he had two sons, Thomas, born in 1743, and William, the subject of this book, who was born at Chichester on November 9, 1745 (N.S.), and was christened at All Saints Church[1] on November 25 (Old Style, no doubt) of the same year.

2

It is at this point necessary to pause a moment to examine what is known about William Hayley's parents, more particularly his mother, since her influence upon his life was considerable. That of his father was much less, as he died when the boy was only three. We will deal with him first.

Thomas Hayley, who had been brought up in the fine red-brick Georgian Deanery of Chichester, which still confronts the inquisitive traveller who passes out of the cathedral cloisters into St. Richard's Walk, had been from the first a young man of considerable expectations. He had been educated at Exeter College, Oxford, and, his parents being affluent, he had settled down early to a life of ease and leisure. I can think of no more fitting symbol of that ease and that leisure than is presented to us by the spectacle of the Deanery in which, built as it was in 1725, he must have passed his later boyhood and adolescence. There behind its wrought-iron gates it stands, square, substantial and assured, with its front door, set in rusticated stone dressings and poised upon four broad stone steps, looking straight down the vista that is closed abruptly by the sky-piercing spire of the cathedral. The great gates stand open, flanked by mellow brick piers that are surmounted by vast balls of stone; and about the whole place is an air of dignity, repose, and absolute security. And, as if this were not sufficient, Thomas Hayley must needs incontinently marry more money in the person of the daughter of an opulent merchant who, as we know, had as incontinently died. Small wonder then that Thomas Hayley, soon after his second marriage, a transaction in which we are told he was "sufficiently affluent to disregard the article of fortune", should be discovered spreading his wings. Living at the time of this marriage in a house in that wonderful quarter of Georgian residences which still stands almost unaltered in Chichester and is known as The Pallant, we consequently find him, in the year 1743, negotiating the purchase of a small estate at Eartham, "a sequestered spot, peculiarly embellished by nature", and some eight miles north-east of Chichester, just off the Petworth road. The previous owner of this estate had been a certain "fantastic mortal" by the name of Sir Robert Fagg, who had been Member for the Borough of Steyning; but though Sir Robert may have been "fantastic" perhaps his heirs were less so, since they sold to Mr. Hayley, along with the estate, only the ruins of a mansion, so that the first thing the new owner was obliged to do was to erect, on a higher spot of ground, "a diminutive villa, a kind of summer house", to which from time to time he despatched his little family, so that they might benefit by the "finer air".

I have put this enterprise first in the works and deeds of Thomas Hayley, since, as future events will show, it was much the most important thing he did. For the rest, what manner of man was he? A matter not without importance, since I think we may trace in his son certain peculiarities which beyond a peradventure spring from the father's side. He was "cheerful and active, benevolent and generous . . . enough of a musician to compose a country dance, and enough of a poet to translate a sportive ode of Horace into spirited English verse". He had a passion for sculpture, painting, and architecture, and was "inclined to amuse himself with Turkish ideas"—a trait evidently derived from his uncle, the Dean who had been to Constantinople—so much so, in fact, that he had, on one occasion, had his portrait painted wearing a turban. More than this, at his death he left unfinished an additional apartment of his house (the one at Chichester, I think), and so singular was the construction of this room that no one could imagine its purpose. At length his son hit upon it: it was intended as a "diminutive representation" of the great mosque of St. Sophia!

Obviously, a man who could conceive such a notion while dwelling in the chastest of Georgian surroundings was no common man; was one perhaps even a little liable to run into excess. And so indeed it turned out, for, one of the periodic military scares being then afoot, poor Thomas Hayley, all too aware of his patriotic duty, rushed forward at once to raise a company of volunteers, who were known as the Chichester Blues. So great was his zeal that he was sent a letter of thanks from the Duke of Newcastle, as well as the offer of a baronetcy. The latter he declined, which perhaps was as well, for, "in supporting the military character", he was speedily led into habits of what his son calls, tolerantly, "convivial intemperance". What made matters worse was his unfortunate custom of terminating a night of revelry by flinging himself into a cold bath, instead of going to bed. His wife remonstrated with him over this practice; and well she might, for it ended by his falling into a consumption. He went in search of health to the Bristol Hot Wells, and there, instead of getting better, he got worse and died in a few weeks. He was buried in a vault near the centre of the churchyard at Eartham, and a monument in that church attests, in Latin, his virtues:

> Vir liberalis admodum, et benevolus.

All the rest of the epitaph, which is a long one, written by his son, deals with the superior virtues of his wife.

His death occurred in 1748, when William was still in petticoats. Poor Thomas Hayley: Southey[3] has provided for him a sour valediction. "He had (says he) the misfortune to have been born rich. Had it been necessary for him to follow some profession, he had abilities which might have raised him to distinction. . . . In the enjoyment of hereditary wealth his talents were dissipated." Just as if he were the first man whom martial conviviality has caused to drink too much, and drinking fall into a decline! I think a better epitaph for Thomas Hayley is to say that he was an odd fellow, and to add that a great deal of his oddity came to its full and perfect flower in that uncommonly odd fellow who was his son and heir.

3

With Mary Hayley we shall not finish so easily. She, obviously, was a being of much tougher fibre than her husband, and she needed to be, since both her children had inherited their father's delicate constitution. Indeed, her elder son succumbed to his, dying two years after his father, a victim of the practice of inoculation which had but recently been invented, and was still a good deal of a hit-or-miss affair. This left the whole of her vigorous disposition concentrated upon her remaining child, William, and it was a good thing for him that it was so, since the record of his juvenile efforts to stay alive will make painful reading, when we come to them.

But first to the antecedents of Mrs. Hayley. She was, as we have said, the daughter of Colonel Yates, an extensive landed proprietor from near Horsham. Her mother was Margaret, the eldest daughter of Sir John Miller of Lavant, and a lady, says Hayley, who always praises everybody, "of singular beauty". Her father, the Member for Chichester, had ruined himself by "improvident habits and the expenses of a contested election" by the time she was grown up, and so Mary Yates was farmed out to live with her mother's sister, the wife of the then Bishop of Ely, Dr. Gooch, a gentleman who is described as "more distinguished by elegance of manners than by depth of erudition"; who had, in short, as Cardinal de Retz said of himself, "*l'âme peut-être la moins ecclésiastique qui fût dans l'univers*" —which for those days was saying a good deal. Still, for all this, the unecclesiastical Bishop took a fancy to his niece and did his best to bring her out, in which endeavour, however, his wife did not co-operate fully. The trouble with this lady was parsimony: her unfortunate niece was often obliged, "from the absolute want of the most common articles of dress", to stay in her room, pretending to be ill. This eventually growing unbearable, she formed the bold, the strikingly bold resolution for those days of assuming a fictitious name and going upon the stage: an enterprise for which, apparently, her face, her figure, and her various talents eminently fitted her. Fortunately, however, while she was weighing up the pros and cons of this desperate step, at that time, as her son well remarks, one "attended both with degradation and danger to the female character", the eligible young widower, Thomas Hayley, turned up, and all was well again. Everything was in his favour, except his extreme generosity and his "propensity to indulge in expensive pursuits"; but Mary Yates, with considerable acumen, got over this last point by making it a condition of her acceptance of him that he should, after marriage, diminish instead of increasing his equipage. The fact was that the iron of poverty had entered her soul; she was afraid of being surrounded by children as necessitous as she herself had been. Yet, for all this, her son assures us she was "far from being an enemy to splendour". She was merely careful.

The wedding-day was fixed, and then the bride was stricken with the small-pox; but she recovered without injury, and the ceremony took place.

4

William Hayley, her son, though he lived to the age of seventy-five, was a man singularly liable to perils and calamities. His troubles, indeed, in a sense, started even before he was born, since, just at the time when that event was anticipated, the French were daily expected to descend upon the coast of Sussex; and no sooner was he in the world than the news came that they had landed at Pevensey and were proceeding at a great rate towards Chichester. The report happened to be false, but no one knew that at the time, and Mrs. Hayley and her infant were urged to fly for safety to Portsmouth. With considerable fortitude, she refused to imperil the baby's life by so doing, and remained where she was, saying that probably the invaders would not get so far, and that, if they did, they would not injure a woman in her situation.

This first escape was soon succeeded by another. Mr. Hayley would not let his wife nurse her baby, lest by so doing she should "injure the beauty of her form", a motive which her son most virtuously observes "ought never to be mentioned without reprehension". The result was that he was handed over to a wet-nurse who was (Hayley again!) "so deficient in the vital treasure" that the poor infant nearly starved to death before it occurred to anyone to investigate the matter.

As time proceeded, further disasters afflicted the family: first, the death of his father; then the death of his brother. In this business of the inoculation, Hayley had yet another narrow shave, since the original suggestion had been that the two boys should be done together. Eventually it was decided that it would be as well to try it with one at a time, and await events. Events turning out as they did, it may be concluded that William's turn never came.

Meanwhile, at the preposterously early age that was then thought proper, the processes of education were unleashed upon the infant William, and he was sent to a dames' school in Chichester kept by three sisters named Russell, who taught him to read. One of them, Philadelphia, gave him a bright silver penny for his pains, and many years later (when he was sixty-three) he returned the compliment by presenting her—still, poor lady! keeping a school—with a copy of his master-work, *The Triumphs of Temper*. In Chichester, also, the first efforts were made to instruct him in the rudiments of Latin grammar, but they were not successful; and Hayley lays all the blame for this on his master.

Perhaps it was the inadequacy of the Latinists of Chichester, or perhaps it was the fact that Mrs. Hayley's income was not what it had been, but the next thing which happened, in 1750, the year in which his brother died and when Hayley himself was five, was that his mother moved to London, and sent him to a boarding-school at Kingston where the master was one Richard Wooddeson. This school, which is now known as Kingston Grammar School, was a place of some repute at the time, and numbered among its *alumni* Edward Gibbon, Steevens, the Shakespearean commentator, George Keate, the poet, and one Edward Lovibond, who distinguished himself by writing a poem called *The Tears of Old-May-Day*. Though neither Gibbon nor Steevens were Hayley's contemporaries at this school (both preceding him), there is a passage in Gibbon's *Autobiography* which is not without a bearing on the future sequence of events. "There is not," says Gibbon, "in the course of life, a more remarkable change than the removal of a child from the luxury and freedom of a wealthy house to the frugal diet and strict subordination of a school; from the tenderness of parents, and the obsequiousness of servants, to the rude familiarity of his equals, the insolent tyranny of his seniors, and the rod, perhaps, of a cruel and capricious pedagogue. . . . By common methods of discipline, at the expense of many tears and some blood, I purchased the knowledge of the Latin syntax; and not long since I was possessed of the dirty volumes of Phædrus and Cornelius Nepos, which I painfully construed and darkly understood. . . . My studies were too frequently interrupted by sickness"; and, to put the matter in a nutshell, he quitted Dr. Wooddeson's establishment—with his life—at the end of 1747.

In 1750, William Hayley succeeded him, and the previous passage may give us some idea of what he had to look forward to. He records, poor fellow, that when his mother drove away and left him, he did not at once join his play-fellows, but sat himself down under a tree alone, and wept. Hayley, in later years, wept a good deal, but this is the first instance that he records, and one cannot help feeling that he seldom had reasons more entirely adequate for his tears. Yet, in this instance he was fortunate, since his master's daughter saw him, and being, I suppose, impressed by his extreme youthfulness, came out to caress and pet him.

This, however, is the only good thing that can be recorded of Dr. Wooddeson's Spartan establishment, for, at the next glance, a highly infectious fever is raging through the school. Gibbon's studies had been "too frequently interrupted by sickness", and now Hayley's very existence was nearly interrupted by it. The mistress of the school, in conjunction with an oaf of an apothecary, doctored the boys herself—rather, one feels, in the manner of Mrs. Squeers—; some of the pupils died; and when at length, on word being sent to Mrs. Hayley that her son was slightly indisposed, she despatched her manservant to see how he did, the servant's report was that, if she did not at once go to him, and bring a physician with her, there would be little hope of saving his life. He presented, says Hayley of himself, with relish, "an amazing and hideous spectacle . . . with distorted body and suspended senses".

Mrs. Hayley was an excellent mother. She proceeded to Kingston without loss of time, taking with her William's nurse, Sarah Betts, of whom we shall hear more hereafter, and the celebrated Dr. Heberden, the same man, presumably, as was then, or later, Dr. Johnson's medical adviser, and is immortalized in Boswell's pages by attending the Doctor in his last illness and refusing to take a fee. The rescue-party arrived, and found the child in so desperate a condition that, though Dr. Heberden promised Mrs. Hayley he would come again the following day, he confided to the nurse that he had only said this to relieve the mother's anxiety, since next day he did not expect to find the patient alive. Then, being a busy man, the doctor asked that word might be sent him if the end should come before morning, so that he might be saved an unnecessary journey; and departed.

Young Hayley's condition was much too serious for him to be

moved; for several weeks his mother and Mrs. Betts took charge of him and nursed him where he lay. He was in the last stage of weakness; his body was strangely contorted—three of his vertebræ, he says, having been dislocated by rough handling; and his mental faculties were in abeyance. He was, in fact, a senseless cripple, and Dr. Heberden told his mother that, should they succeed in keeping him alive, he would probably be no better than "an ideot".

But Mrs. Hayley was undaunted: she prayed earnestly; her devotion knew no bounds; and at length her exertions were rewarded. Years later, in lines which Gibbon admired, and which Lamb declared notoriously the best that Hayley ever wrote, her son addressed to her memory a tribute which harks back to this period:

> In life's first season, when the fever's flame
> Shrunk to deformity his shrivell'd frame,
> To blank confusion and her crazy train,
> 'Twas thine with constant love, thro' lingering years,
> To bathe thy idiot orphan in thy tears,
> Day after day, and night succeeding night,
> To turn incessant to the hideous sight,
> And frequent watch, if haply at thy view,
> Departed reason might not dawn anew.

At length he was strong enough to be moved, and his mother carried him off to her abode in Leicester Fields; and, as summer approached, Dr. Heberden advised that they should take a lodging at Richmond, where the patient might be under the eye of a Dr. Lewis of Kingston, who, among other things, later read lectures on chemistry to George III, and published a volume with the staggering title of *Commercium Philosophico-Technicum*, or *The Philosophical Commerce of the Arts*. Under this redoubtable physician all manner of "unusual expedients" were tried, though we have, unfortunately, no record of what they were; and every day the patient was taken for an airing in a carriage in Richmond Park. He was sunk into a lethargy and appeared to notice nothing, and so the joy of his mother may well be imagined when at length, one day, a hare starting up before them, he roused himself and called out excitedly: "Mamma! Mamma! there's a hare!"

After this things went a little better; first his limbs, then his faculties were restored. He learnt to walk upon crutches; then without them "on legs of unequal dimensions". It may be said here and now that this affection of the legs never entirely left him. He walked all his life with a limp; and in his later years used both a stick and an umbrella to assist his progress.

This illness is of the greatest importance in considering the future career of Hayley. In the first place it prevented him from taking part in the sports usual to boyhood, and induced instead a shrinking from such practices which, when later on he went to Eton, rendered him unduly retiring. No healthy boy likes to be lame, and to have the fact noticed by his fellows who, in those days, were even less likely than they would be now to refrain from commenting on it. And, in the second, it was during these years of helplessness that his mind first assumed the bias towards reading and study that possessed it all his life. It was natural enough; it is almost always the sickly child who turns to literature as a substitute for the life of action which he is unable to enjoy. Besides, his mother, and oddly enough his nurse also, were strongly addicted to poetry. The former had been instructed by her uncle, the Bishop, in the art of reading verse aloud; and she evidently took pleasure in doing so. Hard on the heels of his major illness, Hayley succumbed to the minor malady of the small-pox, which luckily he had only mildly, thus getting off more lightly than his unfortunate brother. While he was confined to bed, his mother bargained with him that, if he would stay quiet, she would read him the whole of the *Arcadia* of Sir Philip Sidney. She did so; and he enjoyed it. Such a boy, and such a parent, it would be hard to find to-day. Even his nurse had read Homer, though only in translation; and, when neither the one nor the other were reading to young Hayley, he was declaiming poetry to them. On one occasion, he tells us, he was indulging them with a spirited rendering of the conclusion of *Othello*, and got so carried away by the part that, upon the words

> I took by the throat the circumcised dog
> And smote him, thus,

he actually stabbed himself, and so severely that a doctor had to be called in who declared that, if the knife had not fortunately struck a rib, he would "probably have destroyed himself".

For all this, however, his education in the other branches of learning was not neglected. A tutor was engaged for him, who instructed him in Greek and Latin. He was also given a pony; and in the summer he and the tutor went into lodgings at Teddington to enjoy the benefits of fresh air and exercise. It was at Teddington that Hayley, always sequacious of the great, met his first great man, the Revd. Stephen Hales, who was then vicar of that parish and some eighty years of age. Unfortunately Hayley was too young to profit as much as he would have liked by his intercourse with this "beneficient and memorable philosopher", though the latter kindly let him look through his microscope at the circulation of the blood in a frog, and through his telescope, wherein he saw (or says he saw, for the thing is a little hard to believe) the races being run upon Epsom Downs.

In later years, in his *Ode* to the prison-reformer Howard, Hayley paid tribute to this venerable friend in the following remarkable lines:

> I see the hallow'd shade of HALES
> Who felt, like thee, for human woe,
> And taught the health-diffusing gales
> Thro' Horror's murky cells to blow:

lines so remarkable, indeed, that they called for a footnote recalling the interesting fact that Hales had invented a ventilator, which had been installed in His Majesty's Prisons; and informing the reader of the precise manner in which he had discovered the principle of this contrivance.

Yet despite this early flirtation with Science, a subject in which he was always interested, as his later exploits will show, Hayley was at this time more devoted to the Arts. All his delights were of a literary kind; he composed an epistle in Latin couplets to a young lady whom he admired; and later on, at about the age of nine, his first verses in English were to a Miss Read who had painted a miniature of him, in Vandyke dress, for a bracelet of his mother's. Learning, he tells us, appeared to him then an agreeable pastime, and life glided on with delicious serenity, under the influence of maternal affection. Alas! it was but an interlude in his career of trials and difficulties, for, by the time he was twelve, he was judged sufficiently robust to be sent once more to boarding-school; and this time it was to Eton, which he entered on August 31, 1757.

5

Eton in 1757 was a rigorous establishment. Hayley, who shared his friend Cowper's views as to the barbarity of despatching tender infants to public boarding-schools, and who, when he had a son of his own to educate, very pointedly preferred to conduct the process under his own roof, does not complain much of what he endured while he was there. But one can read a good deal between the lines, if only from the fact that in this particular instance his customary loquacity is lacking, and he says remarkably little about it. It does not need much imagination to tell us that the lame and sickly only child, whom constant intercourse with his mother and his tutor must have rendered precocious, could not have enjoyed his schooldays to any great extent.

What he does tell us is that he was severely flogged for neglecting to prepare a Greek lesson, and that the injustice of this proceeding almost tempted him to give up the study of Greek; and that, moreover, in later years, the incident still rankling, he contemplated a poem "in several cantos" to be called *The Expulsion of the Rod*, which was to have dealt exhaustively with the abolition of corporal punishment. This project, to the great detriment of all future generations of schoolboys, he abandoned; but his views remained unchanged.

There was, perhaps, one bright spot. His tutor at Eton was a

Dr. Roberts, who was himself a poet and indeed produced, in 1774, a vast epic, *Judah Restored*, which is closely based upon *Paradise Lost*, and is really not at all a contemptible production. Roberts was kind to young Hayley; he was pleased with his Latin verses, which he was now writing with great facility, and I daresay he encouraged him also in the composition of his English ones, since he now completed, before his fifteenth birthday, an *Epistle from Sophonisba to Massinissa*, and a somewhat embittered *Ode to Ingratitude*, of which the following sample is more than sufficient:

> Ingratitude! such rank offence,
> To all the plainest rules of sense. . . .

And that, with its implication that he was a boy who could be led by kindness better than he could be driven by fear, is almost all he has to say of Eton, save for a couple of revealing anecdotes. The first concerns his passion for splendid books, which lasted all his life, and tells how, wishing to have his early exercises preserved, he took them to that extraordinary artist, Roger Payne, then a young man and living at Eton or Windsor, and had them bound up in his best manner. There were six of these volumes, and it would be interesting to know where they are to-day.

The other story also casts its shadow ahead, for it tells of Hayley's first relations with the theatre, that institution which was to harass him during the greater part of his long life with prospects of quite unattainable riches. In the company of a boy named Manly, he went secretly to London, to see a play. They had the misfortune to meet a local apothecary, who betrayed them; and they were both beaten. Manly, who, as befitted a boy with a name like that, "had a frame of adamant", never groaned. But poor Hayley, who had contemplated with deepest admiration his comrade's fortitude at the block, was obliged to bite his underlip almost through so as to emulate it. However, as he remarks, even as he endured his punishment he found himself looking forward to the day when he should be able to enjoy a well-acted tragedy "without any hazard of paying for his diversion with his blood".

Though he was studious and retiring, he was not, as this story, and the whole course of his future life, bears witness, at all a namby-pamby sort of boy. He grew up into a large and powerful-looking man with an alert and military bearing. It was only inside himself that the sensibility engendered by his early misfortunes continued to flourish, to bear fruit eventually in his copious and characteristic works.

6

In 1763, after six years, he left Eton and went to live with his mother, who now possessed spacious lodgings in Bedford Street, wherein was arranged to the best advantage the "copious library" of his late father. He had entered himself at Trinity Hall, Cambridge, a college he had specially chosen because, in those days, its students enjoyed certain exemptions from the public activities of the University, on the pretext that they were immersing themselves in the study of the civil law; and this, he deemed prudently, would enable him to devote the greater part of his time to literature and art. Indeed, so he tells us, there were then but two lecturers at Trinity Hall, one of whom specialized in civil law, and the other, oddly enough, in Longinus. Both, he says, were dull, though diverting; and there is the further implication that Hayley felt himself already possessed of sufficient classical learning not to be perturbed by the attainments of either. This, he confesses, had the effect of making him idle.

But we anticipate. Before he went up to Trinity Hall in the autumn, a long summer stretched before him, which he and his mother spent in apartments near the Cloisters, in Chichester. Among their nearest neighbours was one of Hayley's guardians, yet another Dean of Chichester, the Very Revd. Thomas Ball, who had been an intimate friend of his father. This Dean was an "amiable divine, of . . . a benevolent and convivial hilarity of temper". His hilarity did him credit, for he had a wife, Margaret, who had lost her reason on account of the death of several of her children. He also had a daughter, Eliza, now about thirteen years of age, and some five years Hayley's junior, of whom we shall hear a great deal more.

This Eliza had been brought back from a school at Chelsea to keep house for her father, whose afflictions and old age prevented him from completing her education. She was a beautiful girl, and Hayley, who was much attached both to her father and to herself, obligingly constituted himself her mentor and began, as he himself says, "to cultivate her mind and heart with the sincerity of a brother". The word 'brother' is significant, since Hayley's warmer feelings were already engaged in a passionate devotion to Frances Page, the daughter of Mr. Page of Watergate, in Upmarden, one time Member for the City of Chichester, and another old friend of the family.

To this gentleman's sequestered seat, some eight miles out in the country, Hayley and his mother were, during this same summer, invited to stay. Frances Page, who was two years his senior, had in infancy been ear-marked by her parents as a suitable match for his deceased brother Tom; and when Dr. Ball casually let fall this interesting piece of information, Hayley's reaction was immediate. "She must certainly belong to me by hereditary right", he said, and declared on the spot his intention of making love to her. The surroundings of Watergate were propitious; it was encircled by groves "peculiarly suited to contemplation and to love". Added to this, a severe thunderstorm broke upon the young couple as they were walking in those selfsame groves. The lady was constitutionally affected by thunder; she fainted in his arms. It was more than enough. On August 15, Hayley presented the following lines to Frances:

> Let not the angry storm, that rages,
> Give thy tender soul alarm!
> From the war, that nature wages,
> Fear, thou dearest girl, no harm!
>
> The thunder's rage, the lightning's flashes,
> Tho' nature's self can scarce endure,
> Tho' cities are consumed to ashes,
> Thy innocence is still secure.

It was a curious species of proposal, but it proved adequate. More verses followed, and with the encouragement of his mother and his guardians, an understanding was reached between the young people. It did not amount to a formal engagement. Mr. Page was apparently a difficult man, and perhaps he had other views for his daughter. A secret correspondence was, therefore, commenced; and, when Hayley went up to Cambridge, it was generally expected that his attachment would have the doubly beneficial result of making him "diligent in his studies" while preserving him from "the coarser affections of youthful liberty". Perhaps it did.

But for all that he tore himself away, before term-time, for a brief visit to East Anglia, where he found, I regret to say, some "cheerful transient acquaintance with some lovely young ladies". A little earlier he had written an *Ode* on the birth of that Prince of Wales who afterwards blossomed out as King George IV. He sent it to Dr. Roberts, his old tutor, who praised it. Then he sent it to the *Gentleman's Magazine*,[4] who printed it. It was his first appearance in print, and he was delighted. He presented his mother with the inscribed proof-sheet of his poem, in recognition of all that he owed her.

7

Hayley's three and a half years at Cambridge must have been uncommonly agreeable ones. Already while in his mother's London lodgings, he had engaged for himself a French tutor, by the hour; and now at Cambridge he seems to have set about the business of his education on the same independent principles. His first step was to provide himself with a drawing-master, named Brotherton; his next with an elderly and distressed Italian, Isola, who gave him lessons in Italian and Spanish: none of which studies, one supposes, had any connection with the normal curriculum of the University. Brotherton introduced his pupil to Jeremiah Meyer, the most celebrated miniature-painter of his time, who had designed the King's head on the new coinage of 1761 and was one of the original members of the Academy. Meyer became a lifelong friend, and one through whose introductions Hayley acquired several of his most eminent acquaintances, notably Romney.

The connection with Isola (who, incidentally, must have been an ancestor of that Emma Isola of Charles Lamb's, who later married the publisher Moxon) was an important one, since in this way, as well as laying the foundations, as he claims, of Isola's fortunes, Hayley was also laying the foundations of his own reputation, which rested very largely on the fact that, in an age not greatly given to such interests, he was extremely well-versed in the unfamiliar literatures of Italy and Spain. For the rest, he formed at Cambridge the usual friendships with congenial spirits; and most of them were life-long. There was Clyfford, a Welshman; Beridge, who became a doctor and settled in Derby, of whom we shall hear more later; and, best loved of all, John Thornton who died young. These young men breakfasted together, and discussed the arts with extreme seriousness. Hayley read Demosthenes with Thornton until one in the morning "without fatigue"; he gave his drawing-master instruction in the art of water-colour painting; he painted himself, copies from Titian and Correggio, some monkeys in the habits of Capuchins, views of Cambridgeshire. The fact that Hayley himself painted, that he was indeed described by Nichols of the *Literary Anecdotes* as "our great painter and poet", must be borne in mind later on when we come to the consideration of his relations with Romney; and with Blake.

More, he did not desist from writing poetry. In 1765 he produced a further piece to his gentle Fanny (of Watergate), on the subject of the fateful thunderstorm, in which, "after indulging his fancy on the probable occupations of the distant nymph, and his apprehensions of what she may be suffering from the severity of the elements", he invites her

> To find a refuge in the folds of love.

And, as if this were not enough, he wrote another long poem on the subject of Tigranes and Arbacia.

In 1766 his activities diminished somewhat: he wrote a few poems, and he painted a fan-mount for Fanny, of Angelica and Medora, from a design of Benjamin West; he also, on June 13 of that year, entered himself at the Middle Temple, as Cowper had done a good many years earlier. However, he neither resided nor practised in that "motley scene of business and dissipation", where, as he asserts, "the professed votaries of Themis devote most of their attention to the more alluring divinities of Parnassus". It is a pleasant picture. We hope it is also a true one.

Hayley's ideas, however, were very different: he was "determined to enliven with affluence the latter days of his admirable parent". He thought he could best do this by writing for the stage.

8

And so, in February 1767, he left Cambridge without a degree, and took a house, No. 5 Great Queen Street, Lincoln's Inn Fields, that was reputed to have once been the abode of Sir Godfrey Kneller. Here he arranged his library, and set to work thinking how he might best storm the citadel of literary fame. The house was lofty and commodious, and a few trees in the area at the back of it gave to his library windows an appearance of verdure and retirement, which was just what he needed.

Nevertheless, for all the verdure and retirement, the gregarious habits which he had acquired at Trinity Hall were, to begin with, too much for him, and, instead of settling down to literature, we find him very soon, on April 24, setting out on a pleasure trip to visit Beridge, who was now studying physic at Edinburgh.

He took the stage-coach as far as Newcastle, and there, since the coaches then went no further, he obtained, with the assistance of the crier, a fellow-traveller to share with him the expense of a post-chaise to the Scottish capital. Here a room was waiting for him in the house in Carruber's Close where Beridge lodged with six or seven other students. The original intention had been that they should proceed to Inverness, "for the sake of visiting the scene of Macbeth", but, the attractions of the capital proving too strong, the friends contented themselves instead with a series of short excursions to such places as Arthur's Seat and the ruins of Holyrood. During the two months Hayley stayed in Edinburgh, he developed a lasting regard for the inhabitants of the North, though he did not "happen to" visit any of the several eminent authors of Scotland. Indeed, he employed his time much more frivolously: he danced, fenced, and exercised himself in the new riding-house which the celebrated Angelo had recently erected in Edinburgh. Seriousness, however, was not utterly forgotten, and, true to the genius of the place in which he found himself, he engaged an instructor in mathematics. This tutor, on May 29, rather surprisingly despatched to his pupil a metrical remonstrance at his having been late for his lesson. It said:

> Dear Sir, compute the worth of time and health,
> How science leads to glory, ease, and wealth.

Truly, as Hayley remarks in this connection, "sincerity and good intention were more prevalent then in Scotland than elegance and refinement".

After these urban delights, the friends proceeded on horseback on an agreeable excursion to take "an extensive view of the country", visiting Glasgow and Stirling, the seat of the Duke of Hamilton, and the falls of the Clyde. Hayley made sketches at Dumbarton Castle, Roslyn Chapel and elsewhere; and kept what he calls a sportive rhyming journal of the trip, which ran after this fashion:

> At Glasgow we walk'd, after tea, up and down,
> To see the fine girls of that beautiful town. . . .
> Having seen all the town, which was busy and full,
> We retreated, and supp'd very well at the Bull.

In Glasgow they also called upon Simpson, the celebrated mathematician, and the Foulis', the great printers, from whom Hayley purchased "a respectable print, very nicely impressed on satin" of Rubens's picture of Daniel in the Lion's Den.

But all such delightful jaunts draw to their end, and, by about the middle of June, he and Beridge were on their way home again. They travelled from Leith to London in a coasting vessel, among an odd diversity of fellow-passengers. There was a young Scottish physician going to practise at Aleppo; an old conjuring Jew who had "visited all countries"; and some entrancing milliners on their way to study the new fashions in London. The voyage, which alternated between gales and unprecedented calms, took eleven days, and one of the milliners was exceedingly ill. It is gratifying to add that she was much soothed and cheered by the humane attentions of Hayley and his companion.

9

Nevertheless "the beautiful damsels of Scotland had not supplanted the fair one of Watergate in the heart of her young poet", though now the skies were beginning to grow dark in that quarter. Hayley did his best. His prospective father-in-law, Mr. Page, as befits a member of Parliament, was interested in politics, and so, later that year, to indulge his tastes, Fanny's lover composed "A Few Thoughts on the Nomination of Members for the City of Chichester", a prose work which was prefaced by a Latin quotation from Sallust, and another English one from Locke. But, despite this, old Mr. Page remained unimpressed, and Hayley goes so far as to call him a reserved and wary old gentleman, and even "a sort of imperious and unfeeling necromancer". In short, it is clear that he was nothing like as grateful as he should have been.

It is a long story, and a sad one, and we need not go into it in any great detail, especially as Hayley hints darkly of secret enemies and anonymous letters. All through the autumn of 1767, he despatched impassioned addresses to Fanny Page, by the hand of his old "sisterly" friend, Dean Ball's daughter, Eliza. Then, in the summer of 1768, when he was lodging once more in Chichester, the same process was pursued, and he indulged himself in sundry clandestine meetings at, of all places, the Deanery, on one of which he presented to Fanny a miniature of himself painted by Meyer, while she reciprocated with a cornelian ring.

But the end was in sight; "dark machinations" of a concealed enemy supervened, and Miss Page, whether by anonymous letters or some other contrivance, was lured from her allegiance. That, at least, is Hayley's version; and we have no other. Perhaps she only got tired of him. Anyway she married someone else, and when, a great many years later, she died, Hayley lamented her end, in verse, after his fashion. And, for the moment, he coped with the situation by writing a poetical epistle called *Resignation*, and returned to London and started to think about composing a tragedy.

His dramatic activities may wait a little, however, while we round off the tale of his amorous complications. In 1769 he despatched an enormous letter to his late confidante, Eliza Ball, suggesting that she had better not call upon the Hayleys, when in London, for fear of scandal. "Such a declaration," he continues in his usual magniloquent style, "must appear very strange, from one who professes himself bound to you by the strongest ties of gratitude and affection. . . . You may say that it is very great weakness to restrain the innocent warmth of friendship, from a servile apprehension that such friendship may be vilely misrepresented by some secret foe. Indeed, my dear girl, such caution does not naturally belong to the heart of your brother; but having once brought upon you a very scandalous insult, I consider it as my duty to sacrifice every pleasure, rather than expose you to the least risk of a second injury."

Now, what was all this about? Well, it would seem that Eliza had been severely censured in an anonymous letter for the part she had played during his clandestine correspondence with Fanny, and that the writer of this letter had, moreover, expressed the conviction that, after such impropriety on her part, no man would think of marrying her. Eliza was now nineteen, artless, modest and lively. Her features and her voice were equally attractive. Hayley was only twenty-four, and, as we have seen, highly susceptible. Eliza had been his protégée; he had taken it upon himself to cultivate her mind. He was in the grip of a strong mortification over the loss of Fanny, and Eliza was very sympathetic.

Consequently, when they next met, what happened is what might have been expected to happen. The poet, enfolding Eliza in his arms, said to her, according to his own version of the matter: "Our enemy has said, my dear girl, that no man will think of marrying you, but I will prove the falsehood of that villainous slander by making you my own wife, if you feel that it is in my power to render you as happy as you deserve to be."

Now this was all very well. The unfortunate thing was that Eliza's mother happened to be a hopeless imbecile, whose only recorded activity was that of cutting flowers out of paper, at which she was reputed very adept. Hayley's mother, in consequence, when she heard of his proposal, most sensibly observed to him: "What should you think of your own conduct, if, after you had made this delicate and charming creature your wife, you should ever see her sink into her mother's most afflicting disorder?"

His reply was magnificent rather than reasonable: "My dear madam, (said he) in that case I should bless my God for having given me courage sufficient to make myself the legal guardian of the most amiable and most pitiable woman on earth."

There is no arguing with that sort of thing, and Mrs. Hayley did not attempt to do so. She merely complimented her son on the purity of his heart, on the strength of his feelings, and on the kindness of his intentions; and she wished him—what we should now call, luck. And, moreover, with considerable generosity, she at once offered to settle upon his bride the estates which were her own jointure.

Hayley introduced his intended to Thornton, who thought her charming. And on May 11, 1769, Eliza wrote to tell Hayley that she had been advised by a lady friend to break the news to her father "as she is certain it would make him leave the world with great satisfaction". Moreover, she added that Fanny Page had conferred her blessing on the match. Who could say more?

The Dean, when told, was more than agreeable. There were no obstacles, none at all. Hayley, in a sudden flush of responsibility, contemplated taking up the practice of medicine to augment his livelihood; but his friend Beridge, who was already practising as a doctor, strenuously dissuaded him. He then thought of the Church; but soon thought again, and decided, instead, that he was

> Born for Love, and for the Muse!

Fortunately he was born also to a private income, and, though this income, and that which would be brought to him by Eliza, were not large, they would, he thought, suffice.

Hayley's vanity as well as his deeper feelings had been seriously wounded by the defection of Fanny. But he was always a mercurial creature, and he was now able to contemplate the delightful spectacle of himself beloved by a beautiful and accomplished girl, whose spirit and imagination "appeared to harmonize with his own". Everything appeared to be just as it should be; and upon October 23, 1769, the wedding took place in Chichester Cathedral, in an atmosphere of general rejoicing.

There was but one jarring note. The service was conducted by the Bishop, Sir William Ashburnham, who combined, it would seem, a not entirely happy married life with an exceptionally fine delivery. After the ceremony was over, Hayley complimented him on his impressive reading of the service. The reply was unexpected, even ominous. "Sir," growled the Bishop of Chichester, "this is the worst service in the church!"

It was a remark Hayley did not forget, and when, many years later, he was writing his *Memoirs* he set it down, without comment, but in a way which shows he must very often have recalled it.

But that is hardly the note upon which to end this chapter. As Hayley himself says: "When he entered the married state, he thought most highly of the sanctity and sweetness of wedded love; and his expectations of deriving from it the purest felicity appeared, to his own mind, to rest on as sure foundations as mortality can afford." From what I know of him, I believe he was quite sincere in saying this. That was the sort of man he was. And the fact that he married twice, and that both his marriages went wrong, does nothing to disprove it. It is just the sort of ironical thing that happens to persons who believe rather strongly in romance, and sentiment, and "pure felicity".

CHAPTER III

LIFE IN LONDON (1769-1774)

I

IN THE MIDDLE OF November, Hayley took his young wife back to Queen Street, where his mother was already in residence; and at once the campaign to capture the playhouses began.

Already, before his marriage, he had decided upon his tactics. They were simple ones. If Dryden had composed four plays a year, he thought himself modest in his purpose of composing only two, and still more reasonable in computing that these should bring him a profit of five hundred pounds apiece.

And so he set to work and, with commendable rapidity, completed *The Afflicted Father*, which was based upon a story he had read in the newspaper. I am not sure whether the plot of this play matters very much, as it was never performed; but perhaps it is as well to adumbrate it as a warning against the sort of newspaper story that appeals to rising young playwrights. This is it: the afflicted father supplies his even more afflicted son, who has been condemned for a capital offence, with poison, to avoid the ignominy of a public execution. The son takes the poison; and then comes the news that he is pardoned. This, Hayley thought, was a theme singularly adapted to moral as well as dramatic effect; and, when it was finished, and his friends had all told him it was first-rate, he prevailed upon a third party, who was acquainted with Garrick, to hand to that eminent man the manuscript, with the following resolute and uncompromising speech: "If you think it unfit for the stage, send it back to me with any mark of rejection, and we will pester you no more on the subject; but if you think as I do, and resolve to produce it, then I will bring you my friend the author."

Some weeks elapsed, and then Hayley was informed that Garrick was delighted with the piece, and wished him to breakfast with him. Everything went most cordially, and another breakfast-date was appointed, at which the minor details of production were to be adjusted. At this second meeting, however, Garrick sang a very different tune. He had, in fact, altered his mind; and the more resolved he grew not to produce, the more complimentary he became. Hayley was very disappointed, but consoled himself by saying that an enemy had been at work. He was always inclined to be one of those fortunate people who are able to believe that their misfortunes are the result of another's malevolence.

However, he was young, and he was resilient; and life in London was very agreeable. With his wife and his mother he attended the theatres with great assiduity, and no doubt derived from the plays he saw many useful lessons regarding the plays he was going to write.

The first taste he had of his wife's unusual quality occurred during the first year of their marriage, and surprised him very much. The occasion for it was curious in the extreme. Eliza learnt that her aged father had resigned his Deanery to the husband of her eldest sister, who was also a clergyman. Though the poor old man was seventy-three years of age, she elected to regard this change as having been brought about by intrigue on the part of her brother-in-law, and she consequently passed three days and three nights in tears. "Incessant tears!" as her astonished husband writes.

The young couple went down to stay at the Deanery, whether with a view to altering the irrevocable I cannot say, and, while engaged upon a little party of pleasure by the sea-side in the village of Felpham, word was sent them that the unfortunate Dean had had a fit and died. Eliza was grieved, but her grief was mitigated by the reflection that his advanced age allowed him but little prospect of preserving his faculties. It seems probable that she regarded his relinquishing his Deanery as an all too vivid proof of this.

Even so, the death of the Dean somewhat improved the family fortunes, for it was after this event, and when they had returned to London in the November of 1770, that Hayley was at length able to provide a carriage for his mother, whose health also had begun to decline. His hopes of eventual affluence still ran high, for now he was busily writing another play, and this time he was not taking his plot from the newspaper, but had followed the advice of his friend Steevens, who had recommended him to play for safety and adapt some accepted success of the French stage. The one which he chose, from Corneille, he christened *The Syrian Queen*, and when it was completed he sent it to Colman, who sent it back to him at express speed, though with a very courteous letter to explain just what was the matter with it.

Dejected by this experience, he decided he would have nothing further to do with the caprices of managers, and resolved instead to begin an epic poem, that should celebrate both the glory of his country, and his own "passion for freedom". The best possible subject for both purposes was, he felt convinced, Magna Charta, with, for his heroes, the Barons and their "venerable director", the Archbishop Stephen Langton. It was much the same conception as was later to occur to Martin Tupper.

However, such an enterprise was not to be hurried: it needed consideration. It was one thing, he said, to fix upon a fine situation for building, and another to erect an edifice there which should ornament rather than disfigure the scene. Consequently, while the project was maturing, he set himself to the composition of a few works of lesser magnitude. One of these, composed in the same summer of 1771, was a Poetical Epistle to the "mild and elegant" Stanislaus, King of Poland, to congratulate him on his recent escape from assassination.

No sooner was this completed than his friend, Thornton, who thought the world of it, set to work and translated it into Latin verse. Then, since Mr. Harris, who was later to become the celebrated Lord Malmesbury, was just upon the point of going, in his public capacity, to Berlin, the two friends gave him both the original and the translation, in manuscript, and besought him to be so good as to have them despatched thence to the King of Poland, in Warsaw. While they awaited the outcome of this transaction, both poets, full of the liveliest expectations, commissioned a miniature portrait of Stanislaus, so that, when the epistles came to be printed, they might have a suitable illustration to accompany them.

It is sad to relate that, after all this preparation, the courier who was conveying the precious documents from Berlin to Warsaw was set upon and plundered by insurgents. The poem was never heard of again. It never reached the King of Poland; and what was worse, and is indeed almost incredible, neither poet seems to have kept a copy of his work. It was lost irremediably.

Nor was this the only vexation of 1771. While staying at a sequestered spot on the Kentish shore, at the farm of Dandelion indeed, near Margate, which, so far as the present writer is aware, is still there, Hayley was moved to compose an Ode in honour of his friend, Theodore Aylward of Chichester, who had been the music-master first of Eliza, and later of the Princesses at Windsor. The purpose of this ode was to befriend the society of decayed musicians. Having written it, Hayley despatched it to Aylward, with instructions that he should set it to music. But unfortunately his friend did not write music, he only taught it: a distinction which Hayley seemed unable to appreciate, for he was much put out by Aylward's non-compliance with his wishes. And what made it worse was the fact that Hayley and Thornton had recently helped Aylward out of a difficulty when, as Gresham professor of music, it had suddenly become necessary for him to read a lecture on music. Neither Hayley nor Thornton knew anything about the subject, but they had not let this deter them. They were always ready to oblige a friend in distress, and so they had written the lecture for him; and he had delivered it. "It was not," says Hayley succinctly, "scientific, but it answered the purpose."

To return to the Epic. Though all his friends were very kind and full of encouragement, the work proceeded but slowly during the autumn and winter of 1771. For one thing, it needed infinite preliminary research, and, for another, it was dogged by the most extraordinary misfortunes. One of these was brought about, inadvertently, by the kindness of Meyer, who had had the beginning of the poem read to him, and had been so captivated by it that he had entreated Hayley to set about getting some suitable illustrations prepared, against the time when it should inevitably appear in print; and to this end he introduced Hayley to the fashionable artist, Cipriani. Hayley at once furnished the latter with a passage sixty lines in length, which, when he described the incident in his *Memoirs* nearly forty years afterwards, he asseverated to be, beyond doubt, the very best verses he had ever written. Cipriani read them, and agreed that they were splendid. He then put them in his pocket and went off at all speed, ostensibly to prepare the necessary designs. He continued for some while to carry the lines in his pocket; and then he lost them. And not only had the unfortunate poet no copy of them, but he was unable to recollect a single line of the whole sixty. They were gone for ever.

This was bad, but what followed was worse, and, curiously enough, it was Hayley's laudable passion for the society of the eminent that was responsible. On May 1, 1772, the *Resolution* with Captain Cook in command, lay in the London river off Erith, all ready to set out on his second voyage, with Mr. Joseph Banks. Hayley with Beridge and Meyer were invited to dine on board, and they not only did so with great enjoyment, but also composed verses to the intrepid explorer, and recited them to him. It was a tolerably fine day, but the wind was sharp and easterly, and it was necessary to make the journey out to the vessel in a small open boat. On this trip Hayley caught a cold in his eyes; and the following day found both of them "drowned in blood". An obstinate inflammation ensued, and for many weeks he was in pain. His eyes were permanently weakened, and he was obliged to give up his painting altogether, and, for a time, his writing as well.

No reader of Hayley's correspondence can doubt that he did in fact, up to the end of his life, suffer considerably from this weakness of his eyes. It is a constantly recurring theme, as an excuse for not having done the things that he ought to have done. In later life he even made it his excuse for not going to church, declaring that the damp walls of the building encouraged ophthalmic inflammation. For the present, the principal result of his affliction was that the Epic, temporarily, was abandoned.

2

Nevertheless, despite this set-back, there still remained much in the way of harmless pastime and pleasure. It was at this time that Hayley developed the habit of conducting his wife and mother upon the most agreeable summer-holiday excursions. In 1772 he had taken them to Derby, where Beridge had settled in practice, and there he had met that very excellent painter, Joseph Wright, with whom he established a life-long intimacy. Wright lent him various sketches of the scenery near Matlock, and the copies which he made of these are his last recorded essays in the art of painting.* His eyes would not suffer him to continue with it; they had grown worse again in consequence of a moonlight ride which he had imprudently taken over the "bleak hills of Derbyshire". Yet despite this, the Derbyshire visit produced two more "poetical flights": "a sportive description of his adventures" not dissimilar, one imagines, from the description some years earlier of his adventures in Glasgow; and a "martial ode" to a gallant warrior whom he had met in the North, one Colonel Gladwin who, when in command of the fort of Detroit, had saved by his vigilance both himself and the men in his charge from being massacred by "an insidious visiting body of Red Indians".

In the summer of 1773, the tour took another direction. Beridge was at Bath, suffering from the gout, and thither the Hayleys repaired, "to cheer him". From Bath they proceeded to Bristol and the Wye Valley, and then back to Bristol again, and, by way of Glastonbury, to Lyme, where they secured "a neat lodging" for the sake of the sea-bathing. From here they took an excursion to Ford Abbey, near Crewkerne, where Hayley met a certain eccentric called Captain Morrison, who had published a pamphlet dedicated to the purpose of restoring the Great Mogul to his ancient splendour. Under the tutelage of this amiable being, Hayley commenced to learn the Persian language, but did not proceed very far with it, as his visit was a short one. One is tempted to say, in parenthesis, that one of the most endearing things about Hayley is just that which is revealed by this incident. What other man would have proposed that he should learn the Persian language from a casual acquaintance, at a week-end party; and what other man would have solemnly set the fact on record after a lapse of more than thirty years?

But the visit to Lyme was responsible for a still more important contact: one which, indeed, plays a part of consequence in certain future transactions that we shall have to describe. It so happened that staying at Lyme, at the time of the Hayleys' visit, was a Mr. Wilson, a tutor, with two of his pupils, the sons of Lord Chatham. Hayley was introduced to this party, and the youngest boy, William, admired his horse, and rode out to show him several romantic spots in the neighbourhood where an earthquake was supposed to have produced "a wild and beautiful singularity of appearance in the face of Nature"—the spot which is nowadays known as The Landslip. This pleasant youth of fourteen who endeared himself so much to the poet was William Pitt, the future Prime Minister, though naturally Hayley was not then aware of it. Often, in later years, he regretted his lost opportunity: that his "poetical reserve" had "prevented his imparting to the wonderful youth the epic poem he had begun on the liberty of their country". What made it still worse was that, if he had but known, the future Prime Minister had himself already written a tragedy. It was bad, of course, says Macaulay; but not worse than the tragedies of his friend.

Their tour over, the family returned once more to Queen Street, for what was to be their last winter in London. The health of Mrs. Hayley senior was failing. Hayley had perhaps had as much of London life as he wanted. He was always a countryman at heart and he found his thoughts turning to Eartham, and to the pleasures of what the eighteenth century was particular to call "retirement". The idea must have been in the air for some while, since during the last couple of years he had been busying himself at odd times in making the neglected family seat habitable. What Eliza thought of the change one cannot say, though one may conjecture. What Hayley thought Eliza ought to think of it is, however, carefully laid down in an *Elegy* which her husband penned at the time, in which, in stanzas not very unreminiscent of Gray's poem of the same name, he expounded clearly the role for which she was intended:

> Eliza too, enamour'd of thy bower,
> Will make thee, Eartham, her peculiar care;
> And court, to grace thee, every coyer flower,
> That yields reluctant to the vernal air.
>
> If aught severe her lovely charge deface,
> Her pitying hand will raise the bending bloom;
> Protect the wounded myrtle's rising race,
> And guard the infant rose's rich perfume.
>
> Nor this alone, but far superior care
> Eliza's gentle, generous heart will know;
> She to th' afflicted cottage will repair,
> And soothe the villager's heart-rending woe. . . .

In return for which self-dedication to the arts of horticulture and of philanthropy, he prophesied:

> The infant tenants will with transport bound,

and proceeded, in similar fashion, to outline the programme of his own activities:

> Perchance, long banished from his failing eyes,
> Th' heroic muse will come with all her fire;
> Yes! in thy shades her sacred form will rise,
> And strike to liberty the lofty lyre!

Part of this agenda was duly carried out: the heroic muse came strenuously enough, even if she sometimes forgot her fire; the tenants bounded with a will, for Hayley was a prince among landlords. But whether Eliza remained enamoured of her bower, the sequel will show. One thing is certain, I think: she fell down on her job in the article of gardening: the bending blooms remained bending; the myrtle was unprotected; the infant rose unguarded.

This, as Hayley calls it, "interesting removal" took place on June 24, 1774. His large collection of books, which he so rightly regarded as "one of the prime luxuries of life", was safely stowed in broad-wheeled wagons (the bibliophilic tenderness responsible for this particularizing of the gauge of the wagons is touching indeed!), and as safely conveyed to the "beloved little villa", which now resembled, owing to hasty enlargements, a sort of rural chaos. The superintendence of the workmen, and the laying out of the garden, absorbed everyone's attention during the remainder of the summer and autumn, while the subsequent winter was occupied in planning future embellishments, "like another Numa" as a contemporary guide-book informs us.[1]

Unfortunately, in the midst of all this turmoil, the health of Mrs. Hayley senior grew worse. The peculiar salubrity of the air of Eartham failed to restore her; she sought remedies more drastic and efficacious, and she found an old friend who had studied medicine in his youth and was fond of giving gratuitous advice. This same enthusiast now presented her with a prescription which he described as infallible in her complaint. A servant was sent into Chichester to have it made up, and the chemist, in some alarm, enquired for whom it was intended, since the dose was lethal. Mrs. Hayley, however, turned obstinate, and so her son was obliged to beg her, if she were still determined to sample the potion, to do so under the immediate supervision of her London doctor. She complied, and went up to lodgings in London, taking the faithful old Sarah Betts with her. She reached London at the end of November, and thought the journey had done her so much good that she went out forthwith and bought a new gown. Whether she took the medicine as recommended, is not recorded; but she would seem hardly to have had time to do so, since on December 3, 1774, she expired in her sleep. She was fifty-six.

The upshot of all this was that Hayley was saddled, so he says, with the reputation of having turned his dying mother out of doors in the depths of winter. It was an imputation which offended him, and he says so, in his *Memoirs*, with some vigour. The vigour is understandable, as, if one thing is certain about him, it is that he was deeply attached to his mother.

He hastened to town and brought back her body for burial at

Eartham; then he settled down to the composition of her epitaph, in Latin.

Perhaps it may be left to that remarkable figure, Mrs. Betts, to have the last word on the subject of Mary Hayley. "My mistress," said she, "ought to be queen of the whole world". And indeed Hayley adds, "Majesty was the characteristic feature both of her countenance and her mind, but majesty so softened by the sweetness of benevolence, that it never appeared imperious or ungentle."

Hayley's language, where his affections are concerned, is so intemperate that one has inevitably a tendency to discount his praises; but I think we may leave undiscounted his praise of his mother. After all, he owed everything to her. Not the least sonorous line on her monumental tablet reads

Uxor inculpabilis, Parens amantissima.

It is ungenerous to doubt it.

CHAPTER IV

EARTHAM (1774-1780)

I

THE PRESENT-DAY VISITOR to Eartham, who arrives in this still secluded village with his head full of the notion that he is about to see the elegant villa in which William Hayley entertained Gibbon and Romney and Cowper, is due for a sharp shock of disillusionment.

True, the little church of St. Margaret remains untouched both as to size and plan; and the little inn, *The George,* looks much as it must have done in Hayley's time, when his son, Thomas Alphonso, presented it with a new sign-board. But Eartham House is now a residence altogether richer and more splendid than one had pictured. It has, indeed, become a most imposing mansion, modernised, and set in the most beautifully kept grounds.

Its situation, it is true, remains the same, since the old house has been incorporated within the new one in a way that is apparent when one proceeds to the interior, and discovers the splendid upstairs library with its three tall graceful windows, and its white marble chimney-piece which Flaxman designed on the spot for Hayley. From this library, too, one may pass to several modest-sized bedrooms which seem to have remained unaltered since Hayley's time; and very soon one sees what has happened, and that the West wing is what remains of the original house, though even this has been raised, and stuccoed, and generally carved about to suit the convenience of subsequent owners.

The building stands low, and near the gates leading from the road. A broad gravel sweep lies before it on this side, and, except for an isolated red-brick and flint circular greenhouse, which at once takes the eye as being the genuine contemporary article, the first glimpse of the place from this aspect is disappointing. It is not until one has passed round the house and reached the garden-front that one understands just why it was that Hayley loved Eartham so well, and that Cowper said of it, when on his celebrated visit in 1792, "I had . . . no conception that a poet could be the owner of such a paradise."

For, upon this side of the house, a great sweep of turf rises slowly to a tree-covered hill, through the very centre of which is pierced a vista that looks out to the sea. On the right-hand side of this eminence, as you stand with your back to the house, the foreground has been artificially levelled, and one surmises that it was here there once stood the famous riding-house within which, on wet days, Hayley took equestrian exercise, and that later was fitted up as Romney's painting-room.

If you want to come closer to William Hayley in the grounds of the present Eartham House, I think the best thing you can do is to make all speed up the grassy slope until you reach the swelling wood that crowns the southward knoll. For here you are soon in the heart of an obviously artificial plantation of box and beech, laurel and laburnum, which is penetrated in all directions by winding sloping pathways that are the very thing for a meditative poet to pace. It is recorded that, upon Cowper's visit, Mrs. Unwin was drawn in a wheeled chair up sundry winding ways by young Thomas Hayley and his fellow-pupil, Thomas Sockett, her "two young griffins" as she pleasantly dubbed them. And, as you mount by degrees to the top of the hill, and pushing through an iron gate come at length to its thyme-covered summit, bare of trees because it is in the line of the vista, you can look back down the slope at the present Eartham House and can perhaps see, in the eye of the imagination, the very much smaller villa that was Hayley's.

You turn, you become lost in the foliage again; and presently you are standing in the heart of a young wood at the foot of a steep rounded hillock. On the top of this mound is an old octagonal summer-house, its conical roof and sides thatched with many-years-dead heath. You climb the steps that lead to the summer-house, and you find that it is open to the south and would command a tremendous view over the flat marshes to the sea at Bognor, were it not that the wood has grown undisciplined, and the trees have defeated the view. The summer-house is rotten with age, but has clearly been carefully looked after. Inside a low bench runs round the wall. You sit down, perhaps, and now indeed you are as near as you will come to the Hermit of Eartham, since a later page will reveal both the date and the occasion for the building of this look-out.

2

It was to this earthly paradise, as he deemed it, that Hayley had transported his Eliza in the summer of 1774; and at first, save for the death of his mother, all went well.

Hayley was an immensely hospitable creature. His idea of felicity was to have a house full of visitors, and, during the first two years of his sojourn at Eartham, he seems to have lived very agreeably. Clyfford and Thornton came on long visits. The former had just got married, and Hayley thought it time the latter should do likewise. So he addressed to him an extensive *Epistle on Marriage*, in which, for reasons best known to himself, he painted a glowing picture of the benefits of matrimony.

His mind, following upon a visit from the newly-married Clyfford in the spring of 1775, had been running on this subject. Mrs. Clyfford combined a warm heart and an excellent understanding with a tendency to melancholy and "fits of connubial altercation"; and, anxious to counteract this by the "influence of benevolent rhyme", Hayley composed for her improvement, first an *Ode to Cheerfulness*, and then a "Matrimonial Ballad", in which he makes, possibly from experience, the unassailably sensible observation,

> Ye husbands! of argument chiefly beware
> That bane of good humour which frightens the fair.

This sentiment, if not in itself striking, is not without interest as coming from the author who, a few years later, was to reform the entire feminine mind of England by the advice laid before it in his influential best-seller, *The Triumphs of Temper*.

During the summer of 1776 Eartham was "a seat of social and poetical pleasure" until August, when the family travelled north to congratulate Beridge on his marriage, which had greatly added to his cheerfulness and had completely restored his health. Hayley addressed a poem to his bride, "Hymen, the restorer"; and resumed his intercourse with Wright, the painter, whom he persuaded to execute "a chiaro oscuro" (whatever that was) of Dr. and Mrs. Beridge. And the trip ended with a delightful fortnight in London, where this year he had acquired a new friend in George Romney, whose star stood now in the ascendant. The introduction had been effected by Meyer,[1] and the purpose of it, in the first place, had been to commission Romney to paint a portrait of Hayley's friend, Mr. Long, the surgeon. When this was done, everyone was so pleased with the result that Romney was asked to execute a portrait of Thornton, and then one of Hayley himself. Furthermore, Hayley found the painter not only so admirable an artist, but also so endearing a man, that he became most attached to him, and forthwith invited him to come on a visit to Eartham, for the benefit of his health.

He wrote on October 22, and this is part of what he said. It is typical of the sort of thing that he was to say in hundreds of other letters:

I entreat you in the name of those immortal powers, the beautiful, and the sublime, whom you so ardently adore, or, to speak the language of your favourite *Macbeth*, "*I conjure you by that which you profess*," to moderate your intense spirit of application, which preys so fatally on your frame—exchange, for a short time, the busy scenes, and noxious air, of London, for the chearful tranquillity and pure breezes of our Southern coast.

To console you for what you will quit, the daily praises of a flattering Metropolis, I will promise you the more silent, but warmer, admiration of a few friends, who join to their esteem of your talents, the most cordial solicitude for your welfare. Nor is this an idle invitation to abandon, even for a short time, either the pleasures, or profits, of your profession; but to pursue both in a manner more consistent with your health, and consequently with that glory in your art, which is, I know, your predominant passion, and which is indeed the only true Promethean fire that can make an artist immortal.

> But vain this vital spark of heavenly flame,
> If toil excessive tears the shatter'd frame:
> Where languid Sickness spreads her sullen shade,
> Imagination's brilliant figures fade . . .

There is more, but that is enough to convey a pretty clear idea of the way in which Hayley worded his invitations.

The point is a not unimportant one, since the common charge against him nowadays is that he was a sort of intellectual tuft-hunter who, without talent himself, inveigled men whose abilities were immensely greater than his own to shed upon his trivial reputation the reflected light of their superior genius. This view I believe to be erroneous. Hayley's attitude towards his friends was conditioned less by their eminence than by his regard for them; and indeed, many of those whose reputation has since outstripped his were men who, at the time, were regarded as of rather less importance than he was. Of course he liked the society of talented people. Who in the full possession of his faculties does not? But that is a very different thing from being a mere lion-hunter.

In the case of Romney, whose health was uniformly deplorable, it seems to me that much the simplest assumption is that Hayley perceived this when he sat to him, and that the idea struck him that a sojourn at Eartham would improve it; and that, at the same time, it would be agreeable both for himself and for Eliza to entertain a man whose society they had come to enjoy. It may seem that I protest too much, but, since this pattern of Romney-Hayley is one that is to be often repeated in the years ahead, it is perhaps best for me to express straight away what is conveyed to me by it.

After all, the proof of the pudding is the eating of it, and the proof in this case is that Romney duly put in his appearance at Eartham, and enjoyed his stay so much that, for the next twenty years, he never failed to repeat the routine of his autumn visit. Moreover, it did him good. He thought so, and he said so, over and over again; and anyone who was able to do George Romney good is entitled to a very decent portion of respect from this, or any other, age.

3

So far the tale of William Hayley's life has been pretty plain sailing, but from now on, as he approaches his apogee, such as it was, our course becomes involved with parallel narratives which require a delicate handling. There is the thread of his domestic life with Eliza; there is the thread of his own so soon to be mounting fame—though the word rings hollowly now; there is Romney; and soon there are to be Gibbon, and Anna Seward.

It may, therefore, at this stage be permissible to exercise a little artifice, and, setting aside strict chronology, to concentrate on a single theme, and pursue it to its conclusion. Since Romney, who now enters the picture, was, with the exception of Cowper and of Hayley's son, the being who meant most to William Hayley, it is, I think, desirable here to go back a little in time, and to give some brief indication of what manner of man he was when Hayley met him.

George Romney, in 1776, was already forty-two years of age, and eleven years senior to his host at Eartham. He had been born at Dalton-in-Furness in Lancashire, the son of a man of many occupations, at various times builder, merchant and farmer. Starting his working life as a cabinet-maker, he had later been apprenticed to an eccentric artist named Steele, who was only a little older than his pupil. This Steele, who for no particular reason elected to call himself Count Steele, became involved in a clandestine love-affair, in which Romney, as every good apprentice should do, acted the part of go-between. When Steele finally eloped with the lady to Scotland, he left behind him a pupil prostrated with fever and sickness, brought about by his "exertions in assisting the escape of the bride". Romney was nursed through his illness by a compassionate young woman, and his gratitude to her was such that, in 1756, when barely twenty-two years of age, he married her.

Unhappily this early marriage did not have upon him the customary effect of making him 'settle down'. Instead he soon resolved "to wander forth alone in quest of professional adventure", and wander he did all over the North, painting life-sized heads at two guineas and small whole lengths at six guineas, until he had managed to save the sum of nearly a hundred pounds. By this time he had not only a wife but also two children to support. It was 1762; he put thirty pounds of the money he had saved into his pocket, gave the remainder to his wife, and set out to London to seek his fortune. He found his fortune, but he did not send for his family to share in it, and indeed, save for a couple of flying visits, he did not see his wife again until thirty-seven years later when, as a broken and dying man, he returned to her in 1799 to drag out under her care his last three years of existence.

Now this, of course, was highly reprehensible; but it is after all Romney's own affair, and it would not be necessary for us to comment upon it here, were it not for the fact that Romney's son, and various other biographers, have made great play with the theory that his virtual desertion of his wife was due to the baneful influence exerted upon him by Hayley. Against this charge, I think it is only necessary to cite the relevant dates. Romney left the North in 1762; in 1773, having raised his annual income to the not inconsiderable figure of £1,200, he went to Italy, with his friend and fellow-painter, Ozias Humphry, where he stayed a couple of years; and in 1775 he settled himself in the substantial house in Castle Street, Cavendish Square, which he occupied throughout the period of his greatest success. By the time Hayley met him, in 1776, he had already had fourteen years in which to have sent for his wife and family, if he had had a mind to do so.

By this time Romney was not only a highly successful and fashionable portrait-painter—"Reynolds and Romney divide the town", Thurlow said of him, rather later—but he was also a man in an advanced state of neuroticism. Everything about him, his dashing nervous handwriting, his stooping habit, rounded shoulders, the sharp apprehensive features which regard you so distrustfully from his various self-portraits, bear out this diagnosis. He was morbidly shy, given to bursting into tears, appallingly indifferent to what he ate. Hayley's friendship, Hayley's invitations to Eartham, were almost the only respites he enjoyed from a life of continuous over-work. His letters are full of a quite unambiguous gratitude to his host. I do not think there is any doubt that he loved Hayley, and that Hayley loved him.

But there is yet another charge against Hayley, which is that, artistically, he was a bad influence upon his friend. It is true that, when the two men first met, Romney was almost exclusively a portrait-painter, while Hayley had very pronounced views on the superiority of what he called "historical painting". Always ready with helpful suggestions, he proposed to Romney sundry subject-pictures, which the latter sometimes executed, and sometimes did not. Some of them, admittedly, were odd. One which he began at Eartham, but did not, I think, finish, represented "a female child of seven years, of the size of life, kneeling by the side of a dead fawn, under a massive tree, split by lightning, which had killed her favourite animal". But—and this is the point—there is no evidence that Romney objected to these suggestions. There is, moreover, very little evidence either that, technically speaking, the pictures thus suggested were inferior to the portraits upon which Romney based his very considerable fortune. Indeed, I think it is fair to say that he enjoyed painting them as a change from the portraits. Still more, to indicate how impossible it was for the unfortunate Hayley ever to do the right thing, we shall see, when we come to the case of Blake, that there the charge is just the opposite one, and that his crime was that he endeavoured to divert Blake from subject-painting to portraiture. So he did, no doubt; and the idea was to enable Blake to make a little money.

At any rate, to set against these possible errors of judgment, there is the undoubted fact that when, in 1777, Hayley composed the first of his major works to attain the dignity of print, the main object of this work, *The Epistle on Painting, addressed to George Romney*, was "to encourage the ambition of the painter [Romney]; to persuade him not to waste too large a portion of life in the lucrative drudgery of his profession [portrait-painting]; but to aspire to practical excellence in the highest department of his art [history painting]". It was a work in which compliment was not stinted; a brief quotation will speak for itself:

> Nature in thee her every gift combin'd,
> Which forms the artist of the noblest kind;
> That fond ambition, which bestows on art
> Each talent of the mind, and passion of the heart.
> That dauntless patience, which all toil defies,
> Nor feels the labour, while it views the prize.

The poem was extremely successful; I think there is no doubt that it did Romney an immense amount of good.

4

And now, once fairly started on his poetical career, there was no stopping Hayley. He emitted poesy upon every occasion, and contrived, usually, to get it printed. At the beginning of 1777, for instance, he had an "excrescence within the lower lid of his left eye". His friend Long operated, and was rewarded by an extensive *Epistle*:

> Health to the friend who passed a wintry way
> To save with healing heart our visual ray.

But this was a mere by-product. The epic on Magna Charta not proceeding as it should, Hayley set to work and addressed to Gray's old disciple, the Revd. William Mason, an *Essay on Epic Poetry*, in which the job was virtually handed on to him, and he was exhorted to "build a national epic poem on the freedom of England". And, in the same year, he apostrophised Marmontel, who had recently written *Les Incas*, in an *Epistle* purporting to have been composed by the Inca of Quito.

This production, we are told, was "rather a favourite" of Hayley's, and he pleased himself with the idea of its leading him into an agreeable correspondence with a foreign writer of distinction. Consequently he despatched his poem to Paris by the hand of a young friend, upon whom he at the same time bestowed a very affecting letter of moral advice on the perilous scene—Paris—that he was preparing to visit. But, unfortunately, Marmontel was not in the capital; the epistle never reached him, and so the agreeable correspondence did not materialize.

However, 1778 saw the publication of the *Epistle on Painting*, and, inspired by its success, Hayley at once set to and composed no less than four tragedies which, though they were at the time flatly rejected by the managers, were later printed, and even, some of them, acted.

The following year was a quiet one, in which the poet published merely an *Epistle to Admiral Keppel* congratulating him on his acquittal from a charge of dereliction of duty, which he duly despatched "with an anonymous billet" to the admiral; and an *Elegy* in which he admonished, for reasons into which we now need not enter, the then Bishop of London. More important still, in view of its repercussions, he also this year started his *Essay on History* which was addressed to Gibbon, the first volume of whose great work had come out three years before.

Early that summer the usual round of excursions began, to London, to Hertfordshire, and to Kent. The Hertfordshire visit was to Thornton, who introduced him to Dr. Cotton, the poetical physician of St. Albans, who, sixteen years before, had taken charge of William Cowper, during the darkest period of his malady. Thornton's health was failing, and he had placed himself under the care of Dr. Cotton. Hayley deemed his friend's malady "partly hypochondriacal", but added, very sensibly, "in all dark internal maladies, the feelings of the sufferer are more to be trusted than the prognostics of his medical attendants". He was, he confessed, hardly able to "tear himself away from a spectacle at once so attractive and so depressing". The phrase tells us a good deal about him.

Yet, for all Hayley's suspicions of hypochondria, Thornton was genuinely ill. So ill that, at the turn of the year, on January 5, 1780, he died. It was the first of the repeated losses that Hayley was fated to undergo. Setting everything aside, he turned at once to the memorializing of his friend, and had soon composed an *Elegy*. In its solemn eighteenth century style, this is by no means so bad as a great deal of his later verse, and so I think I might do worse than quote a few lines from it, as much for the light they throw upon Hayley as for that which they throw upon Thornton. First then, see Thornton, the partizan of awakening talent:

> Friend of my opening soul! whose love began
> To hail thy Poet, ere he rank'd as man!
> Whose praise, like dew-drops which the early morn
> Sheds with mild virtue on the vernal thorn,
> Taught his young mind each swell of thought to shew,
> And gave the germs of fancy strength to blow!

Cambridge:

> Ye towers of Granta, where our friendship grew,
> And that pure mind expanded to my view,

> Our love fraternal let your walls attest,
> Where Attic joys our letter'd evening blest;
> Where midnight, from the chains of sleep reliev'd,
> Stole on our social studies unperceiv'd!

Indeed, there is a sincerity in this lamentation which, as loss succeeded loss, grows ever fainter. Hayley even strikes out a couplet which conveys with real accuracy the feelings of anyone who has been bereaved:

> At evening's pensive hour, or opening day,
> He yet shall seem the partner of our way;

though he ends his poem on a note which, neat as it is, is highly characteristic of his century:

> So may we still in this dark scene of earth,
> Hold sweet communion with thy living worth;
> And, while our purer thoughts thy merit scan,
> Revère the Angel, as we lov'd the Man.

The death of Thornton had one other consequence. He had been the chief supporter of the Epic. With his departure from the "dark scene of earth", Hayley set that work aside for ever, and no one now knows what English poetry has lost. It is, of course, permissible to conjecture; but it is kinder to do nothing of the sort.

5

No man's activities were less predictable than Hayley's. No sooner had he composed his *Elegy on the Death of Mr. Thornton* than he repaired to his writing-table, and, upon January 28, 1780, addressed himself to the venerable William Melmoth, "an excellent critic and amiable writer", who lived at Bath and was a perfect stranger to him.

He wrote as follows: "Dear Sir, Though I have never had the pleasure of conversing with you, my vanity has for some time taken the liberty to reckon you in the list of my friends." He went on to tell Melmoth about Thornton's inscrutable disease, and to assure him that "under the pressure of this recent affliction, I have found a very soothing satisfaction in reviewing your excellent translation of Laelius . . . I am not," he added proudly, "afraid of your suspecting this to be the language of flattery; for you are too well acquainted with the human affections, and know that the voice of sorrow, though frequently impertinent, is not addicted to adulation". And he enclosed, for Melmoth's perusal, the Elegy which he has written upon their, apparently mutual, friend. He concluded with his usual invitation to Eartham, failing which: "May I solicit the consolation and pleasure of seeing you in your letters?"

Melmoth's reply was favourable; the correspondence thus solicited was established; and the *Elegy* was published in the spring.

Likewise, in that same spring, Hayley published his *Essay on History*, addressed to Gibbon; and his *Ode to Philanthropy*, which sang the praises of John Howard, the prison-reformer. The *Essay on History* was duly despatched to Gibbon, with a covering letter in which Hayley declared himself "apprehensive that I resemble the famous pedant of antiquity, who read a tedious lecture to Hannibal on the art of war", but added that "eager as I am to cultivate your regard, you will perceive that I am not afraid to censure you, in the very moment that I am soliciting a distinction so honourable as that of your Friend, a title which I should by no means despair of gaining, were I certain that my composition did justice to the idea which I entertain of yours". He need have had no fear. Both Gibbon and Howard received his advances with extreme graciousness; both visited him; and much epistolary intercourse ensued.

Meanwhile, as Hayley's literary fortunes thus prospered, a diversion occurred, when, at the beginning of June, 1780, the Gordon Riots broke out in the metropolis. Hayley chanced to be staying at the time at the house of a friend in Hart Street, Bloomsbury, and, at about four in the morning, he was awakened by the sound of firearms. He arose, and, looking out of the window, saw a dead man being carried by on a butcher's tray. Still worse, he perceived that Bloomsbury Square was on fire, and, recollecting that the female servant of another of his friends was alone in a house near the scene of the trouble, he courageously resolved to dress and go to her assistance. Passing through groups of "most fiendlike wretches" he was able to contemplate the burning of Lord Mansfield's house, which was now well alight. The first thing he noticed when he reached the premises of his friend was "a dead glazier", left leaning against the iron-rails of the house. How he knew the man to be a glazier I have no idea, unless it was that he carried the insignia of his trade. He knocked; he was admitted. He cheered and fortified the old servant who had remained faithfully at her post, and he stayed with her until things grew quieter. Then he returned to breakfast in Hart Street; and went home again to Sussex.

That summer, at Eartham, he meditated and composed the work that was to prove the most popular of all his poems, *The Triumphs of Temper*: an extensive performance, as he calls it, for the extreme success of which we can now perceive singularly little reason. Later we shall discuss this master-work in rather more detail, but for the present we can confine ourselves to saying that the essence of the poem, and, it is to be presumed, the source of its success also, was the simple doctrine that, if a young woman wants to secure a good husband, the chief quality she requires is a good temper.

That he should have written such a poem at such a time is significant, since it was in this same year of 1780 that it first becomes apparent that his marriage with Eliza was not an unqualified success. The simplest possible demonstration of this fact is provided by the birth, on October 5 of this year, of his son, Thomas Alphonso. As this may seem, at first sight, a strangely unconvincing proof of domestic infelicity, it may be as well to explain, without more ado, that the mother of Thomas Alphonso was not, as might have been expected, Mrs. Hayley, but a certain Miss Betts, housemaid at Eartham, and daughter of his deeply-read old nurse, Sarah Betts.[2]

CHAPTER V

ELIZA: AND ANNA SEWARD (1780-1782)

I

Mrs. Hayley is a figure of so much importance in our story that she requires somewhat extended consideration. To take her good qualities first, she was, her husband tells us, "a peculiarly interesting and lovely young woman". Her features were delicate and expressive of sense, vivacity and good nature; her hair was light and beautiful, her complexion rosy. Her speaking voice was musical; and, though the acquisition of music was "rather an irksome labour to her, yet, by the long attention which, from the continued advice and entreaty of her husband, . . . she bestowed on the cultivation of her voice, she sang with great sweetness".

There, however, the catalogue of her virtues stops abruptly. Her mother, as will be remembered, was mentally deranged, and it was Hayley's simple contention, throughout the whole of his *Memoirs*, that the daughter, his "pitiable Eliza" as he habitually calls her, was similarly afflicted. He does not mince matters, either. There were, says he, in her "marvellous organization, inscrutable sources of suffering, which rendered her occasionally one of the most truly pitiable of mortals"; and he proceeds to illustrate his point by quoting the dictum of "one of her most attentive medical friends": "Her whole frame is full of pins and needles; at every turn they run into her, and she imputes the blame to the first cause that occurs to her agitated fancy."

Well, the point is a moot one, upon which it is hardly possible, at this time of day, to arrive at the truth, especially as almost all that we know of Eliza is what Hayley himself has to tell us, and he is not, in this connection, a very impartial witness. That she was flighty, and volatile, and sexually frigid, I think we may with some degree of safety assume; and, if the story which, years later, Hayley confided to Walter Scott of the circumstances of her birth be a true one, all this is hardly to be wondered at. It will be remembered that already at the time of their engagement, Mrs. Hayley senior had expressed her doubts.

But the facts with regard to the pitiable Eliza are so elusive that it is best to marshal them together. Apart from what Hayley himself has to say, the fullest description we have of her is that contained in a letter of Anna Seward, who knew her well. This letter was written to a Mrs. Gell on December 3, 1797, after Miss Seward had heard the news of Eliza's death; and here is the relevant passage:

Dear Mrs. Hayley has died! . . . We met at Derby last spring. She then appeared in the strongest-possible health. Never was there a firmer constitution. I have not known her to complain of bodily indisposition. She had a Gallic gaiety of spirit, which the infelicities of her destiny could but transiently, however violently, impede. The short paroxysm of anguish passed, the tide of vivacity returned, and bore down everything before it.

Nature, after striking off this one singularly characteristic impression, broke the mould in which she made Mrs. Hayley.

Fire in her affections, frost in her sensations, she shrank from the caresses even of the husband she adored. Hence, while she had a morbid degree of tenaciousness respecting his esteem and attention, she was incapable of personal jealousy; and would amuse herself with the idea of those circumstances, with which she could so perfectly well dispense, being engrossed by another.

Alike during the years of their union, and in those of their separation, she gloried in the talents of her bard, as she used to call Mr. Hayley, and delighted to praise his virtues, perpetually producing specimens of the first, and giving instances of the latter.

While her heart was warmly attached to the many whom she believed her friends—for to wish and to believe were twin feelings with Mrs. Hayley—while she could not bear, without visible pain and ardent vindication, the slightest word which had a tendency to question their pretensions to talent and virtue; yet, respecting strangers, or acquaintance that did not interest her, she had a quick sense of the ridiculous, which produced very pointed satire;—but, never tired of placing an absurd speech, or mean action, in new lights of ludicrous exhibition, the fertility of her imagination counteracted the fine edge of her wit, worked her theme thread-bare, and fatigued her auditors.

With sportive fancy; with no inconsiderable portion of belles-lettres knowledge; with polite address, and an harmonious voice in speaking, and with the grace of correct and elegant language; with rectitude of principles, unsuspecting frankness of heart, and extreme good humour; she was, strange to say! not agreeable, at least not permanently agreeable. The unremitting attention her manner of conversing seemed to claim; her singular laugh, frequent and excessive, past all proportion to its cause, overwhelmed, wearied, and oppressed even those who were most attached to her; who felt her worth, and pitied her banishment from the man on whom she doated. . . . Yet her rage for society, and excessive love of talking, were so ill calculated to the inclinations and habits of a studious recluse, as to render their living together inconsistent with the peace of either. However, while their separation was the quiet haven of his spirit, it was, unfortunately, a source of pain and mortification to her. . . .

Her unhappiness in the disunion, came on by sudden violences of sensation, like the grief of the Otaheiteans, who, when the thought of a lost friend occurs, start into agony, shriek, and wound themselves, and then, as instantly recovering, laugh, sing, and dance.

I am extremely curious to know how and why she died; as the event, simply announced in the newspapers, is all I know. If her intentionally blameless spirit slid out of existence by any of those countless doors which disease and accidents open, her death will relieve Mr. Hayley's mind from much anxiety, occasioned by her total want of common-life discretion, and of economy. . . . I hope there was no self-violence;* but her strong health, the extreme, though transient bitterness with which she felt every new mortification, would prevent my being surprised, if information that her expences were likely to banish Mr. Hayley from his beloved home, had produced a rashness. Alas! should it be so, Mr. Hayley's quiet will have received a cureless wound. If not, he will be the happier for this removal.

And, to the passage marked with an asterisk, Miss Seward, in her printed version of the letter, attached this foot-note: "The author, soon after the date of this letter, had the satisfaction of learning that Mrs. Hayley died of an epidemic fever, and that her fears of self-violence in the case had no foundation."

This passage, when it was published in 1811 in the *Letters of Anna Seward*, occasioned Hayley a great deal of distress, not, it would seem, because of the imputation that "those circumstances with which" Eliza "could so perfectly well dispense" had been "engrossed by another" (because by then he had quite ceased to keep up the fiction that Thomas Alphonso was his adopted rather than his natural son), but because of the strictures contained in it upon his late wife's "permanent agreeableness"; though I cannot myself see that Miss Seward's brilliant character-sketch comprises any ingredients which are not present, over and over again, in Hayley's own account of her.

But he evidently thought otherwise, since he now took it upon himself to address to Walter Scott, who, though not editor of these particular volumes, was editor of the poetical part of Miss Seward's remains, the following private and confidential missive,[1] of September 15, 1811, to which I have already alluded. In this, hoping to make matters better, and really making them a great deal worse, he wrote:

I promised you some particulars of a *mysterious nature* concerning the cruelty and ingratitude of our unhappy and vindictive Anna Seward towards the memory of my piteous Eliza. . . . The manner in which Seward indulged her vanity and spleen by writing a very indecent and injurious character of that hapless and in some points angelic Lady has appeared to me more reprehensible because Seward was confidentially acquainted with a *Secret History* relating to the marvellous Organisation and Infelicities of that singular Personage which ought to have filled our intelligent Poetess with a tender and delicate Respect for her Memory, especially as the Poetess had received from Mrs. H. many proofs of the kindest hospitality at Eartham. The *Secret History* alluded to is *so extraordinary* that to give you the clearest Idea of it, I will transcribe the following Passage from a private piece of Biography intended for a posthumous Publication:

"Though William Hayley in the year 1769 had married a young Lady in the Bloom of Health and Beauty, he might justly regard himself in one point of view as having *no* wife. He had married a person to whom Nature not only refused . . . the privilege of producing a child, but even those natural desires which she has wisely and tenderly given to Modesty herself for the preservation of the human Race. The astonishing existence of a beautiful female Form with an affectionate Heart and a very feeling Mind, yet *so organised*, was owing to a circumstance *not less astonishing*. The excellent Mother of this singular, pitiable Female had fallen into a state of Insanity from a Cause that justly excited the most tender compassion. She had the misfortune to lose several children. Her husband, of a very affectionate but irritable Temper, could hardly bear these repeated Losses. In striving to mitigate the excess of his grief she suppressed her own; and that suppression (as medical men imagined) involved her in the Calamity of absolute distraction. The celebrated Dr. Batty, most eminent at that period *as the Physician of Insanity*, having tried, with no success, to effectuate by Medicine and Regimen the cure of this interesting sufferer, said—with the boldness of desperate Humanity—to her afflicted husband: 'Sir, as your amiable wife lost her senses from the Loss of her children, it is possible that the birth of another child might restore them.' The most affectionate of Husbands endeavoured to realise an Idea so delightful to his Heart, unrestrained by all that cool Reason and considerate Nature might suggest against it. His wife conceived, and brought forth a Daughter without any consciousness of conception or childbirth. That daughter, by a series of many surprising Incidents, became the wife of William Hayley; and from the marvellous Infelicity of her Frame, though he loved her as a Bosom Friend, he considered himself as singularly exempted from a strict observance of the nuptial vow. . . .

"I have mentioned these extraordinary Circumstances not to justify but to palliate his Conduct. Violations of Divine Law ought never perhaps to be stated as *innocent*; but there may be many occasions on which they occur (and this is probably one) where enlightened Humanity will pity, condemn, and forgive."

That then is Hayley's own story; and for all we can tell now to the contrary, it may well be the true one. And yet, as one follows the progress of Eliza through such independent evidences as are vouchsafed us, one wonders a little. On January 3, 1799, for instance, Joseph Farington notes in his Diary[2] a conversation which he has just had with Flaxman, an old and faithful friend of Hayley, in which the matter is put in a rather less melodramatic light: "Flaxman told me . . . Mr. Hayley married the daughter of a Clergyman. . . . She had no children by Hayley & expressed a wish that He would take the daugr. of his Nurse, (His foster sister) into his House *in Her place.*—This Hayley did, and they all lived together cordially, and by this young woman Hayley had the boy. . . .—Mrs. Hayley was very excentric in Her conduct, would often on a sudden, when in Sussex say she must go to London, and would accordingly drive off, and while her spirits lasted go much into public places.— these dashing excursions were succeeded by fits of lowness of spirits and by degrees Hayley & she finding their lives rendered uncomfortable when together amiably agreed to part. They accordingly separated & Hayley allowed Her what He could afford.—She had about £7000 as her fortune—The nurse's daugr. now lives at a house belonging to Hayley"; which, in fact, lay just outside his estate.

This account seems to me less highly-coloured than Hayley's own, as given at enormous length in his *Memoirs*; to which, after this involved but most necessary digression, we can now return.

After a month in London during the autumn of 1780, where Mrs. Hayley had singing lessons, the family returned to Eartham, and Hayley takes up at once the tale of Eliza's plight: "The health of Mrs. Hayley had been ever irregular. The fluctuation of her spirits was rapid to an alarming degree." They had gone back to Eartham in November (Thomas Alphonso, it will be remembered, had been born on October 5), and now her medical advisers recommended that she should reside for some time at Bath. Hayley, although his "passion for retirement and literary enterprise conspired with his slender finances to make him a recluse", yet most willingly took upon himself the expense of providing for her in the most comfortable manner. Her nervous infirmities, he thought, admitted "only of such palliation as might be gained by tender and liberal care"; and, accordingly, he sent her to Bath, where his new friend, Mr. Melmoth, volunteered to look after her.

2

And so, by the beginning of 1781, an animated correspondence between Mrs. Hayley and her husband was in full swing. She had met the awe-inspiring Melmoth, who had at once introduced her to Gibbon, to Gibbon's step-mother, and to the sister of his friend, Lord Sheffield. Gibbon had been most gracious: he had enquired solicitously after the progress of *The Triumphs of Temper*, and had also "rallied" Eliza on the subject of matrimony.

Hayley was delighted both with her social successes, and with the "exquisite" style in which she narrated them. He told her to put herself entirely into Melmoth's hands in the matter of her "conduct"; adding, a little oddly, that the world might not understand, as he did, how "much more of the angel than of the woman" was "blended in her constitution".

Soon Eliza had begun the Waters, and had also been invited by Gibbon to attend, under his chaperonage, the fantastic ceremonial of the Bath Easton vase. She added somewhat acutely regarding her new mentor that, "though he has condescended to interest himself concerning my health and establishment", he really "wishes me to *look up to him*".

By February, however, the old trouble was reasserting itself, and she confessed that, with the novelty of Bath wearing off, her customary ennui had set in. To this Hayley briskly responded with a long screed to say that he had been looking into his finances, and that he would deem it on the whole most fortunate if she were soon to be seized with a "passion for retirement" equal to his own.

To this thinly-veiled suggestion that it was time for her return, Eliza made no response. Instead, she despatched forthwith a glowing account of the junketings at Bath Easton, in which she dilated with relish on the vase "elegantly ornamented with laurels and pink riband", and begged her husband instantly to compose a poem for her that she could enter for the prize.

It was March now, and Hayley, feeling perhaps that it was the only way to get her to come home, complied and sent off some lines upon *Content*, which were duly submitted at the next Thursday meeting, and as duly received the myrtle-wreath that was first prize. He acknowledged with gratification the receipt of this wreath which was at once forwarded to him; but added with determination that he was proposing to escort her back to Eartham on April 11.

In the meantime, *The Triumphs of Temper* had reached Bath, and Eliza basked in reflected glory. It had, she told its author, quite banished her headache. Hayley, in reply, informed her that his old nurse was reading aloud to him the recently-published second and third volumes of *The Decline and Fall of the Roman Empire*. When each double page was completed, she handed the book over to him, for him to examine the footnotes. Mrs. Betts, it appears, did not unreservedly approve the tone of the work. During some passages describing the capture of Rome by the Goths, "where the grave historian talks a little too facetiously about the captive virgins, &c", she observed roundly: "In my mind this is a sad pack of stuff to put into so fine a book."

Eliza, I fear, must have wriggled out of her proposed date for returning, for, though no letter of hers on the subject is preserved, Hayley's next is composed more in sorrow than in anger:

> My dear Eliza, as you think a longer residence in Bath of real consequence to your health, you have my full permission to remain there, till the last moment that you wish to do so. In all points remember it is my ardent and invariable wish to promote your welfare and happiness, to which I am ever ready to sacrifice both my fortune and my pleasure.

She got her own way after all. It was not until May that Hayley went up to London to escort her home. She had then been away nearly five months. The expense must have been terrifying.

But, before they met, there is one more incident that can hardly be passed over, since it relates to a typically Hayleian imbroglio. Miss Hannah More, "the fair poetess of Bristol", had paid tribute to the moral excellences of his newly-published *Triumphs of Temper*; and Hayley, always impulsive, had sent her a poem of thanks. The last stanza of this effusion ran as follows:

> How may he scorn all human harms!
> How blissful his condition!
> Who shall encircle in his arms
> So lovely a magician!

The magician in question being, it is perhaps necessary to state, Miss Hannah More.

Now, as a rule, Hayley had the wise custom of submitting everything he wrote to his friend Dr. Long, but upon this occasion he could not do so, because Long was on the road to Salisbury. But when he was next available, the verses were duly shown to him, and he expressed the view, which alarmed Hayley very much, that the conclusion of them was "rather too warm". "He was", Hayley wrote, "surprised to see a composition with a spark of animation from a poor poet, whose animal spirits he had just been draining, by four leeches, and two blisters. . . . They appear to me without a shadow of any thing that can appear too strong for the eyes of the most delicate and modest of women. I would not offend my fair poetical encomiast; but I think she must be very prudish indeed, (which I am very far from supposing her to be,) if my verses offend her in that point of view."

Well, well; it is pleasant to reflect that Hannah More also was young once. There is no evidence that she was offended. Indeed, I don't suppose she was. After all, there was an occasion, on Friday, April 20, in this same year of 1781, when, at a party at Mrs. Garrick's, a much more outrageous observation was made in her hearing. And what did she do? She "slily hid her face behind a lady's back who sat on the same settee with her". James Boswell was also present, and has immortalized the incident.

3

It is clear enough that the domestic affairs of the Hayleys were approaching a crisis. Eliza, though nothing in her conduct at this time gives support to Hayley's contention that she was insane, was evidently extravagant, giddy, and profoundly self-centred: was, in short, very much the sort of person that Anna Seward had described to Mrs. Gell.

If further proof were needed of her sanity, one may be brought forward in the fact that she had actually, at about this time, published a book, though it was only a translation of the Marchioness Lambert's *Essays on Friendship and Old Age*.[3] This, however, is a point that I will not stress unduly, because, on reflection, I am not at all sure that the publication of a book is an action that any reputable Court of Law would accept as a guarantee of sanity.

Hayley, when he reached London, to escort his wife home, soon found his most gloomy prognostications fulfilled. The waters of Bath had rendered no essential service to her singular state of health. She seemed, he thought, merely to have amused her mind, and to have had a number of excellent music-lessons. He deemed himself, he says rather pathetically, agreeably rewarded for the expense of her residence at Bath, by the increased powers and sweetness of her voice, and consoled himself by the reflection that music might well be the best antidote that could be found for the agitation of her nerves.

But all these things, including the fashionable music-masters, had turned out hideously expensive, and so Hayley returned to his poetry with increasing ardour, during the summer that ensued. He worked zealously on his *Essay on Epic Poetry*, in the hope that it would produce "sufficient supplies". He found time, also, to send a few verses to the redoubtable Anna Seward, in praise of her recently published *Elegy* on his old (and now eaten) acquaintance, Captain Cook; and this secured for him the friendship of that formidable lady.

In November, Eliza returned again to the distractions of Bath, thus enabling Hayley to accept an invitation to visit Miss Seward and her father "in their hospitable mansion", the Episcopal Palace of Lichfield. He arrived at noon on December 15 at the house of his friend, Beridge, in Derby, where were "two pleasant girls", one of whom obligingly sang the "Skirmishing Song" to the strains of the Doctor's flute. Here also he met the celebrated Dr. Darwin, later to be his poetical competitor, and by him sent on a note to Miss Seward to announce his approach. He wrote to Eliza from Derby, telling her he was going to visit his old friend, Joseph Wright, and he concluded, rather affectingly: "I touch not on the material article in your last letter, *money*; because I find Dodsley [his publisher] intended to send you a fresh supply of that important commodity."

On December 18 he was installed in the Episcopal Palace, and wrote again. Thus:

Behold me seated, my dear Eliza, in a very noble and comfortable house of the church, where divinity and poetry form a very uncommon and agreeable alliance! [I arrived yesterday soon after twelve.] The fair Muse perceived my chaise as she was sitting in a neighbour's window, and hastened home to receive me.... My reception was gracious in the highest degree.... She is a handsome likeness of those full-length pictures which you have seen of Queen Elizabeth, where the painters gave her Majesty all the beauty they could consistent with the character of her face. The Muse laughs at herself as fat and lame; yet the connoisseurs in woman would still pronounce her handsome. . . . She is famous for her elocution . . . and reads with peculiar force and propriety. . . . The execution is fine, though the instrument is imperfect.

4

Anna Seward* is a personage, a portent, so characteristic of her age that it is perhaps permissible at this point to say a little about her. Though she did not spend much time with Hayley, their meetings being confined to that which we are describing, to a return visit which she paid to Eartham in the summer of the following year, and to a brief encounter, again in Lichfield, in the May of 1789, they were indefatigable correspondents, and, though their friendship sadly enough turned sour from a variety of causes long before Miss Seward's death in 1809, there was, while it lasted, nothing to touch it for sheer frenzy of mutual admiration. A rhyme current at the time,[4] the work of Dr. Mansel, the witty Bishop of Bristol, hits off fairly enough the orgy of public complimenting which ensued when Anna Seward and William Hayley got together:

> *Miss S:* Prince of poets, England's glory,
> Mr. Hayley, *that* is you!
> *Mr. H:* Ma'am, you carry all before you,
> Trust me, Lichfield Swan, you do.
> *Miss S:* In epic, elegy or sonnet,
> Mr. Hayley, you're divine!
> *Mr. H:* Madam, take my word upon it,
> You yourself are—all the Nine!

Even so, Miss Seward's correspondence is to be treated seriously enough, as one of the chief sources of information which we now possess upon the subject of this memoir. It is, therefore, important to know the sort of person she was. Born December 12, 1747, she was two years younger than Hayley, and was consequently thirty-four years of age at their first meeting. The description Hayley has already given of her says that she was still handsome, and the phrase in which he speaks of her laughing at herself as "fat and lame" is revealing, since she had been, according to Scott at any rate, "exquisitely beautiful when young". Unfortunately, in her early twenties, she had had a fall, and had broken her kneecap, which caused her to walk with a limp and to become unduly stout. Very feminine and romantic by nature, she had had two affairs of the heart in her youth with young soldiers named Vyse and Taylor; and in her middle years she became exceedingly attached to Dr. Erasmus Darwin, and had fully expected him to marry her after the death of his first wife. He did not do so, however, and she spent her latter years in a platonic but strong attachment to John Saville, the Vicar-choral of Lichfield Cathedral. I do not doubt that there was a good deal of personal feeling in her early enthusiasm for

* Who, incidentally, pronounced her name See-ward, not Su-ward.

Hayley's work, nor that it was a feeling which could easily have turned to love, if he had not happened already to be married. It was this original strain of tenderness in her regard for him which caused her later attitude to become so uncommonly embittered.

Anna Seward is a difficult person for us to understand nowadays. For one thing, her verse is unreadable: one wonders indeed how it was ever read. For another, almost all the writers that she admired are writers we no longer admire, or even remember. "Matchless" Jephson, Mundy, Sargent, William Newton the Peak Minstrel, Mrs. Yearsley the Bristol Milkwoman—never was there, it would seem, such an appalling collection of non-stayers. And, moreover, when a writer of quality did happen to arise, Miss Seward was not at all quick in picking him. Her views on Johnson, and Boswell, are well enough known; she thought the former an envious boor, and the latter a sycophantic fool; she greatly preferred *Ossian* to the works of Cowper; and Southey (of *Madoc* and *Joan*) to Wordsworth (of the daffodils). Despite which, save where matters of taste were concerned, she was very far from stupid. She was a woman of solid and robust intelligence, and, though she wrote habitually in a most elaborate and high-flown style, she had a great deal of humour, and considerable shrewdness. Though she was capable of describing woodcocks as "the transmigrating gentry of dusky pinion", she was equally liable to come out with such sensible observations as the following, with regard to Dr. Darwin's *Botanic Garden*: "Young women who could be endangered by such descriptions must have a temperament so unfortunately combustible as to render it unsafe to trust them with the writings of our best poets. . . . *Paradise Lost* presents more highly-coloured scenes than any which pass in the floral harems; so does the song of Solomon. . . . Do not suppose that a virtuous girl, or young married woman, could be induced, by reading the *Botanic Garden*, to imitate the involuntary libertinism of a fungus or a flower. . . ." It is in the grand manner, of course, but the grand manner grandly handled. And how surprising, critically considered, is the following observation (in a letter to Mrs. Hayley) on Dr. Darwin's poetical principles: "His system demands, that all poetic apartments, from the saloon to the water-closet, should be covered with pictures, allowing not an inch space between them."

Besides, Anna Seward had an immense zest for life; she could never resist a show: laughing hyaenas, mad dogs, the Chevalier d'Eon, the Ladies of Llangollen, the French officers captured in Ireland in 1798, the Cambrian Orpheus, Randall "the Meonides of the pedal-harp", fire-balls "the size of a melon", thunderstorms, which make her "extremely irrational", Dr. Parr "in clouds of tobacco", animal magnetism, Æolian harps, Mrs. Delany's celebrated *hortus siccus*, Mr. Saville's green-frog—anything and everything that was out of the ordinary amused and delighted her. And she revelled consistently, her whole life through, in the music of Handel, and "crosses wild hills" to hear it performed in Sheffield, and other unlikely places.

Indeed, her love for variety comes out even in the subjects she chose for her flat and turgid works. How stimulating, one would fancy, should be a "Runic ode with a funeral forest at midnight, an Amazonian nymph, opening her father's tomb by magic spells, and forcing thence an enchanted sword, which ascends in a pillar of fire from the withered hands of a warrior's corse". That it fails to stimulate is perhaps not our fault; but it is a great mistake to think that Miss Seward, in herself, was as dull as her lamentable poetry.

Besides, she was a patron, and in her way a generous one. She 'thought Hayley's poems (oddly enough) "equal to Dryden", and setting her own beside them said "faint one day will be *their* bloom and odour, compared with the magnolias, roses, and amaranths of the Haylean wreath"; she fostered the early muse of Cary, the translator of Dante, and of Lister, whose principal production was his son, who was once memorable as the author of the novel called *Granby*; and she waxed extremely indignant because the whole of Southey's profits for a year's sale of *Madoc* amounted to the sum of £3 17s. 1d.

In fact, I fancy that if she had not been so unwise as consistently to belittle Dr. Johnson, we should regard Miss Seward a good deal more kindly than we do. Boswell, of whom she thought but poorly, has extinguished her even more effectually than she has contrived to extinguish herself. And it is a pity, for she can be very rich.

5

Hayley wrote again from Lichfield on December 23: "A country town is a scene so very unfit for poetical studies" that he is "amazed the Muse can write at all". They have been inundated with a multitude of female visitors, and a host of divines; Mr. Saville's voice has astonished him; but all the same, "in the midst of honours and flattery", he has found himself sighing for the silence and solitude of Eartham.

Mrs. Hayley replied: "Your descriptions are so descriptive." She regrets the deplorable state of his health, and goes on to tell him about Mr. Glover, the author of *Leonidas*, who is at Bath; and that she is not only going again to Bath Easton, but is also about to meet Mrs. Siddons. And she concluded by asking him to wonder and admire at the discretion of a Bath lady who has spent three evenings in succession alone in her apartment, at the height of the season.

A week later Hayley wrote to congratulate Eliza both for the affection that her letter breathed and the expedition with which it travelled. But he added that, though truly delighted with Miss Seward's wonderful talents and most pleasing manners, he has resolved to beat a hasty retreat to the solitude of Eartham. Money is the cause of this decision, for, as he says, "the prosaic visitants of a country town absolutely rob me of all literary powers, and not even the sublime Muse of Lichfield can counterbalance their lethargic influence".

One cannot help feeling that he did not enjoy his stay at Lichfield quite as much as he had hoped to do. At any rate, Anna Seward had no such reservations. She accompanied her departing guest on his road to London as far as Coleshill, and in the chaise, on her way back, she commenced an *Epistle to William Hayley Esq.*[5] that starts in the following arresting fashion:

> 'Tis past!—the shades of deprivation lour,
> Numbing with influence cold, the heavy hour.
> Thy joys, O Friendship! fly ere well begun,
> Like the mild shining of yon liquid sun
> Through this short winter's day:—and yet I hear
> Haylean accents vibrate on my ear;
> Still on that countenance I seem to gaze,
> Whence mingled stream the intellectual rays. . . .

Further on in the same opus we catch a glimpse of Hayley's manner of passing his time at Lichfield:

> And late ye saw, at evening's solemn hours,
> As sigh'd the winter-blast amid your towers,
> Britain's distinguish'd Bard beneath you stray,
> And bend through your long aisles his musing way,

to which passage is appended the clarifying footnote: "It was Mr. Hayley's custom, during his fortnight's residence at Lichfield, to walk in the side aisles of the Cathedral during choir-service at evening prayers, which are always performed by candle-light in winter . . . [giving a] fine effect of dubious light and shadow."

Back again at Eartham, Hayley was able to reflect with complacency on a good year's work, on the publication of his *Triumphs of Temper*, and on the completion of his *Essay on Epic Poetry*. And now, in addition, he had the little Alphonso, whose infantine endearments had "infinite influence over his heart and imagination".

Moreover, it really seemed that when Hayley and Eliza were apart, nothing could be more affable than their relations. She wrote again, proposing "a tempting horse", and he replied, declining the horse not only on the ground of the difficulty of conveying the beast to Eartham, but also on the even greater one of paying for it. This factor of expense, he said, had nearly persuaded him not to go to Lichfield, but he is glad that he did, since now he is going to shut himself up and work hard, "to procure the last requisite" both for Eliza and for himself.

To this she replied with an enquiry as to the number of Alphonso's teeth. "And does he eat hearty?"

On January 20, Hayley, emerging from perfect solitude and a redoubled fury of work, engendered by the sight of his Christmas bills, answered her enquiry, saying that Alphonso regards her return with "affectionate gallantry" (Alphonso being now some fifteen months old). "I shewed him the other day your miniature portrait from the cabinet, and ever since he never enters this room without running to the cabinet, and begging to have the picture produced. . . . He is very lively and fond of play. Books are his favourite playthings; you would be much diverted to hear him *pretending to read*, and still more to see him imitate Nurse reading with her magnifying glass; for this purpose he has seized an old brass buckle to a door, and holding it by the screw, he directs his eye through the circular part of it, held over a book."

It is a touching picture, but Mrs. Hayley, though she told her husband that she delighted in it, exhibited no inclination to come home and share his domestic joys. Instead she regaled him with literary anecdotes.

Hayley, overworking, fell victim again to his eye-trouble, and developed thoughts of engaging a secretary. "You know", he wrote, "I am as magnificent in my projects, for a poet, as my Lord Chatham was for a minister." Mrs. Hayley thought the notion excellent, but before she had time to urge him to carry it out, his volatile mind had moved on, and he was confessing to her that he was experiencing "parliamentary ambitions". These, he added quickly, he "violently repressed", since, despite his "unquenchable passion for freedom", he was, upon reflection, able to see in provincial politics "nothing of which he could perfectly approve". Perhaps it was as well, though imagination cannot help conjuring up an engaging picture of Hayley addressing the House of Commons.

By April he was writing to his still absent wife to enquire if she had had any tidings of Gibbon, whose revenue had been sadly diminished by "the annihilation of the Board of Trade", and hoping that "some equivalent will be found to support the dignity of the Roman Eagle. Otherwise I apprehend he will retire to France . . . and that will be a disgrace to our country. . . . Indeed, I think our nation should form some kind of establishment to ensure ease and independence to her most eminent men of letters, a subject I intend to touch upon in one of the notes to my new poem." And he added, rather plantively: "A *certain* increase of annual income would be undoubtedly a great comfort to me, and it would make me perhaps a *better*, at least a *correcter*, poet."

It is to be feared that, already, Eliza's disbursements at Bath were heavy. So too were Hayley's, for the extensions and improvements to the house and park at Eartham, that were already well under way. And, indeed, in the following month, the same theme recurs, *fortissimo*. Eliza had arrived at last in the metropolis, and Hayley was to bring her home. "As to the weighty sums you have expended," he wrote, "if I am able, as I trust I shall be, to repay the dear friend who has supplied them, I hope they will never more give you an uneasy thought." It is an agreeable beginning, but he goes on in a more ominous tone: "The state of our exchequer . . . will certainly make it proper for me to adopt . . . a future plan of economy. . . . It will be necessary for me to employ as many hours of my life as my eyes and health will permit, in literary labour." And, in a note even deeper, he adds: "But a life so employed will necessarily produce at times some degree of *dullness* and *taciturnity* . . . and, as you have been used of late to more idle and gay companions, I would prepare you to look on my peculiarities with *affectionate indulgence*; as my works are to supply us both with the comforts of life, if the *author* frequently spoils the *companion*, I flatter myself the motive of his application will endear to you even the dullest effects of it."

This, I think, is an important letter, and one which, though couched in Hayley's most Micawberish style, reveals the true source of incompatibility between him and his wife. That his style upon such occasions has a ring of incomparable priggishness is not, I fancy, a difficulty. Coleridge's letters to his wife strike an almost identical note. It is very nearly impossible for the writer to plead his cause with the worldling without an appearance, at least, of preciousness. And, moreover, the case is the same whether the writer be one of the calibre of Coleridge or, merely, a Hayley. The reason for this is that it is just as exhausting to be a bad writer as it is to be a good one. The difference resides in the man himself; not in the energy expended.

6

That summer Hayley was busy seeing his *Essay on Epic Poetry* through the press. When it appeared, in June, he sent a copy of it to the Revd. William Mason, to whom it was addressed, with a "friendly letter", to which he soon received a reply that was, to say the least, chilly. "You have, I fear (Mason wrote), hazarded some of your great and deserved popularity, by so very partial an address to a writer who perceives his own credit with the public much on the decline; but who feels it without chagrin . . . sitting perhaps too easy to the taste of the times, and paying too little deference to the leaders of that taste."

Hayley decided that Mason was old—as he was—, and disappointed—as he was also, no doubt—, and consoled himself for the rebuff by the circumstance that Gibbon had declared, among other pleasing observations on his poem, that "since Pope's death, I am satisfied that England has not seen so happy a mixture of strong sense and flowing numbers".[6]

By June the cavalcade of summer visitors had commenced, headed this time by Miss Seward's friend, Mr. Saville, who had been sent, it would almost seem, to spy out the land for his more distinguished patron. For, as Hayley observes, "his grateful account" of his entertainment next induced Miss Seward herself to venture upon a visit of several weeks. Romney was there also, as usual, and both the pen of Hayley and the pencil of Romney became at once "most cheerfully employed" in delineating this good lady's various endowments, and in trying to entertain her in a manner congenial to her own "sprightly and cultivated mind".

It is not easy to-day for us to imagine the cultivated and sprightly fashion in which the hours of this visit were passed. Something may be gained perhaps by the inspection of Miss Seward's portrait which Romney painted a little later; something more by the famous interchange of verses which are to be found alike printed in the collected works of Hayley and of Anna Seward. It would seem that the August of 1782 was uncommonly wet, and Hayley, consequently, set to and produced a mock-heroic poem about it:

> Whence are these storms? an angry poet cried,
> Who saw his shady summer haunts defaced,
> Saw o'er his shatter'd grove, black whirlwinds ride,
> And deeply mourn'd the unseasonable waste.

To him, with sundry ghastly and striking circumstances, Eolus, the God of the Winds, uprears his head, and observes:

> Know thou, vain bard, within thy mansion dwells
> The wondrous source of all this wild uproar,
> Thence round my cave the din of discord swells,
> And I my rebel offspring rule no more.
>
> To own my law my madd'ning sons refuse,
> All, all are deaf to my paternal power,
> Struggling alike to kiss that vagrant Muse,
> Who deigns to visit thy sequester'd bower.

In short, all the winds want to kiss Miss Seward, and that is why the weather is so bad; and, in nine stanzas more, Hayley goes into the full details of the business; Boreas, Auster, Zephyr and Eurus each of them stating his case, until, at last, their contention is resolved by the suggestion of the poet that they shall all have a turn:

> Let each in order taste the tempting bliss
> ... Each unmolested take one precious kiss.

On September 5, Anna Seward started for home again, but on the preceding day she had been careful to pen the lament for her departure:

> To-morrow's dawn must bring th' unwelcome hour,
> When my reluctant spirit's kind farewell
> Shall mourn in sighs, through Eartham's beauteous bower,
> The vanish'd pleasures of the sylvan cell.

She then indulges in scenic description for several stanzas, and comes at length to an evocative passage:

> Groves *half* as fair as these may meet my eye,
> Thy bowers, O Litchfield, lovely scenes afford;
> But ah! what keen regrets shall wake the sigh
> To miss the pleasures of the Haylean board!
>
> Where, as his *pencil*, Romney's *soul* sublime
> Glows with bold lines, original and strong;
> While Fanny's lays and kindred spirit chime
> With fair Eliza's wit, and sparkling song.

Eliza we know, and Fanny was a Miss Heron, of Portsmouth, a friend of the family, much given to singing. Miss Seward, it may be noticed, had nothing to say of Miss Betts, the mother of Tom, and no wonder, since one of her greatest grievances against Hayley was that, upon this visit, he deceived her by leading her to believe that the child, now nearly two years of age, was by no means his but rather the offspring of an orphan youth, named Howell, who lived in the house under his protection, and of whose sad fate we shall hear later.

"He either chose to deceive me on the subject", she wrote in September 1800, "or I strangely misunderstood him."[7]

I do not think Miss Seward misunderstood him. I think the story she was told regarding Tom was that which was then in general circulation. It was, to be sure, very accommodating of Howell to shoulder the burden, particularly when Mrs. Hayley knew all about it. I even incline to think that it was Mrs. Hayley's not unnatural desire for the concealment of the true facts that was responsible. Who, at this distance of time, would wish to blame her?

CHAPTER VI

FRIENDSHIPS: AND THE DRAMA (1782–1785)

I

WE MUST NOT, however, permit the zeal with which we have followed the fortunes of Hayley and his Eliza to carry us past other landmarks. As his fame grew—and he was now, since the publication of the *Triumphs of Temper*, the leader (or at least the best-seller) of his profession—so also did his friendships. Romney, Wright and Meyer have already been noticed, and now, in the eighties, we come to the beginning of his relations with Gibbon and Flaxman; to say nothing of a host of lesser figures.

The case of John Flaxman (an important friendship since it was the one which later brought Blake into Hayley's life) is simple enough in its inception. Romney had been one of the earliest patrons of the young modeller, and it was he who introduced him, probably in 1783, to Hayley. The occasion for his introduction must, I fancy, have been the commissioning of Flaxman with the monument in Chichester Cathedral to Eliza's parents, since a letter of his of February 10, 1784,[1] to Hayley, reveals that he is already busy upon this work, and that, moreover, he has paid a visit to Eartham in connection with it, and has, rather strangely, been presented by his host with a hedgehog. In the same letter there is a reference linking Swedenborg with this hedgehog, which implies, I think, that Flaxman who was, or was about to become, a disciple of that curious prophet, had lent some of his sacred books to Hayley. The matter comes in a postscript, as follows:

> Pray when you have a favourable opportunity let me have Swedenborg, which reminds me of the Hedg-hogg who is very well and we have a tender regard for him on the giver's account.

This visit was followed by another in the autumn of 1784, in connection with the new library which Hayley had started building some while before, and was now approaching completion. He and Romney, upon the latter's usual autumn visit, had been discussing the appointments of this admirable apartment, and what could be more natural than that the name of Flaxman should occur to them as a suitable designer for the mantel-pieces.

The ungainly young sculptor, then a man of twenty-nine, revisited Eartham in September, and not only superintended the sculptural ornaments of the new library, but also executed portrait heads of

Hayley and Romney. When he was back in town he wrote to his host: "I had the happiness of living such a fortnight at Eartham, as many thousands of my fellow-creatures go out of the world without enjoying."

Flaxman's chimney-piece may still be seen in the library at Eartham, embellished with the muses of music and painting, with their attendant trappings of lyres and palettes. Hayley, moreover, was not the sort of man to be backward in securing other commissions for a friend. From the monument to the Ball family sprang directly that series of memorials with which, in later years, Flaxman enriched the cathedral of Chichester. In 1795 he executed the famous cenotaph to William Collins, the poet; then the memorial to Mrs. Jane Smith; and, in 1800, that to Agnes Cromwell, the most beautiful of them all. Certainly Hayley's introduction to Chichester had been well worth while to Flaxman; and he was never to forget the fact. Indeed, of all Hayley's friends, he was to remain the most constant.

It will, however, be noticed that between the date of the monument to the Ball family, and that erected to the memory of Collins, an interval of more than ten years had elapsed; and this circumstance was not due to any lack of vigilance on the part of Hayley. The explanation rests simply in the fact that, after they had been acquainted for some four years, during which time Flaxman had enjoyed several holidays at Eartham, he had, in 1787, betaken himself to Rome, to study the antique, for a period lasting seven years. Because of this he comes into our story here only to vanish again, and then to appear later as one of the most important characters in it: as, indeed, the master and mentor of Thomas Alphonso, to whom Hayley was wont in his more elevated moments to refer as the Young Sculptor.

But for this phase we must wait until Thomas has grown up.

2

Perhaps of all the great men whom Hayley called friend, Edward Gibbon is the most difficult to explain, if one assumes, as one commonly does nowadays, that Hayley was no better than a pompous ass without a single valuable quality. In the case of his artist friends there is perhaps always present the possibility that they thought him useful as a patron who, though not wealthy himself, was at least in a position to advertise and recommend their wares to others more affluent, such as his eccentric and extremely powerful neighbour, Edward O'Brien Wyndham, the third Earl of Egremont.

This, of course, could not be the case with his literary associates, and it is indeed worthy of note that, in fact, with the exception of Cowper (to whose case very special reasons apply), he did not number among his intimates many literary figures of the first rank. For this there are several reasons: one of which is that he flourished in a period in which there existed few such figures; and another is that Hayley's own productions were such as were unlikely to secure for him the esteem of those few of his contemporaries who knew good work when they saw it. His relations with Dr. Johnson, for example, are instructive. He had early been infected with Anna Seward's prejudice against her plebeian fellow-townsman, whose old schoolmaster, Mr. Hunter, had been her maternal grandfather; and besides, Miss Seward's intimate knowledge of Johnson's family-circle, of the Porters and others, had rendered it difficult for her to take seriously his vast London reputation. Because of this, Hayley neither sought for nor desired an entry to the Johnson circle, and never spoke of it save slightingly. And Johnson, throughout the whole of Boswell's pages, counters effectually by entirely ignoring him. Indeed, the only reference I have been able to find to Johnson's opinion of him is contained in an anecdote by Mrs. Rose (the wife of Samuel Rose), who says:[2] "Much pains were taken by Mr. Hayley's friends to prevail on Dr. Johnson to read *The Triumphs of Temper* when it was at its zenith; at last he consented, but never got beyond the first two pages, of which he uttered a few words of contempt that I have now forgotten." Hayley, possibly, did not forget so readily; in two of his publications he caricatured Johnson, very badly it must be admitted, and he certainly never lost an opportunity to attack him for his disparaging comments upon the poetry of Milton and Gray. He thought, as Miss Seward thought, that the crowning disfigurement of Johnson's genius was envy; and it is indeed instructive to observe with what infinite tact Boswell skirts round and glozes over this weakness in the constitution of his hero.

Even more were Hayley's works and his success anathema to the waspish genius of Horace Walpole, whose letters to Mason on this subject are most amusing. On June 25, 1782 (after the publication of the *Essay on Epic Poetry*) he wrote: "I find there is a correspondence commenced between you and Mr. Hayley by the Parnassus post. I did not know you were acquainted. . . . If you love incense he has fumigated you like a flitch of bacon. . . . For Mr. Hayley himself, though he chants in good tune, and has now and then pretty lines amongst several both prosaic and obscure, he has, I think, no genius, no fire, and not a grain of *originality*. . . . I doubt your new friend will write his readers and his own reputation to death; every poem has a train of prose as long as Cheapside, with a vast parade of reading that would be less dear if it had any novelty or vivacity to recommend it."

But Walpole's references, all in this spirit, are too many to quote. Perhaps the choicest of all is that which he wrote to the Countess of Upper Ossory on January 7, 1783: "Mr. Hayley has been put into a course of breast-milk, and sucked the nine muses, and is now as tame as a lamb."

Consequently, when we come to inspect Hayley's purely literary friends, always excluding the special case of Cowper, we find ourselves in the presence of a somewhat ragged regiment: Charlotte Smith, Mme. de Genlis, Joseph Warton, and, of course, Anna Seward. It is for this reason that the one really great name among them, that of Gibbon, stands out and sets us asking questions.

Some of these questions have interesting answers. In the first place, Edward Gibbon was a historian, and not a poet: there was therefore no question of rivalry. In the second, Gibbon was nearly as unhappy with Johnson as was Hayley: there was a ground for sympathy. In the third, Hayley was (albeit sincere) an adept at flattery; and I rather think Gibbon was not immune from a liking for incense. They had met, it must be remembered, through the praises which Hayley had heaped upon Gibbon in his *Essay on History*. And they had, on the whole, met sparingly. Besides, the historian had encountered Mrs. Hayley at Bath, as has been related, and had found her vivacity rather to his taste.

So far as one can tell, the first meeting between the two men had taken place at Eartham either in the May or June of 1781. Hayley had despatched to the historian at Brighton a rhymed card of invitation, which commenced in this ultra-modest fashion:

> An English sparrow, pert and free,
> Who chirps beneath his native tree,
> Hearing the Roman eagle's near,
> And feeling more respect than fear,
> Thus with united love and awe,
> Invites him to his shed of straw.

The Roman Eagle, on his return to Bentinck Street after this visit, had sat down and written to Lady Sheffield, saying: "I spent a very pleasant day in the little paradise of Eartham, and the hermit expressed a desire (no vulgar compliment) to see and know Lord S."[3]

Since Hayley does not himself refer to this visit, we have no further details, and are obliged to proceed to November 2 of the same year, when Gibbon, writing this time to Mrs. Gibbon from Brighton, says: "I had almost forgot Mr. Hayley; ungratefully enough, since I really passed a very simple, but entertaining day with him. His place, though small, is as elegant as his mind, which I value much more highly."[3]

Four days later, Robertson, the historian, wrote to Gibbon: "By the bye (he asked) who is this Mr. Hayley? His poetry has more merit than that of most of his contemporaries; but his Whiggism is so bigoted, and his Christianity so fierce, that he almost disgusts one with two very good things."[3]

This is an illuminating reference, since Gibbon, it will be remembered, was by no means a lover of Whigs; while Hayley, in after years, was regarded in religious circles with the gravest suspicion on account of his association with the not very "fiercely" Christian Gibbon.

In 1782, Hayley's protégé, Howell, was promoted into a regiment destined for the Indian service, by the good offices of Gibbon who at that time held a small post in Lord North's government; and in January 1783, Hayley, indulging in somewhat tortuous negotiations with the publisher Cadell, enlisted his friend's help to arrive at a settlement. On January 16th they met again in London, and Hayley despatched news of their encounter to Eliza: "You will rejoice to hear that the Roman Eagle flew safely to his nest from Bath. [The figure is one unaccountably risible to anyone who recollects the rotundity of Gibbon at this period of his life.] He arrived last night, and I visited him at ten this morning. His cordiality towards me has given me more pleasure than anything I have met with in the course of my travels. He has promised to sit to Romney for me on Saturday; and we are to change the scene, from the house of the friendly painter to Bentinck Street, and dine all together under the roof of the great historian. He is impatient to see my new work. . . . He is to hear one of my Comedies on Saturday evening."

He wrote again, Saturday night, January 18: "We are this instant returned from the Roman Eagle, who has proved his generous and imperial spirit, by the reception he gave us. Romney has seized him most happily on canvass, and I have been doubly delighted by the success of the Caro Pittore, and the applause which the great historian has bestowed on my *Two Connoisseurs*, which I recited to him in the course of the evening. He called it the boldest of poetical attempts; but declared himself astonished and delighted by the happiness of its execution."

To us, who have read the *Two Connoisseurs* also, the astonishment and delight is all for the forbearance of Gibbon's verdict, but no matter. Hayley concluded by saying that, in his negotiations with Cadell, Gibbon had behaved most kindly.

Nothing, indeed, could well have been more genial than were the relations between the Roman Eagle and his friend, the Sparrow, at this time. Gibbon even went out of his way to tell Hayley that the Duchess of Devonshire and Lord North (Lord North!) were great admirers of his *Triumphs of Temper*. Because of this kindly intimation, Hayley promptly dedicated his next work, his *Plays*, to the former, and had looked forward to the volume being presented to the Duchess by Gibbon himself, had he not been obliged several months before, in September 1783, to "escape from the political tornado" which had reft from him his lucrative appointment and forced him to take refuge at Lausanne.

"Poor Gibbon!" Hayley wrote in May, 1784, " . . . he is sunk into the most deplorable depression; is a striking example that no author should depend too much on his talents and reputation. . . . His books (I shudder while I relate it,) are to be sold by auction next winter."

However, Gibbon did not have to sell his books after all. He continued, on and off, to correspond with Hayley, who particularly felt his absence when he visited London in May, 1784, to see represented the two dramas which that "friendly critic had most warmly applauded in a private perusal". Besides, Gibbon was well employed: he was completing *The Decline and Fall of the Roman Empire*. He did not return to England until 1787, and we can for the time leave him to his labours at Lausanne.

With one curious footnote, however. In 1788 he made his first Will, and therein appointed Hayley beneficiary in respect of any emoluments arising from his unpublished works. In 1791 he made a second Will, from which this clause was omitted. Hayley, so far as one can tell, took this with perfect equanimity, and, as we shall see hereafter, zealously assisted Lord Sheffield in the preparation of these posthumous volumes, which were published in 1796, and which included the immortal *Autobiography*.

3

In completing the record of Hayley's friendships of the 1780's it is unnecessary to expend much time upon those whom time has obliterated, though they are often figures of interest.

One of them, who bulks tolerably large in the *Memoirs*, is John Sargent, the author of *The Mine*, a poetical drama, published in 1784, which deals with the affecting case of Count Alberti who was condemned to the quicksilver mines of Idria, as a punishment for duelling. Sargent was a neighbour, a fellow-squire, of Woollavington, who married an heiress and in later years blossomed out as M.P. for Seaford. One of his sons was an evangelical clergyman, of the species known as a Simeonite. He held the family livings of Graffham and Woollavington, and we shall find him at Hayley's death-bed, some forty years on. And, rather strangely, while one of the Simeonite's daughters, Emily, appropriately married that Bishop Wilberforce, of Winchester, who was known to the irreverent as "Soapy Sam", another of them, Caroline, espoused a young Anglican curate named Manning, who was later to become Cardinal of the Church of Rome.

Hayley, as usual, was all enthusiasm over his brother-poet's publication, and hailed it with a few stirring lines beginning:

> Away with diffidence and modest fear,
> Thou happy fav'rite of Castalia's quire!
> Withhold no longer from the public ear
> The rich delight thy varied lays inspire!

Sargent, it would appear, had been chary of venturing upon publication, which would seem a pity since, according to Miss Seward, Hayley deemed his piece a worthy rival to Milton's *Comus*. Miss Seward did not agree: she placed it on a level with Mason's *Caractacus*.

There is yet another literary character—a lady: now forgotten, but then very much alive, and important in our story for the connection which she had with Cowper's visit to Eartham. Charlotte Smith, born Charlotte Turner of Bignor Park, Sussex, was a near neighbour of Hayley's, and a most unfortunate woman. She had married before she was sixteen, and very unhappily. Her husband, who was a spendthrift, speedily presented her with an enormous family (one authority says it consisted of twelve, and another of seven, children), and with little else. By the time she had reached her thirties, both she and her husband, and presumably all the children as well, were in the King's Bench prison for debt. When she was released, after seven months, she left her husband and was seized with the notion that she might best restore her fallen fortunes by writing sonnets. She fled to "a gloomy château" in Normandy, and did so. Then she sent them to Dodsley, who rejected them; and to Dilly, who did likewise. In despair she appealed to Hayley, who was known to her by repute, as well as by being a neighbour, and he, in his usual good-natured way, permitted her to dedicate to him her thin quarto volume of *Elegiac Sonnets and other Essays*, which, though printed at Chichester at her own expense, was then, through Hayley's persuasion, published under Dodsley's imprint in 1784. It was extremely successful, and a second edition came out in the same year. By 1789 it had reached its fifth edition.

Then Mrs. Smith turned to novel-writing, commencing with *Emmeline, or the Orphan of the Castle*, which appeared in 1788 and was vigorously praised by Hayley. Other novels followed, as we shall see.

Meanwhile on September 28, 1784, the year of the dedication of her Sonnets, an odd encounter took place. I do not think it can have been Hayley's first meeting with the poetess, but it was certainly his most sensational, and may as well be told in his own words, as related in a letter to Eliza:

> About one o'clock, I was surprised by an exclamation from Nurse, "Lord sir! there are three strange ladies in the garden."—"Find out who they are."—My ambassadress, however, did not return . . . and when I descended to make further enquiries, I found the veteran Charlotte Collins, with Mrs. Smith and her daughter, in a piteous plight, in the parlour.
>
> Our tender sister of Parnassus had been seized with spasms in her stomach, which had obliged her to quit her horse, and creep, like a poor wounded bird, through the garden.

I played the physician with some success; and by a seasonable medicine soon restored the sick Muse.... I insisted on their taking a poetical dinner, to which they consented after many apologies.

Apart from this bizarre incident, there is one other singular circumstance about Mrs. Smith: which is that Anna Seward, who could tolerate almost anything in the way of verse from Jephson or the Peak Minstrel, could not, for some reason, stomach *her* sonnets. More: she could not let the poor woman alone! To one correspondent she wrote:[4] "You say Mrs. Smith's sonnets are pretty;— so say I;—*pretty* is the proper word; pretty tuneful centos from our various poets, without anything original." And she continues, I regret to say, in a most modern manner; she says: "It makes me sick." And later, much later, sixteen years later, she is still on the same tack, calling those unfortunate sonnets "everlasting duns on pity", and complaining that she "pules with the pertinacity of a pea-hen, though we must not allow that she is puny".

Well, such severity on the part of Miss Seward, who was normally so idiotically indulgent towards her contemporaries, seems to call for some explanation, and I must confess that the thought has, at times, crossed my mind that perhaps she might have been jealous of that lady's near proximity to the then highly esteemed Hayley. For—and this is the peculiar thing—though Mrs. Smith's sonnets are not anything that we should now get excited about, they are, nevertheless, a good deal less objectionable than the mass of stuff that Anna Seward was always so busy praising. Her observations of nature were occasionally just, and, though her verses were of a gloomy turn, that was not unusual in her day, and she had, indeed, plenty to be gloomy about.

Coleridge, in 1796, in fact goes so far as to say that Charlotte Smith and Bowles were "the first who made the Sonnet popular among the present English", and he proceeds to give a definition, interesting in itself, of what at that time was meant by a Sonnet. It was, he says, "a small poem, in which some lonely feeling is developed".[5] Mrs. Smith's "lonely feelings" had a reasonably long run. As late as 1859, for instance, the guide-book to Bognor was quoting with appreciation her sonnet upon the church at Middleton, near Felpham, which had been washed away by the sea, and commenting with prophetic frenzy "lines which outlive the edifice and the authoress".

In this sonnet the authoress contemplates various bones that have been washed out of the crumbling churchyard, and she concludes her verses with a reflection upon the difference between herself and the previous proprietors of those bones:

> While I am doom'd by life's long storm opprest,
> To gaze with envy on their gloomy rest.

It is hard indeed to see what Anna Seward could find to take exception to in those sentiments: they are so exactly like what she and her colleagues had penned a hundred times.

No: I believe it *was* jealousy.

4

And that, perhaps, is enough to be getting on with, though, to be sure, one must not forget Dr. Guy, of Chichester, Hayley's physician and friend, of whom much will be heard later; or Richard Vernon Sadleir, of Southampton, of whom the main thing was that he was exceedingly old, and who, though hailed by Hayley in 1777 in an *Ode* commencing

> Business be gone! Thou vulture, Care,
> No more the quivering sinews tear
> Of Sadleir's mortal frame!

yet lived on to correspond in 1810 with Walter Scott.

Again, there was Dr. Joseph Warton, poet and headmaster of Winchester College, under whose aegis the scholars mutinied three times, until at length he resigned and retired to the Hampshire village of Wickham, where Hayley visited him, and whence, in the fullness of time, he was conveyed to Winchester Cathedral, where he rests beneath one of Flaxman's best monuments that represents him paternally instructing sundry angelic boys who, being composed of marble, are incapable of mutiny.

All these, and others, were from time to time guests at Eartham, during those agreeable summer days when Hayley laid aside his indefatigable pen and indulged in that festive hospitality which was meat and drink to the mercurial Eliza.

All this gaiety, however, had to be paid for, and it was in the autumn and winter that he worked. It is time now to consider his next attempt to make money, which was by a return to his earliest love, the Theatre.

5

Already in the autumn of 1782, Hayley, whose previous theatrical experiences had embittered him, was at work upon his volume of plays, which consisted of three comedies in rhyme and two tragedies in blank verse, which he proposed to publish in book-form under the title of *Plays for a Private Theatre*. "Dramatic composition", he says, "had ever been a favourite of his fancy, and the ill-treatment he received from various managers, instead of extinguishing his passion for the drama, only led him to indulge it, without exposing himself to mortification at their hands."

This autumn, however, as he toiled at these truly unreadable works, his old eye-trouble reasserted itself, and the idea came to him once again that he would be well-advised to engage a secretary. Accordingly he proceeded to do so, in a fashion truly Hayleian. Even in his humblest associates, Hayley was always on the look-out for talent. His earliest protégé, Howell, was, according to Hayley, incredibly gifted; and his later finds, to which we shall come in due course, were all, on his own showing, thoroughly out-of-the-way people. On this occasion, the subject who fired his ardour was a poor boy whom Guy, his doctor, had discovered in Chichester, who after working all day at some nameless employment, went fishing all night to procure the wherewithal to buy books. This was quite enough for Hayley, who at once conceived a very high idea of his genius, and supposed him a second Chatterton.

The lad was engaged, and promptly walked the eight miles from Chichester to Eartham. On the way he was stricken with ague, and when he arrived Hayley and the Nurse took him for a "poor crazy fellow". When they discovered who he was they decided that he was much fitter to be a patient than an amanuensis, so they put him to bed "and gave him some electrical fire". This electrical fire, which was, of course, static electricity produced by a friction-machine, was one of Hayley's great stand-bys both for the villagers, whom he habitually doctored, and for himself; and we shall meet it again at an important juncture in the history of Cowper.

Next day, between nine and ten, the amanuensis arose, and Hayley, who could not find it in his heart to send him back to Chichester, set him to work copying out the rough draft of his tragedy. But alas! "the ardent desire to learn turned out to be a very different thing from genius". The poor lad could write only very slowly; and he could not read Hayley's by no means difficult handwriting at all. He had, for instance, written *nose* when he should have written *those*, and he was quite unable to perceive anything wrong when questioned about his emendation.

I fear the new secretary did not last very long, and think it probable that Eliza was roped in once more for the fair-copying. All through the autumn and winter of 1782, Hayley laboured at his collection of plays. He calls it "a singular enterprise". He is quite right. He used his old Nurse as a test for the comic passages, and she obliged by shaking her sides with hearty laughter. Perhaps they were the only sides ever shaken by those passages.

6

In January 1783, Hayley went to London to carry through, with the assistance of Gibbon, the enterprise of getting back his earlier copyrights from Dodsley. This he eventually managed to do by making the quite substantial payment of five hundred pounds. He then transferred all his works to Cadell's imprint, and, in the following year, that publisher produced his *Plays for a Private Theatre*; and, the year after that, the six volume collected edition of his *Poems and Plays*, which comprised all the poems he had previously published, together with a few new ones, and five of the aforesaid plays.

Before these eventful occasions, however, one or two other things had taken place. At the beginning of 1783, his mother-in-law expired at last, and Hayley memorialized the event in a long effusion which he called "*On a Lady who laboured under an Insanity of many years, and recovered in the close of her long life an imperfect use of her reason*". In it he paid tribute to his father-in-law, saying:

> For her he shuns gay friendship's festive band,
> To share insanity's insensate hour;
> To mark her babbling lips, or aid her hand,
> Her trifling hand, to frame the mimic flower.

With this graceful compliment to the deceased lady's skill at making artificial flowers (an art which was evidently hereditary, since Eliza was also proficient in it) everyone, strangely enough, was very pleased, and, as it does not appear in his collected works, Hayley treats us to most of it in his *Memoirs*.

Next he turned to the succour of his friend, Wright of Derby, who, like Romney, was neurotic, and had lately been suffering from deep depression. Consequently Hayley rushed to the rescue with an *Ode to Dejection*, specifically designed to cheer him up, and ending with characteristic vigour:

> Thro' WRIGHT's warm breast bid tides of vigor roll,
> Guard him from meek Depression's chill controul,
> And rouse him to exert each sinew of his soul!

In this case, as we are informed, his kindly action worked wonders. The amiable valetudinarian revived, and Hayley followed up quickly with a little good advice on the question of painting a picture of Penelope. Wright replied: "You mention the boy Telemachus being pale and feverish; pray is there any authority in history for it? . . . When I know this I shall make a sketch of it, and consult you further about it."

Is it to be wondered that Hayley should, later, feel himself perfectly qualified to give William Blake any amount of good advice? I make the point here because it seems relevant, and I shall make it again in the proper place.

When at length, in the spring of 1784, the new volume of *Plays* appeared, the irony in which all things literary are involved at once manifested itself. Hayley's plays were probably no better than their predecessors, which the managements had turned down so peremptorily. Indeed, it is difficult to believe that they were any better, because it is difficult to believe that any plays could be worse. They were, however, in print and not in manuscript, and perhaps theatrical managers were no better then than they are now at reading manuscript. However it was, one thing was clear: at once all the managements started tumbling over one another to secure the rights of performance.

On March 23, Colman, of the Haymarket, wrote to Cadell saying that he had read with pleasure Mr. Hayley's plays, and that "as a theatrical trader" he could not but regret they had lost their edge of novelty by publication. Hayley, of course, was overjoyed when he heard this, and negotiations commenced forthwith, protracted negotiations, which culminated at length in the production, though not until the following spring, of his tragedy *Lord Russel*, and of his comedy *The Two Connoisseurs*, both at the Haymarket, and for both of which, sadly and strangely enough, he did not receive any payment. However, he did not know at the time that this would be so, and when, later on, he did, he consoled himself by the reflection that the *praise* bestowed upon his works had afforded him "much lively gratification".

In the May of 1784, while his negotiations with Colman were still proceeding, Hayley at length had the pleasure of meeting, at Romney's house, his idolized exemplar, Mason. It was a curious encounter. Mason was ill and melancholy; his conversation upon life and literature showed many signs of his having "suffered his own enjoyments to have been sadly overclouded by the ebullitions of a spleenful spirit". He told Hayley that whereas public criticism teased and vexed him, public applause, on the other hand, gave him little or no pleasure. And "his countenance confirmed what his discourse discovered".[6]

Or so Hayley thought, though perhaps Mason was only recalling the intended compliment which his fellow-poet had once paid him:

> Sublimer Mason! not to thee belong
> The reptile beauties of invenom'd song.

It is pleasant to relate that the two poets parted with many expressions of reciprocal regard. They did not meet again.

7

No sooner were the plays off his hands than Hayley broke out in a new place, and in a very odd style, by starting to compose his prose *Essay on Old Maids*, a project he had evolved in consultation with Dr. Warton and Sadleir.

This, though it is the most readable prose work of Hayley's that we have (if you except his biographies), was also the one which, at the time, did him most harm, for all that it was published anonymously. It is not really so surprising. Old Maids, at the best of times, are touchy subjects for semi-humorous treatment; and even Miss Seward, an old maid herself—though one hardly dares to think of her as such—was affronted. She said that the book "so wantonly betrayed the cause it affected to defend that she could wish it had never passed the press". It is, indeed, to be feared that Miss Seward never got over the *Old Maids*. The clarion call on Hayley's behalf never again sounds so clearly in her letters.

More, and worse still, the book was deemed indelicate; and so, by certain standards, no doubt it was. It is tolerably tedious reading to-day, though lit here and there with certain flashes of Hayley's rather laborious humour. I shall discuss it in more detail later on, for it is a scarce and rather original book, and I think it improbable that it will ever be reprinted.

Meanwhile his progress in writing the *Essay* had been considerably accelerated by an accident. At the beginning of 1785 his *Memoirs* state, in their usual arresting fashion, "Hayley was in imminent danger of being destroyed." We read on, and find that he was merely thrown from his horse while taking exercise in the hundred-foot-long riding-house which he had constructed at Eartham. A friend had presented him with a horse "of extraordinary stature" but fortunately also of very equable temper. This "lofty steed" slipped in the riding-house one day, and dragged him, with his foot in the stirrup, the whole length of the building, though luckily refraining from kicking him. This accident further injuring his already defective hip, he was ordered to bed for six weeks. He erected a tent bed in his library, and pursued his literary work on his pillow. "The honest old virgins," he said, "were very quiet and pleasant bedfellows in the season of my confinement."

Later, at the end of May, he went to London on two sticks to get a second opinion from the famous Dr. John Hunter, and, at the same time, visited his two plays at the Haymarket Theatre. And then he came home and worked at his *Old Maids* until the book was finished, and his hip was better.

The *Essay* was published that December, and, for all the hostility with which it was received, it did well. Hayley, conscious, as he says, of his "pure intentions in composing the essay, only smiled at the mistakes of those rigid ladies who reviled the production as indecent and irreligious". Moreover, he "exulted in the applause of those who regarded it an elegant and moral performance, that truly deserved the thanks and esteem of their society". Which particular old maids these last were, he does not tell us. Indeed, I fear that the whole of his observations upon the reception of this work smack more than a little of self-complacency.

CHAPTER VII

"THE CALAMITOUS PRESSURE OF CONNUBIAL INFELICITY" (1786-1787)

I

AND NOW THE CENTRE of the stage must be given over to Eliza, whom we have been neglecting. The fourth Chapter of the seventh Book of the *Memoirs* (which possesses, indeed, pretty nearly as many books as *The Iliad*) is portentously entitled: "Of Unsuccessful Endeavours to Counteract the Calamitous Pressure of Connubial Infelicity"; and the chapter begins as it means to go on: "The year 1786 was in its commencement peculiarly unfavourable to the domestic peace and literary pursuits of Hayley."

He proceeds to elucidate matters, to explain that, so long as he was able to retain his own health and cheerfulness, he could keep under reasonable control "the marvellous mental infelicities of his pitiable Eliza"; but that, when his own spirits were too low to divert her volatile mind with "lively sallies of fancy", then the fat was in the fire indeed, and she regarded Eartham as no better than a dungeon. And, in fact, became so disagreeable that, in the February of this year, he found himself obliged to convey her to the house of their intimate friend, Mrs. Nicholas, the sister of Mr. Mundy, the poet, who had "immortalized his name by his two excellent compositions on Needwood Forest". Mrs. Nicholas lived in Argyle Street, London, and no sooner was Eliza safely bestowed upon her than schemes began to be discussed for an amicable plan of separation, which, says Hayley, his friends now considered absolutely necessary "to preserve his life". These are strong words, but Eliza was always a subject upon which Hayley felt strongly; and, after many painful cogitations, it was all arranged that she should be packed off to Derby to live under the care of his friend Dr. Beridge.

Everything settled, Hayley returned home, and passed just ten days in sweet serenity; and then matters went horribly wrong. I will give the sad story in his own words, from a letter which he wrote, that August, to his ancient crony Sadleir:

Yes, my dear Sadleir, could you see every suffering of my soul, since I wrote to you last, you would candidly confess all your own troubles in life very tolerable indeed, when compared to mine. You are no stranger to the apprehensions that my dear departed mother entertained, concerning my poor Eliza. These apprehensions have, in part, taken effect. Though she is not, and perhaps never may, fall into absolute insanity, yet ... the state

91

of mind, to which she has long been subject, is to all who tenderly regard her, an evil much more distressing than madness itself; it is a state not easily described. At times suspicion and pride (the two frequent forerunners of absolute insanity,) appear its chief characteristics; at other times, depression and melancholy. This severest of human distresses so severely afflicted my shattered health, that by the advice of some friends, I attempted, in February last, to obtain a little respite, and relief to myself, by removing my dear though half-crazed companion, to Derby under the eye of my excellent medical friend Beridge. I thought I had adjusted this difficult and torturing business. I had left her in London and returned to Eartham, when I was surprised by a letter, to say that my excellent friend of Derby (whose health also has been much shaken) found the idea of the important charge too heavy for himself and his tender-minded wife. I set off at three o'clock in the morning, through a deep snow, to save poor Eliza the shock of hearing this disappointment from any other quarter, and brought her tolerably composed to Eartham. Since that time, finding my condition such that no *human friend* could relieve me, I have sought refuge only from Heaven.

Poor Hayley! Beridge's defection must have been a sad blow. It was not until 1789 that he was able to pack Eliza off once more (and again to Derby), and in the meantime, though he endeavoured to "grow more and more of a philosopher every day", his peace of mind was broken, and he found himself totally unable to engage in any literary works that might promise future profit. And this was bad, since there can be no doubt that he was now extremely hard up, and in that worst of all possible ways, for which a man receives no sympathy at all, because it is quite patent that he is living in a fine house and is surrounded by every evidence of refinement. It is at such a point always worth while to call to mind Mr. Micawber's pronouncement on the importance of the relationship between income and expenditure.

2

Meanwhile, with an Eliza on his hands who, even if we should not call her mad quite so readily as Hayley did, was beyond question a trying housemate, matters at Eartham during 1786 and 1787 proceeded less eventfully than in preceding years.

Thomas Alphonso was growing up, and this may well be a good opportunity to take a glance at his earliest performances. To do so is not difficult. Indeed, when one recalls that, after his death, his bereaved parent memorialized him in a biography that runs to some five hundred pages, it may readily be understood that the chief difficulty with Thomas is one of compression.

Fortunately, the first ten years of his life are beyond even Hayley's ingenuity to make much of. The first thing we are told of him is that his father developed the pleasing habit of causing him to deliver to Mrs. Hayley, upon each of his birthdays, including the first of them, what he described as a Lilliputian ode. The earlier pages of Tom's *Life* are devoted largely to these effusions, which, one would have thought, might have been more properly addressed to Miss Betts. Still, Mrs. Hayley appears to have entered into the spirit of the thing; there is no doubt that she was fond of the boy; and, since she was agreeable, I do not see that it is any business of ours to cavil.

The first of these productions, running to forty-two lines, is, as Hayley considered suitable to a "Little Hero" on his first birthday, of an uncommonly brief metre, and goes after this fashion:

> 'Tis a year,
> Lady dear,
> Since this earth
> Saw my birth,
> Who desire
> Nothing higher
> Than to be
> Page to thee. . . .

As he grows older, so the metre lengthens:

> To-day I'm told
> I'm two years old. . . .

And this game was kept up by the unfortunate Thomas so long as Mrs. Hayley continued to reside on the premises.

Soon Hayley was exercising upon the child all the powerful theories which he possessed with regard to education. By the time he was three, he could "spout Shakespeare". He was governed solely by love, not fear, was "compelled to nothing", and was so, it is alleged, "open to tender and rational persuasion". It all sounds very up-to-date. His father was his sole preceptor and playfellow. Hayley did not believe in boarding-schools. He frequently said, "Were it the will of Heaven to take the life of this boy to-morrow, I might still be thankful that he has enjoyed several years of the rarest felicity." And, moreover, Dr. Warton (who should have known something about education) is reported to have observed, when he saw the child, still in petticoats, playing among the books of Hayley's library: "I perceive that this boy, rolling about among your noble heap of books, and taking them as his playthings, will prove a better scholar than I can make in my school."

Yet, for all this, Tom was by no means deprived of the benefits of a formal education. On the day after his fourth birthday, his father started him in Latin, and before he was five he suddenly astonished everyone by repeating an ode of Pindar in Greek. This was remarkable, since Hayley had not yet started to teach him Greek. What had happened was that he had heard his father repeating the ode out loud, and had memorised it. When this anecdote was related to Gibbon, he remarked in his inimitable way that Hayley ought to have recorded the day and the hour of an incident so singular, adding that it was more extraordinary, as a proof of mental power in childhood, than anything recorded by Klefekerus in his *Bibliotheca Eruditorum Praecocium*.

By the time the Ode for his sixth birthday was composed, Tom was able to report his prowess in the matter of Pindar, and also to state "Homer with transport I repeat", to say nothing of French. But, besides all this learning, he was, in the epithet which his father describes as "undignified but very desirable", a *handy* boy. He could bridle a horse most rapidly and neatly, could fence, and write a clear hand. When he was only six he emulated his parent by bursting into rhyme, in a poem to Romney, of which all that now remains is the unexceptionable sentiment:

I love thee, Romney, for thy painting well.

It was a curious life for a little boy: when one reflects how curious, one wonders that he did not grow into a most appalling little prig. It is to Hayley's credit, one feels, that he did not. Perhaps, after all, there was something to be said for his theories of education.

3

It is taking matters a little out of their turn, but, since we have been discussing the processes of education, it is perhaps permissible to recall here that Tom was by no means the only boy upon whom Hayley exercised his flair for instruction. In June, 1790, for example, he paid a visit to Romney's friend, the Revd. Thomas Carwardine, and brought back with him, as a fellow-pupil for Tom, Carwardine's son, Henry; and, a little later, Carwardine's second boy joined the party. This arrangement did not last long, however, as Henry Carwardine fell ill and had to be taken home again the following December.

The next resident scholar was Thomas Sockett, on whom, as he belongs to the Cowper episode, I shall here say no more than that, by his transit in 1792 from Olney to Sussex, he laid the foundations of his future fortunes, which were various and extensive.

And then, with Sockett still in residence and promoted, as it were, to the role of assistant pedagogue, there came, in 1795, the longest and most important of Hayley's tutorial jobs, when he took into his charge young George Wyndham, the natural son of his remarkable neighbour, the Earl of Egremont.

The circumstances surrounding this commission were curious. Egremont, who lived to a great age and died only in 1837, was that fabulous peer who is admirably portrayed in the pages of Greville

A great patron of the arts, and enormously wealthy, he had allied himself to a certain Elizabeth Iliffe, the daughter of a clergyman, by whom, in the carefree fashion of the time, he had begotten six illegitimate children.[1] Miss Iliffe, who was known as Mrs. Wyndham, had, in the early spring of 1794, lost "a most lovely little boy", who was the godson and the namesake of William Hayley. Consequently, when Lord Egremont, in great distress, rode over the Downs from Petworth to break the news to the child's godfather, and when, moreover, he burst into tears in Hayley's library, the latter at once became all sympathy, and arranged that Mrs. Wyndham and her surviving children should remain with him at Eartham until the funeral was over. So impressed were the Egremonts on this occasion by the charm and cultivation of their host, and by the manners and accomplishments of young Thomas, that it was then suggested that, at a later date, their eldest boy, George (who later inherited Petworth and was eventually created first Baron Leconfield), should be boarded with Hayley as a pupil. "I never", Lord Egremont observed, "saw a boy educated so completely to my fancy as the boy of Eartham." It was a pretty compliment, for Lord Egremont's standard was not a low one.

Poor little George Wyndham had previously been to boarding-school, where he had contracted a fever which had almost "destroyed him". Hayley, remembering his own school-days and his own illness, was glad to do what he could to save the boy from what he himself had suffered. He had his pride, however; and he refused to take payment for his services. But since his plan involved the retention of Sockett as his assistant, he agreed that his expenses should be reimbursed. Of course, Egremont was a man of enormous influence in the county of Sussex, and there is little doubt that the connection was one calculated to do Hayley, and his friends, any amount of good. Even so, there is no reason why his action should not be taken at its face value; George had been miserable at school, and Hayley knew all about that.

For two years this arrangement endured, and then Hayley was obliged to relinquish his charge. He had had, he said, "much cordial gratification in making the early life of his little friend a scene of cheerfulness and improvement".

4

One of Hayley's favourite words is "benevolence"; and, while we are discussing his turn for the practical exercise of this virtue, it may be as well to take a glance at the way in which, from a medical point of view, he interested himself in the welfare of his humbler neighbours. He had always been interested in medicine, and even, as may be remembered, had once entertained serious thoughts of entering the profession. Consequently, his therapeutic activities in the parish of Eartham were considerable. It is easy enough to laugh at him now, but in those days, when it is to be presumed that there was no doctor nearer than Chichester, his nostrums must have been very welcome. "It was", he says, "his constant custom, while he resided at Eartham, to supply his rustic neighbours with such medicines as their simple maladies required"; and he was accustomed to add that he considered himself highly fortunate in having acted as the village doctor, for more than twenty-five years, without having reason to apprehend that he had shortened the life of a single patient.

Both in the case of Romney and of Cowper, as we shall see, he was prolific in remedies, and often they were of a nature which, for the time, were remarkably up-to-date. His favourite specific was sea-bathing, which, at the latter end of the eighteenth century, was still something of a novelty. On any and every occasion, Hayley would "plunge into the ocean", and he would, moreover, encourage others to plunge. What is more, he would thus plunge at periods which, to our softer ideas, seem positively inhumane. October bathing, for instance, was nothing to him, though it is seldom practised nowadays save by the truly Spartan.

And another favourite specific was the electrical machine, which we have already seen in action upon the person of the embryonic Chatterton who, for a few days, filled the role of amanuensis. Later, with Mrs. Unwin, the electrical machine rises into the dignified realm of literary history.

Most curious, perhaps, of all his medical devices was the newly-invented shower-bath which Dr. Austin presented to him at Christmastide, 1792, and which he rigorously used all through the winter, to his extreme benefit. This object consisted of "a little wooden tower, stationed in the hall, which had a very large circular tin vessel on the top of it, which, on pulling a string, revolves, and throws a deluge of water on the head and limbs of the prisoner in the said tower, which admits only a single person. I had (he says) no conception of the force and effect of this mode of bathing, . . . but I now prefer it to every other kind. . . . It requires no moderate degree of resolution, I confess, to persevere in such a cold discipline these dark mornings; so apparently tremendous, that my boys shudder at the thought of it, and at the sound of the cataract, which pours upon me so furiously, that, in truth, I was almost stunned by the force of the water upon my head."

No wonder then that young Thomas Alphonso was, at this juncture, destined for a medical career, and engaged to be articled to the obliging Dr. Austin. But the gods saw otherwise: Austin died unexpectedly; while as for Tom—well, the only connection he ever had with medicine was that of patient.

5

Meantime, it will never do to lose sight of Romney, the dearest, most valued of Hayley's friends. As year succeeded year, each autumn visit to Eartham brought them closer together. Hayley had a portion of his riding-house partitioned off as a studio for the artist; who, in return, painted a whole series of imaginary portraits representing Serena, the placid heroine of the *Triumphs of Temper*. And, moreover, though there were a good many signs that Romney's nervous peculiarities were increasing, his work had not yet suffered, and his reputation was still on the upgrade. In 1786 he painted portraits which brought him in three thousand five hundred and four guineas, at a time when his price for a three-quarter length was twenty guineas. Upon his return from Italy in 1775, the price of the same article had been fifteen; rising to eighteen in 1781, and again in 1787 to twenty-five. In 1789 it increased again to thirty, and thereafter to thirty-five.[2] So much for Romney's worldly condition.

In addition, as early as 1782, an important event had occurred. A Mrs. Hart had been brought to him by the Hon. Charles Greville, to sit for a three-quarter length with a little spaniel dog under her arm. At almost the same time, Romney had commenced a fancy portrait of her as Circe, but had not finished it because there had been some difficulty in obtaining models for the beasts which the enchantress had metamorphosed.[2]

Poor Emma Hart, later to be Lady Hamilton! Her contemporaries were a good deal more severe to her than posterity has been. Romney's son, the Revd. John Romney, is especially severe, as befits a clergyman, no doubt. He says of her, loftily: "Fortunate would it have been for Lady Hamilton, if she had conducted herself with the same prudence and discretion after she was married to Sir William Hamilton, which distinguished her behaviour while she was"—and here, as also befits a clergyman, he breaks into Greek (and in Greek characters, too)—"*hetaira* of Charles Greville".[2] And on he goes to explain that, throughout his father's whole intercourse with her, she was treated with the utmost respect, and sat only for the face—even in the case of the Bacchante, "which was as modest as the character would admit of".

That, of course, is very probable; but what is important is the fact that Romney, once he had seen her, had eyes for little else. He painted her as Calypso, as a Magdalen, a Wood Nymph, the Pythian Priestess on her tripod, and St. Cecilia. And, what is still more to the point, as Sensibility, a picture which later became the property of William Hayley, and in the composition of which he took a principal and most characteristic share.

It was, he tells us, in the November of 1786 that, visiting Romney one morning in his studio, he found him contemplating a recently coloured head on a small canvas. Hayley expressed his admiration, saying, "This is a most happy beginning; you have never painted a female head with such exquisite expression; you have only to enlarge your canvas, introduce the shrub mimosa, growing in a vase, with a hand of this figure approaching its leaves, and you may call your picture the personification of Sensibility."

Romney was struck with the notion. Hayley, "exulting that his idea had been so kindly adopted", exclaimed: "Without loss of time I will hasten to an eminent nurseryman at Hammersmith,* and bring you the most beautiful plant I can find."

He did, and Romney painted the picture. Hayley bought it, and it hung for many years in his library. When it was sold in 1890, it fetched the sum of £3,045.[3] Once again, is it so odd that Hayley should have ventured to make suggestions about his pictures to William Blake?

But it is a pity, now that we have introduced her, not to complete the story of Lady Hamilton, so far as she comes into our picture. As John Romney goes on to relate, she enjoyed sitting to his father; from what he tactfully calls "the peculiarity of her situation", she was excluded from society, and her only resources were reading and music at home, and coming twice a week for her sitting, always in a hackney coach, and always with her mother. Early in their relationship, Greville had taken her to Ranelagh, where she had created such a stir that it had caused him pain. And so she had put off her gay attire there and then, and never again went out but in the humble dress of a lady's maid.

Unfortunately, Greville growing unable to support her, he was obliged to think of some honourable means for her subsistence, and so, recalling what a fine voice she had, he packed her off to Naples, under the safe conduct of the painter Gavin Hamilton, to take singing lessons. There, as everyone knows, instead of having her voice trained, she met His Britannic Majesty's Ambassador, Sir William Hamilton, who was then approaching sixty.

And so, in the summer of 1791, Romney, after a long interval, was surprised once more in his studio by the apparition of the fair Emma, in a Turkish habit, and upon the arm of Sir William Hamilton, whom she announced, with tears, she was shortly to marry.

All through this summer Romney was like a man in a dream. "At present," (he wrote to Hayley) "and the greatest part of the summer, I shall be engaged in painting pictures from the divine lady. I cannot give her any other epithet, for I think her superior to all womankind. . . . She says she must see you, before she leaves England, which will be in the beginning of September. She asked

* Probably Mr. Lee, of Messrs. Lee & Kennedy: see *The Beautiful Lady Craven*, by A. M. Broadley and Lewis Melville, v. 1, p. xxxvi.

me if you would not write my life:—I told her you had begun it:—then, she said, she hoped you would have much to say of her in the life, as she prided herself in being my model."

On August 8, he wrote again: "In my last letter I think I informed you, that I was going to dine with Sir William and his Lady. In the evening of that day, there were collected several people of fashion to hear her sing. She performed, both in the serious and comic, to admiration, both in singing and acting; but her Nina surpasses every thing I ever saw, and I believe, as a piece of acting, nothing ever surpassed it. The whole company were in an agony of sorrow. . . . My mind was so much heated, that I was for running down to Eartham to fetch you up to see her. But alas! soon after, I thought I discovered an alteration in her conduct to me. A coldness and neglect seemed to have taken the place of her repeated declarations of regard."

In response to this, Hayley, perfectly aware of how much the power of Romney to exercise his talents depended on the tranquillity of his mind, sent him, by return, the following lines which were intended as a peace-offering, and, of course, purported to be of the painter's own composition:

> Gracious Cassandra! whose benign esteem,
> To my weak talent every aid supplied;
> Thy smile to me was inspiration's beam,
> Thy charms my model, and thy taste my guide.
>
> But say! what cruel clouds have darkly chill'd
> Thy favour, that to me was vital fire?
> O let it shine again! or worse than kill'd,
> Thy soul-sunk artist feels his art expire.

Fortunately, the soul-sunk artist was not obliged to have recourse to these lines. The next time he saw Emma, she was quite herself again, seemed even more friendly than usual, and asked him to begin a picture for her mother. "She is", he wrote, "as cordial with me as ever; and she laments very much, that she is to leave England without seeing you."

At last the Hamiltons returned to Naples, and Romney retreated to Eartham, worn out by his labours. Poor Romney: "His health (Hayley said) was too much impaired to allow him to participate in our usual salutary amusement of sea-bathing."

Even now the story was not quite ended. On December 20, 1791, Lady Hamilton wrote to Romney from Caserta.[4] She had a message for him to pass on:

Give my love to Mr. Hayly. Tell him I shall be glad to see him at Naples . . .—Tell Hayly I am allways reading his *Triumphs of Temper*. It was *that* that made me Lady H., for God knows I had for 5 years enugh to try my temper, and I am affraid if it had not been for the good example Serena taught me, my girdle would have burst; and if it had, I had been undone, for Sir William more minds temper than beauty. He therefore wishes Mr. Hayly would come that he may thank him for his sweet-tempered wife. I swear to you that I have never been once out of humour since the 6th of last September [her wedding-day].

It is a handsome testimonial. It shows an unexpected modesty in Hayley that he did not print it himself. Perhaps he did not know of it. What he did know was that, in the following February, Romney received yet another letter from Naples, inviting him there, and extending the invitation to his friend of Sussex. Unhappily he was too busy to accept, and Hayley could not afford to.

When next Lady Hamilton came to England, in 1800, Romney was already a dying man, in Kendal. She wrote to Hayley, expressing the most friendly solicitude as to Romney's health, and also some solicitude as to the portrait of her which he had promised to paint for her mother. Hayley unearthed the picture in Romney's deserted studio, and conveyed it to her. Romney, hearing an account of this transaction, wrote to his friend: "The pleasure I should receive from a sight of the amiable Lady Hamilton, would be as salutary as great; yet I fear . . . I shall never be able to see London again."

It was but too true; and already Emma Hamilton had passed on to a greater destiny.

Sir Herbert Maxwell takes Hayley to task[5] for the part he played in this abortive romance. What he says, in effect, is that, instead of persuading Romney to behave as was becoming in a man of fifty-six when he thought Emma was treating him coldly, Hayley aided and abetted him by writing the ridiculous lines to "Gracious Cassandra" as a peace-offering. Life, one feels, would be a very dignified proceeding if it was arranged exclusively by people with the views of Sir Herbert Maxwell.

Elsewhere, in Ward and Roberts' *Life of Romney*, we are treated with shocked horror to a little episode of a pretty French model, called Thelassie or Thalassie, who, so late as May, 1791, when Romney was fifty-six, and Hayley forty-five, puts, as Messrs. Ward and Roberts smugly phrase it, "the matter beyond all doubt". Hayley, it seems, introduced the lady; but informed Romney that, when he had ceased to interest himself in her, he would be glad to know of it. The period was the latter end of the eighteenth century: Messrs. Ward and Roberts seem to have lacked an historical sense.

6

From Emma Hamilton back to Mrs. Hayley is rather a leap, but perhaps it may be mitigated by considering the fashion in which

Hayley employed his time at Eartham during the first couple of years after his failure to despatch that pitiable lady to Derby.

Briefly, these years, 1786 and 1787, were not fruitful ones, so far as the Muse was concerned. One may guess why. Eliza, though now thirty-six years of age, was still in ardent pursuit of pleasure. But, unfortunately, Hayley either would not, or could not, any longer subsidise her visits to Bath, and the result was as might have been expected: "My dear unhappy companion ... is subject to more variations than the weather. ... I keep her as much under my roof as possible and contrive all the quiet amusements I can for her." "It is", he adds, "no easy task", particularly as all his friends shrink from "an office so oppressive". This leads him to feel that the only assistance he is likely to obtain is that which derives "from the Almighty". The mood was a recurrent one.

It was no wonder that his pen was idle; though he assures us that, "in spite of his incurable domestic affliction", his fervent desire to "obtain new distinctions in the fields of literature" was by no means quenched. All that he wrote, however, in 1786, was a single *Ode* which he sent anonymously to *Maty's Review*, and this, as usual, was designed to animate and encourage somebody: in this case Mr. Bruce, the Abyssinian traveller.

Meanwhile, Eliza becoming, one fears, more than ever difficult, Hayley, in October, betook himself to London, to stay with Romney. While he was away from her, he wrote almost daily, displaying (he says it himself) his incessant solicitude for the amusement and tranquillity of her mind. His own health was extremely unsatisfactory. It continued unsatisfactory for the next thirty-four years. In fact, until his death. All the same, London did him good. It always did. Intelligent and affectionate friends were to him, he said, the best of medicines. With them he felt his imagination stirring, and was able to entertain the hope that such talents as he had were not utterly destroyed.

It was during this autumn visit that Hayley had more than a finger in the fashioning of that singular, and famous, pie: the Shakespeare Gallery of Alderman Boydell. The scheme was, Boydell tells us, started at a dinner which took place in his house at West End, Hampstead, towards the end of 1786, at which were present Benjamin West, Romney, Mr. Braithwaite of the Post Office (one of Romney's earliest patrons), Hoole, the translator of Ariosto, George Nicol, the bookseller, and Hayley. The Gallery, which bulks largely in the history of late eighteenth century art, was a project whereby the best artists of the time were commissioned to paint pictures that represented scenes from Shakespeare's plays, which were then to be engraved by Boydell (who was a printseller), and sold in large quantities to the public. A number of them were done by Fuseli, and Romney painted several. It was, Hayley explains, the thought of the benefit which this project would exert upon the work of his "dear Romney" that principally caused him to bestir himself in its favour. What he meant by this was that he hoped the scheme would lead to Romney's abandoning, to some extent, his highly profitable trade in portraiture, for the sake of painting subject-pictures.

Nor was the Shakespeare Gallery the only artistic project which engaged his attention during this autumn. There was also the serio-comic business of The Opera. The Opera was a popular German one, the musical score of which Meyer, who had been on a private mission to Germany, had brought back with him, in manuscript, from the court of Wirtemberg. Meyer, whose private mission was "directed to adjusting a point of much domestic importance to Mrs. Warren Hastings", connected, no doubt, with her former husband, Baron von Imhoff, the German artist from whom she had been divorced to marry Hastings in 1777: Meyer, we say, had brought back this manuscript, in the "sanguine benevolence of his heart", because he considered it likely to produce emolument amounting to little less than a thousand pounds, which he hoped to see fortifying the "too much exhausted exchequer" of his friend. Upon this work, therefore, a conclave duly sat, consisting of Hayley, Romney, Meyer, Long, the surgeon, and Clyfford, the barrister. Meyer, who was of German extraction, assisted Hayley to translate the libretto, wherefore the latter triumphantly wrote to Eliza: "We are preparing one of the prettiest musical dramas that I ever saw." When completed it was to be sold to Harris, the manager of Covent Garden, who was eager to have it, and, what was more, to pay handsomely for it. Everyone, accordingly, was in transports, and all through November the good work went on.

The further history of this Opera is so pleasantly fantastic that we will anticipate events, and pursue it to its end. By June the following year that work had been enriched by the addition of certain supernatural properties, and was now consequently referred to as "our magical Opera". Harris, it seemed, had not approved of it as first translated, so Hayley, nothing daunted, invented both new characters and new scenery, while condescending to retain the original music. The Green Isle, the former scene of the action, was now metamorphosed into the Rock of Gibraltar, which was just then very much in the news. The period, however, was not the present, but that of the Moorish Caliphs. Still, Hayley was able, "by the aid of magical personages", to get round this little difficulty, and the performance was made to terminate with a contemporary compliment to the gallant defenders of the Rock. All seemed well, and once more, in February 1788, he again presented the piece to the management of Covent Garden; to have it again rejected. In consequence, in April, we find him, indefatigable as ever, writing to Eliza: "Meyer and I are now laying our heads together to set our poor enchanted Prince on his legs in the Haymarket."

A few days later he wrote again, to tell her that he and Meyer were due at Colman's Richmond villa on the following Tuesday, for a full conference on the piece. Managerial opinion had been highly flattering concerning it; though of a curious and disturbing inconsistency. Harris, it appears, had admired the songs but disliked the serious scenes in blank verse. And now Colman thought the blank verse just the thing, but suggested that the drama would be greatly improved by leaving out the songs. It might be the history of every musical drama that was ever written. However, Colman was still agreeable to retaining the music in the magical scenes; and Hayley remained unconquerably sanguine.

Four days later they had seen Colman with the manuscript of *The Enchanted Prince*, as it was now entitled, and Hayley wrote: "The petty monarch received us graciously, and said many flattering things." However, he wanted time to consider it, and, as usual, said that everything depended on getting the right leading lady. The pair of dramatists returned from Richmond not much wiser than they had set out, but with fresh hopes, and Hayley concluded by saying, with what seems laudable restraint, "Patience is necessary".

And now a cloud descends until the October of the following year. In the interim, Hayley's dramatic coadjutor, Meyer, had died and been buried in his parish church at Kew; and Hayley, who was in touch with Harris again, over the representation of his tragedy, *Marcella*, told that manager that nothing in the world would give him so much pleasure as the production at his theatre of the ill-fated Opera, so that he might be able to raise, out of the author's profits, a monument in Kew Church to the "admirable artist and most benevolent man" who had originally imported it. "Much more I said", Hayley remarks modestly; and Harris agreed that he would read once more, and reconsider, the piece.

Yet again Hayley re-modelled the Opera, and, reducing it to a mere afterpiece, sold it outright to Harris for a hundred pounds. Duly it was represented under its new title, *The Trial of the Rock*; and duly it failed, despite the new characters, and the compliments so seasonably introduced to the brave defenders of Gibraltar.

However, all was not utterly lost. Out of his hundred pounds Hayley piously erected the monument to Meyer, from a design by Dance; and there it is in Kew Church to this day—probably the only funerary monument in existence to be paid for out of the profits of an unsuccessful comic opera. He had intended to meet the full expense of the work, but Meyer's widow insisted that they should go halves. Hayley, having written the epitaph upon the memorial, agreed to her proposal. Honour was satisfied.

CHAPTER VIII

SEPARATION: AND THE REFUSAL OF THE LAUREATESHIP (1786–1790)

I

THE ONLY OTHER transaction of 1786 upon which we need to touch was a domestic one. Sarah Betts was growing old, and Hayley felt, in the circumstances, that it was his duty to make provision for her. He did so by selling the family house in Chichester, and by purchasing for her, out of the proceeds, an annuity of twenty pounds a year, with which she went to live in retirement at Petworth. As for her daughter, the mother of Tom, the last reference to her that I have been able to discover comes in a letter to Flaxman, of July 1800,[1] wherein Hayley expresses the hope that she will "pass a respected and tranquil evening of mortal existence in a neat and comfortable little mansion" at Eartham.

This year Hayley had acquired another friend who, though little known to posterity, yet played a considerable part in his life. This was a "pleasant and polite divine", Dr. John Warner, who besought his cooperation in a design for the erection of a public statue to Howard, the visitor of prisons; and no doubt Hayley was approached on the strength of the Ode which, some years earlier, he had addressed to that gentleman. Moreover, as was his custom, Hayley at once seized upon Warner's project, and started to add improvements: his conception of the statue was that Howard's effigy should hold in its hand a lamp which should shed around him "a splendid and perpetual light". Miss Seward, when she heard of this amendment, was enraptured. She wrote at once suggesting that she should be appointed the vestal that guarded the lamp. "Such an appointment," she said, somewhat bitterly (for she had not forgiven the *Old Maids*), "might exalt, to some degree of dignity, the derided state of stale maidenhood."[2]

Sadly enough, however, Howard, with true evangelical modesty, deprecated the proposal, and nothing came of it. "Nothing came of it" are words which one writes all too frequently, when discussing the projects of Hayley.

However, in May 1787, Hayley, who, while Eliza remained at Eartham, seems to have got rather out of his habits of retirement, met Howard himself in London, whither he had just returned from his investigations into the "penitentiaries of Turkey". The philanthropist not only listened with great sympathy to an account of our hero's domestic troubles, but also offered him the use of his house in Bedfordshire, if he deemed it might be of service in "amusing the unquiet spirits of his pitiable Eliza". Hayley did not accept his offer, so, instead, Howard presented him with a Turkish towel for her use, the same, he said, as the delicate ladies of Constantinople employed for their complexions.

That summer came yet another book: *Dialogues* in which were compared the styles of Johnson and Chesterfield, much to the detriment of the former. It was no great success, save among the detractors of Johnson; though Gibbon kindly remarked of it that it would "be appreciated by time".

Romney's visit that year was earlier than usual. Meyer was also of the party, and the riding-house must have witnessed animated scenes. It was a charming spot, "screened on three sides by foliage, in its front to the south a very broad gravel walk with borders of evergreens, commanding an extensive view of sloping and level land, terminated by the sea, which, when the spectator was so stationed that his eyes lost the intermediate vale, had the appearance of being delightfully near the building, especially when the water reflected a brilliant sky".

Yet, for all these amenities, Hayley seemed increasingly unable to settle down alone with Eliza, for, in October, we find him again in London; and this time not staying, as was his custom, in a friend's house, but installed in an "airy set of chambers" in Barnard's Inn. The ostensible purpose of this arrangement was that he might attend to his literary business and, at the same time, encourage the spirits of Romney, which were more than usually low. It may be so. At any rate, so airy and so tranquil did he find his cell that he assured Eliza, "I shall fancy myself at College again". Breaking-point, it seems, was near: Hayley at last had tacitly admitted that he could no longer work in the same house as his wife.

2

This autumn visit was brightened by the reappearance from Lausanne, after an absence of four years, of the Roman Eagle. On November 1 they met again, in a lodging-house in Pall Mall. The Eagle had "just alighted on his new and temporary perch", and Hayley found him extended on his sofa in perfect solitude, having just finished his dinner. Gibbon, "with his usual force of expression", exhibited most flattering signs of surprise at seeing his old friend, and admitted that he was ashamed at having written to him so infrequently. Hayley, ever frank, confessed that he was afraid some third party had "poisoned Gibbon's mind" against him. The historian eagerly reassured him, and bade him attribute his long silence to his habitual indolence. He might have said also that he had been reasonably well employed in writing the last three volumes of his History.

Hayley found Switzerland had much improved his health: his colouring was better, and he was less corpulent. He was, he told his visitor, only in London for a fortnight, and was then due to visit his step-mother at Bath. Very flatteringly he pressed Hayley to join him at Lord Sheffield's, when he returned there; but Hayley warmly replied that he would rather see him under his own roof than beneath that of any Lord in the land.

Upon their next meeting, a few days later, he found Gibbon prostrated by the gout, but otherwise very ready for literary conversation; and, two days after that, he wrote proudly: "I am going this evening to read an hour or two to the imprisoned Eagle, who is highly affectionate and flattering in his behaviour to me."

The evening of his reading to the "confined historian" was a memorable one, and one upon which the mind of posterity may dwell with a certain awful fascination. Picture the scene! The work Hayley had selected for the diversion of the gout-stricken Eagle was a manuscript poem of his own, in cantos, of which only the first had been completed. I do not think the portentous business can be described better than in his own words. He started by saying to Gibbon, "I will frankly tell you a perplexing circumstance concerning the commencement of a work that I have brought, in the hope of amusing you. The single canto that I have finished, has been submitted to two of my intimate critical friends. One says 'Proceed, by all means', the other tells me I had better not. Will you favour me with your casting vote in this perplexity?"

"I will give you my sincere and unreserved opinion", said Gibbon, with great cordiality, "if you will favour me by reading the canto." (And somehow, as he says this, one can see him with his swathed and bandaged leg, fidgeting to get it into a more comfortable position for the audition.)

Hayley began, and was not a little pleased to observe that the story had seized the attention and interested the heart of his illustrious auditor, who made, however, no sign either of approbation or disapprobation. (The fearful thought seizes one that he was perhaps asleep!) But no; when all was over, Gibbon exclaimed, with great animation: "You have gratified and obliged me in no common degree. When you began to read, I was suffering not a little from my tormenting complaint, the gout; but you have gradually charmed away my sense of pain, and I assure you, with perfect truth, that I have been highly entertained. If your poem proceeds as it begins, I am persuaded it must have great success."

We have already touched upon Hayley's enterprises as an amateur medical man. It is a great pity that one is not able to specify with any degree of accuracy which poem of his it was that possessed such remarkable therapeutic properties as to have charmed away the gout of Edward Gibbon. Alas! it is doubtful if it is even in existence, since we are told that he was prevented from pursuing the completion of the work by a recrudescence of his dramatic activities. Irresistibly one is reminded of the White Knight, and of the wonderful pudding which he invented during the meat course: "I don't believe that pudding ever *was* cooked! In fact, I don't believe that pudding ever *will* be cooked! And yet it was a very clever pudding...."

There is, indeed, the more one thinks about it, a great deal of the White Knight in William Hayley.

3

But Gibbon went away to Bath, and Hayley, after an agreeable jaunt with Romney and Meyer to Windsor to see the Raphael cartoons and the King's pictures, where they found West hard at it painting historical pieces, was due for home. While at Windsor, Hayley seized the opportunity to visit his former tutor at Eton, Dr. Roberts, who in the meantime had become Provost; and then reluctantly he nerved himself to a winter of Eartham and of Eliza.

That it was a winter of some complexity may be gauged by the fact that, as early as the following February, he was back in London again, in pursuit of his dramatic projects. In April he was still there, writing to Eliza about his forthcoming introduction to the Lord Chancellor, Thurlow, which was to be effected through Carwardine, to whom Thurlow was patron.

Meanwhile, Romney was still low-spirited; and Hayley himself experienced yet another misfortune in the loss, by drowning, of his protégé, Howell. On April 29, as he was proceeding to make enquiries of Howell's colonel in Berkeley Square, he met at the colonel's door an officer of Howell's regiment, who had known him well. Together they went into the colonel's vacant parlour, and conversed for an hour, not without shedding tears. For it now transpired that Howell had set sail from Bengal almost two years previously, in a Dutch ship which had not since been heard of. This was a severe blow to Hayley, and accordingly, bursting frequently into tears, he determined to return at once to Eartham; but, on second thoughts, refrained, since, right on the tail of this disaster, he received an invitation to dine at Cadell's, at a function designed to celebrate at once the fifty-first birthday of Gibbon, and the publication of the final volumes of his Truly Classic work. He had not, however, the heart to face these festivities. Instead, he called upon Gibbon and told him poor Howell's fate; and then he proceeded to write several stanzas in praise of the historian of the Roman Empire, which he despatched to Cadell to stand proxy for him at the banquet. The verses were duly recited upon the great occasion, while Hayley returned to Eartham, together with the new volumes of the *History*, which the author had presented to him.

Unfortunately, perhaps because of the tears he had shed, his eyes were bad again and he could not see to read *The Decline and Fall*. Eliza, too, was very temperamental. So he despatched her to lodgings in Felpham for the sea-bathing, and sent for his old nurse, from her retirement, and besought her to read aloud to him, as she had done before, the new volumes of the History. Though her imperfect articulation often injured the harmony of Gibbon's language (he says), her serious and comic remarks on his merits and foibles made most amusing amends for all the defects of her elocution. Besides, she had known Gibbon personally when he had stayed at Eartham, and this made the reading more interesting to her.

It is, I think, a spectacle upon which the mind rests with some affection: the afflicted bard of Sussex listening in his lofty library to the resounding strains of his friend's History, now for the first time reverberating round the world; and listening, moreover, to the strains as transmitted through the homely accents of old Sarah Betts.

Some years later another reading took place, in which the part of Hayley was played by an old gentleman of the name of Boffin, while the lector was a literary man (with a wooden leg), Silas Wegg. It is pleasing to reflect that, in each case, the book was the same.

4

Then, for yet another summer, Romney came, and stayed longer than usual. He was still ill, and Hayley persuaded him to leave London earlier than was his custom. Accordingly, he remained at Eartham throughout the whole of August and September, and returned to London much revived; though Hayley was still uneasy on his account. At least, that is the reason he gives for his retreat to his cell at Barnard's Inn as early as the ensuing October, though the matter may be somewhat complicated by the fact that he was also engaged in seeing through the press a *Centenary Ode upon the Glorious Revolution*, with which, as an advanced Whig, he was naturally in sympathy. This poem he despatched in manuscript to his new friend, Thurlow, who replied, almost by return, "It gives a bright relief to the subject. . . . Liberty itself derives advantage from this dress."

This compliment, happily, pleased Hayley to an excessive degree. "Can any poetical vanity wish for more?" he wrote.

Poetical vanity, however, without sales, is not much good, and, as the Ode did not sell, Hayley was soon deflated again, though a breakfast with the Chancellor was some compensation. This went off splendidly. Thurlow was extremely agreeable, so much so that his guest was emboldened to confess that he was "such a hermit, and such a humourist", that he had a horror of dining with a great man: to which Thurlow very graciously responded by asking him to dinner on the spot.

At the same time another death—a most important one for his fortunes, as it turned out—took place. It was that of Beridge, his doctor friend, the same that had so woefully failed, earlier, to take Eliza off his hands. Hayley, writing to Eliza shortly after the event, on October 20, 1788, expressed his grief, and also sent her the epitaph he had composed, which, in the circumstances, was handsome:

> These hallowed stones an English heart enfold;
> Warm, tender, steady, simple, just, and bold.
> A Christian who fulfilled his Saviour's law,
> To man with charity, to God with awe.
> This praise, dear Beridge! to thy tomb is due,
> Pure as thy spirit, as thy friendship true.

When, however, on November 29, he returned home, it seems probable that he was no longer able to regard the demise of his friend as an entirely unmitigated calamity; since the fact that Mrs. Beridge was now in rather reduced circumstances caused him to hope that there might, before long, be a resuscitation of the project of depositing Eliza at Derby. She, he alleges, looked forward with satisfaction to this prospect, for she had many friends in that part of the world; while as for Hayley himself he was now adumbrating a scheme of taking Thomas abroad for a few years, to enjoy a survey of Rome in the company of Flaxman, who had been settled there for a twelvemonth, and had constantly been despatching to Eartham glowing accounts of its glories.

And so, however he managed to contrive it, as early as the February of 1789 all was arranged, and Mrs. Hayley accepted her fate. All through the winter of 1788–89 the versatile Hayley had been busy upon another literary project, of which more hereafter, and it was not, in consequence, until March that he was ready to put into operation the removal of Eliza to the North.

He effected this delicate transaction by easy stages, conveying her first to the villa of their invaluable friend, Mrs. Nicholas, who was now living near Goodwood. From here, on March 26, Eliza wrote to him, pathetically, and not one would have said very insanely, "I thank you for your kind attention, which increases the comfort and quiet of mind I at present enjoy."

Next it was arranged that he and Thomas should precede her to London, to prepare a lodging for her there, and to treat her to a week of sight-seeing, prior to conveying her to Derby. Tom was now rising nine, and it was his first visit to town. He was, naturally, highly delighted at the prospect; preparing, as Hayley typically observes, "as eagerly as the young Anacharsis[2] could do for a survey of Athens".

By April 2 the young Anacharsis and his father were in London, and, while Hayley sallied forth eagerly in the hope of catching the peerless Howard in his lodgings, which he did, and had a charming half-hour with him discussing his projected expedition to Egypt, Aethiopia, &c., to "visit the sources of the plague", Tom was indulging in a visit to the pit of Covent Garden, where, in the company of Romney and Carwardine, he enjoyed the spectacle of Mr. Walker's Eidouranion, or immense orrery.* Tom liked the orrery very well, but relished even more his next visit to the playhouse, when he saw a piece called *Miss in her Teens*.

Already, before his London adventure, he had shown a liking for the drama, and had even composed a play of somewhat singular character. It commenced with a man shivering and pretending to see spirits, and concluded, in the second scene, with a youth in love, asleep under a tree, and contemplated by his parents. This curious work might well seem to betray the influence of William Blake, were it not for the fact that neither Hayley nor his son had, as far as anybody knows, so much as set eyes upon Blake at the time.

As for the Eidouranion, we have pretty conclusive evidence as to the way it affected our young philosopher, as there still exists a charming letter in which he gave Mrs. Hayley his impressions of it. This is what he says:

DEAR MAMMA,
    I am very much obliged to you for your letter. The magnificent scene in the playhouse is beyond my description; it was so beautiful; but I have saved a little book, to give you an account of it.
                              I am your most affectionate
                                          TOM TIT.

Hayley spared no pains to see that the week Eliza was to spend in London should be an agreeable one. He provided a commodious lodging for her in Great Queen Street, he arranged to secure a place for her in the house of a friend in Fleet Street that should enable her to see comfortably "the grand show of the day". Since this show was the triumphant Procession of Thanksgiving to St. Paul's with which King George III was celebrating the recovery of his reason, the choice may perhaps, to one in Eliza's situation, have seemed a

---

* This, on a larger scale, must have been similar to the masterpiece that Wright of Derby painted in 1766, and is now to be seen in the Corporation Art Gallery at Derby under the title of *The Orrery*. Adam Walker, the initiator of the Eidouranion, was an interesting man. The son of a woollen manufacturer, he was born in Patterdale, Westmorland, and, after lecturing on astronomy at Macclesfield, established a seminary at Manchester. Later on he gave scientific lectures all over the country (some of which we shall notice hereafter) and, in 1790, he planned the rotatory lights on the Scilly isles.

little unfortunate. Hayley, however, had no such doubts. In fact, as he says in an outburst of perhaps slightly apprehensive self-approbation: "Perhaps no man, on the point of removing from him a wife, with whom he felt it impossible to live, ever showed more tender or more sincere anxiety, to promote her ease, comfort and welfare."

I daresay he did. Hayley was not a brutal man. It was simply that he had had as much of Eliza as he could stand. It was a struggle for survival. It is the very fact that his conscience was so uneasy; that he protests so much; thåt makes us willing to believe the urgency of his case. He should not have protested so much; but perhaps he felt that, if he did not, then nobody would believe the gravity of his situation.

The last stages are soon told. Eliza had her week in London, and was then duly escorted by her husband, on April 27, to the house of Mrs. Beridge, in Derby. He remained with her for a few days to arrange that her new lodging should be to her liking. And then he bade her adieu, "with much tenderness and anguish of heart", and "threw himself" into a post-chaise. He must have felt the scene very much; he may even have feared that at the last moment Mrs. Hayley might repudiate the whole arrangement. At any rate, he looked ghastly. He tells us that Harry, his "intellectual and affectionate valet", exclaimed to him, as soon as they were off the stones, that is, out of the town, "I thank God, Sir, you are now got safe out of that town, for I have for many hours been afraid, that I should see you drop down dead, in the midst of it."

It was a triumph of sensibility, no doubt, Hayley's ghastly pallor; but, for all that, the die was cast, and he was free. He never saw Eliza again; though they corresponded with extreme animation until nearly the end of her life.

And now, with the swift wheels of the chaise rattling under him, Hayley forgot for a while, I think, "she with whom he had found it impossible to live, and equally impossible to be indifferent to", as he sped towards the comforting presence of his Sister of Parnassus in Lichfield, Miss Seward, whom he had not seen for nearly seven years, and with whom his relations had deteriorated considerably since those sportive days at Eartham during the wet summer of 1782.

5

Anna Seward, in 1789, was not at all the same woman as in 1782. For one thing she was now forty-two; for another she was a success—relatively speaking. She was the authoress of *Louisa*, which in 1784 had received the highest encomiums from the first literary characters of the age, and she was also the close friend of the most successful poet of the day, Erasmus Darwin, the first part of whose

Botanic Garden had been published that year. In 1782 she had been, relatively, starry-eyed, and Hayley had appeared to her a very great man. No, it was not quite the same.

And, besides, he had been negligent in his letter-writing, and that was a thing which Anna Seward was unable to forgive. In 1784 it had been: "Suffer me then, my dear bard, to express my gratitude for the kind attention and ardent welcome with which my poetical offspring has been received in Eartham's lovely precincts." In 1785: "My pride, my heart exults in these distinctions conferred by the transcendant English bard of the present aera." Early in 1786: "Dear Mr. Hayley, with those burning eyes of his." (This was before she had read the *Essay on Old Maids*.)

Later in that year, however, after she had given Hayley her views on this production, we have: "You inquire after my correspondence with the illustrious H——. It is not what it was; but the deficiency, or cause of deficiency, proceeds not from me. I honour and love him as well as ever; yet I feel that the silver cord of our amity is loosening at more links than one."

Then, in 1788, Hayley despatched to her Romney's portrait of himself, and the embers burst again into flames: "See how we little satellites move around you, our Jupiter!" On June 1 that year, the flames rise even higher as she learns the intelligence of Howell's death, whom she had met at Eartham. Since, for all her nonsense, Anna Seward was a kind-hearted woman, it may perhaps not be amiss to give at some length the effusion in which she strove to comfort Hayley for the death of his protégé.[2] It is, besides, for the connoisseur in such matters, an admirable piece of Sewardese:

> Indeed, dear Mr. Hayley, my heart bleeds for the intelligence your letter brings—mournful, bitter disappointment!—I, who on this occasion grieve infinitely for you, grieve not inconsiderably for myself. I had taken the most lively interest in the destiny of that gallant, accomplished, grateful young man, whom you had so generously adopted, and so admirably instructed. I had nourished the hope of one day being honoured and happy in his friendship, through your kind interposition.
>
> Almost two years since he committed so precious a freight to 'that fatal, that perfidious bark!'—Were you not alarmed by so long silence?—You probably formed some method of accounting for it, that preserved you from the rack of terrified suspense;—more agonizing than even that certainty, which, alas! must have been yours from the instant you knew how long it is since he sailed for England. . . . O! my dear Mr. H. that I could have been with you at Eartham, to have softened your griefs, by sharing them!—the only possible consolation in so deep a sorrow. . . . You have great, great trials, my dear Mr. Hayley—God Almighty support you under them, and prevent their utterly destroying your precious health!—The sweet boy—he would be a comfort to you. May you find in his talents, his affections, his virtues, and his prosperity, that happiness denied you from so many sources whence you had a right to expect it.

What a similarity in your fate to Milton's—the visual powers pained and impeded, though, thank God, not quenched;—and now you mourn a Lycidas sunk beneath the waters!

After this it is with some surprise that we find her on September 25 of the same year, confiding to her young friend Henry Francis Cary (Lamb's "Dante-man") that "the dear illustrious bard's . . . affections are subject to ague fits. Sure I am, that I never deserved to lose one atom of that fervent friendship which Mr. Hayley's letters, during the first year of our correspondence, pledged to me should be eternal. The letters with which he has honoured me, during the past three years, have had intervals of several months between their dates, are shorter and less affectionate than those which blest me in the years that are flown. Never will he find a being more devoted to his genius, more interested in his happiness, more attached to his virtues".

This now is odd, and not very explicable. One can only guess; and it is my guess that Miss Seward's impassioned letter on the death of Howell did not receive quite the response from its recipient that Miss Seward deemed suitable, after she had taken such pains with it. There is, as a matter of fact, another and later episode in her career which gives some colour to this conclusion; and it is to be found in a letter to Joanna Baillie from no less a personage than Sir Walter Scott:[4] "The crossest thing I ever did in my life (wrote Scott) was to poor, dear Miss Seward; she wrote me in an evil hour (I had never seen her, mark that!) a long and most passionate epistle upon the death of a dear friend, whom I had never seen neither, concluding with a charge not to attempt answering the said letter, for she was dead to the world, &c., &c. Never were commands more literally obeyed. I remained as silent as the grave, till the lady made so many enquiries after me, that I was afraid of my death being prematurely announced by a sonnet or an elegy."

It looks then, as though, if there were one thing that Anna Seward could not bear, it was to be disregarded when she had given of her best.

But be that as it may, Hayley's third and last meeting with her, to which we left him speeding, was a disappointing, and a disappointingly brief, one. Perhaps he was too overcome by his emotions at leaving Eliza; perhaps Miss Seward really did not quite approve the transaction. All that he has to tell us of their few hours together was that he anxiously did his best to engage her to show every civility to his unfortunate wife.

Miss Seward herself is a little more illuminating, but not much. What she says is: "I found on my return, the illustrious, the graceful Hayley, in my dressing-room. He is going to Rome, and the rest of the Italian cities. He had been to Derby to settle Mrs. Hayley in lodgings there, during his absence. . . . He said indispensable business called him immediately to town, and he set out the next morning. I travelled with him to Coleshill. He looks vastly well, but I dread the influence of sultry climates on an habit so feverish."[2]

Now, with regard to this passage, there are just two observations to be made: the first is that it seems probable that the story Hayley related to his hostess, regarding the separation, was a rather disingenuous one, and that he represented it as purely a temporary affair, occasioned by his proposed Italian journey. The second may be put more briefly: Miss Seward did not, this time, compose any lines upon her guest as the chaise brought her back from Coleshill.

Even so his visit to Lichfield did not remain unsung, since Cary promptly weighed in and wrote a sonnet on the subject of Mr. Hayley's excursion to Italy. It was a splendid subject, and it is a pity it should have had to be wasted. But it was. Hayley did not go to Italy.

6

What with the commotion of jettisoning Mrs. Hayley in Derby, two matters of some moment have been left behind.

The first of these was the death on January 19, 1789, of Hayley's oldest painter friend, Meyer. We have already noticed the extraordinary transactions which led up to the erection of Meyer's monument, but we have had little occasion to speak of his decease, because of the somewhat odd circumstance that Hayley, who was literally nearly always in at the death of his friends, really seems to have missed Meyer's. I conjecture that it must have taken place at the height of the controversy with Mrs. Hayley on the matter of the separation, since we find in the *Memoirs* practically nothing about it. But, as we have seen, Hayley soon made amends, and anyone who wants to know what he thought of his friend has only to go to Kew and read the tablet in the church there. And, while you are at Kew, you should take a look at Ebor House, which faces the church upon Kew Green, and in which Meyer and his family lived for many years. Hayley kept up his friendship with the widowed Mrs. Meyer and her children, and in after years we shall often have occasion to speak of his visits to Kew, and of the Meyers' visits to Eartham.

That is one of the omitted incidents: the other is the production of William Hayley's only novel, which he composed, as we have already hinted, in the winter of 1788–89, basing it, as he tells us, partly upon the "amorous adventures of Betts A.B.", the son of his nurse, and partly upon a suggestion which he had made to Charlotte Smith. As regards this last aspect of the work, a little elucidation is desirable. What happened was this: while revising one of Mrs. Smith's novels in manuscript, Hayley took exception to the ending of it, and, with his customary willingness to oblige, evolved an alternative one. When the lady, who had already thought of a new conclusion for herself, decided that she did not require his, Hayley deemed it too good to perish utterly from the earth, and so he composed, in four volumes of letters, the work which was brought out, anonymously, under the title of *The Young Widow, or the History of Cornelia Sedley*. His publisher paid him the substantial sum of two hundred pounds for it; and did not profit by it. So little indeed did he do so, that Hayley's heart was softened and he presented him, free gratis, with a further anonymous prose work, entitled *Eulogies of Howard, a Vision*, which commemorated the death of that illustrious friend of suffering humanity. As this slender pocket volume passed through what Hayley cautiously calls "more than one edition", it is to be hoped that the publisher just about broke even.

But, even if he did not, he could hardly blame Hayley; for, of all the singular actions of this unaccountable man, I am inclined to bestow the palm on what he now did, in order to ensure the success of *The Young Widow*. It was, he tells us, a highly moral work. Who, then, was the highest moral authority in the land? Obviously, the Archbishop of Canterbury! And so, just as in previous years he had despatched missives to the King of Poland and Monsieur Marmontel, so now, without more ado, in the March of 1789, just after the novel had appeared, he sent all four volumes, together with the following —manifesto one might almost call it, to the Primate of All England. Unfortunately though he chose to maintain his anonymity, an action for which he gives due, if not convincing, reasons:

MY LORD,
  The questionable shape, and the title of the work, which is here presented to your Grace, might lead an hasty spirit to censure, as an insolent impertinence, what is truly designed as an act of serious and cordial respect.

As there is, perhaps, no species of composition so universally read as a novel, and as much harm has been often done by works of this class, it is surely to be wished, that a vehicle so alluring might be effectually employed in the service of religion. . . .

The chief aim of the work before you is, to exhibit an elegant young widow, struggling between her maternal affections, and an attachment of the heart to an engaging infidel, supported in her severe conflict by sentiments of piety. And to shew in the other sex, that the most dazzling and attractive qualities produce only misery in their possessor, if they are destitute of that primary grace in an accomplished character, a proper sense of religion.

It is not recorded that the Archbishop made any reply. Perhaps he preferred to promote the fortunes of the elegant widow and the engaging infidel by private and personal recommendation. Indeed, it is a little difficult to understand just what Hayley *did* expect the Archbishop to do. Perhaps if he had mentioned the book in his pulpit . . . or issued a pastoral letter on the subject . . . or even written to the papers about it? . . . But no; the dreams of ambitious authors are curious. Sometimes even a shade impractical.

7

And now we can return to Hayley, as he resumed his course, free at last of Eliza, back from Lichfield.

No sooner had he returned to Eartham than large schemes were at once under way, of retrenchment, reform, and the higher education of Thomas Alphonso. Punctually each week, he now despatched to Eliza lengthy missives in which he explained to her the inner workings of his new system of management; how that he and his little companion were the "most cheaply-supported pair of hermits in the country"; how poor Harry Hammond was sorely oppressed by an attack upon his lungs; and how old paralytic Richard was faring. And, more than all, just how Hayley was treating his invalids, and with what striking success!

The first visitor to the reconstituted Eartham was an early one. In June, Dr. Warner arrived, and at once set Hayley a medical problem which nearly turned out beyond his wits to solve. To explain the nature of this, it is necessary to say a few words about Hayley's own regimen in the article of food and drink. Contrary to the usual practice of that full-blooded age, he himself ate very sparingly, did not smoke at all, and drank no wine. Coffee was his strongest stimulant. Dr. Warner, a man of fifty-three and accustomed to good living, perceived how well Hayley looked under this dispensation, and at once determined to follow suit. He left off wine, and he left off tobacco; he even tried a basin or two, I think, of Hayley's favourite supper-dish, bread and milk. And the result was that Dr. Warner, who was unused to such austerities, became ill; very ill. He sank into a debility and a low obstinate fever. He applied to Hayley for advice. Really, it was very puzzling! The more healthily Warner lived, the more precarious grew his health. At last, in a flash of inspiration, Hayley hit upon the remedy: his friend's constitution was accustomed to a more generous mode of life, and could not easily be weaned from it. He prescribed at once tobacco, wine, plenty of meat, and a speedy return to the pleasures of London society. Warner incontinently took his advice, went away, and very soon was quite himself again.

All the same, it was a pity that he was thus obliged to send his friend back so soon, because now Hayley's eyes were bad again, and Warner's "rapid pen and powerful voice" had been extremely useful to him in his literary avocations. Moreover, this year Romney was exceptionally busy, and late in coming to Eartham; even by the end of October he had still not put in an appearance.

Under the stimulus of all these disappointments, Hayley was imprudent enough to write that autumn to Eliza, complaining of the trouble his eyes were giving him. Her reply was immediate; precipitate; and most alarming. She said she would come back and read to him during the long winter evenings. Hayley's letter, of September 13, in reply to this amiable proposal, shows very clearly just how much the prospect perturbed him. The letter is so revealing that I shall give it almost in full. The reader will not miss the high comedy of the implication that it is the strain upon *Eliza's* eyes that is really worrying Hayley.

MY DEAR ELIZA, (he wrote) Your kind and generous letter affected me with singularly mixed emotions of pleasure and of pain. Let me first speak of *yourself*, the most *important personage* in the world, for my consideration! I feel as gratefully as I ought to do the extreme kindness of your offer, to dedicate your winter to reading entirely with the sequestered invalid: but the more I feel the generosity of such a proposal, the more my heart and spirit oblige me to decline it. Indeed, nothing could make me so wretched as the having suffered my infirmities to lead you into a situation so very ill-suited to your delicate health and spirits. Recollect, my dear Eliza, how many a winter evening I have seen you overwhelmed with the dread that you might lose your eyes, by reading to the sickly hermit, or by weeping for his misfortunes. The bare recollection of your sufferings of this nature is painful to me in the extreme; and my sincere and invariable solicitude for your real good, must prevent me from incurring the hazard of renewing them. As I have, by happy exertion, settled you in the midst of such respectable and pleasant society as I wish you to enjoy, I should detest myself if I permitted you, from any kind and useless attention to me, to forego those promising advantages, which I have so satisfactorily secured for the tranquillity and amusement of your life. As to myself, in one particular, you know I resemble cats, and whenever I am ill, I rather choose to seclude myself from my friends, than to court or admit their society. Never, I believe, did two persons wish more sincerely to be serviceable to each other; but trust me, we can never obtain this end by living together, unless Heaven should restore to me the very high and lively spirits I once possessed, or make me rich enough to support a carriage for you, and all those elegant conveniences that can enliven female life in a sequestered village. Allow me, therefore, to enjoy the satisfaction I feel, in having placed you in a state that I think most conducive to your real good; and let us be contented in administering to the comfort of each other, in the only way that our very peculiar circumstances will allow, I mean, by the frequent intercourse of affectionate letters. At a time when I possessed, perhaps, some social talents, I devoted my best days to your amusement and instruction. Now that many disappointments and infirmities have made me fit only for solitude, (for which Providence had kindly given me an early passion,) allow me to spare you the frequent sight of melancholy alteration, in the person with whose gaiety you were formerly entertained; and remember that he has always been influenced by romantic generosity, in what he gave and what he denied; and that, resting on the firm ground of his own good intentions, he is naturally firm in his opinions, and inflexible in his conduct. So much for your kind proposal, my dear Eliza! which I shall ever remember with affectionate gratitude. . . .

Poor Eliza! Life with Hayley must have had its maddening moments. Though there was high comedy in their relationship, it has its tragic, or at least its pathetic, side as well.

8

The vicissitudes of the would-be dramatist are ever curious. Just as in 1784 offers to perform two of his plays came to Hayley out of the blue, so, in this autumn of 1789, he suddenly again received, for no particular reason, a most polite letter from Mr. Harris of Covent Garden, asking permission to represent his *Marcella*, another tragedy from the same collection. Hayley wrote at once to tell Eliza the good news. But he was wiser now: "Though I have too often been duped by managers to be very sanguine in my expectation of theatrical riches, yet it is pleasant to be thus flattered by one of those monarchical gentlemen." Though much displeased by Harris's previous treatment, he gave him the permission he desired, and, at the same time, as has been related, contrived to sell him, as makeweight, the famous Opera.

Every time, however, that poor Hayley got near to the "expectation of theatrical riches" something untoward was sure to happen; and the production of *Marcella* proved no exception. No sooner had Covent Garden announced the presentation of his play for November 8, 1789, than the management of Drury Lane proclaimed that they also were producing it, on the preceding evening, with John Philip Kemble in the part of the villain; and, moreover, apparently without seeking, or even considering it necessary to seek, the consent of the author. The manager of Drury Lane, in the course of the warfare which he was then waging with the manager of Covent Garden, appeared to regard the mere author as a kind of inoffensive neutral whose territory he could invade as and when the exigencies of war demanded. "It is curious indeed*!*" Hayley reflects, "after having shut me out of their houses for twenty years, to see the managers contending to represent a play of mine." Indeed, he first thought the Drury Lane production must be that of another play that happened to have the same name as his. It was not so, however: it was the same play, but got up so hastily and produced and acted so wretchedly, that it was calculated to wreck the chances of the better-mounted production at Covent Garden. Such, at least, was Drury Lane's intention. It is pleasant to be able to relate that the plot failed. The Covent Garden production of *Marcella* was tolerably successful, after all; oddly enough, to be sure, for it is an intolerable work.

Moreover, when Hayley called upon Mr. Kemble at Drury Lane to request an explanation of his strange behaviour, he was mollified by a full, candid and flattering apology. That, after such treatment, a mere apology should have put him in perfect humour with Kemble speaks volumes for the essential mildness of his disposition; though perhaps he was only magnanimous because the manœuvre had not come off.

Even so his good fortune did not last long. December brought yet another death: this time that of his college-friend, Clyfford. Thornton had gone, and Beridge, and now it was the turn of the last of his cronies. It was a bitter destiny, he said, for a poor invalid like himself, who ought, in the common course of probabilities, to have departed for Heaven before any of them.

It was on Christmas morning that he learnt Clyfford's illness had taken a turn for the worse. Eartham House, as usual, was full of villagers, who had assembled for the festivities. In a tempest of wind and rain he travelled post, to catch a last glimpse of his old friend, and arrived in London on Christmas night. He saw Clyfford, and shook his hand; but the dying man could not speak to him.

Still, Hayley was for ever given to finding silver linings. "The cordial sorrow" he felt in losing Clyfford, "prepared him (he wrote) to support with the more philosophy the lighter misfortune of seeing his hopes of honour and emolument from the theatre suddenly blasted". Towards the end of January, 1790, another of his tragedies, *Eudora*, was produced; and produced in so wretched a manner that he determined it should be withdrawn forthwith, in fact after a single performance. Romney and he witnessed this performance from one of the upper boxes, and, when all was over, Hayley informs us that "no author could have supported such a disappointment with a more philosophical cheerfulness of spirit". It was just as well. It was the last of his works to appear on the stage. Moreover, throughout the whole course of his dramatic career, if we except the hundred pounds he obtained for the Opera, he had not, he assures us, received one penny in payment. Indeed, on several occasions he had been obliged to pay for his own seat, at his own play.

9

At Eartham once more, in the spring of 1790, Hayley confined his energies to the educating of Tom, and to ministering to the illnesses of his villagers. One of these, the farmer, John Bailey, who would have no truck with doctors, was a long-standing patient of his, and he visited him, during a protracted period, three times a day. At length he succumbed, and Hayley wrote his epitaph. In fact he wrote a couple, one of eight lines, and one of two. Then he consulted Thomas Alphonso, aged ten, on the question of which was the better, and was delighted by his son's ingenuity when he suggested that the "best parts" of each should be "melted together" into one final version.

April saw him in London again, visiting Romney, and Carwardine at Earl's Colne in Essex. And also, and in parenthesis, we learn from a modestly casual reference, not in Hayley's own *Memoirs* but in those which he wrote of his son, that he had yet other business to transact in London. Thomas Warton, the Laureate, had died on May 21, and, by the good offices of various friends, the vacant post was offered to Hayley. He declined it graciously, in a few well-chosen verses addressed to the Prime Minister; in which he also gave Pitt his own views upon the qualities desirable in a Poet Laureate. Why he refused the honour, I do not know; and he does not tell us. Perhaps he was truly modest, and did not think he deserved it; perhaps he thought there were others who deserved it more. What is more probable, I think, is that he deemed his "passion for Liberty" and his pronounced Whiggish views incompatible with an official situation of this kind. All the same, that he was in a position to decline the office must have been gratifying. The post was given to Pye instead; and Hayley returned to Eartham in June, with Henry Carwardine, upon whom he was about to exercise, as has been related, his talents for juvenile education. Tom was growing up now, and in need of a playfellow; and, while Henry was forward in the art of drawing, and instructed Tom in the use of his pencil, the other, whose ability in the matter of languages was tremendous, helped Henry on with his Greek and Latin.

CHAPTER IX

THE WORKS TO DATE (1778–1790)

I

So far, while a good deal has been said about the events of Hayley's life, little has been made of his works; and this, at first sight, is reasonable enough, since they are, according to the taste of the present time, pretty well unreadable. They are also difficult to procure; to be run to earth in no collection with which I am familiar.

It is, however, just this inaccessibility of The Works which now tempts me to feel I had better say a little more about them. Because, after all, what was once very popular must always be of interest as a mirror of at least one aspect of the age in which it was popular. I think there can hardly be a better place for us to examine these works than at the point to which we have just brought the author of them—his refusal of the supreme honour of his tribe: the Laureateship.

Hayley's writings up to the period at which we have arrived may roughly be classified in four groups: his epitaphs, some of which in their own kind are very good; his didactic poems, which are dull but sometimes important in their influence on contemporary thought; his occasional poems which, to use words of which he was fond, are often "sportive and sprightly" in a fashion that Cowper, and no one else at the time, had successfully mastered; and his plays which, whether they are blank verse tragedies, or comedies in rhyme, are frankly unbearable.

The favourite epithet used by critics with regard to Hayley's poetical writings is "feeble". It is a severe expression, though hardly an unjust one. A kinder pen would, perhaps, amend the word to "playful". It is rather odd, indeed sometimes it is rather embarrassing, that so powerful and soldier-like a man, one so given to plunging into the ocean and galloping about the countryside on his charger, could, on occasion, be so kittenish. Leigh Hunt, in his *Autobiography*,[1] makes this point very well, saying, "I looked upon him as a sort of powder-puff of a man, with no real manhood in him", adding how surprised he had been when he had finally met Hayley, and had found him to be the kind of fellow who could have "snatched up the 'vigorous' Gifford, and pitched him over the hedge into the next field". For this playfulness the taste of the age was chiefly responsible; the taste of the age, and the fact that Hayley, like Byron at a later date and to infinitely better purpose, was an ardent admirer of Ariosto, Tassoni and the other master of the Italian mock-heroic.

2

Hayley's epitaphs (to take the best of his categories first) are numerous, amounting to some hundred and forty all told, and they are often felicitous and dignified. In fact, one of them is, I think, the best poem he ever wrote. It is that which celebrates the memory of Henry Hammond (whose defective lungs we have heard about earlier), the Parish Clerk of Eartham. Here it is:

> An active spirit in a little frame,
> This honest man the path of duty trod;
> Toil'd while he could, and, when death's darkness came,
> Sought with calm hope his recompense from God.
> His sons, who loved him, to his merit just,
> Raised this plain stone to guard their parent's dust.[2]

Then there are the lines he wrote for the tomb of his old nurse, Sarah Betts:

> Farewell, dear servant! since thy Heavenly Lord
> Summons thy worth to its supreme reward.
> Thine was a spirit that no toil could tire,
> "When service sweats for duty, not for hire".
> From him, whose childhood cherished by thy care,
> Weathered long years of sickness and despair,
> Take what may haply touch the blest above,
> Truth's tender praise, and tears of grateful love.

It is, indeed, curious that his best epitaphs are generally those which he composed for comparatively obscure people. Here is one upon Thomas Payne, the elder, his bookseller:[3]

> Around this tomb ye Friends of Learning bend
> It holds your faithful tho' your humble Friend.
> Here lies the literary merchant, Payne,
> The countless volumes that he sold contain
> No name by liberal Commerce more carest
> For virtues that become her Votary's Breast.
>   Of cheerful Probity, and kindly plain,
> He felt no wish for disingenuous gain.
> In manners frank, in manly spirit high,
> Alert good nature sparkled in his Eye.

It is pleasing to know that, at any rate once, there existed a bookseller who "felt no wish for disingenuous gain".

Better still, perhaps, are the lines on the elder William Aiton, the Curator of Kew Gardens:[3]

> Flowers that, assembled from each foreign Spot,
> Here bloom by royal aid and bless your Lot

> In circling Rows a radiant Glory frame
> Round this memorial of your Aiton's name;
> His patient care, his pure benignant Mind
> Rank and Distinction to your Tribes assign'd;
> With you permit no venal bard to bend
> In just Regard of Flora's buried Friend,
> 'Tis Hers his living Monument to raise
> Proof of his Toil and Herald of his Praise,
> Nor ends the plaudit of his Virtues here
> Those who embellish Earth to Heaven are dear.

It is not quite 'fair Fidele's grassy tomb', but the gap is not immeasurable; and I think we ought to be grateful for the picture of the flowers blooming "by royal aid".

And now, in conjunction with the other epitaphs which occur in the body of this book, enough evidence has, I hope, been provided to show that, as a writer of memorial verses, Hayley was uncommonly neat, within the framework of his period. Moreover, what a worker he was! It is doubtful whether any contemporary of his whom he had so much as passed the time of day with, escaped his attentions. Beyond a peradventure, he enjoyed writing epitaphs, and had a flair for doing so. It is rather curious that the one epitaph which he did *not* write—that to the blacksmith in the churchyard at Felpham—is the one which is most commonly attributed to him. However, though this was certainly not his composition, it is probable that it was his selection, from a book of existing epitaphs. Funerary inscriptions were, evidently, a matter of which he made a study.

3

As for our second classification, the didactic poems, which, in chronological order, deal with the following Arts and practitioners of those Arts: Painting (Romney), Philanthropy (Howard), History (Gibbon), Epic Poetry (Mason), and Good Temper (Serena)—for I will leave out of consideration for the present the *Essay on Sculpture* and the *Triumphs of Music* which belong to a later period and are rank madness—perhaps the best way in which to tackle these is to quote a few lines from Hayley's own introduction to these works in the collected edition of 1785. He begins his exordium by saying that it is by no means his design to assume the office of a legislator, and that, moreover, he thinks it may be said of all didactic poems, that the parts of them which do not pretend to teach, are those most productive of pleasure. This is fair enough and so is his further apophthegm which declares that "precepts . . . can never make either a Painter or a Poet", and likens those who imagine that no one can produce a good Poem without being acquainted with the Poetics of Aristotle, to those who imagine that no one can become a parent without perusing a treatise on Anatomy.

This is reasonable, and so is the apologia which succeeds it: "My principal design was to present a general view of the art in question, with a just and animating character of its most eminent professors . . . to inspire an enthusiastic passion for some particular art, [and] . . . an ingenuous delight, in the glory of its Heroes."

"An ingenuous delight in the glory of its Heroes": in that phrase, I believe, we really touch the root of the matter. Hayley for all his sillinesses was a hero-worshipper, and he wrote his long didactic poems with two purposes in mind, both highly laudable. The first was to do good to his Heroes, to whom, as symbolical leaders in their respective arts, he addressed the various Epistles; the second was to do good to the public by arousing in them as keen a pleasure in the matters he praised as he himself had been able to derive from them. I am, of course, aware that philanthropy of this description is no part of the equipment of a literary artist, and that, because he was not, or was only very seldom, such an artist, Hayley's exercitations did not, or did not for long, produce the fruits he had anticipated. This is a pity, but it is not a crime; and moreover, paradoxically enough, there is little doubt that it was not his poems at all, but his highly informative notes to them which, in the end, did the most to further his intentions.

It has to be remembered that the one really important thing about Hayley, in the period in which he flourished, was that he possessed a far greater knowledge of both Italian and Spanish poetry than was common; and that the trails, in these connections, that were blazed by his notes were trails that succeeding generations trod with some alacrity. Dante, for instance, had never been done into English at all until Hayley, in the Notes to his *Essay on Epic Poetry*, furnished a version, in terza rima, of the first three cantos of the *Inferno*. It was a very literal version: *fastidiosi vermi* was rendered "fastidious worms"; but still it was a beginning. He was soon followed by Boyd and others, and the process culminated in the masterly, and still standard, verse-translation of his young friend, Henry Cary.

And Spanish, too. Many years after Hayley had referred in his Notes on the same poem to the *Araucana* of Ercilla, Lord Holland confessed that it was what he had read of it in that place which had induced him to learn Spanish—in those days an uncommon accomplishment for an English nobleman. Indeed, Southey goes so far as to sum the whole thing up, perhaps even a little too generously (if generosity be a fault in this connection), by asserting that "a greater effect was produced upon the rising generation of scholars by the Notes to the *Essay on Epic Poetry* than by any other contemporary work, Percy's *Reliques* alone excepted".[4] That the effect was not invariably a good one, and that a good deal of the Minerva Press nonsense at the end of the century stems from the same source of inspiration is, for the moment, beside the point. It is sufficient to say that Hayley stands as at any rate the spiritual father, of Cary's *Dante*.

4

For the rest of his serious minor works: his Ode to Wright of Derby; his Ode to the Countess de Genlis; his sonnets to Gibbon, Melmoth, Sargent and so forth: it is necessary to say little. The intention was always admirable, and designed to cheer the subject addressed. But the effect was often otherwise. In the ode to the ambiguous Mme. de Genlis occur some lines which display, very typically, the gulf which so often yawns between Hayley's intention and his execution:

> No more let English pride arraign
> The Gallic Muse, as light and vain,
> Whose trifling fingers can but weave
> The flimsy novel, to deceive
> Inaction's languid hour. . . .
>
> Too often, in the giddy fit
> Of wanton or satiric wit,
> The rash and frolic sons of France
> Have sketch'd the frivolous romance;
> While reason stood aloof;
> While modesty the work disclaim'd;
> And griev'd religion, with disdain inflam'd,
> On the licentious page pronounc'd her just reproof.

In this, as in so many other pieces of highly serious intent, one feels that the frankly "sportive and sprightly" side of Hayley has taken the bit between its teeth, and bolted from the awful solemnity of his subject. It is, therefore, rather a relief to turn to the occasions when he was both sportive, and intentionally so.

Of this aspect of his Muse, I think my favourite manifestation is the lines[5] (which I have never seen in print) with which he begins a very light-hearted letter to Cowper on July 1, 1792. The occasion of them was the poem which Cowper had sent him a few days before, in celebration of the marriage of Sir John Throckmorton's brother: a poem that may be found in Cowper's works under the title of *Catherina: The Second Part*. In it, Cowper makes play with the fact that he had wished Catherina to be "queen of the Hall", and now she is; and so, having been successful in one wish, he ventures another—that she will soon become a mother. It is at this point that Hayley's reply becomes intelligible:

> As so fully the wishes prevail
> Of us Bards, unincumbered with Sins;
> Dear Cowper, your Friend cannot fail
> To enrich her good Sposo with Twins.

> If we in a Wish have such vigour,
> Let great men befriend or neglect us,
> By wishing we'll make such a Figure
> That the World shall for ever respect us.
>
> Yet 'twere well, Brother Bard, by your leave,
> That my verse were another Specific;
> That some by your wish might conceive,
> Some by mine escape being prolific.
>
> We thus may have Cash in a Lump,
> While the sex has a want, or a whim;
> Much many will give to be plump,
> And many give more to be slim.
>
> I see the dear Creatures confounded;
> They fear that we only have vapour'd;
> Yet Tribes run to you to be rounded,
> And waddle to me to be taper'd.
>
> God bless them, say I, one and all,
> Tho' our spirits they frequently harrow:
> I love them, when round as a Ball,
> And I love them, when strait as an arrow.

It is not very refined, perhaps; not quite the thing, one would think, to send to the author of the *Olney Hymns*; yet strangely enough neither Cowper nor Mrs. Unwin seemed to mind ("Your humorous descant upon my art of wishing made us merry, and consequently did good to us both"); and it gallops, I think, gallops decidedly. Every now and then in his lighter verse Hayley does achieve this effect, and though, of course, it is no great matter, it is sometimes pleasing, in the same way that the *New Bath Guide* is still pleasing.

One of these lighter pieces has a certain adventitious interest in that it depicts, with a reasonable measure of detachment, the deplorable condition of the contemporary stage upon which he had, for some twenty years, sought to triumph. *A Receipt for a Tragedy* it is called, and here it is:

> Take a virgin from Asia, from Afric, or Greece,
> At least a king's daughter, or emperor's niece;
> Take an elderly Miss for her kind confidant
> Still ready with pity or terror to pant,
> While she faints and revives like a sensitive plant;
> Take a hero, though buried some ten years or more,
> But with life enough left him to rattle and roar;
> Take a horrid old brute, who deserves to be rack'd,
> And call him a tyrant ten times in each act;
> Take a priest of cold blood, and a warrior of hot,
> And let them alternately bluster and plot:
> Then throw in of soldiers and slaves *quantum suff.*,
> Let them march, and stand still, fight, and halloo enough.

> Now stir all together these separate parts
> And season them well with Ohs! faintings, and starts:
> Squeeze in, while they're stirring, a potent infusion
> Of rage and of horror, of love and illusion:
> With madness and murder complete the conclusion.
> Let your princess, though dead by the murderer's dagger,
> In a wanton, bold epilogue ogle and swagger;
> Prove her past scenes of virtue are vapour and smoke,
> And the stage's morality merely a joke;
> Let her tell with what follies our country is curst
> And wisely conclude that play-writing's the worst.
> Now serve to the public this olio complete,
> And puff in the papers your delicate treat.

Occasionally Hayley also wrote songs, and some of these were set to music and sung by Eliza and others. He was evidently rather proud of one or two of these, since they are referred to by name in the course of his *Memoirs*. Here is one, the best of an indifferent lot:

> From glaring shew, and giddy noise,
> The pleasures of the vain,
> Take me, ye soft, ye silent joys,
> To your retreats again.
>
> Be mine, ye cool, ye peaceful groves,
> Whose shades to love belong;
> Where echo, as she fondly roves,
> Repeats my STELLA's song.
>
> Ah, STELLA! why should I depart
> From solitude and thee,
> When in that solitude thou art
> A perfect world to me!

A characteristic theme, you perceive: the blessings of Retirement!

5

As for the Plays: the comedies in rhyme, *The Happy Prescription*, *The Two Connoisseurs*, *The Mausoleum*; and the pseudo-Shakespearean tragedies in blank verse, *Marcella*, *Lord Russel*, and so forth: perhaps it is kindest, both to Hayley and to the reader, to draw a veil. One may, with some degree of assurance, say that the tragedies are worse than the comedies, and that *Marcella* is the worst of the tragedies. For the rest, few things in the world are more tiresome than rhymed comedies. Hayley wrote a preface to prove that this need not be the case, but his practice did not live up to his theory. As a sample of the sort of thing it is, I will quote a brief passage from *The Two Connoisseurs* relating to Harry, a servant, because I like to think that when Hayley wrote it he had in mind that same Harry who was so grievously disturbed by his master's pallor during those terrible parting hours at Derby:

> Harry's warmth is affecting.—'Tis pleasant to win
> A regard unconstrain'd from the low ranks of life,
> Which are falsely suppos'd full of baseness and strife.
> How mistaken is he, who incessantly raves,
> That domestics are nothing but idiots or knaves!
> When nature oft shines, with a lustre most fervent,
> In the zeal of an honest, affectionate servant.

There is, however, in *The Mausoleum*, as well as an idiotic caricature of Johnson, over which we need not linger, a portrait of two poets, Trope and Facil, which is interesting because it almost certainly represents what Hayley thought to be the truth about himself and the Revd. William Mason. Trope-Mason:

> Talks in a high strutting style of the stars,
> And the eagle of Jove, and the chariot of Mars;
> And pompously tells, in elaborate lines,
> That now the moon glistens, and now the sun shines:

but it is the character of Facil-Hayley which is really revealing, for, whatever it does or does not indicate, he would be a bold man who would suggest that it indicates conceit, or any undue sense on Hayley's part of his own capabilities. Of Facil he writes:

> Whose verse is the thread of tenuity,
> A fellow distinguish'd by flippant fatuity,
> Who nonsense and rhyme can incessantly mingle,
> A poet—if poetry's only a jingle.
> Poor Facil wants force; yet may frequently please
> By a light airy mixture of mirth and of ease.

And he adds, with real discernment:

> Too quick in their birth are the brats of my brain:
> My Muse is no parent inur'd to long pain. . . .
> She with lively dispatch, like a provident mother,
> Soon as one child is born thinks of getting* another.

These passages are illuminating because, even if what a man writes about himself may not be the whole of the truth, the fact that he thinks it is so, or wishes others to think that it is, is important.

As for the Tragedies: Cary in his essay on Hayley in the *London Magazine* says the kindest thing: "His tragedies are some of the most endurable we have in what a lively modern critic (my friend Mr. Darley) has termed the rhetorical style. Yet he had some skill in moving compassion."

I record that verdict, while feeling no impulse to endorse it. The only compassion I felt, as I read them, was for myself.

---

* Rather curiously, I derive this reading 'getting' from a pencilled emendation in the Manchester Central Library copy of the plays, where the word is actually printed 'rearing'. I have little doubt that the emendation is correct, but cannot help wondering how it got to Manchester.

6

I have left to the last that piece of Hayley's verse which it is most difficult to expound: his great success, *The Triumphs of Temper*, a work which ran into fourteen editions, and is, consequently, the only one of his books that is come across at all frequently nowadays.

It may have been noticed that, in my earlier classification of Hayley's verse, I put the *Triumphs of Temper* in the didactic category; and this I did advisedly because, though it often pertains to the "sportive" side of his muse, I am sure it was this aspect of it which was responsible for its great success. It was, in fact, a didactic work on the Art of Good Temper, in women, one might almost say in wives, and it was written—and this is the irony of it—when Hayley was living with Eliza during what, in a painter, might have been called "her best period". It was, in consequence, written from the heart; and, coming from the heart it proceeded to the heart, though strangely enough not so much to the heart of the unfortunately-married male, as to that of the would-be happily married female. We have already noticed the high testimony paid to the work by Lady Hamilton, who attributed her capture of Sir William to its benign influences; and, later on, we shall find Amelia Opie writing to Hayley to tell him that "one of my earliest recollections is a sense of obligation to you; as 'the triumphs of Temper' was one of the first books of poetry which I read aloud to my mother; and as she judiciously held up its admirable heroine as a model for imitation, the delight which I felt in the beauty of the poem was encreased by a consciousness that it improved, while it pleased me".[6] Moreover, Hayley himself tells us the pleasure it gave him to be informed by the "mother of a large family", that she was beholden to the poem for a "complete reformation in the conduct and character of her eldest daughter", who, "by an ambition to imitate Serena was metamorphosed, from a creature of the most perverse and intractable spirit, into the most docile and dutiful of children". This, he says, was the greatest reward he ever received as an author.

In July, 1800, Hayley still thought well enough of his poem to present a copy of the tenth edition to William Blake. It had been the property of his son, and he inscribed it in phrases that are revealing:[7]

> Accept, my gentle visionary, Blake,
> Whose thoughts are fanciful and kindly mild;
> Accept and fondly keep for friendship's sake,
> This favour'd vision, my poetic child!
>
> Rich in more grace than fancy ever won,
> To thy most tender mind this book will be,
> For it belong'd to my departed son;
> So from an angel it descends to thee.

Ozias Humphry, the painter, who had accompanied Romney to Italy, said a neat thing to Farington on May 15, 1803, which may fairly be taken as applying to this poem: "Hayley was the *workbasket poet* of that day,—His verses were upon every Girl's Sopha".[8] But, as late as 1806, Anna Seward, though otherwise much out of temper with Hayley, was still writing, and to Scott of all people, that the *Triumphs of Temper* was a "bright diamond".[9] And Anna Seward was no mother of a refractory daughter, nor had she, by reason of the poem's precepts, scored the triumph of a Lady Hamilton, or even of a Mrs. Opie.

But we have revolved in wonderment long enough around the covers of this portentous volume. It is time we opened them. What do we find inside?

Well, in the first place, we find a preface in which, since Hayley, whatever his faults of periphrasis and euphemism, was a writer who, in prose at any rate, was able to make his meaning clear, is provided a pretty full statement as to the purpose, genesis, and manner of the poem. "It seems (he writes) to be a kind of duty incumbent on those who devote themselves to poetry, to raise, if possible, the dignity of a declining art, by making it as beneficial to life and manners as the limits of composition, and the character of modern times, will allow."

Excellent; and on he goes to speak of Alessandro Tassoni, the inventor of modern heroi-comic poetry, and of Pope and his description of the Cave of Spleen. "I imagined (he says) it might be possible to give a new character to this mixed species of poetry, and to render it by its object . . . more noble than the most beautiful and refined satire can be . . . to delineate the more engaging features of female excellence." And then he tells us how he proposes to do it, by shifting from real to visionary scenes, in alternate cantos. "I wished, indeed, (but I fear most ineffectually) for powers to unite some touches of the sportive wildness of Ariosto, and the more serious sublime painting of Dante, with some portion of the enchanting elegance, the refined imagination, and the moral graces of Pope"—a programme which, to say the least, was comprehensive.

We find ourselves faced then with six cantos and three thousand one hundred and thirty-two lines of rhymed heroic couplets, in which is set forth the history of Serena; her rather crusty father, Sir Gilbert; and his old-maidish sister, Penelope. During the course of the performance, Serena crosses a lake and enters the abode of Spleen; and one has the uneasy sensation that Dante's *Inferno* has, as it were, chastely broken loose in the drawing-room. One has other sensations: there are times when one thinks of Scrooge and his visiting Spirits; and, throughout the whole piece, the undistinguished couplets jingle relentlessly upon their way. It is not perhaps, without a period charm, of a sort; what is astonishing is that it should have been *avidly* read. Here, for instance, is an average passage: a description of a London morning:

> For now the heralds of the London day
> Sing their loud matins in th' uncrowded way;
> Th' impatient milk-maid now, with early din,
> Screams to the rattle of her pail of tin;
> With sweep's faint cry, and, latest of the crew,
> The deep-ton'd music of the murmuring Jew.

And, again, transmuted to a properly feminine note, we hear the old theme of the vanity of human wishes:

> To thee, sweet maid, whose pleasure-darting eyes
> Joy in this favourite vest, an hour shall rise,
> When thou shalt hate the silk so fondly sought,
> And wish thy silver-spotted gauze unbought.

Perhaps, too, we may catch a side-glance at Eliza, in such a passage as:

> The voice, that health made harmony, disowns
> That native charm for langour's mimic tones;
> And feigns disease, till, feeling what it feigns,
> Its fancied maladies are real pains.

Shall I go on? No! Serena's temper triumphs over a variety of not remarkable vicissitudes, except of course her sufficiently exciting visit to the pantomime Cave of Spleen, over the entrance to which, by the way, is written, in laudable pursuit of "the more serious sublime painting of Dante":

> Justly they feel no joy, who none bestow,
> All ye who enter, every hope forego!

and, in the end, we are quite assured she is so good-humoured that she is bound to get the nicest of husbands; someone, in fact, very like Hayley himself. Moreover, when she does get him, one feels confident there will be none of that nonsense which the poor author was obliged to put up with from Eliza. For

> Mild *Serena* scorn'd the prudish play,
> To wound warm love with frivolous delay;
> Nature's chaste child, not Affectation's slave,
> The heart she meant to give, she frankly gave.

Well, there it is. It suited his public immensely, and it brought him a considerable amount of money. I cannot conceive that it did any of his young-lady readers harm. On the contrary, it is more than likely that a whole generation of sweet-tempered and affectionate wives was reared upon it. The only person whom it did harm was Hayley himself, since for the rest of his life he was saddled with the reputation that it was his masterpiece. What was worse, because it was successful and his other poems were not, he often managed to convince himself that this was so, and attempted to repeat its success with works of a similar kind. The results were too terrible to contemplate here.

One thing is certain: like the lean kine in Joseph's dream, the *Triumphs of Temper* ended by swallowing up his other poetical works. Its popularity, especially as a present to children calculated to improve their dispositions, was perennial. I have seen a copy of the 1809 edition which was, as late as 1815, inscribed by Charles Lamb as a gift to "little Lizzie Hazlitt", presumably the niece of his great contemporary.[10] And even now, if anyone knows Hayley's name as a writer, it is always this work that they are sure to mention. I have tried, in the earlier part of this chapter, to show that his poetical situation is not quite so desperate as that.

7

After his collected *Poems and Plays* were issued in 1785, Hayley published a regrettably large quantity of verse of which we shall take little notice; and he also produced a great deal of not so disreputable prose, of which a word will have to be said in due season. So as to clear up his works, however, to the date we have arbitrarily chosen, we have still to touch on his earlier prose writings. Of these, I have nothing to say of his novel, *The Young Widow*, for I have not read it; nor, I incline to believe, has anybody now living. Tempted as I was by the thought that it was based upon the "amorous adventures of Betts A.B.", I did, I confess, for a few moments toy with the idea of doing so, but I abandoned it in favour of his other prose-work of that time, *The Essay on Old Maids*. This, I can assure you, makes very singular reading.

The *Essay*, though the description is by way of being an understatement, since it runs to three volumes, is a work that is still, in parts, readable, and is always, to say the least, peculiar. It not only has a good deal to tell us about Hayley himself, but it also furnishes us with a pretty clear idea of why his reputation in such circles as Miss Seward's was always a shade ambiguous. While I should not for an instant be prepared to say that the *Essay* is a good book, I should, I think, be willing to go so far as to assert that it is one which only a man of considerable scholastic attainments could have written; and this, in itself, is to the point, since a reader who only knew Hayley's work through his *Triumphs of Temper*, or his lamentable comedies, might well be excused for believing that he had never had any education at all.

It is a scarce book now; and this, I think, justifies me in saying something about it here. What is it about? Well, as might be expected, it is about Old Maids, or rather what Hayley, with that sometimes sickening facetiousness of his, chooses more frequently to call "ancient virgins". The strange thing is that, benevolent as ever, he was quite sincerely of the opinion that he was propounding a defence of this section of the community. When actual old maids fell upon him from every side and reviled him, because he had made fun of them, he professed himself deeply grieved, and I have no doubt that, in his muddled way, he was.

But let him speak for himself. "A celebrated philosopher of France", he says, "(Mr. d'Alembert) has written a benevolent and admirable essay on those unfortunate beings called Authors; and a contemplative, indefatigable philanthropist of our own country [Jonas Hanway] has, with equal goodness and propriety, produced a treatise on Chimney-sweepers. . . . I flatter myself with the idea of surpassing both the French and English philanthropist, by directing my lucubrations to an order of beings, whom I think still more entitled to the regard and protection of an enterprising philosopher; I mean the sisterhood of Old Maids. . . . I devote myself, with a new species of Quixotism, to the service of Ancient Virginity."

That is all very fine, though perhaps it is a little difficult to see how three volumes are going to follow such a beginning. It may be that the best way of giving some idea of the often amusing intention of the book is to provide a brief résumé of its Contents. The first part, then, deals with the failings peculiar to Old Maids, with chapters devoted to their Curiosity, Credulity, Affectation, and Ill-Nature. The second lists their good qualities: Ingenuity, Patience, and Charity. In the third, the fun begins as, with mock-seriousness, he traces the Old Maid in Ancient History, with Conjectures concerning the existence of Old Maids before the Deluge; among the Jews, Aethiopians, and Other Nations of Antiquity; the Old Maids of Greece; and of Rome, which includes the Vestal Virgins. Part Four is devoted to Old Maids after the Christian Aera, when an infinite increase in their numbers took place: with some consideration of the early Christian authors who have touched on Virginity —Tertullian, St. Cyprian, Methodius Bishop of Olympus, St. Athanasius, St. Basil, and St. Gregory Nazianzen. Part Five continues this with references to St. Gregory of Nyssa, St. Ambrose, St. Chrysostom, St. Jerom; on Some Miracles ascribed to Monastic Virgins; on the Decline and Fall of Monastic Virginity; on some Monastic Old Maids distinguished by Literary Talents; and on some Old Maids of the New World. The final Part discusses what the English Poets have had to say on the subject; the Medical Influences ascribed to the state; and Various Devices supposed to ascertain it.

It sounds dull, you think? And so, in parts, it is. It is, on the whole, an undisciplined farrago, part parody of Gibbon's historical style, part interpolated romances of a highly sentimental nature, part "characters" of the kind one finds so much better done in, for example, Law's *Serious Call*; part, too, is sheer Ossianism and madness, as in the long and unbearably tedious account of an Antediluvian Old Maid. Such virtue as resides in the book may, I suppose, be summed up under two heads. First, there is really a good deal of curious learning in it; and second, there are here and there individual sketches and phrases which, in their own right, are entertaining.

A sample or two will give the flavour. There is a rather shrewd hit at the Old Maid whose failing is a quality in which Hayley himself was not deficient: the affectation of an extreme sensibility. Such a one, he tells us "can pluck a withering flower from the nosegay in her bosom, and drop a tear of tenderness in remarking the transient beauties of vegetation. . . . A lap-dog, a parrot, or a monkey, is the object of her caresses. . . . She professes to have an aversion to children, because she is distracted by their noise; yet, so inconsistent is affectation, she has chosen for her constant companion, and even for her bedfellow, a great surly Pomeranian dog, whose incessant barking is more offensively loud than the most noisy infant that ever squalled in a cradle". This is agreeable enough, and enough in the tradition of the *Tatler* and the *Spectator* to pass muster; but occasionally, in a phrase here and there, Hayley's bite is sharper:

"At the age, then (says he) when ladies allow themselves to be forty. . . . I advise them to avoid every kind of personal decoration, which custom has in any degree appropriated to youth, and, above all, the use of pink ribands, to which they have a particular propensity."

"As the Roman empire was founded on a rape, and no less than six hundred and eighty-three Sabine virgins were forcibly converted into wives, according to the account of that accurate antiquarian Dionysus of Halicarnassus, we cannot expect to meet with many Old Maids in the early period of the Roman history."

"The panegyric which St. Gregory of Nyssa composed on virginity is the more remarkable, as we have positive evidence that he was himself a married man."

Embedded in the middle of these pseudo-Gibbonian solemnities we find an interesting echo of Hayley's own early experiences with anonymous letter-writers. This takes the form of one of the small novels with which the work is interspersed, and tells the story of Miss Winifred Wormwood, an envious Old Maid, who "made it her chief occupation . . . to frustrate every promising scheme of affection and delight". This person's victim was the amiable Amelia Nevil but the really interesting character is Mr. Nelson, beloved of Miss Nevil, who "lost the use of his reason" when his "destined bride was burnt to death. However, he later recovered it, together with "a great portion of his former spirits", and the way he did so was, I think, unique: he evolved "a singular plan of benevolence" which consisted in searching for "female objects of charity, whose distresses had been occasioned by fire".

Enough has been said, I hope, to indicate that this is no ordinary book. It was an odd work for a man of Hayley's years to have written, and to the end of his life he nourished the delusion that by doing so he had struck a blow for the more sympathetic treatment of Old Maids. Indeed, behind all his mock-solemn learning, one obscurely detects, I think, a sincere belief on his part that the lot of the unmarried woman was an unsatisfactory one. What he did not realise, however, was that his contemporary Old Maids, who were what they were through necessity rather than choice, could hardly be expected to be agreeably impressed by his championship of their cause.

The work was dedicated to Mrs. Elizabeth Carter, the learned translator of Epictetus. She did not accept his tribute in the spirit in which it was offered. She was furious with him. She thought he was making game of her.[11] And so, with hideous unanimity, did all the other Old Maids of the island of Britain. Unfortunately, among the reading-public of the day, they represented a powerful contingent.

Hayley, though ostensibly unperturbed, was much put out that his "benevolent intentions" should have been so misconstrued. He interested himself no further in the cause of the Old Maids.

8

And now, one pendant, before we leave, without undue regret, the subject of Hayley's earlier writings.

Of all the Old Maids in literary history, one reigns supreme. Her library was small, and it is not known with any certainty of what it consisted. She lived, in the days we are considering, at Steventon in Berkshire, and she had, by 1795, completed a novel, then known as *Elinor and Marianne*. Among the few books which she certainly possessed was a set of Hayley's *Poems and Plays*.[12] I do not say that she ever read them. They were the sort of thing which, I imagine, was, in those days, chosen as a safe New Year's gift by an affectionate relative, for a young woman of literary tastes. There is, in fact, in her own works, no indication whatever that she was influenced by Hayley's writings. Indeed, quite otherwise.

But, later on, when *Elinor and Marianne* was reshaped and published in 1811, under the title of *Sense and Sensibility*, it contained a character, Miss Marianne Dashwood, who, I am confident, had in her youth been an ardent admirer of the Hayleian muse.

CHAPTER X

THE PARIS VISIT: PRELUDE TO COWPER
(1790-1792)

· I

IT IS TIME NOW to return to the summer of 1790, and to an event of considerable moment: no less than Hayley's first, and only, trip to the Continent.

Few things are more remarkable in the career of the subject of this biography than his inveterate propensity for staying in his native land. Ever since the Scottish journey of three-and-twenty summers before, Hayley had not once quitted the soil of England. This, in the case of a fox-hunting country squire would not have been out of the way; but, for such a man as Hayley, a cultured dilettante, a student of foreign languages, it was quite extraordinary. Especially when one reflects that this was pre-eminently the age of the Grand Tour, the age when no gentleman's education was considered complete until he had mused in the ruins of Rome, had meditated upon the fountains of Vaucluse, and wandered sentimentally among the groves of Meillerie. It is true, no doubt, that the slightly earlier Europe that Boswell and Horace Walpole had visited had been a more peaceful one. War with France had for some time been sporadic; and in 1789 the French Revolution had begun. Nevertheless, neither in those days, nor later, had such considerations done much to deter the really obstinate traveller—as may be demonstrated by the feats carried out in this respect by Hayley's friends, Gibbon and Flaxman.

No, I think the reason for Hayley's home-keeping habits is a much simpler one: chronic shortage of ready money. This is a point of some importance, since most of the writers who deal with his relations with Blake persist in regarding him as a rich and pampered dilettante. He was a dilettante, of course, and he lived in comfortable style. But he was never really well-to-do. He lived far too near the extreme edge of his income for that, and besides, Eliza was an uncommonly expensive luxury. His works, for a time, brought him a welcome addition to his revenue. There is an unconfirmed note on a letter of his to Cadell, of July 29, 1785, to the effect that, during seven years prior to that date, his poetry had earned him a sum of just over a thousand pounds. But this money was spent almost as soon as he got it. The benevolences of which he writes rather too largely were, often, real and considerable.

Be this as it may, 1790 saw him at last uprooted. Dr. Warner was the immediate cause of the excursion. He had been appointed chaplain to Lord Gower, the British Ambassador in Paris, and had consequently invited Hayley to visit him. Now Paris, in the summer of 1790, was a very interesting proposition indeed to an ardent and romantic lover of Liberty. It was, Hayley says, "a spectacle of chearful curiosity, and of hope so magnificent in promises of good to mankind, that philanthropy could not fail to exult in the prospect."

In addition to himself, Romney and Carwardine were to be of the party; and Hayley had, as well, the best of all possible reasons for wishing to go to France: one that affected the welfare of his son. Already for some time this reason had bulked large in his mind. As early as the preceding August he had written to consult Anna Seward about it. The question was no other than that of engaging a governess to superintend Tom's education; and, moreover, since he wished the boy, whom he then intended to be trained as a physician, to have a knowledge—indispensable as he thought to such a career—of French, he had contemplated the dangerous notion that the governess should be a French one.

Miss Seward's concern when this project was mooted to her was comic, even pathetic. She felt she knew only too well what both Hayley, and French governesses, were capable of. She wrote to him on August 17, 1789,[1] in the following strain:

When you urged the necessity of an assiduously attentive friend and secretary to yourself, and an occasional preceptor to your darling, when indisposition or literary employment of another species should make it inconvenient to you to attend to him, I mentioned Mr. W.—as a person I know to be in every way qualified for those trusts. I fear it will not be easy to find another companion of your travels so eligible in either sex, especially in ours. France may, however, perhaps supply you with what I think England could not, an amiable and accomplished woman, who durst put her peace and fame into the hazard of living domestically, during some years, with the most dazzling and engaging of mankind. Nothing but a considerable independent fortune can enable an amiable female to look down, without misery, upon the censures of the many; and even in that situation, their arrows have power to wound, if not to destroy peace. Surely no woman, with a nice sense of honour,—and what is she worth who has it not?—would voluntarily expose herself to their aim, except she has unwarily *slid* into a situation where the affections, making silent and unperceived progress, have rendered it a less evil to endure the consciousness of a dubious fame, provided there is no real guilt, than to renounce the society of him, without whom creation seems a blank.

While I cannot be entirely certain what she means by her last sentence, it is sufficiently clear that her disapproval was unreserved. But Hayley was an obstinate man; it is one of his most notable characteristics; he would have nothing to do with the impeccable

Mr. W—; and Warner's invitation gave him just the opening he required. He set forth to France determined to return with a real French governess.

The trio departed from Eartham on Saturday, July 31, in great style, in a post-coach specially purchased by Carwardine for the occasion; and, proceeding by way of Brighton and Dieppe, they reached Paris on August 3, where they were cheerfully received by Dr. Warner, and lodged in the Hotel de Modene.

Festive scenes followed. The party dined twice with Lord Gower at the Embassy; they inspected the latest work of the French painters, David and Greuze, both of whom dined with them. David escorted them in return to the Luxembourg gallery where they were able to admire his Death of Socrates, his Paris and Helen, and his Horatii. All the while the heat was tremendous. They visited the theatres and found them delightful, particularly the women, says Romney; who added that the acting, especially in comedy, was much beyond what England could provide. They also inspected the Palais Royal, and found that "the whole of the apartments over the shops (as Romney records[2] for the benefit of his son John, the budding clergyman) . . . are let to ladies of pleasure, whose windows look down upon the people walking in the arcades and the square; which renders it one of the most licentious and splendid places in Europe". The letter containing this animated description ends, pleasantly enough, "I am pleased to hear you pursue your studies with vigour".

Perhaps the *pièce de résistance* was a series of visits to that energetic female, Stéphanie-Felicité du Crest de Saint-Aubin, Comtesse de Genlis, to whom earlier, in 1784, Hayley had addressed an Ode. She, in gratitude no doubt, was courtesy itself, and entertained them in the convent *de la belle chasse* in which she resided; in another convent on the outskirts of Paris; and in the villa of Rancy, the seat of the Duke of Orleans. Romney was delighted with the "sprightly benevolence" of this admirable lady, and so was Hayley, though I daresay both were still more delighted with her charming and most enigmatic companion or pupil, Pamela, now a lovely girl of fourteen. Pamela, later to be the wife of the unfortunate Lord Edward Fitzgerald, is a figure that needs judicious treatment. At the time nearly everyone believed her to be the natural daughter of Mme. de Genlis by the Duke of Orleans, in whose family the lady was preceptress—governess is a word of hardly enough weight in this case. Mme. de Genlis, on the other hand, asserted, with what at that time seemed the merest perversity, that the girl was in fact Anne Stéphanie Caroline Sims, daughter of Guillaume de Brixey and Mary Sims, and a native of Fogo Island, Newfoundland. And, oddly enough, modern research seems to incline to the view that her version—however improbable—is the true one.

The trip to Rancy must have been most enjoyable. The party was augmented for the occasion by the addition of Mme. de Genlis's pupils, the Duke of Chartres and his brother and sister. The former was a fine young man of sixteen, and both he and his brother and sister conversed fluently in English. The equipage which carried them was enormous. It contained twelve people, and was drawn by eight horses. It was, says Romney, "a very comfortable and sociable way of travelling".[2]

At length, on August 21, the tourists bade their adieux to these enchanting ladies at a breakfast, and Hayley, ever ready to rise to the occasion, presented their united thanks for courtesies received in a poem which neatly contrived to be gratifying both to the pupil and to the mistress:

> So great the favours shewn us here,
> Which time can ne'er efface,
> Our gratitude can scarce appear
> Proportioned to their grace.
>
> In this distress sure aid I seek,
> Dear Pamela, from you,
> If those sweet lips will deign to speak
> Our thanks, and our adieu!

All this was well enough; but what was even better, he had succeeded, despite Miss Seward's animadversions, in doing what he had intended. He had captured the French governess.

She was, he tells us, a "very singular little woman, full of noble sentiments and odd fancies . . . and admirably adroit in teaching manners to little folks". She was passionately fond of books, and wrote a diminutive delicate hand; though she hardly ever spelt two words together aright in her own language (which might well have been a disadvantage in a teacher of little folks). However, she read excellently, particularly tragedy. That must have settled it with Hayley. She had married young, and unhappily. Her husband had ruined himself by gambling; and then he had died and left her with a baby, and quite unprovided for. She had charming manners, and Hayley was entranced by the thought that she would be able to impart these to his son. In short, his experiment was a complete success, and though his friends pulled his leg a great deal about the governess, he did not mind. He knew when he had secured a treasure.

The party returned the same way as it had come, and reached Eartham towards the end of August. Romney was ill; and no wonder. The crossing had taken twenty-two hours, and the travellers had lain in bed all the time, while outside the rain fell incessantly, though it still remained intolerably warm.

It may perhaps be as well to conclude here the story of the

governess, who remained at Eartham until the summer of the following year. Far from exhibiting the artful rapacity which is so often imputed to governesses, and especially to French ones, she was generous and charitable to a quite uncommon degree. So much so, in fact, that when Hayley eventually found it necessary to dispense with her services, she begged him to take back the whole of the modest salary he had paid her. Indeed, she did more than beg; she sent the greater part of it back to him, and it is pleasant to relate that he kept the money by him, and later returned it to her at a time when she was genuinely in need of it.

Nor, I think, is this the last word she has to say in our story. I believe we can trace her hand in a very extraordinary transaction of the following year: none other than the composition by Hayley of a comedy in five acts and in the French tongue, entitled *Les préjugés abolis, ou l'Anglois juste envers les François*. This work dealt with the adventures of an English gentleman named Mr. Trumore, the son of an old Peer who was outrageously prejudiced against the French. Its heroine was a French damsel, *la tendre Emilie*, who comes to England in quest of her old persecuted father, and, falling into indigence, is assisted, virtuously assisted be it said, by Trumore; ultimately, by her own magnanimity and that of her discovered parent, converting the outrageous old Lord Trumore to an at least modified form of Republican enthusiasm. The hand is the hand of the governess, I think, though not, I hope, hers the spelling. By the end of February, the piece was finished, and Dr. Warner was pressed into service to negotiate it with the Parisian managements. But there, unhappily, a sad hitch arose. Hayley had not considered with sufficient care the propriety of the Parisian stage. Among his secondary characters he had introduced that of a courtesan, and, as he quaintly puts it, "the delicacy of France could not tolerate any person confessedly destitute of continence". The play was consequently returned to him, and so ended his brief dream of dramatic success in a foreign land and an alien tongue.

Was he daunted? Not at all. Both he and Warner had "a considerable fund of philanthropy and enthusiasm", and had therefore exulted as all right-thinking men should upon the destruction of the Bastille. They had cherished from the beginning "ideas of the loftiest kind" concerning the destiny of France; and so, when Edmund Burke brought out his eloquent *Reflections on the French Revolution*, Hayley without a moment's hesitation began to compose a refutal of them. Fortunately perhaps, he did not complete it, as he was interrupted by the illness of Henry Carwardine, and was obliged to rush him up to London to see Dr. Austin, of shower-bath fame. Dr. Austin gave the sufferer a bottle of bark, and, by the time they had returned to Eartham, Hayley's desire to put Burke in his place had unaccountably vanished.

2

It was during his three weeks in Paris that Hayley entered into yet another of those pseudo-parental relationships which were a speciality of his. This time it was with that frigid piece of political machinery, William Huskisson, who, because he was the first man in this country to be run over by a train, is now best known to posterity as an occasion for public statuary.

At this time, however, Huskisson was a mere youth of twenty, with his way to make in the world. He was attached to the British Embassy as private secretary to Lord Gower. There Hayley must have met him; and met him, moreover, for a comparatively short while. But in a Hayleian friendship time was of little consequence. Hayley's impulsive nature seems always to have led him to propound to any young person of either sex to whom he chanced to take a fancy those sentiments which were once celebrated as the slogan of the proprietor of a well-known business college: "Let me be your Father!" And so, in the Huskisson Papers at the British Museum, one comes upon a file of letters[3] the first of which, of February 18, 1791, starts in no uncertain fashion: "Mon très cher cher Père, Honteux de m' appeller votre fils, I should not have had the confidence to make use of the expression had not" etc., etc.

I must confess that, when I first came upon these words, I rubbed my eyes, and started jumping to conclusions: conclusions which broadened when I found Huskisson alluding to Tom as his "little brother", and asking for Hayley's "paternal benediction". But alas! it was not to be. Agreeable as it would have been to have discovered in the impeccable William Huskisson a natural son of William Hayley, by degrees, as I read on, enlightenment came. What I was up against was not an interesting scandal, but a very pretty piece of eighteenth century sentiment. Huskisson was an ambitious boy, and Hayley was a great man. When a great man bids an aspiring youth to call him 'father', the aspiring youth obeys, particularly when he thinks it to his advantage.

Yet, despite this disappointment, the correspondence is an interesting one, though more for the light which it throws upon the assiduous climber Huskisson than for that which it casts upon his mentor. It endured with a good deal of warmth for some years; and Huskisson, returned from Paris, paid several visits to Eartham. In 1792, for instance, it seems that he had applied to Hayley for "literary counsel", since the latter replied: "I shall be willing to give you [this] with all the affectionate sincerity of a parent."[3] Huskisson, it turned out, was on the verge of his "first appearance as an English author".

Soon, however, his projects were much more grandiose than mere authorship. He was in the War Office, and a rising man. The warm expressions of the earlier letters diminish. By 1794 he is Hayley's "affectionate friend".³ By 1795 he is writing official letters of such crushing import as this to some wretched contractor: "Mr. Huskisson presents his Compliments to M. Le Cointe, and is very much astonished that he should have so much mistaken his character as to have renewed an offer on which Mr. Huskisson had already made Him acquainted with his Sentiments."³ Clearly this was no sort of adopted son for the gentle hermit of Eartham!

Still, in April 1799 he married, and Hayley obliged with a nuptial sonnet.³ And in 1800 – but 1800 is some way ahead, and we shall come to Huskisson again in due course.

3

The year 1791 started for Hayley in the spirit of the morning after the night before. The French holiday had been costly, and none of his numerous projects were producing any money. In February he was obliged to dispense with the services of his valet, the affectionate and intellectual Harry; and Tom was promoted to the post of keeping the family books. Before January was out, Hayley was writing to Eliza in a familiar strain: "As I find economy is the only thing that a spirit so independent as mine can safely trust, in regard to this world, I am growing a minute economist, in respect to my household; keeping no footman, and only two diminutive maids."

This being so, it is typical that the next of his activities should be a new expenditure: the purchase of a furnished cottage, no less, in his favourite village of Felpham. He excused the extravagance on the grounds that it would enable him to teach Tom to swim, a point he had much at heart so as to preserve his life from accidental calamity. Also he thinks it will probably cure his own headaches, which have been severe.

Soon, however, after a glorious interval of calm, Eliza began to grow restive. Perhaps she was lonely. At any rate, she requested Tom's society at Derby, and Hayley consented to let the boy pay her a visit. This necessitated the disbandment of the governess, he gave her a resounding reference, and then took both her and Tom up to London, whence he despatched her to her new post in Monmouthshire, and Tom to Derby. The latter, it may be presumed, travelled with the unusual item of baggage of a bow-and-arrows. This, at least, is what one infers from Mrs. Hayley's letter to her husband of September 10: "The archers and archeresses assemble at the Kiddleston Inn, once in every month. The former shoot for small prizes, the latter only for honour. I have been invited to dine in this party; but have put off the scheme for the arrival of Thomas. ... You will equip him with a proper bow and arrows, and I desire to have the honour of presenting him with a green coat, on which

I shall work a golden arrow, and put the buttons of the Derby archers. The waistcoat also, which is to be buff, with a simple laurel leaf in ribbon (as I have been wont to work for you and your friends,) will also take a little time."

Tom arrived safely in Derby, and stayed there until the beginning of November. Hayley, alone at Eartham, missed him tremendously, though he was somewhat consoled by receiving from Mme. de Genlis the gift of her latest work upon child-education, together with a very pretty drawing from the hands of the enchanting Pamela. Both these ladies had by now reached England, events in France rendering desirable a temporary change of scene; and, throughout the month of November, a diverting little comedy of errors was played out by Hayley as he endeavoured, vainly, to lure the distinguished birds of passage to Eartham, that he might repay the hospitality he had received in France. He wrote to Dover; but they had left. Then to Brighton and to Arundel; with similar results. He made all possible preparations for their entertainment, and the next news he had was that the elusive couple had reached Bath.

In the interim he had had to speed up to London to receive Tom on his return from the North. As some compensation to Eliza for the boy's departure, he then kindly despatched to her the portrait of Tom which Romney had painted that autumn, in which he figured as Robin Goodfellow, flying on a cloud and crowned with a chaplet of flowers. On this picture Tom wrote to Mrs. Hayley with some maturity: "We are much diverted with the observation of the lady who took the clouds in the picture for a muff."

The winter of 1791 was notable for the sickness which raged in the village of Eartham. Hayley set boldly to work with his remedies, and, according to his own account, grappled single-handed with the epidemic. One invalid, however, was beyond even his aid. On January 2, 1792, Sarah Betts, who had been nearly fifty years in the service of his family, died at the age of seventy-five at Petworth. The epitaph Hayley wrote for her has been quoted earlier; and she was not without other distinctions. She was, after all, Thomas Alphonso's grandmother; and she had been drawn by George Romney in the character of an ancient sibyl.

Whether Tom knew of the relationship I cannot say, but if he did not there was a singular propriety in the request he made. He told his father that he had never seen a corpse, and that he would like to. So Hayley took him to see the faithful old Sarah as she lay in her coffin. The same day, Hayley records, with a fitting sense of the bizarre quality of existence, Tom danced with a countess, presumably at Lord Egremont's. He was, however, equally silent on his reaction to both experiences.

Then, early in 1792, there came at last, and quite unheralded, the crowning moment of Hayley's life: the date was February 7.

4

Crowning moments, when they arise, seldom seem so important as to the eye of retrospect. That February was, on the surface, nothing out of the ordinary run. Hayley was entertaining guests, Dr. Warner over from Paris, and the "very amiable American poet", Joel Barlow. It was a brief visit, only of three nights' length; but during it Hayley retired to his library and wrote a letter which completely diverted the course of his existence. The immediate cause of this letter was a paragraph which had caught his eye in a newspaper, to the effect that he and William Cowper were competing with one another in producing rival editions of a *Life of Milton*.

This is what he wrote to Cowper:

DEAR SIR,
I have often been tempted by affectionate admiration of your poetry, to trouble you with a letter; but I have repeatedly checked myself, in recollecting that the vanity of believing ourselves distantly related in spirit to a man of genius, is but a sorry apology for intruding on his time.

Though I resisted my desire of professing myself your friend, that I might not disturb you with intrusive familiarity, I cannot resist a desire equally affectionate, of disclaiming an idea which I am told is imputed to me, of considering myself, on a recent occasion, as an antagonist to you. Allow me, therefore, to say, I was solicited to write a Life of Milton, for Boydell and Nicol, before I had the least idea that you and Mr. Fuseli were concerned in a project similar to theirs. When I first heard of your intention, I was apprehensive, that we might undesignedly thwart each other; but on seeing your proposals, I am agreeably persuaded, that our respective labours will be far from clashing. . . .

To you, my dear Sir, I have a grateful attachment, for the infinite delight which your writings have afforded me; and if, in the course of your work, I have any opportunity to serve or oblige you, I shall seize it with that friendly spirit which has impelled me at present to assure you both in prose and rhyme, that I am,
                Your very cordial admirer,
                          W. HAYLEY.

And the inevitable sonnet followed.

As he composed this missive, natural reserve, he tells us, caused him to hesitate. He consulted Warner, and Warner told him he was sure Cowper could not but be pleased with such a letter. Moreover, he offered to convey it himself to Cowper's publisher, Johnson, as he passed through London on his way back to Paris. Hayley concurred. Barlow, the friend of Tom Paine, returned to get on with the French Revolution; and Warner went up to town with the fateful letter in his pocket.

And, for a long time, nothing happened. Hayley, who felt snubbed, took no further action, and proceeded to other affairs: to toying with the idea of sending Tom to school in Derby; to toying with the idea of going abroad and taking the boy with him; to toying with, and finally agreeing to, Romney's plea that he should write the *Life of Milton* already mentioned, which was required to preface the magnificent folio edition of that poet which the Boydells were bringing out. Romney's urgency was not entirely disingenuous; he fancied, or so Hayley thought, that his friend's compliance with their wishes would persuade Messrs. Boydell to pay him better for the work he was executing for the Shakespeare Gallery. And so Hayley settled down cheerfully to two years of diligent application upon a project for which, he says, the pecuniary reward was trifling.

Meanwhile, his letter to Cowper was lying, unforwarded, forgotten, as charged with potentialities as a stick of dynamite, in publisher Johnson's office, by St. Paul's.

Looking back, with a knowledge of subsequent events which at the time it was given to no man to see, one can still feel the almost physical tension that involves the destiny of our hero during that fateful spring of 1792.

CHAPTER XI

WILLIAM THE FIRST AND WILLIAM THE SECOND (1792)

1

FORTUNATELY THE TENSION did not last. One day, some six weeks later, someone at Johnson's office came across the errant letter and re-addressed it to Weston Underwood; and, a little later, it was in the hands of the author of *The Task*.

Now, since this book is a long one, and since William Cowper is a figure of credit and renown, who, moreover, in his own letters has given us as living a self-portrait as any man has ever done; I think it must be taken for granted that the chief happenings of his life up to this date are familiar to the reader. Cowper in 1792 was already sixty-one years of age; it was twenty-nine years since his first attempted suicide and most serious bout of madness; it was twenty-seven years since he had retired to Huntingdon, and twenty-five since his arrival, with Mrs. Unwin, at Olney. He had published his first book of poems at the advanced age of fifty-one in 1782; and three years later had leapt into considerable eminence with the appearance of his masterpiece, *The Task*. Furthermore, the move from Olney to Weston Underwood was already six years old. Lady Austen had passed out of his life; John Newton was passing out; and William Unwin was dead. The chief figures in it now were: the devoted Mrs. Unwin; his "restored cousin" Lady Hesketh; the Throckmortons at the Hall; Samuel Greatheed, the minister of Newport Pagnell; and his young admirers, Samuel Rose, the budding barrister, and John Johnson, the budding clergyman, son of his maternal uncle's daughter, and better known to posterity as "Johnny of Norfolk".

In addition, Cowper had in the previous year published his translation of Homer, and was now turning his attention to his annotated edition of Milton which, with a variety of other misfortunes, was before long to send him mad once more.

And Hayley: Hayley was forty-seven. No mere boy like Rose or Johnson, though in ardour he was soon to excel them all.

2

So far as I know, Cowper's reply to Hayley's first letter has not been preserved, but this does not matter, since, writing to Lady

Hesketh on March 25, he tells her pretty exactly what he said in it. Rose had been staying with him when the long-delayed missive arrived, and it had been sent back to London in Rose's pocket, so that he could show it to Lady Hesketh. Cowper continued: "Mr. Hayley's letter slept six weeks in Johnson's custody. It was necessary I should answer it without delay, and accordingly I answered it the very evening on which I received it, giving him to understand, among other things, how much vexation the bookseller's folly had cost me, who had detained it so long; especially on account of the distress that I knew it must have occasioned to him also. From his reply, which the return of the post brought me, I learn, that in the long interval of my non-correspondence, he had suffered anxiety and mortification enough; so much that I dare say he made twenty vows never to hazard again either letter or compliment to an unknown author. What, indeed, could he imagine less, than that I meant by such an obstinate silence, to tell him that I valued neither him nor his praises, nor his proffered friendship, in short, that I considered him as a rival, and therefore, like a true author, hated and despised him. He is now, however, convinced that I love him, as indeed I do, and I account him the chief acquisition that my own verse has ever procured me."

This is warm enough, but better is to come, for, though we do not exactly know what Hayley replied "by return of the post", we can guess well enough from the tone of Cowper's letter of April 6 which, one presumes, is in reply to it:

My dear Friend,

God grant that this friendship of ours may be a comfort to us all the rest of our days, in a world where true friendships are rarities, and especially where suddenly formed they are apt soon to terminate! But as I said before, I feel a disposition of heart toward you, that I never felt for one whom I had never seen. . . .

It gives me the sincerest pleasure that I hope to see you at Weston; for as to any migrations of mine, they must, I fear, notwithstanding the joy I should feel in being a guest of yours, be still considered in the light of impossibilities. Come then, my friend, and be as welcome, as the country people say here, as the flowers in May! I am happy, as I say, in the expectation, but the fear, or rather the consciousness, that I shall not answer on a nearer view, makes it a trembling kind of happiness, and a doubtful.

Hayley, no doubt, had issued his customary invitation to Eartham, and Cowper had responded with a counter-proposal. The letter continued with a brief explanation of Mrs. Unwin, and concluded:

Bring with you any books that you think may be useful to my commentatorship, for with you for interpreter, I shall be afraid of none of them. And in truth, if you think that you shall want them, you must bring books for your own use also, for they are an article with which I am *heinously unprovided*: being much in the condition of the man whose library Pope describes as

> No mighty store!
> His own works neatly bound, and little more! ...

Tell me, my friend, are your letters in your own hand-writing? If so, I am in pain for your eyes, lest by such frequent demands upon them I should hurt them. I had rather write you three letters for one, much as I prize your letters, than *that* should happen. And now, for the present, adieu—I am going to accompany Milton into the lake of fire and brimstone, having just begun my annotations.

Hayley's reply to this was curiously all his own. He had, evidently, already confided to Cowper his trouble with his eyes, and now, while knowing nothing of the tragedy of Cowper's life, he plunged into a dissertation upon his own sorrows, saying (April 11):[1] "[I] wish you had known me before long years of ill-health, and the miseries of a marvellous life had diminished a native Gaiety of Spirit, which might have rendered me perhaps a more amusing companion to you, had our Stars thrown us together more early in Life!—Yet as I delight in such mental chemistry, as draws Good from Evil, I sometimes please myself with an Idea, that a reciprocal account of our past misfortunes may furnish us with more pleasing and useful Topics of Conversation, than we could have derived from any wit or vivacity of our younger days." And, moreover, he promised: "However deficient you may find me in Talents, I flatter myself I possess *one advantage over you*, which it will gratify me to *hear you confess*—I mean the advantage of having endur'd *calamities*, which even your Imagination, powerful and sublime as it is, *could not reach*, and which, when you know them, may I trust, lead you to regard your own as infinitely less, than they before appear'd to you.—This is the *only sort of Triumph* I can ever *meditate over you*, for as to Genius, I declare by the Almighty Giver of it, I esteem your poetical *Powers* far above those, that I ever thought myself possess'd of in my vainer days—when I had certainly an uncommon quickness and facility in composition—of late years I have reckon'd my Fancy almost as much crippled as my limbs."

There are occasions when the irony of circumstance becomes painful beyond bearing; and this is one of them. I need hardly add that the italicisings are Hayley's very own.

The letter ends with the announcement that he intends to stay a fortnight at Weston, "if", he adds diffidently, "you are not tired of me *sooner*." And, on April 27, he wrote yet again, with a slight variation of the compliment to Gibbon: "The red-breast of Eartham is not a little impatient to visit the sky-lark of Weston."[1] Later too, in the same letter, comes a passage rather touchingly modest: "If I had, at *any time*, the power *of shining*, I believe the season is over, and I am shorn of my Beams—they are not, however, worth regretting, for had they been shorn, like a sheep's coat, at their full Growth, they would not have made a golden Fleece large enough to have loaded a mouse." It is, of course, easy enough to call this sort of thing mock-modesty: one can do no more than judge the passage by one's own ear: to mine it rings true, and I like Hayley the better for it.

Then on May 6 yet another letter[1] was despatched to Weston, in the highest of spirits, commencing: "Age! take care of yourself!—William the Second is coming—Well said, my dear Lady! and this William the Second is coming with a *spirit so imperious* that he would carry off not only your Mary, but your Castle, your Garden, and even your River Ouse with its Poet, if He could transport all this radiant Spoil to enrich his favourite scenes of the South.

"There's an Invader for you!—what were your Norman Williams to this?"

He hoped, he said, to arrive on Tuesday, May 15, and he praised Cowper for some self-depreciatory remarks he had made in his last letter: "I love you for your modest kindliness in preparing me so well for the New *Ignoramus* I am going to see." And then there follows a very characteristic passage, touching in its thoughtfulness:

> Ladies, I know, are sometimes *alarm'd* by an expected visit from an Invalide, because in general it is very difficult to satisfy such visitors in Articles of the Table; but William the Second is, in truth, a simple Hermit in his diet—He drinks no wine and eats only a small portion of Milk and Bread for his supper. Forgive me for talking of such things, but I could not rest under an Idea of exciting even a shadow of domestic Inquietude in the friendly spirit of that Mary, for whose affection I profess myself a very aspiring and anxious Candidate.

His letter ends, as it began, with a playful allusion to the circumstance that both he and his "poetical brother of Weston" are Williams: "I will bring you a Heart and Soul so dispos'd to take an affectionate Interest in all your Works, that I flatter myself I may be able (as an Ally to the dear Mary) to drive that depressive spirit of Melancholy you once mention'd, to such a distance from you, that it shall have no chance of invading you again. Then I shall be *William the Conqueror*."

In this same communication, Hayley said that he knew his road as far as the *George* at Wooburn, and sought instruction for the way thereafter; and he also wrote "me with my old and only valet in petticoats", which would seem to imply that, since the disbandment of Harry, he had been valeted and accompanied, with a fine and free disregard of convention, by a female servant. It is unusual, but it doesn't matter. If it was good enough for Cowper and Mrs. Unwin, it is quite good enough for us.

3

And now, at last, we have no more need to be groping and delving among things lost and forgotten, since the scene to which we have come is suddenly as brightly lighted as any in our literary history. The Lodge at Weston Underwood stands out in the vivid illumination of Cowper's genius, and almost every detail of the picture may be seen by those who will take the trouble to read those incomparable letters of his. Besides, the moment is one charged with significance, for we are standing on the brink of one of the periods most ominous in the appalling story of his life. Assuming that Hayley arrived, as he said he was going to, on Tuesday, May 15, the two new friends were able to enjoy together just a week of delightful study and gossip and rambling the countryside, before the blow fell. On Sunday, May 20, Mrs. Unwin was tolerably well; on Tuesday, May 22,[2] she was attacked by her second, and most serious, paralytic stroke.

But before this calamity, Hayley had had time to dash off a few enthusiastic lines to Romney, describing the delights of Weston:

Carissimo Pittore, . . . My brother bard is one of the most interesting creatures in the world, from the powerful united influence of rare genius and singular misfortunes, with the additional charm of mild and engaging manners.

Then as to the grand article of females . . . here is a *Muse of seventy*, that I perfectly idolize. . . . This is a wonderful scene. . . . Few things in life have given me such heartfelt satisfaction as my visit to this house; and the more so as my kind hosts seem to regard me as sent to them by Providence, for our general delight and advantage. . . .

As to myself, I feel I have now found the thing I most wanted—a congenial poetical spirit, willing to join with me in the most social and friendly cultivation of an art dear to us both, and particularly dear to us as the cement of friendship.

And Cowper, in his turn, had reciprocated the compliment in a letter to John Johnson, of May 20, in which he said: "Mr. Hayley is here on a visit. We have formed a friendship that I trust will last for life, and render us an edifying example to all future poets."

Too soon, however, all these delights were at an end, and tragedy took the stage. On the afternoon of May 22, the poets returning from their walk were met by Mr. Greatheed, the minister, who came out of The Lodge with a face expressive of very ill tidings. He did his best to prepare them for a great shock; and then came the dreadful news that Mrs. Unwin was, at that very moment, in the grip of a fit.

Cowper rushed into the house, and a few seconds later came from Mrs. Unwin's room in a state which bordered upon frenzy. He had seen her who had been his prop and stay for nearly seven-and-twenty years, speechless, helpless, convulsed. It was true then, what he had always believed: that he was accursed of God! As he staggered from her room, Hayley met him in the passage. "There is a wall of separation between me and my God," Cowper cried in his anguish.

And then Hayley said one of those unaccountable things which make him so curious a character, and one for which we can hardly fail to feel real affection. Looking fixedly into Cowper's distracted eyes, he answered with an equal vehemence of expression: "So there is, my friend, but I can inform you, I am the most resolute mortal on earth for pulling down old walls, and by the living God I will not leave a stone standing in the wall you speak of."

He wrote this, of course, long years after the event,[3] and I find it impossible to believe that he made his bravely-silly speech in just those stilted terms. But what he did say was to the purpose, for in his foolishness he had been wise enough to answer Cowper in the only way that he was, at the moment, capable of understanding. For, Hayley continues, at this fantastic reply, "he examined my Features intently for a few moments; and then, taking my Hand most cordially, said, 'I believe you' ". The crisis was past, and it was Hayley's inspired imbecility that had averted it.

In his *Life of Cowper*, Hayley does not tell this anecdote. He probably thought no one would believe it. He, as it were, paraphrased it, saying, "His first speech to me was wild in the extreme:—my answer would appear little less so." But it was its very wildness that had rendered it effective. "From that moment", says Hayley proudly, "he rested on my friendship . . . [and] . . . regarded me as sent providentially to support him."

That was the point: Hayley was to him now the direct minister of providence. I think Cowper's letter of May 24, to Lady Hesketh, describing the catastrophe, bears this out: "It has happened well, that of all men living the man most qualified to assist and comfort me, is here, though till within these few days I never saw him, and a few weeks since had no expectation that I ever should. You have already guessed that I mean Hayley! Hayley who loves me as if he had known me from my cradle."

4

Meanwhile Hayley had passed rapidly, and with his accustomed energy, from ghostly counsel to measures of a practical nature.

It has already been related how, among his *materia medica* at Eartham, there was that new-fashioned cure-all, an electrical machine. Hayley was convinced that, if only he had his machine, it would do Mrs. Unwin a great deal of good. He had used it upon himself to counteract his habitual inflammation of the eyes—

Heaven knows how!—and now he was determined to try the effect of this "powerful, though uncertain remedy" upon a case of paralysis. The question was: could such an apparatus be discovered in Weston?

It is at this point that the Sockett (or Socket) family enter the story. Mr. Sockett had been a stationer and bookseller in a small way of business, a trade he was later to enter upon once more in London. At present, however, he was rusticating at Weston. Cowper, who knew him, thought highly of his gentle manners and his ingenious mind; and, what was still more important, his ingenuity of mind had been responsible for his becoming the possessor of just such a machine as was required.

Hayley called and found Mrs. Sockett at home and perfectly willing to lend the appliance. It was one of the usual contrivances for producing static electricity by the friction against a revolving glass cylinder of a rubber made of silk or leather and stuffed with hair. It was, in fact, a similar article to that which Shelley had later employed at Eton for his alarming electrical experiments. The cylinder was revolved or whirled by a handle, which necessitated an assistant, since one operator's time was fully employed in passing the spark so obtained through the unfortunate patient's body, *via* the tongue, the teeth, or whatever member was deemed most proper. For his coadjutor in this business of turning the handle of the machine, Hayley therefore pressed into willing service the fifteen-year-old son of Mr. and Mrs. Sockett, Thomas.

Nor did Hayley stop at mere electricity. He also wrote urgently to his friend in London, Dr. Austin, and procured various prescriptions, which he had made up. Under the influence of all, or some of, these remedies, Mrs. Unwin slowly grew better, and Cowper's spirits also improved. By May 26 he was able to report to Lady Hesketh that the patient "daily recovers a little strength, and a little power of utterance". Hayley, he added, "has been all in all to us on this very afflictive occasion. . . . Where could I have found a man, except himself, who could have made himself so necessary to me in so short a time, that I absolutely know not how to live without him."

It is clear that the conquest had been complete. Cowper, always affectionate, always willing to lean upon those he deemed stronger than himself, was captivated by Hayley. And, judging by the evidence available, it seems obvious that anyone would have been.

Because, very soon, it becomes apparent that it was not only in the matter of medical advice that he was anxious to serve his brother-poet; but also in another respect, equally important. To understand what this was we shall have to examine a little the state of Cowper's finances. These now, for many years, had been parlous. Though his poems had brought him renown, they had not brought him wealth, and, though the way of life which he and Mrs. Unwin had adopted had been frugal in the extreme, he had, nevertheless, been living beyond his means—and hers. His whole fortune consisted of a few hundred pounds invested in the funds, together with the rent from the chambers which, as a young man, he had purchased in The Temple; and he was both improvident and extremely charitable. As early as 1765, he had confessed to Joseph Hill, who administered his affairs, that "he had contrived to spend . . . in three months the income of a twelvemonth". After he went to live with the Unwins, things for a while were better. His family helped; so did his friends; and Mrs. Unwin, besides being an admirable manager, had a little fortune of her own. Yet, for all this, as the years went by his state grew no better, and, what was much worse, Mrs. Unwin's little capital steadily dwindled.

Thus, by the time of Hayley's visit, the position was desperate. The shock of Mrs. Unwin's seizure doubtless released Cowper from his natural disinclination to discuss his financial affairs with a stranger. Or it may even have been Mrs. Unwin herself who confided in Hayley her fears of what might happen to Cowper when she was gone. Twelve hundred pounds of her fortune were spent; and, if she were to die, Cowper's situation would be hopeless. It is not precisely known how Hayley ascertained all the facts, and indeed it does not matter. What is important is that he knew them, and that, directly he realized the seriousness of the position, he decided in his customary style that someone had got to do something about it, and that that someone was himself. His own finances were in a bad way; it was impossible that he himself should play the *deus ex machina*. He made up his mind at once that the only solution was a Pension from the Government. The more he meditated the matter, the more certain he grew that this was the only hope. "It became", he tells us, "the most darling project of my sanguine spirit."[3]

Now, in this most darling project, he had one invaluable card. Thurlow, the Lord Chancellor, had been a school-fellow and friend of Cowper's; and Hayley, as we know, was acquainted with Thurlow. As long ago as 1762, Cowper had jestingly said to Thurlow, then a rising lawyer: "Thurlow, I am nobody, and shall always be nobody, and you will be Chancellor. You shall provide for me when you are." Thurlow had smiled, and answered, "I surely will." In 1778, what Cowper had prophesied came to pass; but Thurlow had forgotten his promise, and Cowper was much too proud to remind him of it. "Our former intimacy", he had said, "would be disgraced by such an oblique application." Nevertheless, Cowper, rather pathetically, continued to remember the incident, and, though in 1782 Thurlow had lacked the common courtesy even to acknowledge the first volume of his poems which he had sent him, he still found himself unable to believe the promise totally forgotten. This story, without doubt, Cowper, proud of his prescience, had told Hayley during his visit; and it was upon this story that Hayley resolved, in the first instance, to base his campaign. There can be no doubt that he told Cowper what he was proposing to do, and that the latter approved it; for, directly Hayley left Weston for London, a series of letters commences in which is related the onset of the negotiations.

Cowper's first letter to Hayley after his departure is dated June 4, and is chiefly devoted to an account of Mrs. Unwin's health; but on the following day he wrote again, saying: "Can I ever honour you enough for your zeal to serve me? Truly I think not: I am however so sensible of the love I owe you on this account, that I every day regret the acuteness of your feelings for me, convinced that they expose you to much trouble, mortification, and disappointment. I have in short a poor opinion of my destiny, as I told you when you were here, and though I believe that if any man living can do me good, you will, I cannot yet persuade myself, that even you will be successful in attempting it. But it is no matter; you are yourself a good, which I can never value enough, and whether rich or poor in other respects, I shall always account myself better provided for than I deserve, with such a friend at my back as you."

In the interval, Hayley had not been idle. On June 6, he paid a visit to Lady Hesketh, and the following day he despatched to Cowper a note in a female hand[1] (the valet, we like to think) saying that he cannot write himself because he is suffering from his old eye-trouble, but that he has secured an appointment for breakfast the following morning with the Chancellor.

Next day he dashed off to Cowper a hurried note[1] in a frantic scrawl which is quite unlike his usual neat and legible hand. It sounds a premature—an all too premature—note of triumph:

Huzza.

I have passed an agreable [sic] Hour from 8 to 9 this Morning with the Chancellor.

Left both Him and Lord Kenyon who was with us so impres'd with warm wishes to serve you that I am persuaded your old Friend Thurlow will accomplish it if possible—

I am fatigued beyond expression.

It is now 4 and I have been busy ever since 7.

And, as postscript: "I decamp to-morrow."

5

So much for what Hayley imparted to Cowper. Now let us look at the picture from another angle. In order to do this we have to consider a very singular work, in manuscript, which is now in the

British Museum,³ and was formerly in the possession of Edward Dowden. This is entitled *Two Memorials of Hayley's Endeavours to serve His friend Cowper*; and it is, for the most part, written in Hayley's own hand. The first memorial (which is all that concerns us for the moment) is thus described: *The first relating to his Fortune—A Singular History in a series of Letters from a Father to his Son, 1794*; in which is set down, with a wealth of detail, the process of the negotiations upon which we are now embarked. There is a good deal besides, in Hayley's best manner. In the prefatory letter, Thomas Alphonso is informed the writer is conscious that, after the father's death, the son will wish to "hoard or circulate hereafter, as Treasures of Affection", the information therein imparted to him; and that, moreover, should he ever be disposed to reflect upon Hayley's failings, the work now presented to his notice may also give him an opportunity of contemplating his *Good Deeds*.

To revert to the first onset: the embroilment of the Lord Chancellor. Hayley set about this feat in characteristic style. His friend Carwardine had recently presented to one of Thurlow's daughters an elegant set of Cowper's *Poems*. Hayley, ever tortuous, wrote to the girl, and asked her to lend him a volume of the work. She did so, and he speedily returned it to her enriched by the following inscription, written upon a blank leaf:

> Sweet nymph, accept a Bard for whom
> Rich Amaranths with Roses bloom
> To deck his moral Lyre;
> Dear, doubly dear, must wit and Truth
> Be deemed by you from one whose youth
> Was social with your Sire.
>
> Apart by different stars impelled,
> Their course as Mortals both have held
> To suffer and to drudge;
> But Genius kept them both in view,
> And to the Heights of Honour drew
> The Poet and the Judge.
>
> Ingenuous Girl, while here you see
> How their Fraternal Hearts agree
> In Energy and Truth,
> May you restore and teach to blaze
> With double Glory's blended rays
> The Friendship of their Youth.

And, at the same time, he intimated to the Chancellor that he desired an interview.

Thurlow "overwhelmed with business and spleen" (for Pitt had had just about as much of his double-dealing as he could stomach, and was even now planning his removal), Thurlow, then, did not wish to see him; and said so. Hayley, however, sent him a further note, to say he was staying in town for the express purpose of waiting upon him; thus forcing his hand. And so, with as good a grace as possible, Thurlow then invited him to breakfast at his house in Great Ormond Street.

Unfortunately, whether by accident or design on Thurlow's part, no sooner were the pair of them seated, quietly and alone, than Lord Kenyon, the Chief Justice, was announced. Hayley, fearful of losing his cherished opportunity, cast etiquette to the winds and proceeded to unbosom himself before both noble lords at once. He spoke at length, and eloquently. He reminded Thurlow that the last time he had seen Cowper had been in 1763, just after the fearful occasion in The Temple when the poet had attempted to destroy himself. Thurlow appeared touched. Ferocious as he was, he was not unkindly; and besides, the very precariousness of his own political situation had perhaps softened him a little. But Hayley never knew when to stop. He blundered on, suggesting that His Majesty George III should bestow a pension on Cowper "as an act of personal Thanksgiving and Gratitude towards Heaven, for having restored him from that mental malady by which this wonderful and most interesting poet has been periodically afflicted". The two Law Lords looked at one another, and Thurlow gruffly observed that such a proposal would need extremely delicate handling.

Hayley glanced at his watch, and perceived he had been addressing his companions for more than an hour, without intermission. He rose to go. The Chancellor did not try to detain him; but saw him out with the "endearing expression", charged with a certain forensic caution: "I am greatly obliged to you for all you have said."

This was the interview which caused Hayley to despatch to his friend the jubilant note, beginning "Huzza", which has been given already. It is, indeed, instructive to regard such a transaction from two differing angles. Nevertheless, for all Hayley's feckless optimism, there is little doubt that the chief reason for the tone of his note to Cowper was—his desire to cheer him up! It was not only laudable; it was necessary.

And then Hayley went back to Eartham, and he and Cowper fell to the milder benevolence of composing each of them an address to Dr. Darwin, who, Hayley rather thought, needed encouragement.

Yet for all this poetical revivification, the medical side of things was not forgotten. On June 20, Hayley was writing:[1] "Now let me speak to you as my medical brother! I am glad you please our dear Patient with your Electrical Process, but in spite of Cavallo's authority I am persuaded you will not find the purple flame sufficiently strong to do any material good." When Cowper replied, three days later, the theme was still electrical:[1] "That silent operation (he wrote) never satisfied me; I wanted a little noise to convince me that some good was done, and shall therefore proceed to sparkle in future as we used to do."

Nevertheless, though it is clear that Mrs. Unwin is still receiving electrical treatment, and that it is still from Mr. Sockett's machine, it is equally clear that, whoever may be turning the handle, it is no longer little Thomas Sockett. For that young gentleman's rise in the world had begun. Hayley with his habitual impulsiveness had brought him back to Eartham. Later he wrote to Eliza to explain the whole proceeding:

> I was induced to bring home from the village where Cowper resides, an interesting youth, who, like myself, had been afflicted with great illness in his childhood. It happened that in my search for an electrical machine . . . I became acquainted with a good woman and her son, who had an electrical apparatus. . . . The lad asked me, if I could recommend him to any situation as a clerk in London, as he writes a very good hand, is deep in arithmetic, and nobly wished to be no longer an expensive burden to his parents. It struck me, that he might be very useful in teaching Tom what he himself learned so well, and by a literary commerce, might acquire more Latin and some Greek from his disciple.

In the interim, Cowper and Hayley were indulging in an almost daily interchange of letters, in which the health of Mrs. Unwin, in all its aspects, was largely discussed; and soon yet another project of moment started to make its appearance. This was none other than the quite amazing conception that she and Cowper should, for the benefit of both their healths, later that summer essay the journey to Eartham, to give Hayley an opportunity of repaying the hospitality he had received at Weston.

I have called this an amazing conception, and so it is, when one considers the circumstances of the case. Mrs. Unwin was nearly seventy years of age, and seriously ill; and Cowper, at sixty-one, had been a recluse for thirty years. Except for his visit to his dying brother at Cambridge in 1770, he had not, since his retirement to Huntingdon in 1765, travelled further than was necessitated by two removals of house—from Huntingdon to Olney, and from Olney to Weston. He had decided that the delicate balance of his reason should on no account be imperilled by excitement, and he had rejected every invitation, whether to London or elsewhere, that had been made him since the time his poems had brought him celebrity. And yet, now, for the newest friend of all, for the friend of a few months, he was contemplating calmly a journey of unprecedented magnitude. Hayley assured him that it would be of benefit to Mrs. Unwin, and no doubt Cowper hoped that it would. But there was more to it than that: at last, in Hayley, he felt he had found a friend for whose sake it was worth risking the perils of the world, from which he had kept himself so long withdrawn. Nothing can show better the quite extraordinary influence which Hayley had in a short while secured over Cowper, than the comparative nonchalance with which already in the early days of the summer this stupendous design was being discussed. By the middle of June, Cowper was writing of the adventure almost as casually as if it were a mere matter of crossing the street, and though as the month wore on his courage seemed to wane a little, he was still able to refer to it as "a delightful and innocent project".

The hand of these letters is still the beautiful, rounded and regular hand of William Cowper; but the spirit is suddenly that of somebody quite different: bold, resolute. Such, in its inception, was the effect of William the Second upon William the First.

6

What, meanwhile, of Thurlow? Nothing, unfortunately. Not a word. On July 1, Hayley, who had just transcribed to Cowper the engaging jingle we have quoted concerning the nuptials of Catherine Courtenay, turned at the end of his letter[1] to that weightier theme: "I have just been writing", he said, "to the quondam Chancellor, and am sending a copy of my bold epistle to you."

The *quondam* Chancellor! In that one word is answer all-sufficient for the silence. Pitt had triumphed, and Thurlow was out of office. As Hayley oddly remarks in his narrative of these events, "I believe the temper and health of the Noble Lord were so embittered at this particular time by Public and Private occurrences, that he was greatly disqualified for social enjoyment and for the common forms of civility." Nevertheless, despite this charitable judgment, he wrote to him again, a long letter, full of gentle reproach, some of it in verse, and some of it in prose. "My dear Lord, (it ran) May I, without Impertinence, speak to you again on paper, after having so recently trespas'd on your time in person, and talk'd, I fear, with more zeal than discretion.

"If I pester you, my Lord, both with prose and Rhime . . .", he wrote, and "Judge of my surprise and mortification . . .", and a great deal more which may be perused at length in Southey's *Life of Cowper*. Some of the verse incorporated in this performance touched with an unexampled tactlessness on Thurlow's dismissal:

> Yes! now your hand with decent pride
> Relinquishes that seal unstained
> Which Bacon, law's less upright guide,
> With many a sordid spot profaned.

But neither prose nor verse stirred Thurlow to any reply, nor even an invitation that he should renew his old acquaintance with "our dear William of Weston" later in the summer, under Hayley's own roof. Like the Tar Baby, Thurlow laid low and said nothing.

At this, Hayley, fired to action as was Brer Rabbit by that other taciturn character, expressed himself once again in verse which he did not this time despatch direct to Thurlow, but sent instead to Carwardine, with the artless request that he would be so good, "if he had courage sufficient" to repeat the lines to his "dumb patron" at a convenient season. The lines began thus:

> Why wrapt in clouds no sun pervades,
> Sullen as Ajax in the shades,
> Why Thurlow art thou mute,
> When courtesy, unstained by art,
> Addresses to thy manly heart,
> An amicable suit?

Whether Carwardine had "courage sufficient", I do not know, but I think it exceedingly unlikely that he would have done anything so imprudent, particularly as the final stanza is, for Hayley, quite remarkably to the point:

> Touch'd by thy silent disrespect,
> Two poets blame thy rude neglect
> With dignity serene;
> *We*, tho' aloof from Public Jars,
> *We* have thy Pride, but, thank our Stars!
> Thy pride without thy Spleen.

It is hardly the kind of thing one reads aloud to one's patron, who is known to be irascible, and has just been dismissed from high office. I think, in the light of future events, we may assume that not only was Carwardine tactful, but that Hayley really expected him to be. If he had not so expected, he might just as well have sent the lines to Thurlow himself.

And that, since no sign had come, and since, moreover, Thurlow was now the very last man who could influence Government, might, by most, have been taken as an indication that all was over in the matter of the Pension. Hayley did not so regard it. He was a man of unabashed pertinacity when a matter dear to his heart was at stake. He retired to regroup his forces; and started to lay his plans for the second assault upon the citadel.

Siege warfare, however, is a slow business, necessitating much gathering of gear; and, before this attack is launched, other ground has to be covered, notably that of preparing for the great feat of transporting Cowper to Eartham.

7

All through July, Cowper's letters, and Hayley's too, are full of practical considerations bearing upon this formidable enterprise. Already by July 1, Hayley had acquired a "charming four-wheeled garden vehicle"[1] for the conveyance about his grounds of Mrs.

Unwin. Moreover, he hazards that the patient, far from being discommoded by the motion of the carriage, will find it "in itself medicinal".

Cowper (who at this very moment was having his portrait painted in the green coat of the Olney Archers) was, as befitted a man actually in contact with the invalid, a little less sanguine; but he assured his friend that "at the very instant we feel ourselves at liberty, we will fly to Eartham". And then at last, on July 22, the great tidings were despatched:

> This important affair, my dear brother, is at last decided, and we are coming. Wednesday se'nnight, if nothing occur to make a later day necessary, is the day fixed for our journey. Our rate of travelling must depend on Mary's ability to bear it. Our mode of travelling will occupy three days unavoidably, for we shall come in a coach . . . with four steeds to draw it;
>
> > —Hollow pamper'd jades of Asia,
> > That cannot go but forty miles a day.

Abbott, the painter, who had now completed his portrait, had been commissioned to engage the coach from London.

> Send us our route (Cowper resumed), for I am as ignorant of it almost as if I were in a strange country. . . . My friend and brother, we shall overwhelm you with our numbers; this is all the trouble that I have left. My Johnny of Norfolk, happy in the thought of accompanying us, would be broken-hearted to be left behind.
>
> In the midst of all these solicitudes I laugh to think what they are made of, and what an important thing it is for me to travel. Other men steal away from their homes silently, and make no disturbance, but when I move, houses are turned upside down, maids are turned out of their beds, all the counties through which I pass appear to be in an uproar. . . . How strange does all this seem to a man who has seen no bustle, and made none, for twenty years together.

This final paragraph gives better than any words of mine could do a picture of the desperate nature of the undertaking as it appeared now to the excited yet apprehensive spirit of Cowper; and desperate is indeed the word, since in his next letter, of a week later, he makes of that word, as it were, his text:

> Through floods and flames to your retreat,
> I win my desp'rate way,
> And when we meet, if e'er we meet,
> Will echo your huzza!
>
> You will wonder at the word *desp'rate* in the second line, and at the *if* in the third; but could you have any conception of the fears I have had to bustle with, of the dejection of spirits that I have suffered concerning this journey, you would wonder much more that I still courageously persevere in my resolution to undertake it. Fortunately for my intentions, it happens,

WILLIAM HAYLEY
From a mezzotint (1779) by Johann Jacobé, after a painting by George Romney (*see* page 53)

GEORGE ROMNEY, 1782
From an unfinished self-portrait (*see* page 203)

EDWARD GIBBON AT LAUSANNE
From a painting by J.-L. Piot

LADY HAMILTON AS SENSIBILITY, 1786
From an engraving by Richard Earlom, after a painting by George Romney (*see* page 98)

ANNA SEWARD, 1786
From a painting by George Romney (*see* page 112)

JEREMIAH MEYER, R.A.
From a photograph of his monument, after a design by George Dance,
in Kew Church, Surrey (*see* page 103)

WILLIAM COWPER, 1792
From a pastel by George Romney, painted at Eartham (*see* page 164)

JOHN FLAXMAN MODELLING THE BUST OF HAYLEY, 1795
(*Reading left to right*): Romney, William Hayley, Flaxman, Thomas Alphonso
From a painting by George Romney (*see* pages 203 and 290)

THOMAS ALPHONSO HAYLEY AS ROBIN GOODFELLOW, 1791
From a painting by George Romney (*see* pages 143 and 230)

EARTHAM
From an engraving after Stebbing Shaw in *The Topographer*, 1791

THE TURRET, FELPHAM
From a pencil drawing (*c.* 1810) by George Engleheart
(*see* page 324)

WILLIAM HAYLEY, THOMAS HAYLEY AND WILLIAM MEYER, 1796
(*reading right to left*)
From an engraving by Caroline Watson, after a painting by George Romney (*see* page 202)

THOMAS ALPHONSO HAYLEY
From a tempera painting done by William Blake for the Library of The Turret, Felpham
(*see* page 266)

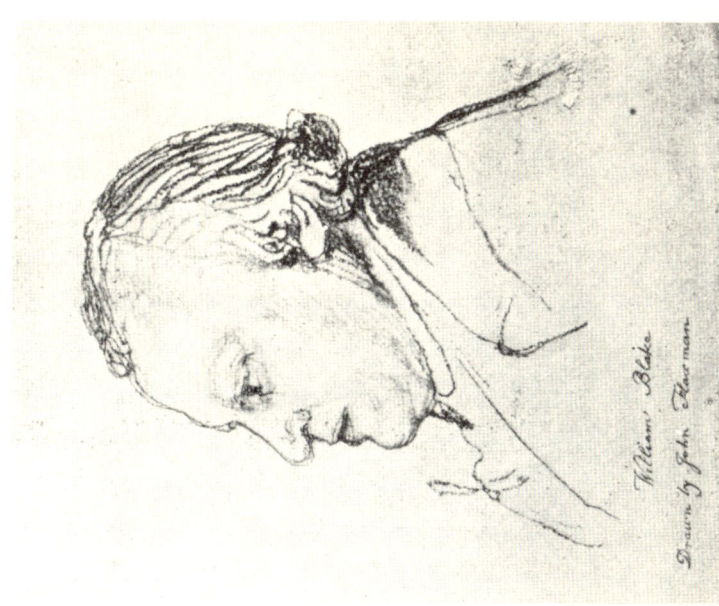

WILLIAM BLAKE
From a pencil drawing (c. 1803) by John Flaxman, R.A.

BLAKE'S COTTAGE AND GARDEN AT FELPHAM
THE VIRGIN OLOLON DESCENDING
From *Milton*, Plate 36 (*see* page 257)

THE DOG

Frontispiece to Hayley's *Ballads*, 1805, from an original engraving by William Blake (*see page* 271)

THE HORSE

From Hayley's *Ballads*, 1805, from an original engraving by William Blake (*see page* 271)

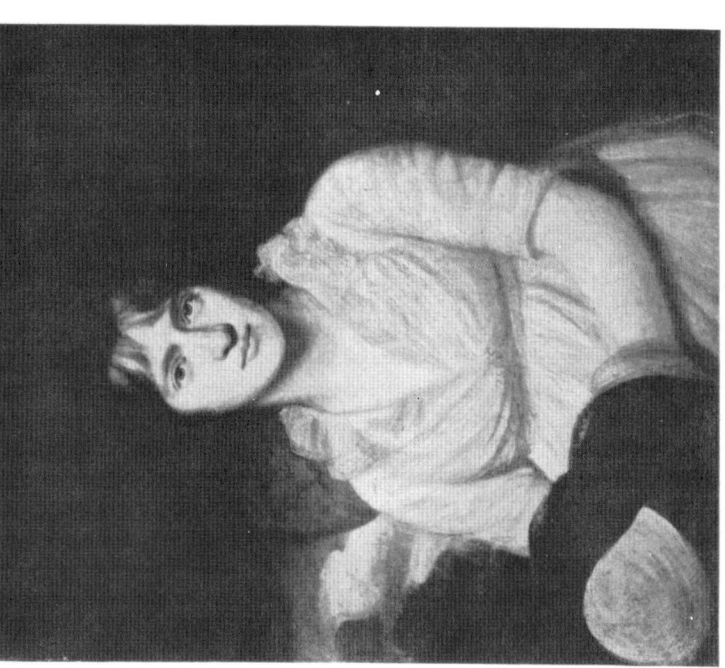

AMELIA OPIE, 1807

From a painting by her husband, John Opie, R.A. (*see* page 340)

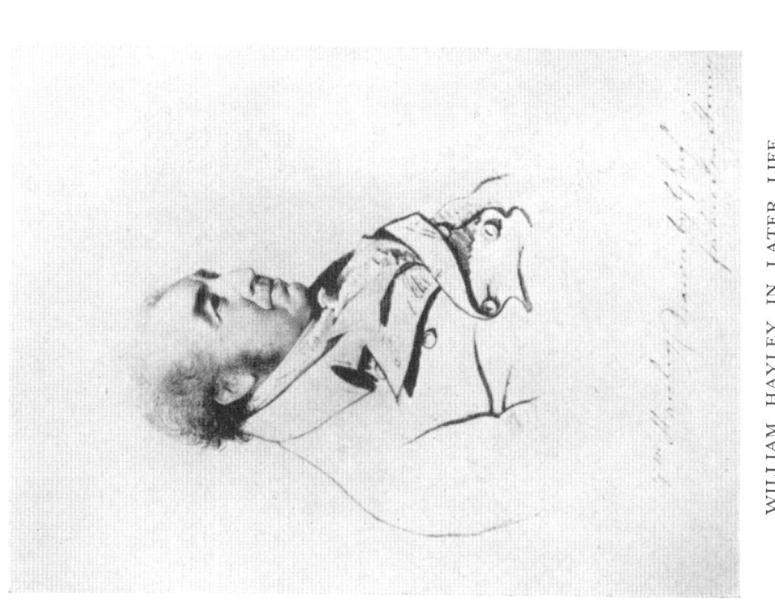

WILLIAM HAYLEY IN LATER LIFE

From a drawing (*c.* 1810) by George Engleheart (*see* page 324)

HAYLEY'S "MARINE VILLA" AT FELPHAM, NOW TURRET HOUSE

BLAKE'S COTTAGE AT FELPHAM

EARTHAM HOUSE, AS REMODELLED BY SIR EDWIN LUTYENS AND OTHERS

that as the day approaches my terrors abate; for had they continued to be what they were a week since, I must, after all, have disappointed you; and was actually once on the verge of doing it. I have told you something of my nocturnal experiences, and assure you now, that they were hardly ever more terrific than on this occasion. Prayer has however opened my passage at last, and obtained for me a degree of confidence that I trust will prove a comfortable viaticum to me all the way. On Wednesday therefore we set forth.

The terrors that I have spoken of would appear ridiculous to most, but to you they will not, for you are a reasonable creature, and know well, that to whatever cause it be owing (whether to constitution, or to God's express appointment) I am hunted by spiritual hounds in the night season. I cannot help it. You will pity me, and wish it were otherwise; and though you may think there is much of the imaginary in it, will not deem it for that reason an evil less to be lamented—so much for fears and distresses. Soon I hope they shall all have a joyful termination, and I, my Mary, my Johnny, and my dog, be skipping with delight at Eartham!

8

Few journeys are more vivid to the eye of the imagination than that which thus commenced on Wednesday, August 1, 1792. The coach must have been a capacious one, since it contained the poet, the invalid Mrs. Unwin, their two servants Sam Roberts and his wife, Johnson, and that eminent spaniel, Beau. The party proceeded by very easy stages on account of Mrs. Unwin, and the first evening found them as far advanced as Barnet, where they put up at the *Mitre*. Already the air of a royal progression clung about the journey; at the *Mitre* they found their young friend Samuel Rose awaiting them. He had walked thither (no mean step!) from his house in Chancery Lane, to spend the night with them. Yet for all this, Cowper had begun his travels with a thousand fears; and during this first evening found himself oppressed in spirit to a degree that could hardly be exceeded. Mrs. Unwin was very tired, and there was such a racket going on (in contrast to the dead calm of Weston), that he feared she would get no rest. He was wrong, however; she rested, though not well, yet sufficiently.

And then the second day went better. They dined at Kingston with Cowper's kinsman, General Cowper, who had ridden over from his house at Ham. They had not met for thirty years, and, as Cowper reflected, but for this journey would never have met again. Mrs. Unwin now seemed invigorated by her travels, and when they called a halt once more at Ripley, on the Portsmouth Road, she and Cowper were in far better condition, both of mind and body, than on the previous evening. The inn at Ripley was quiet, and held that night no visitors but themselves; and there they slept well, and arose refreshed. Now the longest of their stages lay before them: through Guildford and Godalming, Chiddingfold, North Chapel and Petworth. They crossed the Downs at Duncton by moonlight—"that majestic range of mountains" as Gilbert White had called them a few years earlier—and here, momentarily, Cowper experienced "some terrors". But, except for this, they had little of which to complain, and when, at ten o'clock at night on August 3, they reached Eartham House, they were at once "as happy as it is in the power of terrestrial good" to make them.

"It is almost a paradise in which we dwell", Cowper wrote a few days later, to Mr. Greatheed; "and our reception has been the kindest, that it was possible for friendship and hospitality to contrive. . . . I have much to see and enjoy before I can be perfectly apprized of all the delights of Eartham. . . . We are in the most elegant mansion that I have ever inhabited, and surrounded by the most delightful pleasure grounds that I have ever seen. . . . They occupy three sides of a hill, which in Buckinghamshire might well pass for a mountain, and from the summit of which is beheld a most magnificent landscape bounded by the sea, and in one part by the Isle of Wight, which may also be seen plainly from the window of the library in which I am writing."

Moreover, the effects of this earthly paradise had already been highly beneficial to Mrs. Unwin. Hayley had forgotten nothing that might serve to render the excursion auspicious: every evening she was treated to her dose of "electrical fire", and twice each day was drawn in her chair by the two Thomases, Hayley and Sockett, round the airy hill of Eartham. Then, in the mornings, there were for the two poets the delights of literature. Eschewing Homer, they confined themselves to a diligent revisal of what each had written relative to Milton, and to a joint translation of the *Adamo* of Andreini. More, Hayley did not fail to "find the sweetest lenitive for his domestic misfortune" in discussing with Cowper that "beautiful and blameless woman" with whom, from her "extraordinary nervous and mental inquietude", he had found it impossible to live. Cowper was very sympathetic, and Hayley's desire to discuss Eliza was not unnatural, since, early this summer, the unfortunate bard had been almost scared out of his wits by evidences of new fractiousness on her part.

It had been in June, while all these delights were pending, that Eliza had announced all of a sudden that she was contemplating a visit to the coast of Sussex. Hayley had been beside himself, and had written at once, with the greatest vehemence, bidding her relinquish all idea of such a project which, he said, was likely to be a source of pain to them both, and particularly liable to interrupt the tranquillity of his studies.

There was less fight in Eliza, apparently, these days, and she agreed under the pressure of his massive flood of remonstrance to abandon her intention. Hayley was nothing if not magnanimous

Once he had got his own way and was assured that the visit of his new friend was no longer likely to be ruined by the sudden appearance of a vengeful or pathetic Eliza, he immediately changed his tune, and, on June 25, responded with a letter of almost comical gratitude:

> MY DEAR ELIZA, I am particularly obliged by the celerity with which you impart to me your kind and generous determination to comply with my request. . . . I thank you speedily for the relief you have thus afforded to my mind; and I thank you *sincerely*, in spite of the little tartness of expression with which you seem to reproach me. . . . At present you think my late requisition harsh, imperious, and severe; but time and reflection will shew it to your mind in a very different point of view; for, in truth, instead of barbarously driving you from any real enjoyments, I have only persuaded you (as tenderly as I could,) to relinquish a project which must have grieved yourself in the end, because it must have been painful and injurious to me, whom, even in an angry moment, you would, I am persuaded, be truly sorry either to injure or afflict.

Well, it is to be presumed that Hayley thought this Pecksniffian production showed him in a creditable light, since he prints it himself; and then he goes on to dilate upon the desirability of the coast of Lincolnshire as a holiday resort. "As for next year," he says, with what in another man would sound uncommonly like hypocrisy, "I think it by no means improbable, that I may by that time rest so peaceably under this earth, that I shall not be able, either kindly or unkindly, to obstruct or direct your movements upon it."

This lachrymose and apparently quite groundless reference to his probable demise seems to have done the trick; and Eliza came to heel without further ado, arranging to take her holiday at Parkgate, near Chester.

She wrote to her husband to announce this decision in a letter which has, I think, real pathos and dignity:

> With sea-bathing, and a change of scene, I hope to recover health and spirits, to feel more comfort myself, and to administer more to my friends, than I am capable of doing at present; but as I have already said, I detest unavailing lamentation. This is therefore the last letter, in which I intend *speaking to you of myself*. In future I will tell you what I am reading, and what I have seen, if I have seen any thing; but I feel to have lived, during the last three years, the life of Mother Goose's Sleeping Beauty; and to have dozed away all my senses: but I hope to rise from the sea, though not a Venus . . . *yet a new-born Minerva*; and on my return to this land of philosophy, to become a philosopher. Hitherto, my natural genius, and habits of society have impeded my progress: but I expect in the cauldron of Medea, as Mrs. Smith calls it, to be regenerated; at present, however, I keep to subjects *unphilosophic*. There was a passage in your last letter but one, which I should have replied to, when I last wrote, had I not been too ill. Till I recollected that *memory* is not required for a poet, I felt surprised at your having *forgot* what I suffered from my father's resignation of the Deanery to the death of my mother, I might say, of my sister, when time and accident

began to *reconcile* me to the loss of my *earliest* connexions. I had not, therefore, an idea, when I spoke of twenty-two years of domestic vexation, of your taking the whole upon yourself. I should indeed be ungrateful, were I not to acknowledge *more* years of kindness, and polite attentions, than I could *now* suppose so lively a character as yours capable of paying to any woman. I have never regretted the time I devoted to you, since I owe to it *powers* of enjoyment, without which riches could afford me little gratification. . . .

For what little proficiency I have made also in music, I am wholly indebted to you. . . . But for your prohibition, I should have given it up. My piano-forte is now my greatest resource, when alone, and a concert (at which I used to tire) is become my highest entertainment. You see, therefore, that I am disposed to end our little *hostile* correspondence by rendering you *ample justice*.

Hayley was so pleased with this letter that he replied in his most gushing style, relating his adventures at Weston; but he burked the more intimate issue by adding suddenly that he had "an oppressive head-ach which rendered him peculiarly unfit for scribbling".

Poor Eliza! It was her last attempt at a reconciliation, and she had chosen the worst possible moment, just when Cowper's famous visit was in the offing. But for this who can tell what might have happened. As it was, however, she was rewarded for her compliance with Hayley's views by a series of letters, in which were described in detail the manifold delights of the visit. I feel sure they must have annoyed her very much.

9

This, however, though a necessary digression, must not be permitted to divert our gaze from the animated scenes now being enacted at Eartham. As I have said, every delight was provided for the gratification of the distinguished visitors, and one of these delights, though Cowper was little accustomed to it, was that of society.

By August 11, after the travellers had had a few days in which to settle down, Romney arrived; and his neuroticism responding to the similar strain in Cowper caused them to get on famously together. Hayley was overjoyed that his two dearest friends should so take to one another, and when Romney set to work and drew in crayons that wonderfully perceptive portrait of Cowper which now hangs in the National Portrait Gallery (and is such a striking contrast to Abbott's more conventional rendering of less than a month previously), his gratification knew no bounds.

Soon the party was augmented by the arrival from Brighton of Charlotte Smith, and Hayley was driven to pass the night on the sofa in his library. He did not mind. The weather was perfect. He could hardly sleep for thinking how happy he was.

Mrs. Smith played up wonderfully, and added to the general impression that Eartham was at last the complete Temple of the Muses. Each morning she remained in her room, writing her daily portion of her new novel, *The Old Manor House*, which she then read aloud in the evening to the assembled company. "This admirable lady," Hayley tells us, "had a quickness of invention, and a rapidity of hand, which astonished every witness of her abilities. Cowper repeatedly declared, that he knew no man, among his early associates in literature, who could have composed so rapidly and so well. Moreover, she read, as she wrote, with simplicity and grace." Romney, always susceptible, admired her immensely, and got out his crayons and drew her portrait too.

What Romney thought of it all is interesting, for, after Hayley's eloquence, his style is a blunt one. When the visit was over he wrote as follows,[4] to his son John:

> I was near a month at Mr. Hayley's, where I met Mr. Cowper, and Mrs. Smith; and yet, in spite of such good company, and bathing, my health continued very poorly.—Mr. Cowper is a most excellent man; he has translated Milton's Latin Poems, and I suppose very well. Hayley is writing the life of Milton, so you may imagine that we were deep in that poet; every thing belonging to him was collected together, and some part of his works read every day. Mrs. Smith is writing another Novel, which, as far as it is advanced, is, I think, very good. She began it while I was there, and finished one volume. She wrote a chapter every day, which was read at night, without requiring any correcting. I think her a woman of astonishing powers. . . .
>
> She and the two poets were employed every morning from eight o'clock till twelve in writing, when they had a luncheon, and walked an hour; they then wrote again till they dressed for dinner. After dinner they were employed in translating an Italian play on the subject of Satan; about twenty lines was the number every day. After that they walked, or played at Coits; then tea, and after that they read till supper time.

This, I think, is the sole reference we have to those Coits. It is a detail that one would have been sorry to have lost.

Meanwhile Hayley had written again to the long-suffering Eliza, describing Cowper at the age of sixty-one: "He is a florid healthy figure . . . with an interesting countenance that expresses intelligence and energy of mind, with sweetness of manners, and a certain tender and indescribable mixture of melancholy and cheerfulness, gravity and sportive humour, which give an admirable and delightful variety of attraction to his character."

Better still, "His venerable muse gains a little accession of strength every day in her injured limbs. I continue to electrify her every evening; and now she walks round the hill with such comfortable use of her legs, as appears astonishing to us all."

Cowper, this selfsame day, August 25, was writing a long letter to the new Mrs. Courtenay, enclosing for her the one poem which he had composed in Sussex, the splendid though sombre epitaph on Lady Throckmorton's spaniel, Fop. But by this time, though pressed to make a longer stay, there was already talk of departure. It had been finally agreed that they should start again for Weston on September 17. The visit, Cowper said, had achieved its purpose, since both he and Mrs. Unwin were marvellously better than when they had set out.

There is yet one more visitor to chronicle. The Revd. James Hurdis, the curate of Burwash near Hastings and the author of a poem called *The Village Curate*,* was already a correspondent of Cowper's, and he had sent him a letter at Weston which had been forwarded to Eartham. This letter had announced the death of Hurdis's favourite sister, and, when Cowper informed Hayley of his friend's loss, the latter at once begged him to invite Hurdis to travel across the county to join them. Neither of the poets at Eartham had met Hurdis, but Cowper assured him, "Here you will find silence and retirement in perfection, when you would seek them, and here such company as I have no doubt would suit you, all cheerful, but not noisy; and all alike disposed to love you."

Hurdis could not resist such an invitation, and by the end of the first week in September he was of the party, which, I fancy, had now been depleted by the departure of the lively Mrs. Smith. Gentle in manner and delicate in person, Hurdis, at twenty-nine, strongly reminded Cowper of poor William Unwin, though he confessed that, at present, under the stress of his bereavement, he lacked the vivacity of that admirable man. Cowper was right about Hurdis's delicate person; but nine more years of life were left to him, and, when he died, as vicar of Bishopstone, near Lewes, it was Hayley's task to memorialize his attainments.

The dwindling September days passed quickly. Hayley and Romney, Tom and Beau went off repeatedly to bathe at Felpham, while Cowper stayed behind to write his wonderful letters to his cousin. Perhaps the first fine rapture was over. He was a man accustomed to take refuge from his natural melancholy in work. Now, as he told Lady Hesketh, "I am so unaccountably local in the use of my pen that, like the man in the fable, who could leap nowhere but at Rhodes, I seem incapable of writing at all, except at Weston. . . . [Eartham] is a delightful place; more beautiful scenery I have never beheld, nor expect to behold; but the charms of it, uncommon as they are, have not in the least alienated my affections from Weston. . . . Here I see from every window, woods like forests, and hills like mountains, a wildness, in short, that rather increases my natural melancholy, and which were it not for the agreeables I find within, would soon convince me that mere change of place can avail me little."

* I am inclined to think that the latest reference to Hurdis which occurs in English literature is to be found in W. H. Hudson's *Nature in Downland*. Hudson, in his early days on the pampas, came upon some extracts from the *Village Curate*: they delighted him, and he did not forget them.

The visit had now lasted for more than six weeks: holiday-time long enough, as Cowper said, for a man who has much to do. He was pining for home, and, perhaps, not a little dreading the return journey. When at last the day of parting came, Hayley presented his friend with the portrait Romney had drawn of himself some fifteen years earlier—a noble gift and one which testifies to the real affection he bore him. There was, however, no room in the coach for the picture; it had to be sent on.

Thomas Alphonso had struck up a great friendship with Cowper during the course of the visit, and now he and his father accompanied the travellers for a mile or more until their coach was clear of the village. In a shower of mutual tears the last farewells were said. The day was wet and cheerless. Hayley later wrote to his friend:[1] "When I arriv'd at my own door after bidding you Farewell in the dripping wood, I was a poor devil indeed—wet, lame, tired." He did the best thing he could in the circumstances and "got into a warm bed for an Hour or two, in solitude and silence". Since then, however, though it was now the very end of September, he had, for consolation, been "throwing myself into the rough ocean". Tom, who had adopted similar measures, had given himself a bad cold.

Cowper wrote at once to his host from the *Sun* at Kingston, where they lay on the second night of their homeward journey. His letter is brief and touching:

MY DEAR BROTHER,

With no sinister accident to retard or terrify us, we find ourselves at a quarter before one, arrived safe at Kingston. I left you with a heavy heart, and with a heavy heart took leave of our dear Tom, at the bottom of the chalk-hill. But soon after this last separation, my troubles gushed from my eyes, and then I was better.

We must now prepare for our visit to the General. I add no more, therefore, than our dearest remembrances and prayers that God may bless you and yours, and reward you an hundred-fold for all your kindness. Tell Tom I shall always hold him dear for his affectionate attentions to Mrs. Unwin. From her heart the memory of him can never be erased. Johnny loves you all, and has his share in all these acknowledgements.

By September 20 the party was safely back at Weston, and involved in all the chaotic readjustments which are the lot of those who travel but seldom. The epic journey had been safely accomplished. They had dined with General Cowper at his house at Ham; they had proceeded from Kingston on the morning of the 19th, starting at twenty after eight, to reach Rose's door in Chancery Lane exactly at ten. Rose had provided a dish of chocolate for them, and had then ridden with them as far as St. Alban's. Thenceforth they met with no impediment, and had reached their own back-door at Weston, in a storm, at eight o'clock at night. Mrs. Unwin was quite worn out, but, after a night's rest, all were well next day.

CHAPTER XII

THE PENSION (1792-1794)

I

AFTER THIS TREMENDOUS experience a sense of anti-climax was bound to set in. Eartham was empty, Tom was ill, Hayley was sad; and Cowper was in the depths of despair. On October 2 he wrote to Hayley: "I will endeavour not to repay you in notes of sorrow and despondence, though all my sprightly chords seem broken. In truth, one day excepted, I have not seen the day when I have been chearful since I left you."

It is a little ominous. When a man has had settled habits for more than twenty years, it is dangerous to break them. Cowper went on to describe how he had been trying to resume work, with indifferent, even disastrous, results; and Hayley, when he was not busy writing almost continuous letters to "cheer the tender spirit of his new and most interesting friend", was himself trying hard to make headway with his *Life of Milton*.

Throughout October and November the letters sped between Weston and Eartham, letters that spoke of powders and laudanum and fevers; also of how Cowper, in the evenings, was endeavouring to entertain Mrs. Unwin by reading Baker's *Chronicle* to her. At last he was able to report some progress. He had completed the sonnet he had wished to write to Romney ever since the latter had drawn his portrait. He sent it to Hayley, to see if he approved it. It was a worthy souvenir of a great occasion:

> But this I mark, that symptoms none of woe
> In thy incomparable work appear:
> Well! I am satisfied, it should be so,
> Since, on maturer thought, the cause is clear;
>
> For in my looks what sorrow could'st thou see,
> While I was Hayley's guest, and sat to thee?

As the hours of darkness lengthened in the quiet house at Weston, so Cowper's melancholy, as in every year, grew in intensity. January was the month he dreaded: the month for voices and madness. Yet that December he heard a voice which was not quite of the usual fearful significance. Hayley, on December 16,[1] commented on his report of this:

I rejoice also that your nocturnal Monitor inspires you with Hope and Confidence—while He speaks *such Language*, I am ready to declare myself his firm and affectionate ally—No mortal, I am confident, can more deserve the friendly whisper of a good angel than you do, and if ever a bad one may dare to approach your ear, I pray to Heaven to make my pen (weak implement tho' it be!) equal to the spear of Ithuriel in your service.

Besides, and what is not unimportant in the now so soon to be renewed history of Cowper's Pension, there was again a visitor at Eartham; and Hayley in this same letter went on to speak of him, calling him "a very engaging young Guest (whom I call my eldest son as He was born in the year I married) . . . He was secretary to our late Ambassador in France, and particularly obliging to me and my Friends during our visit to Paris . . . We had not met since, and having a million of subjects to discuss, we have talked incessantly to each other for seven days".

The guest, of course, was none other than the serious Huskisson, and, beyond peradventure, one of the matters discussed between him and Hayley, during their seven days of incessant conversation, was the question of Cowper's financial position, and the set-back which Hayley's plans had encountered in the fall of Thurlow.

Huskisson, whose name Hayley oddly enough does not mention in his manuscript account of this transaction (though it is significant that a page has been torn out of the record at the place where his part in the business would naturally have come), Huskisson was now back from France, and installed with his patron, Lord Gower (now the Marquis of Stafford), in Whitehall. He was clearly a man who could be expected to know how delicate affairs such as these should be pursued, and there is little doubt that it was upon his advice that Hayley's next step was made.

It was a step both grandiose and resplendent, one quite in keeping with his earlier address to the Archbishop of Canterbury over the matter of *The Young Widow*. On December 11, 1792, Hayley composed a long letter to the Prime Minister of England, William Pitt, who was, of course, at that date very much occupied in coping with the French Republic. It will be recalled that years before Hayley had met the future Prime Minister at Lyme Regis, and that he had also had dealings with him in 1790 over the matter of the rejected Laureateship; yet, despite these contacts, he evidently did not feel that he knew the great man particularly well, since he now set about the business of delivering this important missive in a way that would seem bizarre to anyone who was not familiar with his methods. He gave his letter to Huskisson, who took it to London and presented it on January 8, 1793, to Mr. Long of the Treasury.[2] Long informed him that it could not possibly be handed to Pitt for the moment, because of the pressure of other affairs; and it was consequently deposited upon his mantelpiece in the Treasury, to await a more favourable season. Hayley made frequent enquiries of Huskisson as to the progress of the document, and learnt on January

18 that it was still upon the same mantelpiece, and still awaiting the auspicious moment. Sometimes Long was sanguine, said Huskisson; sometimes otherwise.

On February 13, Huskisson reported again, no doubt in response to further frantic enquiries, that the seal of the letter remained unbroken.

As, what with Mr. Huskisson and Mr. Long, this was going to be the state of the unfortunate letter for a long while yet, we may as well fill up the interim by breaking the seal ourselves, and seeing a little of what it contained:[3]

> As I was partly influenc'd by a sincere tho' perhaps a romantic Zeal for your Glory in declining the Post of Laureate . . . my honest pride suggests that I have a little Kind of right to speak to you on the private Interest of a Great poet who is worthy of your regard.

And on he goes, four close pages of it, setting out Cowper's financial position very exactly, and relating the expenditure of full twelve hundred pounds of Mrs. Unwin's little capital. There is a dig at Thurlow: "His honest pride has been wounded by a Friend with whom He was intimate in the Temple who since became great and has neglected him." And he concluded by apologizing for "this very long letter".

Long as it was, however, it was not to be thought that Hayley would end it without dropping into poetry. Here is the poetical portion:

> Some maladies, dear Pitt, are Gifts divine;
> Not ills, but antidotes:—and such be Thine!
> Behold a Pacquet, that, in friendly stealth,
> Has watch'd to seize a moment of thy Health.
> Watch'd but in vain:—thy Health is Britain's treasure,
> And They, who love her, scarce can wish Thee Leisure.
> Yet Friends (no selfish supplicants to Power!)
> May ask one moment from thy sickly Hour;
> O grudge not one to Him, whose spirit free
> Aims to confer a Benefit on Thee,
> While thus he gives thy liberal mind to prove
> Genius and Virtue sanctified by love.
> To aid them, as thou canst, I press Thee not;
> There is no Joy more poignant in thy Lot;
> And I have wish'd Thee, from thy boyish days,
> The noblest pleasures, and the purest praise.

Now, Hayley being Hayley, it is clear, I think, that he read this effusion to Huskisson before handing it over to him; and equally clear, I fancy, that Huskisson, being Huskisson, would be certain to reflect that his career would in no wise be assisted by the tactlessness of pestering a much harassed Prime Minister, in time of war, with a document—to put it mildly—of so leisurely a character. And so I am inclined to believe that all Huskisson's talk about Mr. Secretary Long was a blind, and that he merely put the letter in his own pocket and kept it there.

At all events, by the time June 1793 came, Hayley was in a frenzy; he could bear no more. The letter still had not been delivered, and he wrote demanding its return. "His affectionate friend" Huskisson, who had already assured him that, if despatched through the normal channels of the post, the letter would be *opened* but not read, cheerfully returned it; and Hayley, on June 9, posted it to Pitt,[3] and received ample confirmation of Huskisson's prescience by obtaining no reply. No reply at all; though he had now fortified the document with a brief memorandum explaining the circumstances of its delay, and, indeed, with the verses, which had not formed part of the original appeal. Pitt was laid up with the gout, hence the poetical references to his health. Hayley for some curious reason thought the moment a propitious one; though it was the tremendous summer of 1793.

Even without the gout, Pitt was no great hand at patronizing the arts. As Macaulay observes, he believed that "poetry, history, and philosophy, ought to be suffered, like calico and cutlery, to find their proper price in the market. . . . Nowhere had Chatham been praised with more enthusiasm, or in verse more worthy of the subject, than in *The Task*. The son of Chatham, however, contented himself with reading and admiring the book, and left the author to starve". And he draws a very pointed comparison between Pitt's treatment of Cowper, and that which Burke, "a poor man and out of place", had given Crabbe.

2

But, as one is apt to do when chronicling the interminable history of The Pension, we have once more run ahead of ourselves. Throughout the winter of 1792–93, as Cowper sank ever deeper into gloom, and Mrs. Unwin failed to maintain the improvement she had exhibited at Eartham, Hayley recruited himself in his new showerbath, and pushed on with his plans for converting Thomas into a physician under the kindly auspices of Dr. Austin.

In January, however, another calamity befell, and Dr. Austin died suddenly, leaving six orphans. Hayley, who, at the very moment he heard of his loss, was writing, by request, a hymn for some female orphans to sing in their chapel, was deeply moved by the coincidence, and imparted some of the emotion he felt to the hymn. He then addressed Eliza and told her that he should be particularly pleased to supply her with "a musical rarity".

At the same time Mrs. Smith was in trouble again. In the same letter as that in which he commiserates with Hayley over the death of Dr. Austin, Cowper refers to that unhappy lady:[1] "Poor Mrs. Smith—chained to her desk like a slave to his oar, with no other means of subsistence for herself and her numerous children." And again, on March 13, came another letter from him[4] which combines a reference to the unfortunate poetess with one, sufficiently heart-rending, that shows The Pension was still uppermost in his thoughts:

> Three days ago I received a swingeing pacquet by the post. Oh ho says I, it is come at last. This can be nothing less than an appointment to some good place under government. Here are the Royal arms, and the bulk of it is promising to a degree that may fairly encourage the most flattering expectations. It must be so, says Mary, and certainly comes from Lord Thurlow.—So I open'd it and found Mrs. Smith's poem. . . . I found myself very easily let down from my imaginary exaltation into the vale of poverty again.

Charlotte Smith was indeed, despite the new poem, in deep waters. Hayley, not content with his efforts to succour Cowper, had rushed to her rescue also, and had applied on her behalf to Cadell, his publisher. A letter of April 12, this year,[5] from him to Cadell, tells its own story, and reveals the straits to which she had now been reduced:

> You astonish me (he wrote) by the mention of *two drafts upon you* by our unfortunate Friend, *immediately after your liberal aid*, in consequence of my first application to you on her Behalf.—I had not the *least Suspicion* of *such a circumstance*; and so far from wondering at your being *hurt by it*, I confess myself *not a little chagrined* on the occasion—Humanity will lead us both to reflect, that the necessities of this wretched sufferer have been extreme.— She must have literally wanted Bread. . . .

In addition to all these endeavours on behalf of other people, throughout the spring of 1793 Hayley busied himself with the *Life of Milton*, diversifying the process with an occasional visitor. One who came early in this year was William Hodges, R.A., the painter who had accompanied Captain Cook on his second voyage round the world, and had drawn the illustrations of the South Sea Islands that embellish his *Travels*, as well as some large views of Tahiti for the Admiralty.[6] Hodges had also lived for a considerable time in India, and he must have proved an interesting visitor to Tom, who, now that his career in medicine had receded, was beginning to take a great interest in drawing, that probably originated in certain lessons he had taken with Wright during his sojourn in Derby in the autumn of 1791.

Hodges did not stay long, and when he left Eartham he proceeded to Bognor, to draw views of that newly-risen watering-place for its founder, the hatter, Sir Richard Hotham. These drawings must have been nearly the last he was to do, since, for a Royal Academician, his future career was unusual. Finding himself unable to gain a comfortable subsistence by his art, he "renounced the pencil, in honest indignation", and took to the more lucrative business of provincial banker. This, however, availed him nothing. The bank failed; Hodges died; and Hayley penned the inevitable epitaph.

As 1793 wore on, the letters from Cowper continued: a sad record of inability to work, and increasing recourse to laudanum. March found Tom despatching to his venerable friend a list of criticisms of his translation of Homer, in a letter which commenced, "Honoured King of the Bards". Cowper's reply was quite in character. He gravely thanked the little boy for his observations (which for the most part were sensible ones), and told him which of them he was going to adopt, and which he was not, giving reasons in each case. It is a charming letter, and one that shows Cowper in a most agreeable light.

At Eartham, meanwhile, *Milton* relentlessly proceeded, though workmen were putting a new roof on the house. This Hayley, in a letter to Cowper, called "preparing a dry and safe nest for the Roman Eagle". For, yet again, Gibbon was in the offing. This time he and Lord Sheffield were paying a visit to Petworth, and Gibbon contrived to steal away from that "festive palace" in August, to devote a few days to the Hermit. Hayley reported to Cowper on his visit. Gibbon was as friendly as ever, and infinitely firmer in his health than could have been supposed possible, considering the little use he made of his legs. "My ideas on religious and political topics (he said), are by no means in unison with those of this wonderful man, but I have great delight in his talents, and still more in the benevolent disposition he shews towards me, and the objects of my regard. Great as he is, as a writer, I think he has equal, if not superior, talents for *conversation*; and you will readily believe it quickened my relish for his society, to find him perfectly inclined to sympathise with me in esteem for you."

Later that August, Romney made his annual visit. He was in an even worse state than usual, and the activities of his host were confined exclusively to resuscitating him. Back in London, Romney despatched his usual letter of thanks. "It was some time," he wrote, "after I parted from you, before I recovered from the grateful impression, that your kindness and hospitality had made on my mind ... How hard I have found it to reconcile my mind, so relaxed with the beautiful scenes of Eartham, to the old habits of mechanical drudgery." It is easy to make fun now of the hospitality of Eartham; but I think that, when it wanted to, Eartham, like Todgers's, "could do it".

Further, with Blake's strictures on Hayley's capacity for interference in mind, it is interesting to come upon a passage such as this in a slightly earlier letter of Romney's, relating to certain ideas or compositions which Hayley had proposed: "I am delighted with

173

the ideas you suggested. I must say you are more happy in forming in your mind subjects suitable for pictures, than all the men of learning and taste, I ever met with, put together. I shall be ever grateful for those you have suggested at various times for my improvement and pleasure, and request you will never neglect me in that point." It is not astonishing that Hayley, after such encomiums as these, should, at times, have felt himself perfectly fitted to give a little good advice to the painters of his acquaintance.

3

All these diversions, however, were as nothing to the splendid plans which had been formed for the autumn of 1793. Hayley had at length completed his *Milton*, and was anxious to show it to Cowper. He had failed this year to bring his friend to Eartham, and no wonder, for all through the summer the shades were drawing ever closer about him. Mrs. Hayley also was agitating for a second visit from Tom, and a scheme was afoot for his attending for a term a school at Derby, that he might thereby improve his elocution. It was at last arranged that all these matters should be combined; that Tom should be taken by his father to Weston, and, after he had spent a few days there, should be sent on, by coach, to Derby.

When the boy's thirteenth birthday arrived, his father addressed to him an Ode some forty lines long, in which it was laid down that his childhood was now over:

> Dear boy endow'd with early sense,
> To-morrow let thy childhood end,
> Let manhood's dearest rights commence,
> And choose me for thy bosom friend. . . .
>
> O learn from me, o'er grief and harm
> Religious empire to maintain;
> Her mild endurance can disarm
> The fierce hostility of pain.

The last couplet was, at least, prophetic.

Shortly after this ceremony of emancipation, the new bosom-friends set out for Weston, and arrived there on October 20. They found a full house. Johnson was there, and so was Rose, who had but recently come over from Lord Spencer's, at Althorp, where Gibbon was shortly expected, and where, a few days later, the Eagle, though now approaching the crisis of his last illness, was able to report "we have completely exhausted this morning [in the Althorp Library] among the first editions of Cicero".[7] Moreover Lord Spencer had very kindly expressed the wish that Cowper should join the party and thus make the acquaintance of Gibbon a project that was as dear to Hayley as was to Boswell that fantastic rencounter which he contrived between Wilkes and Dr. Johnson.

But this engaging conjunction was not to be. Cowper was too shy, and Mrs. Unwin too ill to be left. Hayley and Rose went over to Althorp instead, to make his apologies.

Before this trip, however, Tom, who had been allowed to stay only a few days, helping with the transcription of Cowper's Homeric translation, had been despatched by chaise to Northampton, on route for Derby. Poor Hayley rode a little way with him to avoid the pain of parting at Cowper's very door; and when he saw the chaise dwindling away in the distance he burst into tears.

There was no real need for them. They soon received a cheerful letter from Tom, saying that "among all my sprightly and young associates you are not forgotten"; and he added agreeably, "I have not half the pleasure in dancing minuets, as I had when at work for Mr. Cowper".

Hayley replied by asking for details of his "literary associates".

To finish with Tom's northern sojourn, though it is slightly out of chronological order, we may add that, on November 29, he voiced a pathetic and unexpected request. None other than that he should be allowed to go fox-hunting! "My very dear Papa, (he wrote) I have now a question to ask you, which is, whether you will give me leave to go hunting with Mr. Pole and Mr. Mundy French, who says he will lend me a safe pony, and take great care of me, at my leisure hours, if I stay in this country, though I had much rather be by your side, and leaping over trees in our north wood." Later, in December, came the first mention of a pony hereafter to be celebrated in literary history as the mount of that strange equestrian, William Blake: "I long to have a ride with you on my favourite little Bruno, in the quiet woods about Eartham." He had been visiting Mamma, in his holiday-time, "to attain politeness", as well as to be instructed in the Italian tongue. And, once again, he had been taking painting-lessons from Wright. Hayley confessed himself charmed that his old friend should condescend to instruct "such an urchin".

4

Back now to Weston, where the Althorp visit, though soon over, was, by reason of Hayley's meeting with Lord Spencer, fraught with important consequences. Rose and Johnson soon left, and the two poets were able to set to work in earnest, and, as Cowper wrote on November 4:

My Homer finds work for Hayley, and his Life of Milton work for me, so that we are neither of us one moment idle. Poor Mrs. Unwin in the mean time sits quiet in her corner, occasionally laughing at us both, and not seldom interrupting us with some question or remark, for which she is constantly rewarded by me with a "Hush—hold your peace." . . . I write amidst a chaos of interruptions: Hayley on one hand spouts Greek, and on the other hand Mrs. Unwin continues talking, sometimes to us, and sometimes, because we are both too busy to attend to her, she holds a dialogue with herself.

Cowper was not anxious, with the dreaded winter coming on, to let his friend go. He persuaded him to prolong his visit, and indeed ended by entreating him to remain the whole winter at Weston, to engage with him in a complete revisal of his Homer. But Hayley had other plans. While, as he says, "I wanted not inclination for an office so agreeable . . . it struck me that I might render much more essential service to the poet, as I returned through London, by quickening in the minds of his more powerful friends, a seasonable attention to his interest and welfare. My fears for him . . . were alarmed by his present very singular condition . . . There was something indescribable in his appearance, which led me to apprehend, that without some signal event in his favour, to re-animate his spirits, they would gradually sink into hopeless dejection." And, besides, the truth had to be faced: Mrs. Unwin was beginning to exhibit signs of imbecility.

And so, after a stay of something more than a fortnight, he was off again, and at work again, in London, on the business of The Pension. This time it was Thurlow's turn, once more. No doubt a new approach to the ex-Chancellor had been discussed during his stay at Weston. It was almost an obsession with Cowper that Thurlow would, and could, eventually implement his thirty-year-old promise.

Hayley now wrote:[8] "My Lord, you *must* point out to me some method by which I may save our poor Cowper; what is it possible to do for him?"

Thurlow, with exemplary patience, again invited him to breakfast; and Hayley immediately came out with the suggestion that some post should be found for Cowper, the duties of which might be carried out by a deputy. "No," Thurlow replied, very sensibly, "an office would only make him mad. You must get him a pension." He did not tell him how to do this; and indeed he did not know. Still, it was a step in the right direction, since up to now Hayley's mercurial mind had wavered desperately between the counter-attractions of The Pension and The Post. Now that point was settled: and he suggested to Thurlow that a private interview with Pitt was the thing to aim at. Thurlow disagreed. He said that Pitt was not a man of much feeling, and that Hayley would do far better to write him a letter. At this Hayley was obliged to admit that he had already done so, without result. "With no more result," he said, rather grimly, remembering the effect of his earlier letters to the Chancellor, "than the letters of little men often produce on great ones." He had been rebuffed, he said, both by the Pluto of politics (Thurlow), and by the Jupiter (Pitt).

This thrust seems to have gone home, since Thurlow replied

somewhat drily: "I do not pretend to know much of political affairs at present—perhaps, as you say you have lately seen Lord Spencer, you know more than I do." And he went on to give Hayley the excellent advice that, if he could only get Lord Spencer to signify to the Minister his earnest desire that Cowper should have a pension, then very probably he would get one.

Hayley, overjoyed by this suggestion, left him, and proceeded once more to give a remarkable exhibition of how not to do things. Instead of going to Lord Spencer direct, he rushed off to Gibbon, who chanced to be in town, and begged him to conduct the negotiation for him. Gibbon's reaction was most unexpected, and indeed remains mysterious. He told Hayley that, while no one in the world more sympathized with Cowper than he did, there were, nevertheless, weighty political reasons which, at the moment, made it inexpedient for him to put the slightest pressure on his noble friend. However, reminding us strongly of Gay's fable of The Hare and Many Friends, he expressed himself, in complete contrast to Thurlow, decidedly in favour of Hayley's original design to seek an interview with the Prime Minister. This was awkward. Hayley was a man of honour, and he deemed that by having first approached Gibbon he had now precluded himself from a direct assault on Lord Spencer. He consequently consulted Lord Egremont; who said that what he ought to do was to write to Lord Spencer. It was unusual for Hayley to recoil from the prospect of writing a letter, but on this occasion he did so. Gibbon's oracular pronouncements had, I think, frightened him. Besides, he was ill, suffering from a fever he had contracted at Weston. He retired to the airy lodgings in Knightsbridge where he was staying with his friend, the Revd. James Clarke, and there gave himself up to meditation. At last, by November 26, he had made up his mind. He wrote and despatched at once to the Prime Minister, a note which ran as follows:

> Mr. Hayley presents his Respects to Mr. Pitt and fervently solicits the favour of a few Minutes Conversation with Him on a private Subject which may prove, he hopes, not utterly uninteresting even to a Mind occupied with the highest National Concerns.
>
> Mr. H. will thankfully wait on Mr. Pitt at any Time and Place that He may have the Goodness to appoint.

To this, strange to say, he received an immediate reply, making an appointment for the morning of Friday, November 29, at eleven o'clock. For this fateful interview Hayley "panted with odd vicissitudes of Apprehension and Desire".

5

We will leave him thus panting while we consider for an instant the society in which we now find him in London. The Revd. James

Clarke was a young divine who had made a protracted stay at Eartham in 1792, during which he was encouraged by his host to distinguish himself by literary application. His grandfather, William Clarke, had been the residentiary of Chichester, in whose house Hayley, in his youth, had passed many social hours.

When I came in my researches to this younger Mr. Clarke, I almost passed him by as one of the few nonentities in Hayley's story. But I reflected that Hayley seemed singularly incapable of attracting to himself nonentities. I probed a little deeper, and found the Revd. James Clarke transformed into the Revd. James Stanier Clarke, the "naval poet", who later became the Prince Regent's Librarian at Carlton House. This at last rang a bell, and suddenly I recalled the events of the autumn of 1815; when a certain literary spinster was shown over Carlton House, and was informed that a dedication would be acceptable.[9] The Revd. James Stanier Clarke further corresponded with this lady, and said he thought it would be a good thing if she would turn her attentions to "an historical romance, illustrative of the history of the august House of Coburg"; or she might perhaps prefer to depict a literary clergyman, resembling himself in history and character, "no man's enemy but his own", in a work that should also advocate the abolition of tithes.

The literary lady was obstinate. She did nothing of the sort. She wrote *Emma* instead; and then *Persuasion*; and incidentally elevated with herself into immortality the name of the Revd. James Stanier Clarke.

6

But it is no good temporising with talk about the Prince Regent's future librarian. Pitt has to be faced, and we, almost as much as Hayley, as the portentous hour draws near, grow unaccountably nervous. "Think of it," he says, with becoming modesty, "this meeting of a hermit, of a little retired and rustic poet with the great Prime Minister and War Minister of England!"[8] He became seized with panic; and at length his agitation grew so great that he fled to Romney for consolation. Romney, sensibly enough, prescribed port-wine, in medicinal quantities only. Thus fortified, though with a stupefying headache, Hayley bade his friend's man-servant, Joseph, "to call a coach and attend him to Mr. Pitt's". Obviously, when you were calling upon the Prime Minister of England, a servant was *de rigueur*. Unhappily, Romney's Joseph was not quite the sort of servant Hayley required in his hour of need. He was, indeed, a servant of a most modern cast of mind: a "delicate domestic" who was terrified of doing anything he deemed degrading. And the result was that, when the coach came, Joseph at once jumped into it and seated himself beside Hayley, instead of perching up behind. Now this was very awkward, with Downing Street as one's destination! Hayley was no bully, but he felt things had gone too far. He turned to Joseph and gently rebuked him, saying: "My good Joseph, I did not mean you should ride with me in the coach, for although I should be very willing to travel in the same equipage with you on a proper occasion, I apprehend it will hardly be right for us to drive to Mr. Pitt's together."

Mildness succeeded where firmness might have failed, and Joseph with an obliging alacrity mounted behind the coach. Once this had been safely effected, poor Hayley, whose nerves were in ribbons, was so tickled by the incident that he began to laugh, found he couldn't stop laughing, and arrived at Pitt's door in virtual hysterics.

However, he was shown into a large and vacant apartment, and this, together with the thought of the solemnity of his mission, soon restored his gravity. He was pondering anxiously how he might best begin the conversation when Pitt entered and immediately put him at his ease by receiving him "not with the supercilious solemnity of a Minister but with the endearing gaiety of a friend". They sat down, and Hayley once more told his story. Pitt was politeness itself. He said how well he thought of Cowper, and how eager he was to help him. He had received all Hayley's communications, and said he would, of course, have answered them at once, if he had but known in what manner he could have been of assistance. At this Hayley produced his well-worn alternatives—Post or Pension. "I think," Pitt said instantly, "that it must be the latter." Hayley was enchanted by his magnanimity; tears came into his eyes, and he kissed the hand of Pitt "in a transport of sensibility". He asked if he might write at once to Cowper, to tell him the good news. At this, ministerial caution reasserted itself. Though Pitt was pledged, he said he would prefer Hayley to wait a little. He would write to him further after he had returned to Sussex.

That now seemed good enough for anybody. Hayley went back in high glee to Eartham, and awaited Pitt's letter. The month of December passed, and no letter came. The year 1793 passed, also. Surely Pitt, situated as he was on "the pinnacles of Political Elevation", had not forgotten all about it! It seemed so, but Hayley refused to despair. "Calamity itself inspired me," he says, "with a new courage"; and out of this new courage he coined the comforting maxim that "to draw good from evil is a noble kind of Chymistry and a kind for which human life affords us inexhaustible occasion".

Of how much more of this noble kind of Chymistry was Hayley capable; of how much more suspense are my readers capable? I think we had better end the story of The Pension here and now.

On January 16, 1794, Gibbon died suddenly, and Hayley at once wrote a very long letter of condolence to Lord Spencer, in which he ventured yet again to urge the claims of Cowper. He was distressed beyond measure by the death of the Roman Eagle; but, at the same time, he was quick to see that his death had opened up that direct approach to Spencer which, when alive, his enigmatic disinclination to act as a go-between had effectually sealed. In this letter Hayley related the circumstances of his interview with Pitt, and begged Spencer to remind the Minister of his promise.

Spencer replied promptly, saying that the state of politics did not bring him much into contact with Pitt; but that he would do his best. And so matters rested until, in February, Rose sent Hayley a letter which contained most disturbing news of Cowper. Spurred by this he roused himself to one more effort, and on February 27 he wrote a final appeal to Pitt in terms which desperation had invested with an unaccustomed dignity:[8]

It is not often (he said magnificently) that a Hermit can be deceived by a Prime Minister; yet I am an example that such an extraordinary incident may happen; for in truth, my dear Sir, I most credulously confided in your kind promise of writing to me soon concerning your liberal intentions in favour of my admirable friend Cowper. Alas! instead of hearing from you such tidings as I hoped would make him happy, I have just heard from another quarter that he is recently sunk into that gloomy wretchedness and half-frantic despondency from which I was sanguine enough to expect that your just esteem and beneficence might preserve him.

Now, perhaps even your kindness may hardly give him a gleam of satisfaction. Your enemies (a great man cannot live without enemies) affirm that you have little feeling; this opinion I have long rejected, from my disposition to cherish an enthusiastic regard for you; but the rejected opinion I am now unwillingly putting to the test. You must have little feeling indeed if this intelligence does not make you lament, as I do most cordially, that an unfortunate delay in providing for a man of marvellous genius may have conduced to plunge him in the worst of human calamities.

How far it is probable that your favour might have preserved him from this evil, or may be likely to restore him from it, perhaps my Lord Spencer may be able from fuller information to judge better than I can at present. He is a neighbour and a friend to the great afflicted poet, yet, if I remember right, not personally acquainted with him; and his Lordship has kindly promised me (should opportunity arise) to recall to your remembrance what I said to you in Cowper's behalf. Lord Spencer enters (as you kindly did when you allowed me the honour of conversing with you) into the cruel singularity of Cowper's situation, and I am confident you both sympathise in thinking that our Sovereign's munificence could not be more worthily exerted than towards this wonderful man, whether it shall please Heaven to bless him with a restoration of his rare mental endowments, or still to afflict him with a melancholy alienation of mind.

I will not utterly relinquish the hope that you may yet be able to serve him; afflicting as the delay has proved, I am inclined to impute it to such difficulties as men, even of excellent hearts and high stations, too frequently find in their endeavours to befriend the unfortunate.

I write in the frank and proud sorrow of a wounded spirit, but with a cordial and affectionate wish that Heaven may bless you with unthwarted power to do good, and with virtue sufficient to exert it.

I retain a lasting sense of the very engaging kindness with which you allowed me to pour forth my heart to you on this interesting subject, and I am most sincerely, my dear Sir, your very grateful though afflicted servant,

W. HAYLEY.

But Pitt did not condescend to make any reply.

On March 5, Hayley heard from another quarter that Lord Spencer would in all probability be able to effect something; and, just a month later, he was urgently summoned to Weston. He arrived on April 16, to find Cowper's collapse complete. Seven days later a letter from Spencer came to Weston, saying that he had seen Pitt, and that a pension of three hundred pounds a year only awaited the Royal sanction.

Hayley's "darling project" had succeeded; and Cowper was now past caring. Through numerous approaches to Thurlow, to Pitt, to Gibbon and to Spencer, Hayley had undeviatingly kept his course; and now when at last his reward came it was too late.

More, though he did not know then that it would be so, the pension was hardly ever paid, even after it was granted. By 1798, one quarterly remittance had been received, and twelve were in arrears.[8] This, naturally, was no fault of Hayley's. It merely illustrated what England thought of her poets.

CHAPTER XIII

INTERIM: THE GIBBON PAPERS (1793-1794)

I

Now with the Pension achieved, we must retrace our steps.

Hayley had returned to Eartham during the first week of December 1793. During his visit to London he had experienced yet another "literary disappointment". His publisher, George Nicol, who was also the king's bookseller, had taken great exception to his *Life of Milton* on account of its unduly democratic tendency; and had told him that he would not publish it unless it were considerably toned down. Hayley, whose manuscript had received the imprimatur of Cowper, would not agree to his work being "dishonourably garbled". The position was difficult; though not beyond his ingenuity.

This is what he did: he told Nicol that he would provide him with an amended version of the *Life*, to preface his illustrations, provided that, in return, the bookseller would furnish him with five hundred impressions of these illustrations for his own use. With their aid, Hayley would then himself bring out a handsome quarto of the book as he had written it; thus characteristically having his cake and eating it too. Hence, soon two entirely different versions of the *Life of Milton* were on the market, and the author was receiving all manner of censures, from Miss Seward and others, for what looked to them uncommonly like double-dealing. "Mr. Hayley's want of judgment in this literary manœuvre (wrote The Swan) is as astonishing as his disingenuousness is lamentable."[1]

The sudden death of Gibbon in January 1794, however conveniently it may have come for Cowper, was a further blow to Hayley, who had been on the point of visiting him at Sheffield Place. On January 29, Romney wrote to express his sympathy: "Poor Gibbon! His last words were, MON DIEU, BON DIEU. They have affected me so much, I shall turn my thoughts more to Christianity than I have done."

With these edifying sentiments, unhappily, Lord Sheffield, who might be expected to know the facts, would have nothing to do. He, on the contrary, asserted that the last articulate utterance of Gibbon was addressed to his valet: "*Pourquoi est-ce que vous me quittez?*"

Hayley, himself so often tarred with the brush of Gibbon's infidelity, commented on this unfortunate discrepancy: "I could wish to persuade myself that the infidelity of Gibbon was nothing more than what he himself called it, in a letter to me, only *supposed infidelity*." And, without more ado, he set to work to contrive an epitaph for his friend, undeterred by the knowledge that the mausoleum at Fletching would ultimately be inscribed with lines from the heavy pen of Dr. Parr. Hayley's version is, one cannot help thinking, the more agreeable:

> Formed for the studious and the cheerful hour,
> Here, Gibbon, rest! thy course of glory run!
> Few thy compeers in literary power;
> And in the charm of social converse, none!
> Thy works immortalize th' historian's fame;
> To fond remembrance let this verse commend
> Worth that delighted by a dearer name,
> Thou sprightly guest! thou sympathetic friend.

Moreover, though now no longer the beneficiary he had once been under Gibbon's will, the time was at hand for Hayley to take his share, with Lord Sheffield, in the editing of the historian's posthumous remains. But, before we come to this, other weighty matters supervene.

2

Since January, Hayley had received no word from Cowper; but on April 8 came heavy tidings: a letter from Mr. Greatheed summoning him at once to Weston, in the following terms:

Lady Hesketh's correspondence acquainted you with the melancholy relapse of our dear friend at Weston; but I am uncertain whether you know, that in the last fortnight, he has refused food of every kind, except now and then a very small piece of toasted bread, dipped generally in water, sometimes mixed with a little wine. This, her Ladyship informs me, was the case till last Saturday, since when he has eat a little at each family meal. He persists in refusing such medicines as are indispensable to his state of body. In such circumstances, his long continuance in life cannot be expected. . . . You, dear Sir, who know so well the worth of our beloved and admired friend, sympathize with his affliction, and deprecate his loss doubtless in no ordinary degree; you have already most effectually expressed and proved the warmth of your friendship. I cannot think that any thing but your society would have been sufficient, during the infirmity under which his mind has long been oppressed, to have supported him against the shock of Mrs. Unwin's paralytic attack. I am certain that nothing else could have prevailed upon him to undertake the journey to Eartham. You have succeeded where his other friends knew they could not, and where they apprehended no one could. How natural therefore, nay how reasonable, is it for them to look to you, as most likely to be instrumental, under the blessing of God, for relief in the present distressing and alarming crisis. It is indeed scarcely attemptable to ask any person to take such a journey, and involve himself in so melancholy a scene, with an uncertainty of the desired success: increased as the apparent difficulty is by dear Mr. Cowper's aversion to all company, and by poor Mrs. Unwin's mental and bodily infirmities. On these accounts Lady Hesketh dares not ask it of you, rejoiced as she would be at your arrival. Am not I, dear Sir, a very presumptuous person, who, in the face of all opposition dare do this? I am emboldened by those two powerful supporters, conscience and experience. Was I at Eartham, I would certainly undertake the labour I presume to recommend, for the bare possibility of restoring Mr. Cowper to himself, to his friends, to the public, and to God.

To such an appeal there was but one answer. Hayley was ill, with, as he says, "hardly enough bodily strength for so trying a scene". And he was so short of ready money that he was obliged to borrow from his neighbours the cash requisite for the journey. Nevertheless, on April 16 he was at Weston, and the very next day despatched to Rose the following outburst of sensibility:

The sufferings of our friend form such a spectacle, as it is indeed most grievous and terrible to behold. Lady Hesketh supports this severe trial of her kindness and fortitude, with a tender heroism that I cannot too much admire and applaud. Heaven, I trust, will supply us both, with strength equal to the calamitous occasion. To me it is a comfort to reflect, that should I chance to lose my life or my senses in excess of anxiety for this most interesting sufferer, you, I am confident, my dear Rose, will act towards my poor little desolate boy, with all the kindness of a father.

It was indeed, as he describes it, "a period of complicated calamity". Cowper had sunk into total apathy; he had exhibited not the least glimmer of satisfaction at the arrival of his friend.

Hayley was almost at his wit's end, when he remembered how well poor Cowper had always got on with Tom. He felt the boy's sojourn in the North had now lasted long enough, and he decided to send for him. On April 25, he wrote to Mrs. Hayley:

My beloved Cowper, though frequently rejecting both medicine and food, will take things from my hand, that he will hardly receive from any other; and perhaps to his dear little favourite Tom, he may be still more complying. At all events, I am desirous of seeing the effect Tom's presence will have on our dear sufferer, who has already, I flatter myself, derived considerable good from my painful visit. . . .

But it is time to direct the journey of your visitor: be so good as to despatch him by the mail of next Tuesday. It stops at Newport, at a public-house called *The Neptune*, where Mr. Greatheed has assured me his servant will wait, and escort the little traveller to his house. The friendly divine will mount his young guest on a fine old horse, and escort him hither on the following morning. In this village, I shall procure him a sleeping-room, under the care of a very amiable lady, who sings in a very enchanting style; and you will enable the little traveller to make the best return in his power for the civilities which, I am confident, he will receive from Cowper's favourite musical friend, Mrs. Courtenay and her husband, if you will kindly furnish him with two or three of my songs, music and words together. He will hardly have time to copy them himself, but he will probably find, in Derby, some person who copies music for hire, and I shall most cheerfully pay the expense. The song I particularly wish to have is, "Stay, O stay," as I think it would particularly suit her voice.

It was at this point the news came that the Pension had been granted: to be engulfed in the prevailing gloom.

On April 30, Tom arrived. He was taken at once to see Cowper, who did not shrink from him as he did "from every creature of full growth"; and for a while it looked as though Hayley's dream might come true. But the effect, unhappily, did not last; and moreover, Hayley's own health was so shaken that he could bear no more.

By May 10 he was in London again, and writing to Eliza:

> Of all the acts of painful exertion that I have known (and many have fallen to my lot) I never experienced a trial more severe than that of forcing myself from the dear sufferer at Weston, who considered my departure from him as the darkest part of his very dark calamity. I took all imaginable precaution to render it as little painful as possible, both to him and to myself, yet it almost overwhelmed me; and in the moment of my quitting him, Lady Hesketh, I believe, thought me almost as much out of my senses as our beloved invalid. . . .
>
> Let me now tell you, my dear fellow-traveller is well by my side: he has just purchased a nice German flute, and seems to have caught such a passion for music, that it is continually at his lips.

It is pleasant to hear of that flute. There is something irrepressible in the spirits of the young.

3

Before they reached Eartham again, Hayley and Tom went to stay a day or two with the Meyers. Hayley had intended to make his visit a week, but Mrs. Meyer was so overburdened with family cares that he curtailed his sojourn. Even so, he found time to take his son into Kew Gardens, where they discovered a most obliging friend in the royal gardener, Mr. Aiton, under whose guidance Tom was treated to a special view of that "magnificent scene of vegetable instruction".

Suddenly there were once more disquieting tidings of Eliza. Hayley had learnt from Mrs. Meyer that she had formed the design of leaving Derby and taking up her residence in Sussex. He wrote to her in great agitation; and with copious references to his slender finances:

> As it is utterly impossible for us ever to live together again, I confess I have wished that your residence in the North should be as permanently satisfactory to you, as the great advantages you possess in our friends of that county have led us to hope it might prove. Believe me, such advantages are not to be found in every county; and as I most cordially wish to promote the peace and comfort of your life, as well as my own, forgive me for expressing a desire that you may well weigh all the arguments . . .

But this time mere arguments were futile. Eliza had set her heart on coming south; and nothing would stop her. Not even the prospect of life in London (for she had pity on Hayley to this extent, and chose London rather than Sussex) on an exiguous income.

Since it is at about this period of her final rebellion that Hayley grows most vehement in his assertions that she was mad, here may perhaps be the best place to insert a word or two concerning Eliza's earlier life in Derby, from such glimpses as we can catch of it in the writings of the one independent witness we have: Anna Seward.[1] On June 14, 1791, in a letter to her friend Mrs. Mompesson, she thus described a visit she had recently paid Mrs. Hayley:

> Mrs. Hayley received me with animated gladness, encompassed with youths of genius—the rising hopes of Derby. They walked with us into Mrs. Hayley's garden, and returned home with us to supper. Next morning we had levees in succession; half the smart people of that town, interspersed with the militia officers. We passed the afternoon and evening with Dr. Darwin. . . . Mrs. Darwin had an immense party to meet us, for whose apprehended amusement she engaged me, by earnest solicitation, to repeat odes and sonnets. If they were not egregious flatterers, the pleasure the company expressed made it impossible to grudge the exertion, even beneath a sky so torrid.

Again, on October 1, 1793:

> I wrote to Mr. Hayley lately. My letter contained a jocular passage to the following effect: "One of my Yorkshire friends [the Revd. Richard Sykes of Westella], a gentleman of considerable talents, conversing twice this summer, at Derby, with Mrs. Hayley, returned to us on the coast, enchanted with her wit and spirit. He thinks it impossible the effervescing cordial should ever cloy. If you could contrive to make his wife, who is a very fine woman, elope with you, there might be a double divorce, and he would certainly marry Mrs. Hayley." . . . Now, if there were an atom of seriousness in all this, what admirable morality it would be!

Glimpses such as these, though they may convey a pretty clear picture of a frivolous mentality, seem hardly to indicate a deranged one. And, even less does the fact that, early in 1796, Mrs. Hayley took a leaf out of her husband's book by publishing yet another work, an essay entitled *The Triumph of Acquaintance over Friendship*, in which she defended the rather unusual position that it was better to have acquaintances than to have friends. Poor Eliza! There can hardly be a nicer indication of the straits to which long years of Hayleian intensity had reduced her.

However, in June 1794, Hayley, with less fight than usual, appears to have bowed to the inevitable, and, when Eliza arrived in the metropolis, "endeavoured to promote her tranquillity to the utmost of his power", going so far indeed, as to despatch to her the following note of welcome:

My dear Eliza, The young traveller and I salute you with a kind wish, that you may find our quiet and airy quarters, in Castle Street, as pleasing a lodging as we did; and we flatter ourselves it may enliven you, after the fatigue of a long journey, to find a letter, on your arrival, expressing our united good wishes.

Who could say fairer? And indeed, to begin with, all seems to have gone well. On November 1, Miss Seward wrote to her:[1]

I rejoice that you are pleased with your situation in the metropolis. May you always find London replete with interest and amusement! . . . You call on Romney sometimes. Assure him of my frequent, my grateful remembrances. The dear bard forsakes me utterly. Newer friends have more charms for him, but none can have a sincerer regard.

Unhappy Hayley! Everything was going wrong. The Pension was achieved, and Cowper was past profiting by it; and Eliza was quite out of hand again. What wonder that he felt ill! What wonder that he should feel uncommonly relieved to accept an invitation from Lord Sheffield to visit Sheffield Place, where, with his host and with Rose, he formed one of "a little cabinet council to sit in judgment on the posthumous manuscripts of the departed historian".

4

Concerning this visit, Hayley, on his return, wrote to Eliza in terms which, in the circumstances, were amiable:

My first arrival under that roof, where I had vainly expected last year to pass many a social and pleasing day with the deceased, affected me so strongly, that I hardly slept an hour the first night . . . but I revived by degrees. . . . I am much pleased with the warmth of heart and considerate fidelity of friendship, which our noble host exerts in regard to the memory and reputation of the great historian, whose life he intends to publish in the course of the next spring.

At the same time, he was writing to his noble host to thank him for the hospitality extended to Rose and himself.[2] They had been examining, since their return, the manuscript of the historian's unfinished work on the *Antiquities of the House of Brunswick*, and he proposed that the account of "Lucretia the wife of the son of Hercules the 1st of Este", or, at least, the "account of her lascivious amusements" should be omitted from it: a passage which he rounds off with two marks of exclamation!!

Now they were pondering Gibbon's *Autobiography*. Sheffield had been kind enough to admit to feeling "disagreeable" since the departure of his guests, and Hayley therefore begged him to visit "his cell, with his two very engaging fair attendants", his eldest daughter, Maria Holroyd, and her friend, Harriet Poole.

Late that September the party reached Eartham, and, while

Maria Holroyd read aloud to the company "the whole life and all the letters of the historian, from the period where the memoirs end", the noble editor expressed his conviction that he would begin to print after Christmas. Together they revised his Lordship's Introduction, and Hayley exhorted him to make every effort to complete his task. Maria and Paulina were charming; the visit was in all ways an agreeable one.

Of one of these ladies, Miss Poole, already familiarly referred to as Paulina, we shall hear much more in future. This is her first appearance.

The visit over, a continual stream of letters from the Hermit reached Sheffield Place. Hayley, for all the veneration he felt for Gibbon, did not mince his criticisms. With regard to his friend's portrait of Brutus, he wrote:[2]

> *Brutus* . . . deserves only to be committed to the Flames—It is an attempt (a very unworthy though artful one) to prove the noble Brutus an *Usurer* . . . I condemn the work as a weak and ungenerous endeavour to vilify an illustrious character.

There was, indeed, something of a breeze about Brutus. Lord Sheffield wrote finally that he had sacrificed Gibbon's digression to "the prejudices of Education", and to Hayley's "democratic spirit". Hayley's reply was suitably magnificent: "You misname my spirit, my dear Lord, when you call it *democratic* . . . It is a *frank, fearless spirit*, yet equally uninfected, I trust, with the Turbulence of Democracy, and the Apathy of Despotism.

"It was the *Infirmity* or *Misfortune* of our lost Friend to entertain a *low opinion* of Human Nature . . . a lamentable defect (to be veiled) in his brilliant mind—a broad speck in a large diamond!"

For Gibbon's *Journal*, on the other hand, he had nothing but praise: "To my Fancy nothing is more gratifying than to be thus introduced to a great author, not expressly *writing a Book* but rather *thinking aloud*." And, early the following year, he was still firing such questions at Sheffield as, "How did the noble Editor settle his embarrass'd Negotiations with the deliberating Gentlemen of the Press?" and suggesting further amendments to his Introduction.

Nor were the fortunes of a minor character unaffected by these transactions. Thomas Sockett, who up to now had been quietly engaged in becoming educated, suddenly pops up as on loan from Hayley to the Sheffields on the task of transcribing the Papers. Sheffield's daughter Maria, writing on June 7, 1794, notes his arrival:[3]

> The wry-necked Secretary is an acquisition lately made, and intended for Country use. . . . It is a very agreeable circumstance, and will save Aunt and I a great deal of trouble. He will be particularly useful, as Papa intends to undertake the Arrangement of Mr. Gibbon's Memoirs and letters for the

Public Eye. The young Man was recommended by Mr. Hayley, who had him from Mr. Cowper.... He is about sixteen; has had a good education, can read Latin and French; and is to have £20 a year and to live with the Servants. It would have been very unpleasant to have a Person in that Situation one of us; and yet there might have been a doubt about the disposal of a Secretary if he were older.

Sockett remained for a year "with the Servants" at Sheffield Place; and when he left a yet more glorious destiny awaited him, at Lord Egremont's.

Meantime, true to form, our hero had been trying to work the new Sheffield connection for all it was worth, first to secure a situation for the son of one of his neighbours, and second for our "worthy little Rose", who, for some reason, he hoped to see made a Commissioner of Bankruptcy, in return for the work he had done in correcting Lord Sheffield's proofs. Youthful merit, he said, can hardly have too many patrons; and again he reminded Lord Sheffield that the Hermit would never ask anything for himself ("except from DIEU & LES DAMES").[2]

All this time, Cowper, under the charge of Lady Hesketh, had made no sign. It was not until the July of the following year that the devoted Johnson was to move him and Mrs. Unwin into Norfolk. The misery of the once cheerful house at Weston is so great that instinctively one averts one's eyes; and I rather suspect that this is what Hayley did too.

And Eliza, back again in London, was ripe for further mischief: another quarter, one feels, which Hayley did not contemplate more than he could help.

This summer of 1794 saw a fresh face at Eartham: the twenty-two year old Henry Cary, who arrived no doubt on the strength of an introduction from his patroness, Miss Seward. Cary may already have been contemplating his great translation of Dante. At any rate, Hayley gave him much useful information on Italian and Spanish literature, and, as usual, was full of Cowper and Milton. He led his guest to an eminence crowned with laburnums where, two years before, the author of *The Task* had walked; and he showed him the Romney portrait. Cary noted his host's propensity for retirement, his abstemiousness, and (perhaps rather a new thing, his guest being, or being about to become, a clergyman) his enthusiasm for family devotion. Much the most interesting of Cary's observations, however, relates to Tom, and throws back to his pathetic appeal to his father, from Derby, that he should be allowed to go hunting. "He spoke to me with some sorrow," Cary tells us, "of his father's refusal to let him join a pack of hounds in the neighbourhood."[4]

It is a revealing touch. It explains why, for all his attainments, there remains something endearing about Thomas Alphonso.

Then it was time again for Romney, who this year came first for a few days in August. He was very busy, but his spirits were lower than ever. Hayley managed to persuade him to pay a second visit in October; and on this occasion his melancholy was so evident that his host and Tom carried him off instantly to inspect the more cheering sights of Portsmouth.

And then, at last, out of all this medley of comings and goings, there arose suddenly one event charged with an extreme significance to the little family at Eartham. A single innocent-seeming sentence, in a letter from Flaxman to Romney late that autumn, carried the news of it. His seven years exile in Rome was over, Flaxman said. He was to "return to London on Lord Mayor's Day".

CHAPTER XIV

THE YOUNG SCULPTOR (1794-1797)

I

THE YEARS 1792-94 which embrace the great happenings of Hayley's life—his friendship with Cowper; the pursuit of The Pension; the death of Gibbon, and the arrangement of his Papers—are so packed with events that the writer who tries to memorialize them often feels like the juggler compelled by professional exigency to keep half-a-dozen balls in the air all together.

It is time for a lull; and the re-appearance of Flaxman provides one. This chapter, as far as possible, will deal with the opening career of Thomas Alphonso, who now, with the return of Flaxman and the temporary eclipse of Cowper, steps straight into the centre of the picture. If it be objected that it is unusual for a child of fourteen to hold a stage that eminent figures have but lately vacated, the only reply is that no life of William Hayley can proceed otherwise, since his next six years were utterly engrossed by the proceedings of his son—the young student, the young sculptor, the young Phidias, as he was wont, in phrases of varying fatuity, to describe him.

Even as early as May 1794, we find Romney writing that he is delighted "dear Tom discovers a growing passion for the noble art of sculpture"; and I think it is certain that during Romney's visit that summer the question was discussed whether it would be possible for him to be apprenticed to Flaxman on the latter's return to England. Evidently the sculptor was approached, since, four days after his re-appearance, he was writing to Hayley to say that he was ready for Tom directly he could find a house, and that he would do all in his power to add a tender friendship for the son to his love and veneration for the father.

Flaxman was now thirty-nine, and had risen almost to the top of his profession. His progress had not been an easy one. The son of a plaster-cast maker of Covent Garden, he had, while still a child, started to practise drawing and modelling. From his twentieth to his thirty-third year he had worked principally on designs for Josiah Wedgwood's great pottery business at Etruria. He had married in 1782, and left his father's studio to set up house for himself. A little earlier, in 1780, he had made the acquaintance of William Blake, and, as we have seen, was introduced about 1783 to Hayley. While in Rome, he had published his celebrated outline illustrations to Homer, which had gained him a European reputation; and he had also maintained his correspondence with Romney and with Hayley. When he came home he found his work in great demand.

One of Flaxman's most endearing qualities was a capacity for gratitude. Hayley had been kind to him in his early days, and he did not forget kindness. His terms with regard to the apprenticing of Thomas Alphonso were exceedingly generous. "If you have quite determined not to make him a physician (he wrote), and if you think he has talents for the fine arts, shew yourself my friend indeed, and accept my offer as frankly as I make it. Send him to me! I will instruct him in all the little I know, and it shall not cost you a farthing. You shall provide his board and lodging in the manner most agreeable to yourselves. The education he should have under me would be a theory and practice of art and science, to make him profound in his profession, and not a drudge for the interest of his master. In your absence I will be his father, and my dear Nancy promises to look to his morals."

With terms such as these offered by one of the leaders of his profession, Hayley could have had no doubt of the course he should pursue. On December 29, 1794, Flaxman wrote to say that he had found a temporary residence at 6, Buckingham Street,* Fitzroy Square; and, proceeding irregularly by way of Sheffield Place, where they spent a few days, Hayley and son arrived eventually at 41, Upper Cleveland Street, a small lodging-house near to the residence of Tom's future master. Here Hayley stayed for some weeks while the boy was settling down to his new profession.

And so, after a long interval, Hayley found himself yet again in the same city as Eliza. Flaxman had already written to say that he had heard of her arrival, and Hayley at once set to work to guard his friend from what, he says, he most apprehended—"annoyance from the active spirit of that pitiable lady".

He laid his plans to obviate, as much as possible, the dangers he anticipated. He wrote to Eliza and told her that he intended to rent a second-floor, either in Flaxman's residence or near it, and that he proposed to place a second bed in his son's room, for his own use, when he was in London. But he added, hastily: "It will not suit my inclination, my health, or my slender finances, to be often in London; but whenever business may call me to town, it is my earnest request to you, my dear Eliza, that we may kindly avoid an interview. . . . We shall meet, I believe and hope, in a happier world."

Unfortunately, Eliza did not receive this letter in the liberal and tolerant spirit he had expected. A set of well-meaning, though

---

* Later, he either moved or the houses were re-numbered, as some of his letters are addressed from No. 7, and Crabb Robinson visited him at this number in 1810.

injudicious, friends of her own sex, "total strangers to the real character of her husband", awakened and irritated what Hayley calls "a sexual pride" in her bosom, by representing his conduct as both insulting and injurious to her. In short, she replied by accusing him of wanton extravagance; and vehemently solicited a formal assignment of her future income. Hayley, fortified by the knowledge that his conscience was, as ever, clear, and that his friends approved his conduct, flatly refused this.

To his refusal Eliza at once returned, by the hands of Tom who had been visiting her, a highly acrimonious reply; and, on the morning of January 17, Hayley seized his pen and composed the following, for him, almost equally acrimonious rejoinder:

My grievously irritable Eliza:

I am more concerned than surprised, that you can so far forget the respect you owe both to me and to yourself, as to send me, by the hands of the dear boy, a letter full of injurious reproaches, and a most artful and malevolent misrepresentation of my character and conduct. Had such a letter been sent to a man of an irascible and vindictive spirit, he would probably punish the writer by abridging the liberal allowance he had assigned to her, from his own narrow fortune. But such kind of resentment I scorn; and when you oblige me to act toward you with an appearance of severity very foreign to my nature, I feel more of sorrow than of anger.

As you are pleased to write with such acrimony and insult, I shall only say that I lament the very wrong point of view in which you represent me, and I request that all sort of intercourse may cease, not only between us, but also between you and the child by whom you despatched me a letter so insulting to me, and so unworthy of yourself. . . .

But it was not in Hayley's nature to keep up for long a tone so lofty. To have deprived Eliza for ever of all intercourse with the child she loved, struck him on reflection as a "barbarous proposition". He consequently soon abandoned it, and gave Tom permission to pay an occasional visit to "the unhappy object of his pity and of his apprehensions".

On one point, though, his mind was made up. He would not meet Eliza himself. Indeed, so great was his determination to avoid this that it even caused him to hasten his departure from London. He left Cleveland Street on February 11, and proceeded back to Eartham, though not without vicissitude. In fact, his adventures upon this occasion were, he tells us, such as might have frightened "an ordinary mortal"; and had it not been for the "cheerful serenity of spirit that Heaven had kindly bestowed" upon him, might well have frightened him too.

For it was a season of snow and flood. Before he reached Kingston, "the water rose near the lock of my great trunk, and I felt some anxiety for my books and the Harmonica". And then, as he forged ahead, magnificently and at great expense, with four horses, enormous snowdrifts blocked the roads. The horses struggled on till they were up to their shoulders, and, when darkness fell, Hayley was obliged to take shelter in a neighbouring farmhouse.

Early next morning a man was despatched to "call forth the rustic pioneers of Eartham", who dug out the coach; and, with this retinue in attendance, he made a triumphal entry into the village seated in his car, "with his royal cargo of plants", and shedding "some delicious tears of honest and tender pride" over the affectionate ardour of his rescuers.

2

Home again, and safe from Eliza, Hayley returned to composition; and what more natural than that, this time, it should be the glorifying of that art of which his son was now a votary. Besides, in such a work, he aspired to promote the professional credit of Flaxman, as, in earlier years, he had performed similar services to Romney, Gibbon, and the ungrateful Mason.

Unhappily, though, when he turned his mind to the subject of Sculpture, he found it was one which required preliminary investigation. And so, for the moment, he set it aside, and diverted himself with minor projects. Among these was a eulogium of Eloquence, which arose from the fact that Erskine had recently distinguished himself by his brilliant defence of Hardy and Horne Tooke in their trial for High Treason. His poem, called *The National Advocates*, was, as usual, designed to fulfil a dual purpose. While, on the one hand, it was intended to honour Erskine, it was, on the other, supposed to benefit in material fashion, not exactly specified, the fortunes of Samuel Rose, who was now painfully making his way up the lower rungs of the ladder of the Law. The plan was, presumably, that by this publication Rose should be brought to the notice of Erskine.

It is, however, unnecessary to contemplate *The National Advocates* at length, for it caused no stir, and there is no evidence that it did Rose the slightest good. All the same, Hayley's next enterprise was of a similar complexion: it was an *Elegy on Sir William Jones*, the orientalist and poet, who had died the year before.

This, once more, was a double-barrelled work, calculated partly to console the widow of that eminent man, and partly to forward Rose's prospects. In this case, advancement was supposed to come to him through some stanzas in the poem which sang the praises of Lord Spencer. When Lord Spencer had read them, he was expected immediately to rush to Rose's assistance. Why, one cannot possibly say. Hayley's reasoning in matters of this sort is never very clear. However, Lady Jones was highly gratified, and Lord Spencer's mother-in-law and her youngest daughter paid the poet a visit at Eartham which, for a while, greatly raised the hopes of both interested parties. But, unhappily, the old lady could not recall Rose at all; and though her daughter was just able to do so, that was about as far as it went.

3

Meanwhile, when not engaged in these benevolent exercises, Hayley was much occupied with his correspondence; in correspondence of an increasingly gratifying nature with his son, and of an increasingly disagreeable kind with Eliza.

With the latter, his rupture was now almost complete. Despite the firm tone of his last pronouncement, she had written to him again, to demand that the allowance he made her should be confirmed by a formal deed. Hayley was always obstinate when he considered a point of principle at stake. He felt his probity questioned; and he felt, too, that an independent income, over which he possessed no control, might well be productive of evils to Eliza that she could not herself foresee. And so, as early as February 25, he despatched to her the very last of the long series of letters which, during more than thirty years, had passed between them. This is what he said:

DEAR ELIZA, Though you indulged an acrimonious humour in writing to me a very insulting and injurious letter, to which illness and occupation prevented my sending so full a reply as I intended, I heartily wish to promote the tranquillity of your life, but can never comply with your improper request. You may, and you ought to confide in my integrity, which has never failed any human being. We parted for our mutual quiet, as it is utterly impossible for us to make each other happy in living together. I assigned you a liberal income, considering the narrowness of my own fortune. That income has been for years most regularly paid to you by a trusty agent, and ever will be so while I live . . . unless you oblige me to abridge it, by a conduct more reprehensible towards me than I will think probable. You are wrong in representing me as a man of ruined fortunes, and destitute of respectable friends. I have been unprosperous, but not dissolute or despicable. My income is smaller than it ought to be, at my age, considering the very studious and temperate cast of my life; but I am contriving by rigid economy to make it sufficient for me in this my favourite retirement, after allotting from it a becoming allowance to those who depend upon my care. . . . Let me advise you, with genuine kindness, and without a particle of resentment, never to revile or doubt the justice of the man, who (whatever the misfortunes or errors of his life may have been) is assuredly entitled to your respect, and who, though it is (to our mutual misfortune) impossible for him ever to live with you, is, I may presume to say, with perfect truth,

The sincerest of your friends.

Perhaps at this point it is fitting to take stock of the relationship that has for so long cast its shadow over these pages. It must be remembered that, throughout, we have only been in a position to give Hayley's side of the story, from the evidence which he himself has provided. To complete his picture, therefore, let us, for a moment, contemplate his own conception of himself as a husband: "Nature had given him a frame so feelingly alive to all the delights of pure and perfect love, with a heart and mind so fashioned for domestic felicity, that if his stars had united him to a consort completely suited to his own character, his life would have been too happy for a mortal." I am sure he believed this. I am not sure, however, that all men do not, concerning themselves, hold similar views.

One final glimpse of Eliza from outside. Anna Seward, on June 19 this year, after the final rupture, wrote to her as follows:[1]

> I am convinced that London is your element, the only one in which your mind can fully and freely expand, without recoiling painfully upon itself. The description of your literary societies, your tea-drinkings, charm me.... Much to be admired is the energy with which you explore new paths of knowledge and science. Middle life is too apt to repose upon the acquirements of its youth, and to shrink from the apprehended labour of extending them....

The picture, I think, grows tolerably clear. There is no longer any need to apportion praise or blame. Hayley suffered because of Eliza; Eliza because of Hayley. The stamp she set upon his mind was enduring; and to its detriment.

4

And now it is pleasanter to turn to the doings of the Young Sculptor. He was bound apprentice to his master by indentures dated February 15, 1795; and thereafter all proceeded delightfully. "The vigour with which I attack the clay," he writes, "makes me eat a good deal." He is modelling; reading history and Greek and Latin. Each morning he reads the Greek Testament with the Flaxmans, and they converse in Latin. And Mrs. Flaxman has taught him to play *Begone dull care* and *The Duke of York's March* on her pianoforte. Flaxman he calls, "good friend, good artist, good man, good every thing that can be named". There were visits to Sockett, at Lord Sheffield's London house, to Romney ("I am quite in his confidence"), and to Lord Egremont. The boy's diary for May 13 ends, very pleasantly, in a transport of delight: "May! monument! me! my model! Flaxman! Eartham! Fido! Bruno! prophet! [Flaxman's name for Hayley] Phidias junior! pleasure! gaiety! love! friendship etc. etc. all in a huddle!"

Upon June 1, Tom left his lodgings and went to live in the Flaxmans's house. July 6 was his master's birthday. They went in the evening to the Shakespeare Gallery, and drank tea "on the other side of the river". On the other side of the river, in Hercules Buildings, Lambeth, resided one of Flaxman's oldest friends, the engraver Blake. Though there is no certainty that it was with Blake that this tea-drinking occurred, I think it a not unreasonable presumption that it was, especially as Tom went on to say that they proposed shortly to visit Stothard, at Hampstead, who, in point of fact, was the friend that had first introduced Flaxman to Blake.

All through this spring and summer, Flaxman was busy upon a project which was dear to Hayley's heart, and for which he had been himself, in part, responsible. This was the monument to William Collins, which is still to be seen in Chichester Cathedral. Collins, who, in his twenty-sixth year, had published those Odes which are almost the finest things his century produced, had died hopelessly insane in 1759. For the last six or seven years of his life he had haunted the cloisters of Chichester Cathedral—a distracted figure which must have been familiar to Hayley as a lad. Upon his death, no monument was erected; but now at last the gentlemen of Chichester had decided the time was come to honour their most famous son. Under the presidency of Dr. Guy a subscription was set on foot, and the commission for the work was offered to Flaxman who, from Rome, submitted various designs at various prices. Then an epitaph was composed jointly by Hayley and Sargent. Thomas Hayley posed for the figure in the design finally chosen, which represents the poet seated reading the Gospel according to St. Matthew. Upon the ground, discarded, lie a lyre and a scroll inscribed *The Passions: an Ode*. The sculpture was first exhibited in London, and then later, in August, Flaxman came to Sussex to fix it in the cathedral, afterwards visiting Eartham, together with his wife. Tom came too; and when the Flaxmans departed at the end of the month, he remained behind, still trying to learn to swim, an art at which he did not prosper.

In September, Romney arrived again, to paint the Egremont family; and Tom executed a medallion of him. Romney was enchanted: "He surprises me more and more (he wrote).[2] I do not know I ever saw such rapid progress before in any or other Art." Then, at the end of the month, painter and sculptor returned together to London, where, during October, the boy worked on the model for his bust of Minerva, of which a good deal will be heard hereafter.

Hayley, as late as October 11, was still bathing. Despite the cloudy and dark evenings, he galloped to the coast on his favourite white charger, Hidalgo, accompanied by Tom's spaniel Fido, who was, he said, "as fierce as a tiger" when he thought anyone was trying to molest him.

Meantime Tom was writing to tell his father that Flaxman had just given him a treat: he had taken him to dine with the great John Wilkes, whose character, with masterly understatement, he describes as "odd".

Nothing much in the interval had happened to Hayley, unless we can interest ourselves in two more of his miraculous escapes from sudden dissolution. The first of these was "a strange attack of internal malady in the night", which he at once took to be the bursting of a vessel in his heart. The other was a fall from his horse, which caught its foot in a frozen rut, and "came down upon its nose". Fortunately, in both cases, he got over it.

With this characteristic flourish of misfortunes, we reach the end of Tom's first year of apprenticeship.

5

The second was, as to its beginnings, not dissimilar. Hayley started it in his best form by galloping over to Petworth to wish his friends the compliments of the season. He also solemnly commenced a diary, to which he confided his regret at the slow progress of his poem on Sculpture. This, however, was chiefly due to the fact that he kept on abandoning it in favour of other projects. This time, for instance, for a work in blank verse, written for the direct benefit of his son, and entitled *The Art of Choosing a Wife*. In April, Rose paid him a visit, and at once had the two first epistles of this composition read to him. He applauded both of them, the second even more than the first, so it was a pity that Hayley's "declining health" and his gathering troubles prevented him from writing any more of it.

Tom, for his part, was as busy as his father. Romney was painting him. Inspired by this he himself took to painting, and composed a design of the Two Angels and Mary at the Sepulchre, which, as we shall discover upon a later page, had the honour of being copied by no less an artist than William Blake. In addition, the marble Minerva was still in process of execution, and a slow process he found it, though "excellent exercise". Nevertheless, it was not all work, for in February young William Meyer came to see him, and they paid a visit to Bedlam, to commiserate with an unfortunate cottager of Eartham who had got himself incarcerated there. They found him, they said, excessively cheerful. And all the time Hayley's letters were arriving, without cessation; very scholarly, and full of Greek. So incessant, indeed, were they, that at length it grew clear even to the loving parent that they were more than his son could cope with. He relented, and thoughtfully offered to make them fortnightly, instead of weekly.

All the while, Tom was reading tremendously. On February 20 he sent his father a little list of the books he required: Aristotle, Euripides, Poetae Minores Graeci, any Greek poet, except Homer and Hesiod ("which I have"), Apollonius Rhodius, Junius de Picturâ, Cicero, Arabian Nights, Diogenes Laertius, Eunapius, Chaucer, Justin, Plato, Geographical Grammar, Josephus.

Hayley responded by recommending that he should read the *Arabian Nights* in French rather than in English; and sent Mrs. Flaxman a present in the form of Mme. Roland's *Memoirs*, which Flaxman read and at once profoundly disapproved.

By March, Tom was so busy that he asked his father, who had been hurt by his ready acceptance of the proposal of a fortnightly letter, if he would, in addition, be good enough to time his letters so that he could answer them upon a Sunday. Hayley responded by requesting the overworked child to make a copy of the head of Pamela which Romney had drawn, as he wished to send it to Mme. de Genlis. "I propose," he said handsomely, "to reward you for your trouble by three French quartos, which . . . contain a selection from the Memoirs of the French Academy of Dissertations . . . and deal with such matters useful to artists as Gorgons, Goddesses, etc." And he enclosed violets, "gathered the instant the sun was rising".

This was in March, and Thomas Alphonso was just fifteen and a half. The pressure was considerable, and it is scarcely to be wondered that, before May, he was ill. All the time the letters from Eartham continued to pour in. Would Tom go to the friendly bookseller Payne, to procure his new Aristotle in octavo; would he send in his next parcel his octavo Aristophanes? "We have got our globes here in order, and are busy with the stars and the earth" (a reference to the education of young Wyndham).

Hardly a week passed now without a new intellectual excitement. Mr. Walker (of the Eidouranion), had given Tom twelve tickets for his new course of lectures; the drawing of Pamela was commenced. Hayley was pleased to hear that he was advanced to a course of philosophy. "Pray do not scruple to furnish yourself at Payne's with any books you may occasionally want." And he thought it might be a good idea if Tom, in his spare time, were to model a bust of the Bishop of Llandaff.

In April yet another commission arrived, though the poor boy was still deeply involved with the head of Pamela, which was giving him a great deal of trouble. This time it was "that singular compound of genius and infelicity", Charlotte Smith, who wanted to send a copy of Romney's sketch of her head to her son in India. Could Tom see to it?

Tom could and would; meanwhile he had been enjoying Mr. Walker's lectures. "Nothing", he said, "is so charming as to investigate . . . the admirable laws by which every thing subsists."

Late in April the sorely driven youth came home for a holiday. After his departure Hayley wrote to ask if he would be good enough to desire his pleasant friend Payne to forward him the *Posthumous Works* of Adam Smith, since he understands they contain some "good remarks" on Sculpture—needed, no doubt, for the Poem.

But the pace had been too hot, and now, almost at once, came misfortune. Tom cracked at last, and, to his father's great astonishment, on May 12 tidings came that he was in Chichester, and ill with a fever. The next day Hayley rode into the city, and brought him back to Eartham. Flaxman, alarmed at his pupil's condition, had sent him home, hoping that the country air might revive him. Hayley, with his customary sanguineness, treated the invalid by reading Homer to him, and an Italian Essay on Sculpture.

6

It is easy to be wise after the event. We who know that Thomas Alphonso had less than four years of life left to him, can experience all manner of facile indignation over what now seems the casual way in which his illness was handled. For this, though, Hayley was not to blame. He at once called in Dr. Guy, who overhauled the boy and said there was nothing amiss.

There was, in fact, a great deal amiss. He was suffering from the first stages of that deplorable malady, a curvature of the spine; which, in the end, rendered him a hopeless cripple. He died, as Hayley was very fond of saying, "a victim to medical mistake". Others, less charitably, ascribed his death to "forcing".

Meanwhile the present respite was only a brief one. By the end of May, Tom was back in Chichester, on route for London. Most of the latter part of his stay had been spent in discussing with his father a project which will shortly take up a good deal of our attention. This was none other than the temporary letting of Eartham to some "more opulent inhabitant", thus saving its owner money which should enable his son, later on, to enter into the full enjoyment of his patrimony. Such a measure, of course, necessitated a new dwelling during the interval of retrenchment, and Hayley had already decided that this should be situated at Felpham, where, as will be recalled, he had already purchased a furnished cottage.

The accommodation of this cottage being insufficient for permanent residence, Hayley's first plan, so typical, so imbecile, was to have built by its side a Tower, a Marine Tower, into which he could enter and shut out the world. To this end he availed himself of the services of a young architect, Samuel Bunce, who had been recommended to him by Flaxman; and, by June 9, this "pleasing little Palladio", as Hayley persists in calling him, was at Eartham, discussing with his patron the "halcyon nest" he was proposing to erect, and, after the fashion of architects the world over, trying to induce his client to face the hard realities of bricks and mortar.

Tom, meantime, had visited Dr. Long, and had, upon his advice, started to take bark. Hayley had got over his fears for him; he recommended him to read Justin, and suggested a pleasing subject for his pencil: "A fine martial youth contemplating a trophy composed of his arms, and perceiving with astonishment and exultation an eagle perched upon his shield, and an owl upon his spear." And, at last, the bust of Minerva had reached completion.

7

Summer came, and Hayley rode on horseback to visit the Meyers at Kew. During this sojourn, Tom came over on a visit, and Hayley proposed to conduct his young friends to Windsor Castle, to entertain them with an inspection of the pictures there. The weather, however, was shocking, and so young Meyer suggested an abridged excursion to examine the collection of Mr. Udney, of Teddington. Mr. Udney's pictures were duly visited, and Hayley was so delighted by a Salvator Rosa and a Correggio which he saw there, that his mind at once turned to Romney, who was suffering from a more than usually prolonged bout of melancholy. These pictures, he was sure, would do him good; and so, the following morning early, Hayley and young Meyer burst in upon the dejected artist. They found him still in bed, and, though they dangled a most alluring prospect before his eyes, he declared himself too ill to move. They cajoled, they reasoned with him; and at length he consented to get up. Then they told him that he would find none but friends at Kew, if he would only venture so far. He agreed to do so; and, once there, the ladies of Kew, and their admirable coffee, soon so inspirited him, that he declared himself ready for Teddington. Once in Mr. Udney's gallery, the Salvator Rosa and the Correggio completely banished all his complaints, as Hayley had been sure they would. The cure was magical. When the party reached Kew again, Hayley was rewarded by his friend's acknowledgement that, though he had felt more than half dead when they had fallen upon him that morning, he had never passed a more delightful day in his life. More, he wrote later: "It was a day indeed; a day I shall never forget; it was very friendly and gallant to me. It was the first step to my recovery." Under its stimulus he had, at last, almost completed the Egremont picture.

I think that when one is tempted to sneer at Hayley—and heaven knows it is easy enough to do so—such a trifle as this may well be remembered in his favour. It is entirely typical of the sort of thing he was, in intention at any rate, always planning.

On August 3 a voice came almost from the grave: "Eartham Gazette Extraordinary (Hayley wrote). Great News! . . . Our beloved Cowper is bursting from his calamitous eclipse of mind.

He is already so far recovered, that he is absolutely at work on the corrections of his Homer, and with such spirit, that he says he never knew how Homer ought to be translated till now." And forthwith he despatched to the "restored bard" a cast of Tom's bust of Minerva. It was a false alarm, but it revealed the extraordinary spring of hope that resided in Hayley.

On August 12, the Meyer family arrived at Eartham, to find Romney already in residence. Hayley sent the news to Tom, and, in the same letter, there comes a reference to the summer-house which I have already mentioned in my description of Eartham: "All were highly pleased with the rustic seat contrived on purpose to contain them all, and raised in grateful remembrance of your recovery." Hayley had scribbled two little compositions—a Sonnet and a Song—which he duly recited "as a sort of poetical consecration of this new rustic bower". It is touching to think of this summer-house now, deeply enshaded in its encroaching wood.

Romney during this holiday appeared in better spirits than usual. Perhaps Mr. Udney's pictures still stimulated him, or perhaps it was the charming Miss Meyers. At any rate, he not only completed the Egremont picture, but also, though an indifferent horseman, was prevailed upon to add equestrian exercises to the usual sea-bathing. No wonder that, under this stirring regime, he should also commence that picture which, in later years, was the pride and joy of Hayley's existence. This, which he called "The Four Friends", later formed the frontispiece of one volume of his *Memoirs*, and represented the Hermit in middle life seated at a table with his right hand resting upon an open book. It is Cicero's *De Amicitiâ*. His face is turned in three-quarter profile as he gazes at the two ingenious youths, Thomas Alphonso and William Meyer. The fourth friend was Romney himself, but his portrait proved so imperfect a resemblance that it was not reproduced when Hayley later commissioned Caroline Watson to engrave the picture.

It is at this point perhaps fitting to introduce a word or two about the extraordinary strictures which the Revd. John Romney in his *Life* of his father, published in 1830, thought fit to pass upon Hayley. His is a venomous production, in which great play is made of the theory that Hayley, all through his relations with Romney, acted the part of evil genius, preventing him from returning to his wife, inculcating in him loose moral principles, and so on. Whether there be any truth in this can hardly be ascertained now; but what is interesting about the book is the very evident way in which John Romney, without knowing it, gives away the reason for his animus against Hayley. Of course he was a moral man, and a clergyman, and poor Hayley was neither; but there was something else: John Romney was obsessed with the notion that Hayley had got hold of a lot of his father's valuable pictures without paying for them!

Now we will say nothing of the many years of hospitality which Romney had received at Eartham, and we will say nothing, either, of the fact that, in the early days of their acquaintance, there is no reason to believe that the portraits which Hayley commissioned Romney to do were not paid for in a perfectly normal manner. We will proceed to the indictment:

In the autumn of 1782 (writes John Romney) Romney began his own portrait, which he afterwards gave to Mr. Hayley; who did not allow him to finish it, but hurried it off to Eartham without delay. . . . Had it, however, been suffered to remain in Cavendish Square sometime longer, an opportunity would have occurred when it might have been finished;— but Mr. Hayley preferred the bird in hand.

Again:

In 1795 he painted that excellent picture Flaxman modelling the Bust of Hayley, attended by his pupil, Thomas Hayley; and Mr. Romney himself looking from behind. . . . It having been claimed by Mr. Hayley, in consequence of some vague expression inadvertently uttered by Mr. Romney, about the time he was sitting, it was accordingly delivered to him in 1802 [at Romney's death]; but only for life. . . .

Finally, and far more serious than all else, there was the horror with which John Romney observed his patrimony being eaten up by Romney's fantastic building schemes at Hampstead, schemes in which he was encouraged by various "worthless people", including Mr. Hayley.

Doubtless it was very wrong of Romney to spend the money he had himself earned upon his own pleasures, instead of dutifully leaving it to his family; but, since he chose to do so, it is not difficult to perceive a reason for the Revd. John Romney's frenetic bias. The subject is not an agreeable one to pursue, particularly as, at the time of his attack, Hayley had already been dead ten years, and could make no reply.

8

So, in varied delights, the summer of 1796 proceeded. The *Four Friends* almost completed, a desire to consult Mr. Bunce on architectural matters became irresistible, and Hayley and Romney, with enchanting oddity, set off for London at two o'clock in the morning of August 29, to waylay him. They reached town at eleven o'clock, and went to Flaxman's to see Tom. Next day, Tom came to visit them, and they found him so feverish that Hayley resolved to carry him back with them on their return. In the interim he bought the boy some medicine, which seemed to do him good; and then the two friends went off to tackle the harassed Bunce, for Romney, even more than Hayley, was at this season bitten with the fever of building.

Back on September 2, after this somewhat wanton excursion, posted the two travellers, taking the sick Tom with them. Romney, all this autumn, was in the best of spirits. It was a last flare up. He put the final touches to the Petworth picture in the painting-room at Eartham; and he also executed a portrait of Dr. Guy, who, he remarked, for "compassionate benignity" of countenance, he would have chosen as model for a representation of his Saviour.

Tom, in emulation, painted his spaniel Fido on a strong tablet of wood, which was then substituted for the almost obliterated St. George that hung as signboard to the village inn.

Finally the great Egremont picture was taken over to Petworth and hung amidst universal applause, and then Romney thought he was really entitled to a little recreation. This took the form of a delightful jaunt, at his expense I suspect, as a sort of return of hospitality. He, Hayley and Tom set out on October 2 for Salisbury, where they spent a couple of nights. Romney's intention was that the student of sculpture should be gratified by a sight of the celebrated collection of statues at Wilton, and by the "stupendous scenery" of Stonehenge. Early on the morning of October 3, they passed several agreeable hours surveying the various works of statuary and painting in what Hayley quaintly calls the "magnificent villa" of Wilton, and Tom made a hasty sketch of a stone Amazon in the hall. They then drank their coffee in the Palladian lodge, and proceeded to inspect the pictures at Longford Castle, the seat of the Earl of Radnor. With fresh horses they next rode to Stonehenge, where Tom made more hasty sketches; and they finished the day with a late dinner at Salisbury. Next morning they turned for home, not forgetting to pay a call on the way on their old friend Joseph Warton at Wickham, and also upon Guy in Chichester.

On October 5, Tom's sixteenth birthday, the cavalcade proceeded to Felpham, to bid farewell to the ladies of the Meyer family who were staying there, and next morning all breakfasted with Lord Egremont at Petworth, and the painter and young sculptor took the road for London.

No sooner were they gone than the architect, Bunce-Palladio, arrived. "He examined the *genius loci* concerning our intended structure," Hayley wrote on the 9th, and, after making various ingenious sketches, finally succeeded in persuading his client that, instead of a lofty round tower, "a singular original cottage, and turret shooting up to fifteen or twenty feet above the roof" would be exactly what the genius of the place, and the genius of the pocket recommended. By which, of course, Hayley meant that Bunce had managed to make him see reason regarding his preposterous proposition of erecting a tower to live in.

On October 16, Hayley was sending his unfortunate son "flannel to protect your body, and Grecian philosophy to invigorate your mind". He, for his part, was still "rushing into the ocean". He was also on the point of writing a long letter to the Bishop of Llandaff, promulgating some elaborate scheme for the general welfare of his young friend, Meyer.

Autumn came on, and the interchange of news continued: Palladio only awaits the spring to start the new building; Hayley is entertaining Dr. Warner; Tom wants to know whether he had not better start studying architecture; the Bishop of Llandaff has responded very kindly; and Rose is laid low with the gout. Moreover, four more casts of the bust of Minerva have set off, by waggon, from London.

Something, however, probably natural restlessness though he says it was the tidings of Rose's gout, prevented Hayley, this autumn, from settling down to his usual routine. His diary during the month of November is full of lamentations concerning his reduced output, both of poetry and prose. Still it cannot be helped, he says; and attributes his decline of productivity to his health. It would, one feels, be fairer to attribute it to his subconscious uneasiness that all was not yet well with Tom, for all that his two long holidays had produced in him a factitious appearance of vigour.

Whatever the cause, however, his next move was a typical one. At three o'clock in the morning of November 16, he set forth on horseback to London, and as he journeyed he entertained himself by the composition of an occasional sonnet:

> Ye stars that, sparkling through November air,
> Behold me starting ere the dawn of day,
> And winging o'er bleak hills my early way. . . .

He had, it would seem, been brooding upon the sad news of Rose's gout, and, fearing lest this malady, if it proved deep-seated, might impede his career at the Bar, the thought had suddenly struck him that, if only Rose could become the tutor to Lord Egremont's children, and at the same time the sub-tenant of Eartham, then that might well entail for him a life of greater ease and security; to say nothing of its being an uncommonly convenient arrangement for Hayley. To this programme there was but one drawback: Lord Egremont would greatly prefer his tutor to be a clergyman of the Church of England. Well, that was not impossible, either, if only Rose were agreeable. Could Lord Egremont's progeny wait while the quondam barrister was hurriedly taking orders? It would need some alacrity, of course; but with good-will and energy all things were possible. No time certainly must be lost! And, when his meditations had reached thus far, Hayley's foot was, I think, already in the stirrup. Hence that fantastic three o'clock in the morning start.

Unhappily there was delay, after all. It started to rain;

prodigously; and he met his brother-poet, Sargent, upon the road, also on his way to town. They stabled their horses, and took shelter in the Godalming coach.

Once in town, Hayley sped to Romney's, and apprised his startled son of his arrival. They passed several very agreeable evenings together, Tom drawing beside his parent, who read aloud, for the delectation of his host. Business, however, was business. He at once rushed to Rose, and laid his proposal before him. Then, because Romney was painting the portrait of "a lovely lady", he took it upon himself to advise him to represent her "in a picturesque greenhouse with some rare and magnificent flower in her hand". Romney had no rare and magnificent blossoms at his disposal, so Hayley arranged for the painter and Tom to ride with him to Kew, where, by the kindness of his old acquaintance, Mr. Aiton, the requisite rarity was obtained. It wilted on the way back; but was much improved by immersion in water.

Hayley returned by coach to Petworth, still deeply perplexed by the problem of Rose's future, and with a sore throat and a headache into the bargain. By one o'clock he was partaking of his coffee at Petworth, whither his horse Hidalgo had been brought to complete his homeward way. He passed through a thick mist on the top of the downs, but when he descended into the vale of Waltham the sunset was a glory all about him.

Then, in characteristic fashion, he approached Lord Egremont, and told him his plans for Rose. The noble lord was perfectly agreeable; the stumbling block was, rather, Rose himself, who seemed a little uncertain about the whole thing. Well, Hayley had done his best. Early and hereditary gout was a sad business; it would be tolerable, he reasoned, in a clergyman and a teacher of youth; but for a man of law quite impracticable.

December found him restlessly riding over to Felpham to meditate his new premises. He made up his mind that it would be better to pull down the old cottage, so that he might thereby be able to have his front-door in the middle of his front wall; and, with a crowning grasp of the inessential, he told Tom he had decided that this should be surmounted by a stone image of the sleeping Fido, from the hand of the young Phidias himself.

Tom replied, rather neatly, though the idea was Mrs. Flaxman's and not his own, that the notion of Fido was admirable, but needed one amendment, viz. that he should be awake.

By December 17, Hayley had at last steeled himself to composition, though only to the extent of twelve lines of his poem on Sculpture, and the translation of a Greek epigram on an iron statue of an oppressive king. The weather had turned bitter, the clay froze as Tom tried to mould it, and Flaxman gave it up and told the boy he might go and skate on the canal in the Park.

Then, at last, tidings came from Norfolk, though the news reached Tom before it reached his father. Mrs. Unwin had died on December 17, and Cowper seemed better. Hayley commented, perhaps a trifle insensitively, that "the release of the poor superannuated lady is likely to produce a very favourable change in the deplorable dejection of our friend".

This good news, for so at the time did it seem to Hayley, was, however, for the moment obscured by a whirl of seasonable activity. The weather was appalling; the roads icy and snowbound. Young George Wyndham, on his way back to Petworth for Christmas, was overcome by the cold, and Hayley was obliged to turn home with him. Travellers in the neighbourhood of Eartham were buried in snowdrifts, and altogether the year 1796 went out like a lion.* It was the last year for some considerable number in which Hayley was to experience anything that resembled peace of mind.

9

It will be perceived, I think, in the somewhat desultory proceedings of this past year, that Hayley, for the first time for a long while, was somewhat lacking an object for existence: a nucleus about which, and on behalf of which, he could exert his extraordinary energies. In the immediate past it had been Cowper; it had for many years been Tom's education; it had been Romney's advancement; it had even been his own. Now, through time and chance, each of these motives was less urgently present. Cowper was beyond good or evil, Tom's destiny lay in Flaxman's hands, and Romney and Flaxman were both too prosperous to need a partizan. Hence, one feels, the sad decline this year to benevolences exerted towards such minor figures as Rose and young Meyer. And Rose, it almost seemed, did not want to be helped!

As for Hayley's own work, one rather feels that his meeting with a real poet, in Cowper, had shaken his never very great pretensions to fame of this kind. His letters to Cowper on his own qualifications were modest enough, and I do not think it was modesty falsely assumed. Besides, his scholastic activities on behalf of the Egremont boy must have been considerable, and were greatly calculated to draw him from the solitude and leisure which he found necessary for his elaborate compositions.

No one perhaps summed up Hayley's character better than Romney, who had, after all, known him longer than most people. He said, according to a letter which Hayley wrote to Flaxman in 1805,[3] "You live upon your feelings." Hayley goes on to expand his theme: "By which singular expression he meant that my wishes

* "Perhaps the coldest day ever known in London was Dec. 25, 1796, when the thermometer was 16° below zero." *Haydn's Dictionary of Dates.*

in regard to works of art were generally influenced by some motive of personal affection." Throughout 1796 he was battling desperately to re-establish within himself this motive of personal affection; and, although he experienced it abundantly, of course, for Tom, he must have frequently felt that, until the boy had at least passed through his apprenticeship, his faculty for artistic eulogy stood little chance of being fully exercised.

10

During the first half of 1797 this situation continued, and one seems to see Hayley desperately investigating a condition of affairs in which he was shut out from doing good. He spent the first days of the New Year quietly engaged in architectural considerations, the results of which were despatched to the harassed Bunce; and then he compiled a prayer for Cowper's recovery, in the form of a sonnet. The previous year had seen yet another death at Dereham: this time of Cowper's famous spaniel, Beau, who, full of years and honour, was duly despatched to London to be stuffed; reappearing this January in all the glory of taxidermical preservation and a glass case.

On January 5, visitors arrived at Eartham, young Meyer, and Captain Godfrey of the Ordnance, Hayley's cousin. They bore in their charge the marble original of the Minerva. While his guests played billiards, Hayley wrote to Tom, to tell him how he had introduced his brave cousin to Lord Egremont, with a view to his future advancement. He thanked Tom for the frequent visits he paid to Romney, and bade him do all in his power to cheer his friend's singularly low spirits.

Tom, in a letter a day or two before, had presented a touching picture of the great painter's dejection: "He is so much alone, and sometimes so low-spirited, that he takes it as a kindness in me to call and sit with him an hour or two."

Meanwhile Rose, it seems, had decided definitely against Hayley's scheme for his advancement, and so the latter's fertile mind turned at once to the notion of converting Captain Godfrey into the tutor desiderated by Petworth. Godfrey, a serving soldier, was much in favour of the idea, which seemed a heaven-sent opportunity for preserving himself from the perils of the West India station, to which at any moment he was liable to be despatched; and, though so far as we know his qualifications as a pedagogue were restricted, he thought that, with Sockett's aid and Hayley's advice, he might be able to make do. "It would" (Hayley wrote solemnly to his sixteen-year-old son.) "give me great delight to place the meritorious captain and his family in this pleasant and honourable asylum from the perils of his present profession." It would also, of course, admirably solve the now urgent problem of what was to happen to Eartham when he himself left it.

On January 19, Hayley went over to Petworth again, to see if he could forward Godfrey's claims. But unfortunately he was unable to get a private word with his noble friend, who was on the point of "sallying forth with a large party for the chase". So he mentioned the matter to Mrs. Wyndham, the mother of the prospective pupils, and found her reaction most favourable.

Hayley's mind, while the processes of benevolence were thus working out, turned once more to architecture, and he despatched to Bunce his notion of a rustic arcade, or covered way, to lead up to the new cottage, in which he might be able to exercise himself during bad weather. It was all a little reminiscent of Mr. Pecksniff and his reiterated observation: "I should very much like to see Mrs. Todgers's notion of a wooden leg, if perfectly agreeable to herself"; but Bunce was most patient, and agreed the idea was a splendid one.

In February the poem on Sculpture took a slow step forward; he had evidently been reading hard for it, since he now related to Tom the strange case of Tisagoras, who had evolved a statue of iron: "Pausanius says, this ironwork of Tisagoras was wonderful; but who Tisagoras was, Pausanius himself did not know."

And then, suddenly, out of all this whirl of culture, wire-pulling and dispersed activity, there came on February 6 a touching letter from Tom which is like a door opening on to the past:

MY VERY DEAR BARD,

Imagine to yourself our front parlour occupied by Mrs. Flaxman and her sister, Mr. Flaxman and his sister, Mr. Howard and a friend of his, (a gentleman painter lately returned from Rome,) looking over Mr. Flaxman's valuable collection of works of art.

Imagine to yourself also, me in the little back parlour *solus*, without fire, scribbling to my dear bard, on my little desk, which I value most highly as his gift, with my watch on the top of it—a pleasant practice which I learned from the bard. Imagine, I say, all this, and you will see me enjoying the greatest pleasure London can afford me. Alone, which I am *but seldom*; apart "From glaring show and giddy noise", which it is my delight to be; and writing to my dear and kind bard, which, next to conversing with him, is my greatest delight. But I am called to supper: there again I follow your excellent example, and, indeed, my own liking, for I eat only a bit of toasted bread, as we used to do at Eartham. Good night!

"From glaring show and giddy noise" is, of course, a compliment to the bard, as it is the first line of one of his songs; and the touch about the watch is inimitable. Poor Thomas Alphonso! I think we come closer to him in this letter than in all the more sophisticated outpourings with which, to please his father, he frequently indulged.

Hayley thought so too, since as soon as he received the letter he carried it over with him to Petworth and read it to his friends there. The reason for this visit was his desire to assist an artist who was then in residence, and who, it seems, being overwhelmed by gratitude to

Lord Egremont, had sought his advice as how best to express it. "You will not, I trust (Hayley wrote to Tom), think superciliously of this good and very *ingenious* man, when I inform you that he is only a painter of four-footed animals. . . . His name is Boltby; of a good northern family, and, what particularly pleased me, near relation of Bage, author of the novels that amused us all so highly . . . Lord Egremont is soon to introduce him . . . to the King, from whom his Lordship has already obtained some commissions. I hope he will soon paint our pleasant acquaintance on four legs at Kew, I mean the family of Kangaroos."

Tom replied most fittingly. He said he should be very glad to make the acquaintance of Mr. Boltby. "Do not imagine," he added, "that I can think more slightly of a man who copies nature on four legs, than of one who copies her on two. . . . I think there is not a more pleasing and interesting study than that of exploring and publishing the bounty and wisdom of the Almighty, as exemplified in brutes of all descriptions."

Hayley was overjoyed by this display of delicacy and good sense. He rode over yet again to see Boltby, found him jaded by over-application, and invited him to return to Eartham for a rest. Boltby said that nothing would please him better, but that he was afraid Lord Egremont would think him lacking in perseverance if he did. Hayley undertook to overcome this visionary obstacle to Boltby's gratification ; did so; and carried him off.

The worthy Boltby was enchanted with Eartham. He was still more enchanted when Hayley read aloud to him the passage from Tom's letter relating to himself and to his own particular branch of art. Then, always with an eye on the main chance, so far as it affected other people, Hayley bade him, should an opportunity arise when conversing with King George III, by no means to forget to press the merits of Flaxman.

Mr. Boltby thus disposed of, Hayley next turned to Tom's request that he should be provided with instruction in the art of reading history. He had perused Goldsmith's Greek and Roman Histories, and now wanted to go further. Should he, perhaps, read Gibbon? Hayley was cautious. He advised that several other authorities should be studied first, to give a proper perspective. Then, "You will always look into our friend Gibbon with a peculiar interest, remembering our affection for the man, and, I trust, without being injured by the sceptical and sarcastic infirmities of the writer."

And then, almost for the first time, one perceives the fact that England has been for some years engaged in war with the French Republic. "Who knows (wrote Hayley to Tom on February 24,) what the wheel of Fortune may produce for us. . . . She has already favoured me, in one of her military lotteries, by giving me an opportunity of serving my country in the new provisional cavalry.

I act like a true patriot, and produce for the aid of dear old England, a much stouter man than myself, and a stronger horse than I have in my stable. There is public virtue for you! which costs me only forty guineas, for such is the current price of substitutes here. My patriotism would have been puzzled a little to find the cash on the sudden; but a rural friend, as generous and as patriotic as myself, managed the business for me . . . and I shall have the pleasure of repaying him in a few days."

Three days later, Tom replied: "What do you think of this invasion, that causes such an alarm? Do you imagine they will attempt any part of the coast of England? If it should be Sussex, I shall set off immediately to join you, and share with you whatever misfortune or glory shall await us. I hear that part of the coast is to be laid under martial law. If it extends to Sussex, I shall be obliged, if I am with you, to serve my country in person, which I should have no objection to, if we were hard pressed, and especially if they should presume to approach the sacred bounds of the Dryads and Hamadryads of Eartham."

Hayley, replying on March 3, struck an heroic attitude:

I delight in your affectionate readiness to share any danger with your friends on the coast, but I would sooner have my old and tattered remnant of life shot at by all the cannon of France, than expose my dear blooming votary of the peaceful Minerva to the fire of a single musket.

Do not apprehend, however, that I mean to forbid your approach to the sea. You know, my dearest bosom-friend, that I am not accustomed to yield to fear, in any shape; and, in truth, I feel no terrors of this projected invasion, which excites so extensive an alarm. I do not think it will be attempted; and if it should, I think we should deserve to lose our island, if we were not able to defend it, even like the brave Welshmen,* with their pitchforks. . . .

But let the storm of war pass away, as I trust it will, like a mere transient cloud, from this lovely island. Let me talk of the dear men of peace and art.

And this he proceeds at once to do, telling his dear diminutive Phidias that the ingenious little Palladio has of late been rather evasive, but that, all the same, his garden walls are rising; "and now we want him, and you also, to hold a conference on the spot to discuss the exact scite of the new structure". And, as in previous years, he sent his son the first violets from his garden.

Bunce, however, continued evasive. Perhaps he took the invasion rather more seriously than Hayley did, and thought it a poor time to start building Marine Villas. Tom called on him, and he said he could not possibly get down to Sussex for three weeks. In the meantime, news had reached town of Jervis's victory off Cape St. Vincent, and the threat of invasion had receded. "This last gallant victory over the Dons (wrote Tom) has enlivened us all amazingly."

* A very contemporary reference to the French landing in Pembrokeshire, February 22, 1797.

It had done more to Hayley. It had inspired him. On March 9 he was writing:

> First let me rejoice in our sympathetic disdain of terror, on the threatened invasion. The victory over the Dons is, as you observe, most seasonably enlivening. . . . It has led me to begin (*entre nous*) a little prose work . . . on a naval topic. . . . I require books for it, despatched on the coach from our pleasant friend Payne's: Lediard's *Naval History*, two folios; and Falconer's *Marine Dictionary*. Pray ask Payne, if the Society for Improving Naval Architecture have published anything on that subject . . . if so send that too.

And he concludes these unusual literary requisitions with the useful and topical reflection: "At this season, when so many folk are frightened by a prospect of invasion, we should animate our spirits by recollecting how nobly the Greeks repelled their Persian invaders."

Tom was enraptured at the prospect of seeing a new production of the bard's, on so noble a subject as "the wooden walls of old England"; and he, for his part, had also a tough job on hand. Dr. Long had presented him with a piece of stone broken off one of the monoliths at Stonehenge, with the modest request that he should convert it into a Druid's head, in bas-relief. Tom found the material of Stonehenge so intractable that he conceded the task might take him some little while.

Neither the French nor the Spaniards could, however, long delay the rapidly advancing preparations for the ceremony of laying the foundation-stone of the *Casina torrata*, the villa at Felpham. Romney had purchased a chaise, and the architect was coming upon a pony. It was presumed that he and Tom would take turns in riding the pony and accompanying Romney in the chaise. But it was uncommonly difficult to assemble all the company at once. First Romney was busy, and then Bunce could not get away. It was not until April 13 that the cavalcade set out from London, and then the tardy Palladio seems to have infected the horses with his sloth, for the party, which had been instructed to proceed *via* Kew, Bushy Park and Cobham, had still not appeared by nightfall. They did not, in fact, arrive before midnight, when their advent was despaired of and all at Eartham were abed. Indeed, the whole journey had been sadly botched: the architect had not taken his fair share of the pony, preferring to ride in comfort and converse with Romney. Tom had consequently ridden it nearly all the way, and arrived excessively fatigued. In view of his state of health this was serious, though at the time he did not exhibit any ill effects.

It was Saturday, April 15, 1797, when Hayley and his three companions rode over to Felpham to witness Tom, with appropriate ceremonial, lay the first stone of the marine turret. It was a great occasion, and, if the members of the party had but known, a sad one. Hayley, moralizing afterwards, says: "How tender to man is the dispensation of Heaven in denying him knowledge of future events. All three beloved artists had sunk into the grave within six years! . . . I am now sitting alone in the dwelling, which their kindness has endeared, and which their ingenuity has adorned."

Yet, for the moment, all was jollity. Tom modelled a resemblance of that "pleasant little round man of art", Bunce; and when Romney and the architect departed on Tuesday, 18th, he remained behind to welcome the Godfreys, who arrived the next day. Alas! the scheme for establishing the worthy captain at Eartham to superintend the education of the Egremont children had by this time utterly collapsed. Hayley had now to find another tenant.

Tom's health was indifferent; he seemed less able than usual to "support exercise". Dr. Guy was consulted, but thought the matter of little moment. On Sunday, May 7, Hayley escorted his son by chaise to Chichester on his road to London, parting with him as was his custom at the pillar which marked the city boundary. The day was wet: Hayley mounted the led horse which had accompanied them, and rode with his servant back through the evening gloom. His mind was grave and troubled, not without reason.

11

One would have thought that all these activities had left Hayley little time for composition; but his energies were still directed, at odd moments, to the preparation of his poem on Sculpture, and he was busy reading all the classical authorities that he could find. The impact, however, of the war, which, as we have seen, was at last becoming noticeable even at Eartham, caused him in the February of this year once more to suspend his labours, as he meditated matter of a different metal. On his visit to France in 1790, his "love of Freedom and his philanthropy" had filled his fancy with visionary hopes that France, on the demolition of despotism, might gradually form a free constitution on the English model; and it occurred to him that "the two nations, who for many centuries had lacerated each other with a barbarous and bloody rivalship, might convert their inveterate enmity into a nobler pacific emulation, and only vie with each other in promoting the true interests of humanity". He had, therefore, begun an extensive historical and moral poem, to show them how to do it.

Unhappily, the excesses of the French Revolution had made the prosecution of such a work appear impracticable, and he had laid it aside until the events of the present year (1797) had (for some inscrutable reason) tempted him to feel that there was once more an opening for such an endeavour. And so he now resumed it, substituting, in somewhat wanton fashion, the Bishop of Llandaff for the Marquis de la Fayette, in the star role of general mediator.

But even this amended version did not get very far. His anxiety over Tom's health was now too great for him to enjoy the peace of mind requisite to establishing the relations between France and England upon a really satisfactory footing.

His transactions for the next few weeks were, therefore, almost exclusively medical. He bombarded Tom with letters of advice; bidding him drink a halfpenny-worth of new milk every morning; to go to Kew for the fresh air; to consult Dr. Latham, to whom he was to take an introductory letter setting forth "all the complicated feelings of a parent". The trouble was now, it was thought, the poor boy's lungs, since he suffered from shortness of breath; and Dr. Latham was just the man to see to it.

Dr. Latham must have been an accommodating person. A month or two later, the distracted parent sent him a sonnet by the hand of his patient, which said, among other things:

> I deprecate distemper's languid sigh,
> And ills that make aspiring genius tame,

and ended arrestingly:

> Save thou the filial darling of my heart
> From malady's malign, though blunted dart,
> Arm his just mind for art's ingenuous strife:
> Not to exist, but well to act is life.

But Dr. Latham, so far as we know, took it all in his stride, and simply prescribed the Mixture as before.

Meanwhile the Marine Villa was growing rapidly: "What think you (wrote Hayley) of our having got thirty-one pillars (for the long arcade) six feet high, out of two cuts from a single oak of my own, that grew in Eartham?"

Tom countered by describing the chimney-piece he was contemplating for the new library: with antique masks at each corner, the pilasters and top ornamented with a single bundle of reeds or fasces, and a bas-relief of several figures round the top. This description stirred Hayley to emulation. He sent Tom a sketch of his own idea of the sculptural lay-out of the library, adding words, "like the sign-painter of famous memory", to elucidate his images. "First, then (he wrote), the grand busts on each side, are Romney and Flaxman; and in a circle under each, the insignia of their respective arts. By the side of the painter, an old lion couchant, and at rest if not asleep. Near Flaxman, a lion younger, and perfectly awake. On each side the juvenile sculptor, two infantine leopards or dogs, with their paws raised upon the block that supports the youth. In the centre of the circular part, below the young animals, a suspended lyre. Under the three busts I would put the famous Spartan words, in the original Greek, describing age, middle life, and youth. Thus, I think, the whole design would afford me a very delightful memorial of my three beloved artists, and of their various periods of life."

Unhappily though, just when most wanted, Palladio was missing again. "Here is Friday morning arrived (wrote Hayley on June 1), but no architect, although an evening coach came last night from Portsmouth, by which the lost little man might have reached us according to his promise. Whether the riotous sailors have tossed his round body into the sea, to make a buoy of it, Heaven knows; but if they have, I hope he will arrive at Felpham, riding like Arion upon a dolphin, with his compasses, instead of a lyre in his hand."

However, a day or two more saw Bunce safe at Eartham, and fresh plans were soon afoot:—for an improvement to the upper room of the turret, which was to be glazed to within five feet of the floor, so that the occupant might enjoy an excellent light without being distracted by external objects: for railings at the top of the turret, so that it might be circumambulated: for the inclusion somewhere in the fabric of "the head of our imperial friend, Alfred, a suitable decoration to the retreat of an old poet, who has ever felt that passion for Liberty. . . ." To crown all, Hayley had managed to purchase a field which lay in the direct line of sight between the Turret and the sea, though he might well have to borrow the money to pay for it. This, he remarked, considering the possibility of invasion, was reminiscent of the spirit of the old Roman who bravely bought the very ground in Italy upon which Hannibal was encamped.

But now, under the shadow of Tom's indisposition, changes were taking place in the interior economy of Eartham. On May 18, Hayley wrote that he had decided to relinquish the education of George Wyndham, so that he might be more at liberty to look after his own affairs. In future the boy was to be educated at Petworth, under the hand of Sockett, whose prosperity he deemed, quite rightly, had now been secured for life. George Wyndham was distressed by the change in his fortunes. When he heard that Hayley was giving up his education, he burst into tears and said: "Oh, then I shall be sent to school again!" Hayley gravely informed him that it might be necessary for Tom to be taken to Lisbon for the benefit of his lungs. "Oh, I would rather be sent to school again, than that Tom should die," the magnanimous young Wyndham responded.

Hayley was entranced by this "genuine stroke of infantine heroism". He told the hero's parents, who were greatly pleased; and then, with incomparable tactlessness, he also told Tom, who responded, graciously enough, that he too was impressed by his friend's nobility; though he added, rather strangely, that it was unlucky for George that he had "too great expectations before him". In this connection, it should be remembered that Tom had been brought up to believe that he should pity the rich, rather than blame them for what they could not help. It was not an evil, Flaxman had assured him, that would be likely to befall him in his chosen profession of sculpture.

And now, very swiftly, the sands were running out. His lungs grew no better; his visits to Dr. Latham increased in frequency; and at last by mid-June he wrote to his father that "if medicine and a blister do not relieve me, I am to come to you for a few months, but so as not to lose any time I am to study, with Lord Egremont's leave, in his gallery". The blister was applied, the medicine taken; but no improvement ensued.

Hayley, meanwhile, frantic with anxiety, was writing to agree to every proposal. Of course he could study at Petworth. If necessary they could travel also to Wilton, and reside there while Tom copied the masterpieces in that gallery. He trusted, however, that this would not for a short time be necessary, since matters at the villa were for the present critical and the workmen needed his constant supervision.

In the interim, poor Tom had, with heaven only knows what labour, completed Dr. Long's Stonehenge Druid, and had conveyed it to him; and he despatched an anxious note to his father on the important matter of leaving a circular opening in the wall of the turret to receive the painted window which he (versatile youth!) was proposing to execute for it.

It was the last flare up. By June 25, news came that he had been ordered back to Eartham. Hayley wrote at once: "My infinitely dear Invalid. . . . Come speedily, but come in the manner least likely to fatigue you. Romney, to whom I write, will escort you in his own chaise to Cobham, or perhaps further. I will meet you in a chaise at Godalmin. . . ."

On June 29, Romney brought the boy to Godalming, where Hayley met them, escorting them both to Eartham. The following day he took them to survey the rising Turret, and the day after he conveyed Romney to Petworth on his road back to London. He was painfully affected by the alteration which he saw in his son, whom he settled down at once to copy a drawing from Michael Angelo, while he himself read aloud to him passages from the life of that illustrious man.

And there, for a while, we must leave them; for now Tom was not Hayley's only concern. A voice out of the past had sounded, in accents that might not be gainsaid; and his distractions were multiplied. On Tuesday, June 20, nine days before the return of his sick son, he had received a letter bearing the Dereham postmark, and in a very familiar hand, though one that he had not seen for some years. It was Cowper's; and it bore no signature.

CHAPTER XV

THE HEAVENLY VISION (1797–1798)

I

"IGNORANT OF EVERYTHING (the letter ran) but my own instant and impending misery, I know neither what I do, when I write; nor can do otherwise than write; because I am bidden to do so. Perfect Despair, the most perfect, that ever possess'd any Mind, has had possession of mine, you know how long, and knowing that, will not need to be told, who writes."[1]

This, now, is a letter which, even after the lapse of more than a century and a half, one cannot transcribe with any degree of equanimity. Its effect upon the sensitive mind of Hayley, coming fresh from his lost friend, may be imagined. All day, and all the next day, he brooded upon its horror; and at last he made up his mind. Very early on the morning of June 22, he saddled his horse and rode over to Chichester. He described to Tom, in a letter in which a certain facetiousness disguises the boldness of his resolution, the first step in the remarkable project he had evolved:

> I sallied forth early this morning, and surprised the garrison in the castle of Guy. The *paterfamilias*, after I had waited some time in his parlour, crept into the room in his night-gown. I felt his pulse, and protested with his own humorous solemnity, that it was highly improper for him to venture out of his warm bed so soon.
> Having rallied him sufficiently, I proceeded to the important subject of my visit; an idea that had struck me concerning our beloved Cowper, from whom I have recently received a few of the most gloomy and pathetic lines that ever flowed from the pen of depression. Guy gave me great pleasure by saying he thought my idea might produce a striking effect on the mind of our dejected friend.

And now, in order to describe the machinations which ensued, it is necessary to carry the reader's mind back once more to that small manuscript book in the British Museum which is entitled *Two Memorials of Hayley's Endeavours to serve His friend Cowper*.[1] The first, as we have seen, was devoted to that immensely involved business of The Pension; the other, which now concerns us, is set forth under the title of "The Second Memorial . . . containing a minute account of Devices employed to restore his dejected spirits", and it is further described as "compiled several years after his decease with an introductory Letter to his favourite Kinsman the Revd. Dr. Johnson", and dated July 1809. In this extraordinary document, Hayley sets forth clearly and in much detail the steps concerning which he had consulted Dr. Guy at that early morning conference in Chichester. They were steps, we may say, of a nature so fantastic that it is doubtful whether any man but Hayley would have taken them; they were, at the same time, steps which, I believe, do him as much honour as any that he took in the course of his singular career.

This is what they were. On June 24 he retired to his library and addressed to Cowper a reply to his letter such as, he says, "perhaps may astonish the reader". Part of this letter ran as follows:

> My keen sensations in perusing these heart-piercing Lines have been a painful prelude to the following ecstatic Vision—I beheld the Throne of God, whose splendour, tho' in excess, did not strike me blind; but left me powers to discern, on the steps of it, two kneeling angelic Forms. A kind seraph seem'd to whisper to me, that these heavenly petitioners were your lovely Mother, and my own. . . . I sprang eagerly forward to enquire your Destiny of your Mother. . . . "Moderate the anxiety of thy Zeal [said she] lest it distract thy declining Faculties! . . . [I tell you that my son's] restoration shall be gradual; and that his Peace with Heaven shall be preceded by the following extraordinary circumstances of signal Honour on earth—He shall receive Letters from Members of Parliament, from Judges, and from Bishops, to thank Him for the service, that He has render'd to the Christian world by his devotional poetry. These shall be follow'd by a Letter from the Prime Minister to the same effect; and this by thanks express'd to Him, on the same account, in the Hand of the King himself.—Tell Him, when these Events take place, He may confide in his celestial Emancipation from Despair, granted to the Prayers of his Mother. . . . [His] Peace is perfectly made with Heaven. Hasten to impart these bless'd tidings to your favourite Friend!"

And, in a postscript, he adjured his friend to tell him if any of the portents to which he had alluded should speedily take place.

Then, at the same time, he notified Johnson what he had done.

Now, of course, it is very easy to sneer at all this, and the part of the scheme which lays itself most open to ridicule is the fact that Hayley had prophesied that Cowper should shortly receive letters from the great ones of the land before he had, in fact, taken any steps whatever to see that such letters should be forthcoming. I think it is not impossible to meet this criticism. Hayley was perfectly well aware that he was dealing with a man whose mind was deranged, and with a man, therefore, whose reactions were totally unpredictable. What he felt was that something *had* to be done, at once, as much for his own peace of mind as for Cowper's; and what he hoped, I daresay, was that his farrago about the Vision might possibly, in the abnormal condition in which Cowper then was, *by itself* afford some relief. If, on the other hand, his letter made no impression at all, then fifty letters from fifty of the most eminent persons in the realm would make no difference. It was necessary first to set the scheme in operation, and then to see whether it produced any effect. If it did, there would be plenty of time to set about procuring the confirmatory letters. Hayley was always sanguine where his heart was concerned.

Meanwhile he sat back, and awaited tidings from Johnson concerning the reception of his missive. I daresay he even thought that Cowper himself might reply to it.

He had to wait some time. Johnson was a dilatory person; and Cowper had, by now, got into the habit of making only the most enigmatic utterances. It was not until July 12 that Johnson wrote to report that the consequences of the letter had been better than either he or Hayley could have believed possible. "He read it in silence, and He heard it in silence. To me who can read [his thoughts] ... these are precious Omens. ... I do from my heart believe, that if any of the letters could be brought about, so as to greet him in the same manner as the vision relates, it would not only *stagger* him, but might give such a turn to his distracted thoughts, as would make us *jump for joy*."

I think from this not altogether committal letter it may be safely inferred that, while Johnson was not wonderfully impressed by the scheme, he was a simple man, with a bias towards optimism, who, being deeply distressed by the state of his patient, was perfectly willing to try anything that was likely to ameliorate it. Anyhow, the next thing he did was to write to Lady Hesketh, enclosing Hayley's letter, and telling her all about it. This lady, consequently, on July 30, replied saying that she could hardly tell which most to admire, "the friendly Heart, which inspired the Idea, or the lively Genius, that executed it". But, she added, putting her hand with feminine promptitude on the weakest link of the whole scheme: "They [i.e. the promised letters] must have made Him *better*, or worse." And she herself wrote to Hayley, enquiring pertinently: "Allow me to ask, what *effect* can we reasonably expect in the *Impossibility* there seems, of getting any part of your Prophecy fulfilled?" If no letters arrive—Cowper will but sink lower in that "cruel Gulph of Despair".

How little, yet, did she know her Hayley! Of course if it was thought expedient that such letters should arrive, then they shall arrive! Hayley was already, with characteristic pertinacity, moving heaven and earth, though, for the moment, recollecting I daresay his heartrending experiences with The Pension, he was not aiming too high.

And now a brief digression must be made. As in the case of The Pension, the machinations which ensued were of an intolerable and vexatious cumbrousness, and took a deal of time. When I was describing the fight for The Pension, I strove to interweave these negotiations into the other events of Hayley's life that were occurring simultaneously. In this case I shall pursue a different method, and shall follow the affair of the Heavenly Vision to its end, believing as I do that the interest of the matter warrants such treatment. Then we shall have to retrace our steps.

2

Lady Hesketh, on the occasion of her letter to Hayley last quoted, had just been, she tells him with startling irrelevancy, driving about on Clifton Downs "in what they call a Jaunting Car—which most resembles two sofas put back to back"; and she confessed that she would like to own such a vehicle herself.

Hayley at once replied to her letter by inviting her to come and pay him a visit. He also told her that he believed Mr. Wilberforce and Lord Kenyon, the Chief Justice, had already written to Cowper letters of the character demanded. He did so because he had taken every step to ensure that they should. And, finally, not wishing that so eminent a personage as Lady Hesketh should consider him either a liar or a madman, he went with some little particularity into the actual mechanics of his Vision, and told her that, "with Eyes cover'd by his Hand, he had seem'd to behold something very like it"—in his imagination.

Now Mr. Wilberforce had been a comparatively simple quarry, and Hayley had approached him directly; but the capture of Lord Kenyon was a more delicate operation. Hayley had met him only once, at the celebrated breakfast at Lord Thurlow's, and so he decided the best way to tackle him was by means of the ever-obliging Rose, who was only too eager to do anything that might serve the interests of Cowper. Accordingly, the young advocate secured an interview with his Chief Justice, who at once bluntly expressed the view that a letter from him upon such a topic would be calculated to do more harm than good.

Rose reported to this effect, but Hayley persisted: "The Letter that I wish Lord Kenyon to write is but a single wheel in a large and complicat'd intellectual machine which I have invented."

Rose, who had not I think been fully let into the secret of this intellectual machine, at this forwarded Hayley's letter to the Chief Justice; and Hayley reported progress to Lady Hesketh, who now, for no very apparent reason, seemed to think that matters were going rather well. But still there were no reassuring tidings from Johnson, and so Hayley asked Lady Hesketh point blank whether she were not acquainted with "any prelate of a tender and feeling spirit" who might be willing to oblige?

In the interim, various enemies of Hayley's had been attempting to poison Lady Hesketh's mind against him, by describing him as an Infidel; and she consequently wrote again, on August 21, to

Johnson, to enquire "how the kindly intended Plot is faring", and expressing at the same time her fears that Hayley was still a stranger to "the great truths of Christianity".

Nevertheless, she did not scruple, almost at once, to take a somewhat mild leaf out of the Infidel's book, by herself writing to her cousin, to say, rather more reasonably, that she had seen him in a dream, quite recovered. And, furthermore, she attacked Johnson—for she was always formidable—for having written his last letter to her too hurriedly, and requested that he would, on the next occasion, reply "in your best manner, as they say of the great Painters".

Shortly after August 9, that is, nearly two months after the promulgation of Hayley's Vision, the first Letter arrived at Dereham: two pages from the obliging Wilberforce, who also kindly enclosed a copy of his latest book. On August 24, Johnson reported this phenomenon, not very hopefully one would say, since he related that Cowper, as he looked at the direction, observed: "The outside tells me, I shall be taken away by Force, and the inside will tell me the Time when." However, he did read the letter "with unusual attention", and made no comment.

On August 27, Hayley was writing again to Lady Hesketh, still on the subject of the unhelpful behaviour of Lord Kenyon. A Lord Chief Justice, he pointed out reasonably, cannot be hurried. "Patience will be necessary. It is not easy to prevail upon *several* persons in elevated stations."

Lady Hesketh responded by suggesting that she herself should approach the Bishop of London, and Hayley replied with enthusiasm: "Yes, my dear Lady! engage our good Lord of London by all means in the plot!" It may be observed that he himself (perhaps remembering his earlier abortive correspondence with the Archbishop of Canterbury) had not yet endeavoured to tackle any eminent ecclesiastics. On the other hand, Thurlow was on a visit to the Sussex coast. What did Lady Hesketh think of him as a possible correspondent?

Lady Hesketh thought less than nothing of Thurlow. "They must all be total strangers," she said. And she went on to speak of the lackadaisical behaviour of the wretched Johnson who, she feared, was about to fall into a state of Torpidity lasting for months together.

By September 25, Hayley had seen Lord Thurlow, who had agreed to tackle Lord Kenyon for him; and had, moreover, himself made a direct approach to the Bishop of Gloucester.

On September 30, Lady Hesketh wrote again. The Bishop of London had risen beyond all expectations. This was but natural, since Dr. Beilby Porteous, as a literary man himself, and author of a large mass of poetry, might well be expected to feel sympathy for a brother-poet in distress.

On September 28 his letter reached Norfolk, and Johnson read it aloud to Cowper. Two days later, with unaccustomed celerity, he was reporting the result. "Never," Cowper had said, "was such a Letter written, never was such a letter read to a Man so overwhelm'd with Despair, as I am—it was written in *Derision*—I know, and I am sure of it."

"Oh no! no! no! My Cousin!" wailed poor Johnson, "say not so, of the good Beilby, Bishop of London!"

"I should say so," Cowper replied, "of an Archangel, were it possible for an Archangel to send me such a Letter, in such Circumstances."

Well—one might have thought this a clear enough indication of the way in which the unhappy Cowper's mind was working; but not so, since the eupeptic Johnson resumed: "I suspect that he was gratified notwithstanding upon the whole—He heard me with the silence of Death; and, except at one passage in this amiable Bishop's letter, never opened his lips at all."

This circumstance was not, however, so remarkable as it seemed to Johnson, since Dr. Beilby Porteous's well-intentioned letter was one of quite excruciating dullness, consisting of five pages and a longish postscript. In the body of it he had quoted, as a pretty compliment to the poet, his own couplet:

> That he, who died below, and reigns above,
> Inspires the Song, and that his name is Love!

"That Love you must possess (he continued) surely in as full extent, as any human being ever did."

It was at this point that Cowper broke his silence. For one, damned as he was, it was too much—these references to heavenly love! His comment was frightful: "Not an atom of it!"

Johnson, after his cumbrous fashion, grew cunning. He asked Lady Hesketh to send back Hayley's original letter describing the Vision, so that he might lay it on Cowper's desk, together with the two others. He thought it best not to speak openly of it, lest a plot be suspected. And, indeed, after the time which had elapsed, it was as well that the patient's memory should be refreshed.

Meanwhile, Dr. Beadon, the Bishop of Gloucester, who was a distant connection of Hayley's which made it worse, had ungraciously refused to have anything to do with the business; and Lord Kenyon was still being unaccountably difficult. Therefore, in desperation, Hayley on October 9 wrote a particularly tactful letter to his old acquaintance the Bishop of Llandaff, saying that his son was contemplating the "aweful project of modelling his countenance", and, without definitely mentioning his Vision, suggesting that a letter of praise from his Grace of Llandaff would be certain to do Cowper a great deal of good, provided that Hayley's own name were not mentioned in it.

Then at last Thurlow wrote to say that he had sent a letter to Lord Kenyon;[2] and the Bishop of Llandaff replied promptly, reporting he had done as requested, to the tune of three good pages.

The arrival of this last missive at Dereham was involved in circumstances almost sensational. When it came, Johnson was engaged in reading aloud to the sufferer that same bishop's *Apology for Christianity*. "Dear me!" said he on opening it, "here is a letter from the Author himself!" "Our poor friend," he added, "was rather startled at the wonderful coincidence, but said nothing."

Then Lady Hesketh took a hand. She declared it was useless merely to lay the letters on Cowper's desk, as Johnson had proposed. He himself must bring the matter up in the course of conversation. This, Johnson replied reasonably enough, was not easy: "After silently suffering the Letters to have lain in the House so many weeks without smelling a rat, it was necessary that I should smell by degrees."

However, he did his best: "I therefore began by sniffing a little one day after dinner, as we were all using the finger-glasses—'Miss Perowne' [Miss Perowne was the lady who attended Cowper], said I, 'don't you recollect something about a Letter's coming to Mr. C. in the summer from Mr. Hayley, containing a wonderful vision, which He had lately had?'

" 'I certainly do remember it,' said she, 'and have often thought of it since.' 'Sam,' said I, 'take away the water-glasses, and set the wine on the table!'—This, as I intended, turned the Subject—but in the Evening, I started up in a great Hurry, just as we were sitting down to Tea—'By the bye I will go and look for Mr. H's. letter.' Mr. Cowper immediately called out, 'No pray don't!'

"Johnny: 'Because it strikes me, there is a kind of accomplishment of what is predicted.'

"Mr. C.: 'Well! be it so!—I know there is, and I knew there would be:—and I knew what it meant.'

... "I slipt out of the room and wrote down [his very words] on the back of a letter. It has not been mentioned since."

Really, after such a scene as this, one wonders that anyone had the heart to continue with the play! But they did.

Lady Hesketh made the next move. She said that if she had first been consulted, she would have amended the Vision by leaving out the Throne of God, as being "rather too *bold* and hazardous an Image". She did not mind the whole thing being a lie, but she did not—as a woman of strong evangelical principles—quite fancy the idea of the Throne of God being dragged into it.

Hayley was indignant. "Could I", he started magnificently, "could I have found expressions stronger and fitter for that effect, than the Throne of God, I should not have scrupled to employ them!"

Lady Hesketh wrote again to Johnson, suggesting that he had not sufficiently stressed the *remarkableness* of the coincidences. "As each letter arrives," she instructed him, "you should express (though not violently or in such a way as to alarm Him) your *surprise*."

Now, however, it was November, and the Heavenly Vision was getting on for five months old. Everyone was beginning to lose hope, perhaps to lose interest as well. Lord Kenyon had still not written; and ultimately, though not until the February of the following year, Lady Hesketh felt constrained to comment to Hayley: "Lord Kenyon has never written at all nor will you, I hope, dear sir, apply to Him any more."

It would not, one feels, have been much use. Hayley, as usual, put a brave face on things. He continued, for the rest of his life, to assert that the experiment had justified itself; that Cowper had resumed work on his Homer, which proved that the Letters must have done him good. And moreover, in justification, and I think true justification, of the boldness of his step, he now for the first time related the full story of that extraordinary conversation he had had with Cowper on the occasion of Mrs. Unwin's seizure. Cowper, he said, had believed his fantastic assertion then; and it was an equal chance that he would believe, and would profit by, his still more fantastic assertion of the Vision.

But he had forgotten that Cowper was now a very different man from what he had been in 1792. In November of this year he started to keep a diary, certain extracts from which Johnson later communicated to Hayley.[1] I think that, if Hayley had known of these extracts at the time, there would have been little more said about the Vision. For they are terrible.

On November 15, Cowper wrote that he had heard these words as the church clock struck nine: "You shall hear that Clock strike many months—in that room—upon that Bed."

In the night terrifying voices cried: "Bring Him out—Bring Him out!"

November 19. Another voice: "You are welcome to all sorts of misery."

Again: "Now Mr. Johnson is gone they will pelt you with stones."

"I saw a Man come to my Bedside last night, and tear my neckcloth off; and it will be so, I know it will."

December 2. Johnson writes: "He told me at breakfast He heard this:

> Sad-win! I leave you with Regret,
> But you must go to Gaol for debt.

'Do you know the meaning of Sad-win, my cousin?' (said I).—'Yes! I do; the Winner of Sorrow.' "

But it is better not to proceed.

3

This then is the story of a failure, though it is not one of which Hayley had any reason to be ashamed. Perhaps the whole thing was foolish and ill-conceived; but it was not ignoble, and it was not unimaginative. Indeed, the trouble was perhaps that Hayley's imagination had, as often before, temporarily got the better of him, and had caused him, for a time, to transport into those thinner and headier regions of the empyrean in which he customarily had his being, not only the solider and more matter-of-fact figures of the Revd. Johnson and Lady Hesketh, but also, for a few brief and eccentric moments, even those of such more gorgeous and imposing creatures as Mr. Wilberforce, and the Bishops of London and Llandaff.

One pendant remains to this narrative, which is that, at the New Year of 1799, Lady Hesketh unexpectedly sent Hayley a present consisting of a most elegant standish for ink, of cut glass and silver, in tribute to the part he had played in the affair.

His reply, thanking her for her gift in a letter[1] of January 5, 1799, may not unfittingly have the last word. "You will not think me (he wrote) either ungrateful or impolite if I say, that a single Letter such as I used to receive from his Hand and Heart would be more welcome to me than all the magnificent Gifts that Art could invent or Liberality bestow."

For all the neatness of the phrase, he never turned one that was more sincere.

CHAPTER XVI

THE END OF TOM (1797-1800)

I

AND NOW WE MUST return to Eartham towards the end of June, 1797, to pursue the declining fortunes of Tom, and the rapid rise of the Marine Turret.

For a while all went pretty well. The gallery of Petworth was open at all times to the young sculptor, and he spent many hours there with his clay, copying Lord Egremont's statues, and often sleeping away from home for two or three nights together.

Flaxman had written (July 12): "I do not believe he has been happy in London; his love of retirement and of his native place seem always foremost in his thoughts." Hayley talked this pronouncement over with the boy, and wrote in reply that Flaxman was mistaken. I do not think Flaxman was merely mistaken; I think he was growing worried by the increasing responsibility. However, on July 19, he wrote once more, giving Tom a remarkably good character. He was, he said, perfectly ready to have him back when he was better.

Tom could still ride and walk without difficulty, though he was developing a shocking stoop. With the onset of the warmer weather, the sea-bathing re-commenced. One shudders to think of the effect of this regimen on the afflicted boy. It would have been as well if he had had courage to take a leaf out of the despised Samuel Johnson's book, and assert sternly to his father: "Sir, I hate immersion." But of course he did nothing of the kind, and soon the party was joined by the poetical Mr. Clarke (later of Carlton House), and, on August 7, by Romney.

Romney was not at all well, either. Hayley's hands were full. Tom modelled a bust of Romney, and Romney began a couple of "historical pictures" in which Hayley was called upon to enact the role of Tobit, while his son figured as Tobias. And there was especially grand company one day this summer: as they returned one afternoon from their bathing expedition, they found awaiting them at Eartham the Duke of Richmond, the Duchess of Devonshire, and Lord Thurlow. Grandeur, beauty and genius, Romney said of the trio; all much in their decline. Thurlow was spending the summer at Bognor, and this visit was one of several. Tom must have been a courageous, as well as a talented, youth. He modelled a bust of Thurlow: "perhaps", Hayley said of it, "the most awful features that an artist so young ever aspired to represent".

It was a season calling for the greatest tact on his part. In an illuminating passage, Hayley compares the spleen of Romney with the spleen of Thurlow: "The first (he said) burst out in rapid and transient flashes, like the explosion of a rocket; the other rolled forth in a gloomy volume like an eruption of smoke, followed by fluent fire, from the labouring Vesuvio." Between the rocket and Vesuvio, he must have had a terrible time. The subject is one worthy of the brush of that great expert in firelight and volcanic effects, Joseph Wright.

Thurlow brought more than his awful features and his spleen, for he introduced Hayley to the Marchioness of Donegall and her sister; and the former came to Eartham to induct Tom into the mysteries of painting upon glass. In return, they were all invited to breakfast with her at Bognor, whence the party proceeded to a survey of the half-finished Turret. It was a windy day and the ladies were rather alarmed at the prospect of an ascent by ladder and scaffold. But Hayley rallied them in the name of their tutelary St. Patrick, and the "fair Hibernians" rose to the occasion. This was on September 30; and the following day Romney returned to town. His plight was a sad one. Hayley noted in his diary: "Paying my last attentions to my old infirm friend, as after cherishing him on this favourite spot for twenty-two years every autumn, I must now consign him to more opulent protectors." Romney, in his turn, wrote a touching valediction of Eartham: "I shall look back with a tender regard for the peaceful shades of Eartham, and almost sigh for some of its social walks, that probably I may never see more. Adieu dear Eartham! and its inhabitants, adieu."

Hayley, it appears, had at this time been driven by the shortage of ready cash to envisage the prospect of quitting Eartham in the following spring, when the new villa should be ready to receive him; and, in order to forward matters, Bunce was sent for to proceed with the design of a "Druidical seat" for the garden of this abode, and sundry other esoteric matters. He, too, was taken to bathe, though it was now October; and later the same month young Meyer turned up, and nearly destroyed himself by falling off his horse.

Hayley, partly because of his young friend's accident, and partly because he wished to talk over with Flaxman his son's future prospects, went back to London with Meyer, taking Tom as well. The question was whether the boy should be entered as a student at the Academy; and, when the matter was put to him, Tom asked his father whether he regarded his return to London as a point of duty, because, if so, "no danger should deter him" from pursuing it. Hayley replied that both his doctors and Flaxman were of that way of thinking; and that he was now deemed sufficiently recovered to endure the rigours of the London winter. The dauntless Thomas bowed to the inevitable. "Duty," Hayley wrote later, "made him send him back", though apprehension constrained him to keep him. It is a pity the voice of apprehension was not a little louder. Poor Tom knew well enough, I think, that he was not cured; but, with the doctors all agreeing he was, what could he do? He made the best of it, and, on the last day of October, resumed his residence with Flaxman.

2

The strange thing about Hayley's life at this time was that the fates appear to have decided he should enjoy no respite whatever. A mere couple of days after the despatch of the allegedly cured Thomas, the post brought a letter from Dr. Long, to say that Eliza had suddenly fallen gravely ill, and was being attended by himself and Dr. Latham. Tom was therefore instructed to call at once upon her, and render any services that lay in his power.

But Mrs. Hayley's illness was more than grave. Within six days, by November 8, she had passed beyond all that either Dr. Long or Dr. Latham could do for her; and Hayley was suddenly a widower.

On November 9 he wrote to Tom: "I wish you to remain under the tender consolation of your excellent master. I shall most probably not move from this spot, till all decent rites are paid to the deceased. It is my intention to honour her remains by placing them next her angelic friend, my own excellent mother, in the vault here, and by a monument to her memory, by our dear Flaxman."

His son replied with due sympathy, and his father wrote again: "Let me now thank you once more, for all your kind and excellent advice to me, particularly seasonable and welcome to the troubled state of my spirits. I say *troubled state*, because nature on these awful occasions exacts a proper tribute from every feeling bosom; and I could not but be deeply affected by the decease of our poor Eliza, though I consider it as a merciful decree of a most gracious and compassionate Providence."

Hayley did not go to London to bring back the body of his wife. Instead he repaired to his library and composed a brief discourse for delivery at her funeral. Moreover, he was so thoughtful as to make a copy of it, which he despatched to Tom, so that he might ("if it proves convenient") recite it out loud to the Flaxmans at the very time it was being given at Eartham Church.

The cortège arrived, and the poor pitiable Eliza was consigned to her grave on Friday, November 17. "The mournful business," Hayley wrote with some satisfaction two days later, "was conducted with all the decorum that could be desired. Our little church was filled, and the sermon was universally felt and approved."

At length, on November 29, Hayley nerved himself to travel to London, to deal with the disposal of her effects. He stayed during this visit, rather singularly, in the lodgings of the departed, at Millman Place, No. 2 Bedford Row, because he deemed this the most convenient for the examination of her papers, and because, also, he felt "a melancholy pleasure" in contemplating the scene she had inhabited and in being thus enabled to hear many particulars concerning her last hours.

It was, he says, "a season of tender remembrance and awful sensibility". He found Tom waiting for him in his late wife's lodgings, and together they passed an evening of "pensive tenderness". To his diary at the end of this month he confided the following extraordinary reflections: "In closing the month, I feel impressed with awful gratitude to Heaven for the merciful manner of conducting all incidents leading to the unexpected fate of my long suffering Eliza, whose decease I ought to regard as a blessing to herself, and a gracious decree of providential compassion towards the evening of my troubled life. May Heaven direct me to feel, and improve as I ought, the kindness of this affecting dispensation!"

The astounding thing is that Hayley himself should have copied out this passage from his private diary, when he came to prepare his *Memoirs*. One can only conclude that he admired it for its style. That was all very well, of course; but, after all, the long suffering Eliza was only forty-seven.

Still, it is useless to blame Hayley. For years now she had been an unmitigated drain upon his purse, in consideration for which he had received no advantages whatsoever. It is true that she had during the last twelve months been much more economical, but even so, with Tom's illness looming ahead and the Marine Turret to be paid for, he found himself quite unable to regard her death as anything other than an unqualified financial blessing. Most men in his situation would have felt the same, but it took Hayley to say so, and to say so in print. There is another thing, however, which I find it much more difficult to forgive: and that is that Eliza did not, after all, receive the monument from the hands of Flaxman which had been promised her. But I think there was a reason for this, to which, though it is not a very creditable one, we shall cöme in a moment.

Meanwhile, as he ran through her neatly arranged papers, his reflections must have been sombre. Her dispositions do not strike us as being those of a lady afflicted with mental derangement: "She had discharged her bills, she had arranged her infinite collection of manuscripts in the nicest order, and particularly the long series of letters that she had received from the poet." Moreover, "of the noble emotions of charity and devotion, she was duly susceptible. Many poor objects might attest the former; and the latter was very affectingly, though not ostentatiously, displayed in her mode of repeating the Lord's Prayer occasionally, during the course of her last illness".

But one further service remained for her husband, and that was what he performed, as a matter of course, for all his friends and acquaintances: to compose her epitaph. This is what he wrote:

> If lovely features and a lofty mind—
> Tender as charity, as bounty kind—
> If these were blessings that to life could give
> A lot which makes it happiness to live,
> Thou, Eliza, hadst been blest on earth:
> But Seraphs in compassion wept thy birth,
> For thy deep nervous woes of wondrous weight,
> Love could not heal, nor sympathy relate;
> Yet pity trusts, with hallowed truth serene,
> Thy God o'erpays them in a purer scene.
> Peace to thy ashes, to thy memory love,
> And to thy spirit in the realms above
> All that from blameless sufferings below
> Mortality can hope, or angels know.

And that, I think, is where things went wrong in the matter of the monument. I fancy that Mrs. Hayley's friends took strong exception to the idea that the bones of Eliza should lie for ever beneath a slab whose sentiments were, to say the least, a trifle patronizing. And so Hayley, his poetic pride aflame, said: "Very well: no epitaph, no monument!" And there was no monument. Considering the profound interest he took in such matters, I think it was about the shabbiest action of his life; especially as now, through Eliza's providential departure, his affairs were in better shape than they had been for years.

Hayley has been called a hypocrite, and indeed, at times, one feels not without justification. But, in this matter of the death of Eliza, one would really have preferred a shade more of hypocrisy than he was able to provide. The fact is, his relief was so great that he was quite unable to conceal it.

3

Alone now at Eartham, contemplating the few memorials of Eliza that he had brought back with him, which included the portrait of Tom as Robin Goodfellow, Hayley had ample leisure to despatch voluminous letters to his son who was enduring the murks and glooms of the London winter. He discoursed to him on Winckelman, and Metastasio, and advised him on no account to miss the "procession to St. Paul's", which I think must have been in celebration of Duncan's recent victory at Camperdown. The winter was a severe one; he could no longer ride to Petworth, or visit Sargent at Lavington; and so he proceeded, without much heart, with his *Essay on Sculpture*. Soon the news from London was disquieting: Tom was ill again. He had rheumatic pains, and Long was dosing him with that inevitable and perilous eighteenth century specific—James's powders.

Meanwhile the winds blew frantically. Windmills were carried away bodily, but the Turret withstood all shocks, greatly to the delight of Palladio, who was once more at Felpham, in his professional capacity. Hayley had bought more land (the first-fruits, no doubt, of Eliza's decease) from that interesting knight, Sir Richard Hotham, the father and founder of Bognor. And, to crown all, somebody had suggested at last that it was high time a biography of Hayley were written. Since this present book is the very first of that species, it will be, I think, salutary for the writer of it to transcribe Hayley's opinion of biographers in general. "If (said he) these humble writers can make a dinner out of it in these hard times, much good may it do them! I have no appetite for their praise, and no dread of their censure."

And now the first violets of the year were back, and were despatched to Tom; and this time they were followed shortly by Hayley himself. He arrived on February 10, and saw at once that his son was extremely ill. The doctors, however, said he was perfectly well. Nothing at all the matter with him!

But Hayley at last had had enough of medical optimism. He packed the boy into a chaise, and, on February 18, brought him back to Sussex, where he at once called in Dr. Guy. Guy applied a blister, and Hayley composed, before daybreak, a sonnet praying for Tom's restoration. Both were equally ineffective, and now, too late, Hayley became really alarmed. On March 5 he asked Guy to conduct yet another examination, and, though that worthy doctor could still find nothing amiss, Hayley himself perceived and pointed out to him "a small obliquity" in the spine of the patient. Books were procured, consultations ensued, and at length Hayley (according to his own account) persuaded the doctor that what his son was suffering from was "that very formidable malady", a curvature of the spine.

During these performances, the patient was, not unnaturally, depressed. His father read him comedies to cheer him up, and eventually moved him into the old cottage at Felpham, since the Turret was not yet ready for his occupation. A curious regime was now in being. Eartham remained unlet, and so Hayley was obliged to remain in residence, while Tom, for his health's sake, was at Felpham. This necessitated endless ridings to and fro on the part of Hayley (a jaunt of some nine or ten miles each way), and almost as much correspondence as when Tom was in London.

In May, Mrs. Meyer and her daughter came on a visit, and, as his son seemed better, Hayley decided to go back to London with them. There he called on Romney, whom he found in a very sad way, with his faculties "beginning to desert him". The fact is that Romney was now almost at the end of his tether. Already in the previous year, Mr. Cocking, a writing-master of Kendal, had been despatched from the North to superintend his declining health; and now the charge was more than he could cope with. At long last, after many years of separation, the painter was constrained to travel north, to confide himself to the care of his neglected, but still apparently affectionate, wife.

Hayley returned to Eartham, together with his architect, on May 27. He rode out to Felpham next day, and thought he found the patient improved. Early that June all were bathing together, and after these exercises Hayley treated his son to a preliminary reading of his *Essay on Sculpture*, as far as it had gone.

On July 20, all the Meyers arrived; and the next day, from the mount at Eartham, signals were exhibited in accordance with a pre-arranged plan, to apprise the invalid of their coming. A few days later, on July 25, part at least of the Turret was ready for his occupation, and he moved in to the uncompleted and no doubt damp and cheerless new building. Eartham was full. As well as the Meyers, Captain Godfrey was there, and so was Rose; to say nothing of a Miss Matilda Greene, who drew all their portraits with a blacklead pencil. There was endless to-ing and fro-ing between Eartham and the sea, and the excitement was none too good for the sick boy at Felpham. At length, perceiving him less well, Godfrey thoughtfully suggested he should take him up to town in his one-horse chair, so that he might again consult his London doctors.

On August 27 they set out, and arrived without mishap; and Tom went to see Flaxman, and Romney, too, who had come back again, unexpectedly, from his northern sojourn. Tom wrote at once, announcing his safe arrival, and Hayley replied, rather like Fanny Squeers and Uriah Heep in unison: "On the receipt of your last, I burst into showers of tears, and exclaimed to myself 'I hope I am grateful enough to Heaven for this blessed account.' "

Then Tom visited his doctors, who were very nice about their mistake, and, now that his real malady had been pointed out to them, genially agreed that it was just as suggested.

By this time, Hayley, hearing that Romney's journey had not benefited him, had written to remind him how often the air of Sussex had set him up, and begging him to try it once again. Romney agreed to do so, and lodgings were found for him in Felpham. Thence the two old friends set out on September 7 for

Brighton, to meet Tom and Godfrey on their way home. They arrived in time for dinner, but the travellers were nowhere to be seen, and did not turn up that night. Hayley was frantic with anxiety, and Romney, I fear, a little fractious. It was not until the next evening that the one-horse chair arrived; and then Tom was driving it, and seemed fairly well, though he had now "lost the use of his legs".

However, they passed "a social evening", and next day returned to Eartham; Tom, who still happily possessed the use of his arms, driving the chair which Godfrey (who did not make one of the party) had kindly presented to him. He was the bearer of a letter from Dr. Long, which did little to allay Hayley's fears. He wrote that their wrong diagnosis of the boy's illness "served to shew the extreme uncertainty of medical knowledge". Nevertheless, Hayley remained sanguine. Though his son could no longer walk, he still dipped him in the ocean, supporting him in his arms.

On September 11 the dejected Romney returned to London, and Hayley began to contemplate the prospect of at last completing his *Essay on Sculpture* in the privacy of his new library, even though, as he said, "it required some fortitude to make any studious exertions in his present state of anxiety". All the while Tom's eighteenth birthday was drawing nearer. Hayley resolved to celebrate it by writing an *Invocation to Patience*, which he forthwith did, reciting it for the first time to the little party of friends that had assembled at the Turret in honour of the occasion.

That the Patience thus invoked was required to cope with the afflictions of the father as well as those of the son, the following excerpt will indicate:

> Descend, angelic Patience, from above,
> Bring me supplies of vigilance and love,
> That in this failure of well-grounded hope,
> With strong calamity I still may cope;
> And, unsubdued by anguish of the heart,
> Act with alacrity a father's part.

That Hayley was proud of this production is shown by the fact that he sent a copy of it to Huskisson, with whom his relations had been cool for some time. Huskisson, on this occasion, behaved with his usual insensibility. He burnt the *Invocation*, by accident, and then hadn't the sense to keep the calamity to himself, but wrote admitting what he had done, and asking for another copy.[1]

Nor was this the only poetical garnish to the festivities. On August 1, Nelson had annihilated the French fleet as it lay in the bay of Aboukir, and Hayley heard the news with tears of delight. He rode over to Felpham, and there, on October 4, after a hasty dinner, composed a "rapid song" on the occasion, which the Meyer ladies adapted to a popular air of the moment and sang, in unison, after the *Invocation* had been delivered.

> Enough of the solemn! of brows darkly bent

(it began); and it proceeded:

> Of our dear cheerful cripple, we joy in the birth,
> That justly may claim celebration;
> When, though cripples, our seamen, uncrippled in worth,
> Have revived the sick fame of the Nation.
>
> The brave little Nelson, of one arm bereft,
> Teaches France to confess from his fire,
> That a Briton, though maim'd, if his heart is but left,
> Is superior to others entire.
>
> To Nature, to Fortune, impute not a fault,
> For a cripple, while Glory will court him,
> Still Genius and Love on their wings may exalt
> Him, who had not a leg to support him.

4

At this point a brief digression seems called for. It will be remembered that, upon a celebrated occasion at Todgers's, the gentleman of a literary turn in that establishment serenaded Mr. Pecksniff in a song of his own composition (and of a classical nature), which invoked the oracle of Apollo, and went on to show that the Miss Pecksniffs were nearly related to Rule Britannia: of which the final stanza ran:

> All hail to the vessel of Pecksniff the sire!
> And favouring breezes to fan;
> While Tritons flock round it, and proudly admire
> The architect, artist, and man!

The present writer has often wondered just what school of poetry it was that influenced the Bard of Todgers's. The foregoing stanzas in celebration of the Battle of the Nile provide, I think, our answer. The Muse of Todgers's was Hayleian in origin. Were it not for chronological difficulties, it would be agreeable to surmise that one of Mr. Bunce's descendants had enjoyed his early training at the hands of Mr. Pecksniff, and that, in some such manner, the tradition had been handed on. . . . But, alas! we do not know if Mr. Bunce possessed descendants.

5

Tom was now hopelessly deformed, but, we are told, he remained "suave". His unhappy father strove endlessly to amuse him. Every morning he awoke at four, and spent the hours before rising in inditing, upon his pillow, brief compositions relating to the invalid's sufferings and virtues. He diversified these exercises by planting in the Turret garden a mulberry tree (which is still there), and by translating some Greek verses which he had found, that not only proved his son's condition was known to the ancients, but also that it was, by the ancients at any rate, curable. This, which is a not unpleasing specimen of his better manner, ran as follows:

> Benumb'd from loins to feet, mere senseless clay,
> Long robb'd of all my former strength I lay,
> A neighbour to the grave, 'twixt life and death,
> A very corpse in all things but in breath.
> Philip the sage, whose statue you behold,
> Restored me, and dispell'd the deadly cold,
> Now Antonine again I tread the ground,
> Walk on my feet, and feel completely sound.

Unfortunately, however, he was unable to find the modern counterpart of Philip the sage.

And now a curious, and, I am afraid, slightly reprehensible passage has to be related. Though Tom was desperately ill, at the beginning of November his father left him once more, while he betook himself on a long excursion to London. The reason he gave for this was his passionate desire to find some means by which his son's recovery might be expedited; and I daresay that this was partly the truth. Partly true, also, is it that Romney was now back in town and in desperate plight, roaming restlessly the lofty apartments of his new mansion at Hampstead, quite unable to work, and all alone save for his young disciple, Isaac Pocock. Hayley did everything he could to animate his spirits. He spurred him on to fresh exertions in his art, he prevailed upon Pocock to read to him, he even took him to see Dr. Milman's picture of St. Agatha by Guido, and a lovely saint by Correggio.

Yet, despite these open benevolences, one cannot help it if the suspicion crosses one's mind that there was yet another magnet which, this time, drew Hayley to London, and kept him there until the very morning of Christmas Day. This magnet, I greatly suspect, was the afflicted Mrs. Lushington, whose story affords a standing example of Hayley's faculty for exercising his beneficence in such a fashion that he was also able to extract from it the maximum degree of adventitious pleasure for himself.

To explain Mrs. Lushington, it will be necessary to proceed a little way backwards in time. It was on July 20, 1798, that Flaxman had first written to Hayley about her:

Mrs. Lushington (of Devonshire-street) has employed me to make a monument, upon the sole recommendation of seeing Collins's in Chichester Cathedral. . . . Mrs. Lushington is a lady under circumstances of extraordinary calamity, and has lost her eldest daughter, her nearest, dearest, and most intimate friend, at the age of twenty-five. She was particularly struck with the verses upon Collins's monument. She is an enthusiastic admirer of your muse, and always procured your works as soon as published. . . .

And, in short, would Hayley oblige with an epitaph?

Hayley was only too willing to oblige. On August 10, he galloped over in the evening to the Turret, to sleep there for the first time, for the purpose of composing, in solitude, the desired inscription. He wished, he said, this work of compassion to be his first attempt in the new mansion; and at the dawning of the day he composed it on his pillow, and read it over breakfast to Tom. The intention of his verses was to soothe the wounded spirit of a disconsolate mother; but what he wrote seems to have had effects even more striking.

He sent the lines to Flaxman, and accompanied them with various enquiries the nature of which may be gauged from the sculptor's reply of August 14:[2]

> At first I thought she was a widow, but from some things which the Parish Clerk of Lewisham Church [for which the monument was intended] . . . said, I now believe her husband is living and that they are seperated [sic]; if her situation is such, cut off from Connubial Happiness . . . bowed down almost to the Grave. . . .

and so forth. Moreover, he added in a postscript: "If chance makes me acquainted with any other particulars of the Lady's history, I will let you know."

In the meantime, Flaxman was busily engaged on the relievo to the memory of Mary Lushington, which may still be seen in the church at Lewisham, together with Hayley's lines beginning:

> Blame not, ye calm observers of distress,
> A mother sorrowing to a fond excess!

while Mrs. Lushington, for her part, was enchanted by the accommodating fashion in which the poet had obliged her. She wrote, I am convinced, to thank him; she even offered him a rich diamond ring in payment, which of course gave Hayley a wonderful opportunity of showing his disinterested spirit. He refused the ring, but said that he would, instead, be very happy to receive a marble bust of the deceased young lady from the chisel of Flaxman. The sensibility of this announcement so delighted Mrs. Lushington that she at once commissioned the bust, for which a clay model was made, though, for some inscrutable reason, Hayley never received the finished article. When he arrived in London, on November 3, his very first business, he tells us, was to make his way to Flaxman's to inspect Miss Lushington's memorial; his next, doubtless, was to visit Devonshire Street to inspect Miss Lushington's mother.

No further reference to the matter can then be found until

November 24, when he wrote, a trifle guardedly, to Tom: "Flaxman and I are more and more pleased with Mrs. Lushington."

It was not until the 29th that the magnificent occasion of his rejection of the diamond was reported to the same correspondent. Mrs. Lushington still had two daughters living, and with them, also, were he and Flaxman more and more pleased. Both possessed great talents with the pencil, even the youngest who, though only eleven, was adept at "historical sketches".

By December 1, he was escorting the whole family to Flaxman's studio, and to Romney's, where they found the unfortunate painter much oppressed by the rainy weather. During this jaunt, Flaxman had been left to get on with his modelling at Mrs. Lushington's house, and (Hayley proceeds): "Mrs. Lushington, who gains more and more esteem from Flaxman and me [still the two of them, it will be observed] . . . is so partial to us, as to consider it a blessing to have formed that attachment to us in her affliction, which appears to be her favourite source of comfort."

A week later he was still protesting: "I went early this morning to . . . Lady Donegall, whom I was under the necessity of neglecting so much, in my incessant attendance on the two deeply afflicted mourners in Devonshire-street. [Who, incidentally, had now been afflicted for nearly two years.] In truth a charitable attention to these very interesting objects in extreme mental distress, has engrossed all the time of the Sculptor and the Hermit." Indeed, Flaxman's solicitude, so Hayley alleged, had been so extreme that there had been serious apprehensions one evening that his health was beginning to "suffer from the influence of extreme compassion". Day after day Mrs. Lushington had deferred her return to Bath; but at last she made up her mind, and on December 8 set out with her daughters. The day before her departure, Hayley visited her to say farewell, but even then, when all adieux were made, he could not refrain from despatching to her, by the evening penny-post, a billet containing a poetical benediction:

> Afflicted parent, whom my prayers would bless,
> Good angels make thy travels safe and calm!
> And teach thy lighten'd spirit to confess
> For sorrow friendship is a sacred balm!

As on the following day he was informing Tom that Mrs. Lushington had received his benediction "about eight in the evening", it is evident that she acknowledged it there and then. "I should have been ungrateful," he added, not very convincingly, "had I failed in attention to her, as her kind solicitude for you has been infinite."

And there, I fear, the Lushington episode comes to an inconclusive end. The monument remains in Lewisham Church; and the bereaved mother vanished to Bath, still drowned in her sorrows; and perhaps in the end she went back to Mr. Lushington. It was a pity. One feels that her sensibility, in conjunction with that of Hayley, might have resulted in an alliance quite out of the ordinary.

6

But Paulina Lushington has distracted us, as she did Hayley, from his other activities. Again he visited Drs. Long and Latham, who were as sanguine as ever about their patient; he walked to Hampstead to see Stothard; and he conferred with Bunce upon a "curious mechanical chair" for Tom, which the architect had kindly caused a "worthy old German" to construct.

Tom, for his part, though it was now November, wrote back with great cheerfulness:

We have had excessively high tides this week. I go down every day at high water, to admire the grand yet desolate spectacle, and see the waves beat over the cliff. The whole shore in mist from the spray and foam. Men and boys running backward and forward on the beach, to try what they can pick up. The wind blowing their hats off, and the sudden dash of a wave wetting them from top to toe. The breakers torn up and floating near the shore, and lastly, the mighty roar of the wind and sea, make altogether a scene that amuses me highly.

Hayley was delighted with this letter. He felt sure that anyone who could take such pleasure in "marine scenery", and could describe it in so robust a manner, was well on the road to recovery.

Soon the mechanical chair arrived at Felpham. It was, apparently, driven by "springs worked by the arms", and it highly pleased the invalid, except that he found it was immobilised by the slightest rise in the ground, which caused the footboard to wedge itself against the earth. Very sensibly he suggested that this might be rectified by having the board hinged and mounted on wheels, "which would permit it to rise and fall according to the ascent or descent . . . it meets with".

A further spate of interesting information reached Felpham: Hayley had been reading the intercepted letters from Bonaparte to his favourite brother, which demonstrated that "even enterprising warriors may be wretched from domestic troubles"; he had received a new novel from Mme. Genlis; moreover, he had formed the striking theory that the root cause of Tom's illness was the escape of waste saline particles from his bones, *via* the urine. Nothing could be simpler than the remedy: "You would oblige me by drinking a little sea-water daily."

Tom replied amiably, poor fellow. His legs, he said, were excessively painful, and prevented him sleeping. "They generally move like two buckets in a well, one up, the other down, which gives me more pain than when they go together." Nevertheless, he begged his father to send him forthwith a few volumes of the new Encyclopaedia.

Hayley did more. He ordered the entire Encyclopaedia to be despatched at once; and sent off as well two sonnets of his own: one on *Devotion*, the other on *Tranquillity*. Nothing but business, he said, now remained to keep him in town; and, as the Encyclopaedia was mysteriously slow in arriving, he despatched, to fill the gap, a copy of the *Meditations of Marcus Aurelius* which he rightly said, "I think you will read with peculiar interest and pleasure, in your present situation".

Tom replied on December 14, in a most touching, most sensible letter. His fingers were so cold he could scarcely hold a pen, nevertheless he thanked his father warmly for the researches he had been making into his case: "The opinions of the *faculty*," he observed, without bitterness, "are so different, and in some instances so diametrically opposite, that I have very little faith in their prescriptions. . . . For the pain in my legs, I should have suffered all my past sufferings to very little purpose, if I could not bear a little convulsive pain in them patiently."

Still Hayley dawdled. On December 18, he reported that he had just been presented with a piece of mechanism "to the value of twenty guineas", that was guaranteed to take the weight off Tom's tortured spine. And, "I have conceived an idea", he added, "that to pass, now and then, three or four days in bed, would be beneficial to you, in the main." With this original conception, Dr. Long, to whom it had been submitted, had concurred.

The Encyclopaedia arrived at last; a box of busts for the library was despatched; and Hayley was still writing eloquently of his hope to reach "his beloved cripple in his Marine Turret by the light of the friendly moon". Yet, unaccountably, he failed to tear himself away. At last, on Christmas Day, after a difficult and snowy journey, he reached Felpham between nine and ten in the evening. The letter announcing his coming had miscarried. Bright moonlight shone on the snow, but the house was dark and shuttered. Everyone had gone to bed. Hayley, however, with his customary vigour, soon rectified all that, and his poor son was shortly expressing, from his bed, sentiments of the utmost gratification at the return of his parent.

It was, moreover, a genuine gratification. Whatever we may think of Hayley's protracted gallivantings in London, it never seems to have occurred to Tom that his father's long absence had been a trifle callous. On that same solitary Christmas Day of 1798, while Hayley had been pursuing his homeward way, Tom had written a seasonable letter to Mrs. Meyer. "My legs," he said, "still refuse to obey me." His spasms, "which the learned say are certain symptoms of returning strength", were giving him great pain; and he prayed Heaven that the learned were right, "for to remain long so inactive, so helpless to myself, and so useless, and even burdensome to others, would be to me, who have been used to active life, a great calamity. But the will of God be done!"

It is a letter sufficiently poignant. He was only eighteen.

7

Hayley, however, was able to stay but one day with his son. He had caught a severe cold on his journey home, and on December 27 he returned to Eartham. Thence he wrote to say that he would be with Tom again on New Year's Eve, as he had asked Dr. Guy to come over for a consultation on the morning following. He went on to tell an odd tale: none other than that he had received a letter from his old Irish friend, Eyles Irwin, which informed him that the Emperor of Russia had despatched his Imperial portrait to Mr. Irwin, so that he might forward it to Hayley as a thank-offering for the pleasure the Emperor (the mad one, Paul) had received from his publications. Mr. Irwin did not say why the Emperor had sent the portrait to him, rather than to Hayley; and I conclude, and so, somewhat reluctantly I think, did Hayley, that the whole thing was merely a leg-pull in rather questionable taste. Hayley did not put it quite that way. He said: "It must be a mere vision of my gentle enthusiastic Irish friend, who is too much of a man of serious integrity and benevolence to invent such a story, as a source of laughable illusion."

On New Year's Day, 1799, Hayley gave his son two presents: the one, an ingenious contrivance made by Flaxman's brother and consisting of a complete suit of miniature armour, six inches high, and made with an infinitude of little joints, so that it could with ease be thrown into a variety of attitudes; the other, a small pocket instrument containing a number of colours, and popularly known as the Claude Lorraine glasses. That same morning, Guy arrived, and a medical conference ensued, at which Hayley inparted to his adviser all the latest information which he had picked up in London. Tom had had a wretched time in the raw and partly-finished Turret during his father's absence, and he now did what was highly unusual for him: he made a request. He asked to be allowed to go back to Eartham. Hayley agreed; and on January 3 he was transferred to his old home. Once there, his father, in order to amuse him, read to him all over again his poem on Sculpture. Tom, ill as he was, took, the author remarks, a "lively and affectionate interest" in the work, and begged that it might speedily be completed. Hayley promised he would persevere, though it was far from easy in the circumstances; but, by the end of January, he managed, in the solitude of the Turret, to finish the Third Epistle.

On February 7, poor Romney, still crushed by melancholy, arrived for his last visit to Eartham. His young disciple, Pocock, was with him, and Hayley, to encourage the youth, addressed a sonnet to him which commenced in good round style:

> Ingenious son of an ingenious sire!
> Pocock! . . .

It was, one fears, a sad gathering. Tom, inspired by Romney's presence, started trying to draw once more; and Romney drew also, a new portrait of Hayley, one of Pocock and Tom, and a self-portrait, in spectacles. "It was," Hayley says, "a singularly affecting sight. . . . While Romney with an infirm hand, was forming a new resemblance of himself . . . the interesting cripple contrived in his uneasy recumbent posture to execute his sketch of the dying Demosthenes."

We are to meet the dying Demosthenes hereafter, when we come to the consideration of William Blake; and the same thing applies to Tom's next design, of a scene between Macbeth and the weird sisters, for which he made use of the miniature suit of armour that his father had given him.

Romney, having completed his self-portrait, went back to London, declaring himself wonderfully revived. His revivification did not, however, last long, and soon he was again engulfed in despair.

All that spring, Tom was painting, copying various portraits of his father's friends, and executing a few original transparent drawings for the glass front-door of the Turret. He seemed neither better nor worse. As each portrait was completed, Hayley hung it up, and, as they were almost all of persons who were dead, he thoughtfully, at the same time, copied out the epitaph he had written for the subject, on the back of the picture.

The gloomy scene was brightened a little at the beginning of April by the re-appearance of Rose. He had been defending a clergyman at the Chichester Assizes, who had been maliciously charged with a "supposedly unchaste attempt" upon the virtue of one whom Hayley, somewhat oddly, calls "an ordinary married woman". Rose had scored a triumph; his client had been acquitted; and Hayley had listened in transports of delight to the oratory of his friend. It was, though no one knew it then, a precursor to another trial, and another acquittal, the results of which would not, for poor Rose, be so happy.

About the same time, Hayley, perceiving the extent of his dying son's attachment to Eartham, did an uncommonly handsome thing. He transferred the whole estate and house to him, on the understanding that Tom should live in but a small part of it, and let off the rest; thus securing to himself both society and an income. His solitary autumn in the Turret had given Tom a distaste for the new building; and, while Hayley was himself determined to proceed with his plan of living there, it does him credit, I think, that he should have respected his son's evident disinclination to do so. It was not, however, in Hayley to effect such a transfer as this in a simple, business-like fashion. The affair had also to have its poetical accompaniments; and Tom found himself the master of Eartham with a couple of sonnets thrown in to make weight. The first of these said:

> In these sweet scenes, salubriously fair,
> From early solitude I sought repose,
> To soothe the pangs of deep domestic woes,
> Which only heaven could teach the soul to bear . . .

From the other, one line alone is needed to give the full flavour. It describes poor Tom as one who

> To coy Hygeia breathes a gentle vow.

8

At the end of April, more restless than ever, Hayley was off to London again; once more ostensibly, and perhaps in fact, in pursuit of measures to promote the welfare of his son. For now the last stage of Tom's martyrdom had begun. He was "a mere helpless heap of emaciated and distorted bones"; he could not use his legs at all, and his arms only with the greatest difficulty. Yet, for all this, he remained as cheerful as ever, and uttered no word of complaint. The spectacle, to one so, as it were, professionally tender-hearted as Hayley, must have been harrowing beyond expression.

By April 25, he was once more seizing a pen at Dr. Warner's, to tell the invalid how he had been examining a "good old crippled woman in the hospital", who, though stricken with his malady, was now on the road to recovery. He had shown Flaxman Tom's latest sketches; and, on April 28, he again visited Romney, and found him in a pitiful condition.

Tom, thoughtful as ever, replied by suggesting that his father should send some of his furniture back from Flaxman's, so that the downstairs breakfast-parlour at Eartham might be fitted up as a sick-room, to save the trouble of his being constantly carried up and down stairs. And, at the same time, he enquired whether Hayley had yet found any tenant for Eartham.

This question of a tenant was now most gravely exercising Hayley's mind; though he does not say much about it. With the completion of the Turret it had become essential to let Eartham, and tenants were less easy to procure than he had hoped. But his search for them was deflected by his social rounds. He had met Joseph Warton, Dr. Long, and the painter, Henry Howard. Most pleasing of all, he had encountered a young lady "artless and pretty", who introduced herself to him by saying: "I have loved you ever since I was ten years old, for then the *Triumphs of Temper* was first put in my hand, and I have ever since longed to call the author my friend." This said, she rushed immediately into the poet's arms "with all the tender innocence and gaiety of an affectionate child", and the poet—can you blame him?—shed tears of pleasure.

But Tom was now too ill for these delightful experiences to be long protracted, and, on May 3, Hayley was home again; and at once decided, with invincible optimism, that the invalid was looking better. Between them a scheme was evolved that the Meyers should rent Eartham, but it soon fell through, and off again to London dashed Hayley, where he sought out Rose, who was comforting and said he was sure to find a tenant before long. The next morning he called on the Flaxmans, and found with them a Mr. Hawkins, who had lately returned from an antiquarian survey of Greece. Hawkins begged him to call the following day to inspect the treasures of sculpture he had brought back from that country; and, in return, Hayley carried him off to look at the famous memorial to Mrs. Lushington's daughter.

Tom wrote: He was suffering from a new swelling in his shoulder, which Guy thought might prove "a material benefit". "Do as you please," the poor fellow said, "about mentioning it to the London gentlemen; I do not by any means wish it." He had had, I think, about enough of doctors by now.

But Hayley mentioned it, nevertheless: to Dr. Long, who was confident that Nature was making "an important effort" in the patient's favour. Then, with a flying visit to Fuseli's Milton Gallery, he hurried back home, for now, despite the fatuous optimism of the doctors, the truth had at last to be faced that Tom was growing weaker. His father did all he could to mitigate his plight. He composed a quantity of sonnets and prayers, which, with an impartial hand, winged to Heaven petitions both for "his sunk darling" and "the tortured sire".

As the boy's sickness deepened, he began to experience a great desire to see his old master once more. But Flaxman was too busy to get away. On July 5, he despatched his excuses in a letter highly characteristic of his stiff though humorous disposition:

DEAR THOMAS, You know what an excellent epistolary correspondent I am, and how regular, this letter is a proof; for, in answer to three kind letters from the bard, I address this to you, so that you see my practice is as uniform as the excuse for what I do. Sculpture! Sculpture! with its studies, and attendant business, leave me little time for any thing beside; so little, my dear Thomas, that it would not be possible for me to visit you in this part of the year, without disadvantageous consequences of a most serious nature. . . . You know the consequence of leaving a large clay figure nearly finished, for several days, in the heat of the summer, together with other models and works which must be done, because honesty and professional reputation are at stake. . . .

Still, he had been gratified beyond expectation by the drawings which Hayley had brought to town to show him. Especially had he been diverted by a comic sketch Tom had made of Romney fencing in his spectacles.

But the mention of Romney brings in again the note of sadness. Now, for the first time in three-and-twenty years, there was to be no summer visit of the painter to Eartham. Gloomy and distracted, he had again returned to Kendal, and to the care of his long-suffering wife. A final glimpse of him comes in Flaxman's letter, last quoted: "I and my father dined with Romney, last Sunday . . . [and were] grieved to see so noble a collection in a state so confused, so mangled, and prepared, I fear, for worse, and not better."

It had been Hayley's oldest and closest friendship; and now it was all over. Romney lingered on for three years in the North, in great distress of mind and body, and died at last on November 15, 1802.

That ended one chapter, and that of Cowper also was drawing to its close. The mad and wonderful idea seems at some time to have entered Hayley's head that Cowper, the devoted Johnson, and Lady Hesketh, should, all three, enter upon a permanent occupation of Eartham, presumably as the desiderated tenants. But it came to nothing, as did Johnson's suggestion, in June 1798, that Hayley should pay a visit to Dereham. He could not, he said, leave Tom: "Had I the wings of a dove or a hippogriff ready saddled, you should not ask me twice." But as things were, it was impossible.

Rose, however, as Cowper's trustee, remained faithful. As early as 1796 he had visited Norfolk; and now, later, he had hopeful symptoms to report from the spot. The poet had shown repeated solicitude for a new coat, and for a sight of his own works in a new and decorated edition. It is at such pitiful straws that people who cannot bear to face the affliction of those they love are obliged to clutch.

Summer visitors of a sort still came to Eartham. In July, Bunce; and then Henry Howard. Hayley read Virgil to his son; confided to his diary that "it is better to hope too much than too little"; and thanked Heaven for his blessings. That he should do so reveals a truly grateful disposition, since, in addition to his other misfortunes, he was also afflicted with money troubles exceptional even for him. He had borrowed heavily, both for his building-project and to assist his cousin, Godfrey, to buy a farm. "The victories of Suwarrow" had, strange as it may seem, seriously affected the Funds; and when it came to replacing the Stock of the friend to whom he was in debt, he found the transaction turned considerably to his disadvantage. The only thing he could do to rectify this was to press on harder than ever with his *Essay on Sculpture*. He referred to this process in one of his many sonnets, describing how: "Lonely I labour by the cloudy main. . . . The weight of literary toil to bear; That study may a monied loss repair."

In September, in the place of Romney, Aiton, the royal gardener, came to Eartham, and Tom accompanied his peregrinations of the grounds in his chair; and on September 24 it was the turn of Hawkins, the "elegant Grecian traveller" whom Hayley had met that spring. Hawkins brought with him a collection of drawings of Greece, and Hayley took him over to the Turret and firmly read aloud to him his new poem, as well as a sonnet addressed to himself, which started:

> Hawkins!
> Well pass'd your early years in Grecian air,
> In happy search of treasures rich and rare,

and terminated, rather happily,

> Graced like Ulysses, be it yours to know
> All his domestic bliss without his woe.

And that, save for the brief appearance of Palladio on the eve of Tom's nineteenth birthday, was the end of visitors for that year. The shadows were growing longer, and Tom at Eartham, and his father at the Turret, were heavily engaged in their own concerns: the latter with his never-ending poem, the other with the business of dying.

9

The end of Hayley's Memoirs of his son is painful reading. The trouble with him is that his grief, though sincere, is couched in terms so exaggerated that—to a modern ear—it does not sound sincere.

Tom now was entirely helpless; he could draw only with the utmost difficulty, and he could hardly do anything else, though the endless succession of notes passing between Eartham and the Turret showed little falling off. Hayley's tears flowed with almost more frequency than did his verses. On September 30 he discovered that Tom had kept, treasured apart, all his letters; and he was so touched that he wrote a sonnet on the subject at five o'clock in the morning, and despatched it to Eartham, together with two peaches, and a novel entitled *The Fair Syrian*, a work "of infinite pathos".

> Thou dearest object of incessant care (said the sonnet)
> For thee before the throne of Heaven I bend.

Tom did not, I fancy, see anything out of the way in missives of this nature. After all, he had been getting them all his life, and was quite accustomed to it.

The birthday passed off quietly. In addition to Palladio, only Guy and his son came over to hear Hayley read the two further sonnets he had composed for the occasion:

> Dear invalid, when last thy natal day
> Awaked the lyre of thy afflicted bard.

Hayley was now writing with frantic facility to keep himself from thinking. He contrived to introduce an episode about Demosthenes into his poem on sculpture, so that Tom's drawing of the death of that eloquent man might be made use of as a decoration to it. By October 12 his manuscript-book of sonnets was full; and he was delighted to find Tom sufficiently cheerful to be indulging in a dream of building a cottage for himself on the Eartham estate, so as to save expense. He found space in his book for yet more sonnets on this project. The fact was that, under pressure of his misfortunes, Hayley was becoming an intolerable babbler in verse. Soon there was no stopping him. He had never been a good poet, but now his fluency was frightful; and it continued so to the end.

Meanwhile, flashes of hope were succeeded by flashes of despair. Guy found the patient better, and all was gladness. But it did not last long. A new abscess formed in his arm, and had to be lanced. Then, pathetically enough, Tom's design of his projected cottage was sent to Bunce, for professional criticism. And, at last, hounded on by his son's reiterated requests that his poem should be completed, the *Essay on Sculpture* was, upon November 22, brought to an end, and Hayley went out into the garden to plant "a few pleasing trees" in commemoration of the feat.

The following day he rode over to Eartham and read the whole poem, once again, to the patient and his doctor. Tom was afraid that warmth of parental feeling had led his father to praise him too much (since there is a good deal about the Young Sculptor in it); but was glad the task was finished. Hayley's next step was to fall like a lion upon the business of compiling the Notes, without which, in those days, no serious poetical work was considered complete.

The winter dragged on, dark and dreary. Hayley's diary is full of observations about resignation, despair, and the desirability of submitting to the will of God. And Christmas-tide brought no relief, save for a brief visit from young Meyer. Tom was now so irked by the mere business of getting up and going to bed again, that he considerately asked his father and his friend to visit him only for a few hours in the middle of the day. Yet, in those few hours, he contrived to remain cheerful, and took the liveliest interest in the portentous Notes his parent was preparing. In fact, Hayley wrote one more sonnet about his usefulness in this capacity, which ends:

> Whatever point I to thy sense submit,
> I feel thy sentiments, angelic youth,
> An emanation of eternal truth.

No sooner were the Notes done, than the proofs of the poem put in an appearance. Tom helped, too, to correct these. When he saw the proof of his own design of the Death of Demosthenes, he was particularly gratified. He might well be so, since the engraver of the plate was that struggling friend of Flaxman, William Blake. Not that the plate met with much approbation from the author of the poem. Indeed, quite otherwise; though that matter must be touched upon hereafter.

10

In 1800—a year of disaster for Hayley—the first blow fell in January: the sudden and unexpected death, on the 22nd, of Dr. Warner. At the end of the same month, however, a more cheerful event took place, to restore the balance, as he trusted. He received, again quite unexpectedly, a letter from Cowper, containing a new translation of that passage in his Homer which relates to the dance of Ariadne (*Iliad*, XVIII, 590–605), for which Hayley had earlier sent him a request. Cowper's hand was as firm as ever, and at once great hopes were entertained that now, at long last, his recovery was imminent.

It was a most illusory hope. By February he was ill again, with dropsy; and Hayley wrote off at once, full of solicitude, to tell how he himself had cured a very bad case of dropsy in a labouring woman, entirely by electricity—drawing sparks from her swelled body and head. He begged Johnson to try "this most easy remedy", or, if that would not do, then "broom seeds roasted like coffee . . . and the frequent use of a flesh brush". And, later, for thirst, he commended *tamarinds* "preserved without sugar, in the pod. . . . I will write to a friend and beg him to send some."

In this same month, Tom developed a fresh abscess, and grew weaker. He could now not use his hands to draw, but instead bravely took to modelling figures in wax. His legs and body were terribly swollen, and Hayley became painfully agitated. He addressed a sonnet to Dr. Guy; and another to his

> Angelic sufferer, whose existence seems
> Supported only by a feeble thread.

It was all he could do, and, though it was not much help, it did at least keep his mind from intolerable brooding. The one bright spot in the whole scene was the serenity of the patient; and, to reward him in some slight measure for this, Hayley was preparing a little surprise for him. Flaxman, early in his connection with Tom, had executed a medallion of him, and this Hayley had had drawn by Howard, and sent to Blake, to be engraved as an illustration to the new poem. Now he longed for its arrival, but Blake was ill and busy, and the engraving was delayed. It was not, indeed, until April 1,[3] that Blake despatched the proof of the medallion to Eartham, and then it was not satisfactory, and Hayley sent it back. Tom was, consequently, never to see the finished version of his portrait, for, though upon April 3 he was still projecting his new cottage, and was, two days later, approving the final version of the Notes, he was sinking very fast. Hayley still, at times, had moods of optimism, which Guy was now obliged, in kindness, to check. All the same, on April 6, the plans of the proposed cottage were sent off to Bunce; and, on the 11th, Godfrey arrived and was taken to see the invalid, whom he found "as admirable as ever in his conversation and affectionate manners".

Now, however, it was necessary to drug him with opium; but still, indomitably, with no thought of death in his mind, he went on making plans for the future. He was, after all, not yet twenty years of age. The newest idea was that his cottage should not now be at Eartham, but at Felpham; so that he might see his father frequently without the latter being obliged to incur the hazard of long rides in the rain. Here he planned a life of incessant industry, in which he should support himself by the production of works of art. It was a brave dream, and, what is astonishing, Hayley still believed in the possibility of it, and even, upon April 27, bought for him, to his immense gratification, a field near to the church at Felpham, upon which his cottage was to stand.

Two days later a terrible blow fell. News came from Johnson that Cowper was dead. He had died on April 25.

"The prospect all dark", Hayley wrote in his diary at the end of the month of April. He still did not quite realize how dark.

On Thursday, May 1, he rode once more to Eartham, and found his son very weak. Guy came, and upon his advice Hayley arranged to pass the night with Tom in the library at Eartham.

The next morning he rose before six. His son's long agony had reached its culmination. The doctor came, and left again. He thought, he said, that the patient would live through the day; for his brain was unclouded, his voice still clear. Hayley did not quit the room. At half past one, suddenly and unexpectedly, all was over. "In death, as in life," his father wrote, "he was most admirable and lovely."

11

He had been a brave boy. Whatever we may think of Hayley and of his educational methods, the life and death of his son demonstrate triumphantly that he knew how to rear a man and a gentleman. To no one had Tom expressed the slightest fear that he was going to die. That he had not done so, Hayley thought (and I think so too), was because he was afraid that such an announcement would too greatly discompose his sensitive parent. Two months before his end, he wrote in a little book a meditation which his father, who knew nothing of it, found after his death. It said: "Although it has pleased God to visit me with a long and enervating illness, by which I have lost, in a great degree, the faculties of my body; yet, in his mercy (for which mercy I hope I am grateful,) he has preserved to me the faculties of my mind, and I have employed them, during my confinement, in that study so important to us as a guard against evil in this world, and as means of rendering us more fit for the next, and yet so little attended to—the knowledge of oneself. I have examined (and, I trust, with an eye tolerably impartial) to what defects and errors of conduct I am particularly liable; and I hope, by being sensible of those defects, I may be able to regulate my conduct in life so that it may be, upon all occasions, such as becomes a man and a Christian."

It is pointless to add anything to this. Hayley tried to do so. He quoted harrowing anecdotes to illustrate the boy's heroic fortitude under his sufferings, and he constantly touched and retouched the description of him which he had incorporated in his *Essay on Sculpture*. In so doing, perhaps he hit upon one fine line which may be left to stand by itself as a memorial to the qualities of Thomas Alphonso Hayley:

> And so the seraph Patience arm'd his soul.

CHAPTER XVII

THE BIOGRAPHER: AND WILLIAM BLAKE (1800)

I

BUT POOR DISTRACTED Hayley was, by no means, content to leave it at that. Beside himself with grief, he set to work to bury his son's memory beneath a colossal pile of platitudinous panegyric. This, however, was not just yet. For the moment, he was prostrated, and, although he was later to write an enormous amount about resignation, and the prospects of a blissful reunion hereafter, it is doubtful whether these were not afterthoughts.

Young Meyer was sent for, and he posted down to Eartham straightway to console his father's old friend; and found him once again engaged in composing a funeral sermon, which the author says, with that curious complacency that is not his most endearing characteristic, was "listened to with peculiar interest in the little church of Eartham".

Hayley, however, still lacked sufficient command of himself to attend the funeral. He bade farewell to his son in his coffin, and scattered upon the corpse some of his favourite flowers, gathered in the garden of the Turret. Meyer went as his proxy to the funeral; and Flaxman came down specially to take a death-mask of his pupil, and expressed his intention of carving for him, at his own expense, a marble memorial.

Hayley, meantime, retreated to his marine residence, and, while the obsequies were taking place, composed a couple of sonnets. Then, with Meyer, he fled to Kew, where, with occasional visits to London, he strove during the month of May to nurse himself to a "firmer tone" of mind and body.

The Meyers were very kind to him; and Rose was sympathy itself. And, endlessly and incessantly, he poured forth a turgid stream of verses, which had, no doubt, a very salutary effect upon his wounded spirit.

That his spirit was wounded, it is impossible to doubt. Tom and Cowper had been the two people he had most loved; and they had died within a week of one another. Hayley was a man much too facile in expression to feel very deeply; but he was capable, if the phrase may be pardoned, of feeling *extensively*, and that was what, at this time, he was doing.

Anna Seward, whose relations with him had of late years grown exiguous, wrote on July 9,[1] with a tempered sympathy: "Prepared as I was for the event, I shuddering, lamented the extinction of your dearest hope. . . . Time and intellectual exertion have balms in store even for such wounds, deep as they are; but the trite arguments of consolation have them not to infuse."

It was not very warm, and, indeed, the trouble with Miss Seward was once bit, twice shy. Nobody living was better able to pull out all the stops of sympathy when she deemed the occasion called for it. Only, unfortunately, she had done so once already with Hayley, in the case of Howell, and had then found, to her great annoyance, that he had not really appreciated it. Besides, she now had another reason: she was extremely jealous of the passionate admiration that Hayley was lavishing upon the works of Cowper. And so, in the following year, on January 5, 1801, she wrote to her friend, Thomas Park, a letter[1] which more sincerely, if less sympathetically, sums up her real feelings:

You say you fear, from the style of his Epistles on Oratory,* and that egotism of melancholy, which so often occurs in their progress, that Mr. Hayley is likely to become, like Cowper, the victim of morbid despondency. His sensibilities have certainly sustained a severe trial, in the long-protracted sufferings, and untimely death of that fondly beloved youth, in whom he had concentred his whole sum of affectionate connection. The very recluse life he has led, and will continue to lead, has an unquestionable tendency to deepen the gloom of this heart-rending disappointment. Yet, I think he will not sink under it. No!—his literary ardour will bear him up. You see, in the course of his last work, and its notes, that he was planning new poetic compositions, even while his griefs were all bleeding fresh. Time does everything for minds of that cast. He who can bewail his sorrows to the world, will not become their victim. There is a mournful luxury in such pains, which has nothing to do with the severity of despair. Mr. Hayley will always love to deplore, and to allude to his lost darling in future compositions. Affliction never overturns the sanity of a spirit which it does not first render indolent.

It is a harsh verdict, but not, I fear, an undiscerning one; because, directly the first impact of his disaster was past, Hayley's reaction was precisely as Miss Seward had suggested. His literary ardour did bear him up. Indeed, there was precious little else left to him that was buoyant, and it would be a severe judgment that should blame him for clutching at this raft in the sea in which he found himself. He was, after all, always able to tell himself that both his deceased friends would have thoroughly approved his conduct; Tom especially, who had, throughout the course of his illness, urged him ceaselessly to complete the poem that was to celebrate the art which he and Flaxman practised.

And so, even while he was at Kew, and even while he was prostrated, he continued with the proofs and the final arrangements for

* Did she mean *Sculpture*?

his *Essay on Sculpture*; and in the early summer of that year it was published, with the three rather inadequate illustrations which Blake had made for it.

It was not a success. It was not even so good a poem as its predecessors, and that is saying something. Hayley consoled himself with the reflection that the art of which it treats had never been sufficiently naturalized in England for a poem on it to become popular.

He did not mind. He was now emitting sonnets and devotional poems like an absolute fountain, and there was, besides, growing more and more clearly in his much chastened mind, the certitude that a destiny of an altogether different kind from any that he had pursued was shortly to open before him. Tom was dead, Cowper was dead, and Romney was mortally stricken. All of these, even Tom to his way of thinking, had been great men, whom he had loved. It is necessary to praise famous men; and suddenly he saw before him, with assurance, the road he had next to tread. For the sake of the dead, and equally for the sake of posterity, the lives of these friends of his had to be chronicled; and, while he was only too anxious to give every assistance to any other person who was willing or able to write of them, he felt convinced that, failing such other, it was his bounden duty himself to provide the necessary biographies.

Tom's was, in any case, his business; he might well begin with Tom. But then, inextricably linked in his mind with Tom was that other whose death had, by a mere week, preceded his. Who was going to write Cowper's life?

On May 31, the same month as that in which his son had died, he wrote to Johnson: "I hope to see you distinguish yourself, as you ought to do, in the character of his [Cowper's] biographer." And he added that, if Johnson were in need of any assistance, then he and Rose would be eager to provide it.

Johnson was a busy parish clergyman, and, as has been suggested, of somewhat slothful constitution. The idea did not, it seems, appeal to him; and, by July 22, Hayley was vigorously writing again, this time to Lady Hesketh, to suggest that hers was the divinely-appointed hand. The Life, he said,[2] "should appear, in a series of Letters addressed to Earl Cowper, and flowing from the *Heart*, the *Memory*, and the *Hand* of *Lady Hesketh*—start not, my dear Lady! . . ."

Lady Hesketh took a few days to meditate the matter, and then wrote back to say that she could not think of executing so delicate an office. It appeared that there was nothing for it: there was the breach, and there the only volunteer willing to fill it—Hayley!

Still, he did not wish, or pretended not to wish, to press his claims to this important office. On August 7 he wrote again to Johnson, saying he had told Lady Hesketh that: "I would not shrink from it myself, if she persisted in thinking me the proper person. . . . I informed her that I had thought of you . . . but that your modesty, like her own, declined the very delicate task." Besides, Johnson had already plenty to do, as he had volunteered to prepare a new edition of Cowper's Collected Works. Hayley expressed his perfect willingness to act as subaltern, under the guidance of the two respected relatives. He felt his position; after all, for all the warmth of their friendship, he had known Cowper a relatively short time.

And so, while thus crying loudly *Nolo episcopari*, he found the task was his, because he wanted it and no one else did. It was his despite the fact that Lady Hesketh was still not at all happy about his religious beliefs. However, Lady Hesketh was a strong-minded woman, and she was willing to take the chance of confiding her cousin's posthumous reputation into the hands of the alleged infidel (who was, after all, a celebrated one), provided she was quite sure he would do everything she told him. There were unfortunate matters which any self-respecting family would wish to have touched upon but lightly: the fact that Cowper was, for instance, for a large portion of his life, insane; and Lady Austen; and things like that.

Hayley was duly tackled on these lines, and promised faithfully to act as requested. It made matters uncommonly difficult for him, and yet it was the only way, because Lady Hesketh and Johnson, between them, possessed nearly all the available material. Besides, he had loved Cowper too, no man more, and had no desire to write a biography which would do other than augment his considerable, and ever-growing, renown.

And so I think we may say that, as early as the August of 1800, Hayley had been officially appointed the biographer of William Cowper. It was a massive undertaking; Cowper had been an indefatigable letter-writer, and vast stacks of documents needed consideration before even a beginning could be made. Moreover, while these stacks were being piled up by the assiduity of Johnson, Rose, Lady Hesketh and others, Hayley, with all the vigour of a thoroughly unhappy man, had flung himself bodily into yet another enterprise. By September 13 he had commenced, and had well on the road to completion, a work devoted to the memory of Tom, consisting chiefly of the devotional and laudatory sonnets which he had composed during the boy's years of illness.

What with this and the Cowper project, and the fact that it was necessary also to get Thomas Alphonso's biography on paper before his memory had grown dim, Hayley, in the summer and autumn of 1800, was an uncommonly busied individual. It is one of the most curious tricks of fate that, upon this scene of frenzied activity, there should now fall, hardly noticed, the shadow and more than the shadow of by far the greatest man that Hayley was destined to know. It was in July, 1800, that William Blake first visited Felpham

to inspect the cottage Hayley had suggested he might like to rent;*
and it was on the following September 18, "between six and seven
in the morning",³ that Blake, Mrs. Blake and Blake's sister set forth
to take up their residence there. For three years this cottage
remained their home.

And so, not for the first time in tracing the career of Hayley, one
finds oneself faced with a most awkward duality of interest: there are
the two strands, and they are not very closely intertwined. To
Hayley, the three years from 1800 to 1803 must have been, pre-
dominantly, the years in which he was compiling the most important
and successful of his many books, *The Life of Cowper*. To us, on the
other hand, one hundred and fifty years later, they are, predomin-
antly, the years in which the strongly opposed characters of Hayley
and Blake were impingeing upon one another; to the general
entertainment of posterity. For Hayley, the history of these years
was composed of the endless, laborious and often extremely exciting
investigations he was making into the past life of his dead friend;
for us, there is a tendency to grasp at every crumb of his story which
helps us to understand a little better that extraordinary genius
whom he was entertaining, like an angel unawares, in a cottage a
few hundred paces distant from his new residence, the Turret. This,
for Hayley, must have been a sad house: he had built it in the hope
of retrenchment, so that Tom might come into the Eartham
estates with capital sufficient to administer them in the way they
merited: and now Tom was dead, and his scheme had fallen to
ruin. Yet, for all this, Hayley had now determined to make Felpham
his home. His son had died in the library at Eartham, and for him
the older house was haunted.

So, as I have said, there are these two strands which intertwine
only at a few points: the *Life of Cowper*, and the Sussex sojourn of
William Blake. It will be necessary to deal with these separately
and in turn; and, while we do so, it will be salutary, I think, to
remember that, whatever conclusion we may come to about
Hayley's relations with Blake, there can be no earthly doubt that,
in his early completion of Cowper's *Life*, Hayley performed a signal
service to literature. Most of those incomparable letters of Cowper
which we now know in better and completer editions, were first
assembled by him. He was the first man to see Cowper's correspondence as a whole, and to realize the extraordinary merit of it. While
he was living, as one might say, in the radiance of this delicious and
memorable experience, he was in daily contact with Blake. That
he did not, as some present-day writers seem to think he should have
done, give up at once all his other activities, and fall down and

---

* Gilchrist places this visit in August, but that can hardly be so, since in Hayley's letter of July 22 to Lady Hesketh (quoted hereafter, p.262), he writes that the cottage is already taken. It may be, of course, that he was enthusiasti-cally anticipating the event.

worship Blake on the spot, is not really remarkable. Moreover, as subsequent proceedings will show, there is uncommonly little evidence that, during the first two years of Blake's stay in Felpham, such exercitations were expected of him. But it is better to demonstrate these points by evidence, rather than by assertion.

2

Hayley's activities after the death of Tom are a trifle obscure, because, as I have suggested, his personal life had, for the time, become swallowed up in his new vocation of biographer. His correspondence of this period deals very nearly exclusively with the material he is collecting. "Are you personally acquainted," he wrote to Johnson on August 7, "with Lady Austen . . . and Mr. Newton? Both [have] . . . materials of consequence." The biographer had engulfed the man; the past, rather than the present, was his life.

Therefore, his own movements are difficult to trace. I doubt whether he returned to Eartham after his stay at Kew. I think it is likely that he went straight to the Turret, and started to work because he did not want to think. He sold Eartham as soon as he could; and he sold it to that unattractive political automaton, William Huskisson, who resided there until the Manchester & Liverpool Railway cut short his career, and he expired, far from home, upon the sofa of the vicar of Eccles.

Huskisson was the first of several wealthy men to inhabit Eartham. He renovated it and added to it, and even before his death it bore little resemblance to the enchanting residence that had known the familiar converse of Gibbon and Romney, of Flaxman and Cowper.

For us, then, the day of Eartham is over, and it is time now to turn our eyes in the direction of Felpham and the marine turret, the joint creation of Hayley and his little Palladio, Samuel Bunce.

3

In 1800, when Hayley took up his abode at Felpham, Sir Richard Hotham, who was then busily creating his new watering-place at Bognor, would have regarded Felpham as a country village, savagely remote from his suave collection of Georgian squares, crescents, and terraces. Bognor was a new, a brand-new, pleasure resort; and Felpham was just a village, like many others in Sussex, which happened to possess a foreshore, and some fine firm sands. In the year 1801, if *Dally's Bognor Guide*[4] speaks truth, the population of this village was 536, of which, very remarkably, exactly half were males, and half females; and the number of dwelling-houses was 82. I am a little dubious about these figures, I may say, since the same authority gives the population in 1811 as only 306, with the still odder fact that, while the females of the parish remain at 221, the males have dropped to a mere 85—a circumstance for which one can only, I suppose, blame Bonaparte. Moreover, as late as 1821, the same source informs us that the number of families then in the village which did not derive their sustenance either from agriculture or trade was, precisely, 14.

It is rather necessary to stress this, because the picture is very different to-day. Felpham now is little better than a genteel appendage to Bognor, with myriads of neat villas that cluster in masses down to the foreshore, which may be approached by a fine concrete thoroughfare known regrettably, if understandably, as Blake's Road.

It is a pity, but there it is. The only thing one can do about it is to exert the eye of the imagination; and that, fortunately, is not so difficult as it might seem, since, in some respects, the vestiges of Blake's and Hayley's Felpham are still there, to be divined as something more elemental imposed upon the flimsy structure of marine suburbia. And, though altered in detail, The Turret, or Turret House as it is now known, still stands where it stood, essentially the same, hard by the church in the middle of the village wherein lie the remains of the subject of this memoir.

The Turret is surrounded, as in Hayley's time, with an enormously high wall composed of large pebbles set in red-brick quoins, which I presume to be the same wall that Hayley, with his mania for privacy, ordered to be constructed even before his house was built inside it. In the middle of this rampart is a vast double gate, with a small wicket in it; and the general effect is that of a jail. However, the fortifications were not intended to keep the inmates in; but to keep strangers out. It was, perhaps, a little overdone. Famous as Hayley was in his day, I should not have thought that he needed such circumvallations to keep out his 'public'; and indeed, I believe the contemporary villagers took a similar view.

Once the great gateway is passed, the prospect that meets the eye is rather in the nature of an anticlimax, since the residence behind the ramparts is by no means so grim or so huge as one would have anticipated from the vast proportions of its out-works. Indeed, in Hayley's time, the contrast must have been more marked than it is now, for contemporary drawings show us a two-storied edifice a good deal more gracious than the very Victorian stuccoed article that stands before us, in which heavy plate-glass sashes, without glazing bars, have replaced the delicate Georgian windows, and a series of incongruous battlements has been clapped on top of the roof parapets. Worse still, the turret has been lowered, and where once arose an elegant structure of wood and glass crowned by an iron handrail, there now only remains a stumpy little tower over the porch. The circular window, too, left specially for Tom's stained-glass, has been removed; and in its place is one of those slit-like embrasures which were useful enough in the days of bows-and-arrows, but have since been superseded. And, over all the windows, a heavy, ecclesiastical-looking drip-moulding has been plastered.

Inside it is much the same: there are some painted ceilings that might or might not be original, showing a blue sky and cupids; there are some painted panels over the doors and on the doors which certainly have nothing to do with Hayley; otherwise it has been converted into flats, hewn into smaller rooms with clumsily erected partitions and generally transmogrified.

It is sad, but it was done long ago; most of it, I surmise, in the middle of the last century; and the only reason I am making a to-do about it in this place is because I should be sorry to have any present-day visitor to the Turret jumping to the conclusion that this not very sightly edifice represents the best that the united taste of Messrs. Hayley and Bunce could do. The old pictures tell a different story. Now the covered way has been pulled down; and, on the east front where the three tall library windows stood, a stuccoed bay has been thrown out. It is perhaps only in the pretty garden, and above all in the mulberry tree, for which I have already given chapter and verse, that we can still find traces of Hayley. There, and in that formidable and melodramatically Gothic encircling wall.

Outside the great gateway in Limmer Lane, a few paces brings us to Vicarage Lane, a still rustic thoroughfare leading to the *Fox Inn*, which, in 1800, was the abode of Mr. Grinder from whom Blake rented his cottage for twenty pounds a year.[5] The *Fox* was unhappily burnt down a few years ago, and is now (in 1949) being rebuilt, though one of its old thatched outbuildings still stands, and part of the walls of the original *Fox* appear to be being incorporated in the new structure.

A short distance past the *Fox*, and on the other side of the road, Blake's cottage remains, facing south and seaward, though now with any number of modern villas between it and the sea. It has been greatly restored and somewhat enlarged, but, though it has risen socially in the world, it is still, in essence, much as it must have been in 1800: two stories high, with three windows on the first floor which would then have commanded a magnificent prospect over fields to the firm sands of the beach, and the wide waters beyond; and, at the back, a thatched roof which comes down to within six feet of the ground. The garden is small, and it was small in 1800. But in Blake's day it was a cottage-garden and raised useful vegetables; and now it is a pleasure-garden, and a pretty one at that.

Then comes the uncompromising concrete of Blake's Road; and villas . . . and villas. And, finally, the wide yellow sands, and the wooden breakwaters. It is not difficult to expunge the villas in imagination, and to replace them with dry-grassed sea-meadows and a great sense of space, that will, perhaps, enable you to see the solitary strand where Blake walked in familiar converse with Milton and Homer and all manner of gods and demons.

The distance from this cottage to the *Fox* is some sixty yards; and from the *Fox* to the back-entrance gate of Turret House not more than another hundred and thirty. Blake, then, and Hayley were, during 1800–1803, neighbours with less than a couple of hundred yards between their garden gates.

That sets the scene; now for the men.

4

Hayley, in 1800, was fifty-five years of age. He had, for more than twenty years been regarded as an eminent poet, connoisseur, and man of letters. He had known most of the great figures of his day that he had wished to know. And now his fortunes were in decline. Such inspiration as he had possessed was on the wane. That is not uncustomary in a poet who has reached fifty-five, and I do not think he regarded it as a matter for regret. He was still uncommonly facile; he continued to write verse out of habit, and because he liked doing so.

What was a great deal harder for him to bear was that he had been singularly unfortunate in reposing his affections upon persons who were either much his senior, or were unhappily short-lived. His real trouble in 1800 was that almost all his friends were dead. His Cambridge confrères were gone: Thornton, Beridge, Clyfford; so were Gibbon and Meyer, and Howard the philanthropist, and Wright of Derby, and Dr. Warner, and Cowper; and, worst of all, his son. And Romney was worse than dead. Such friends as he had left were for the most part his juniors and men of second-rate quality: Rose, and Johnson, and young Meyer. Flaxman was almost the oldest friend he had, certainly the oldest who was of any real stature. And Blake was the friend and the protégé of this oldest friend.

Blake, on the other hand, was already forty-three. His life had been a long struggle with poverty, task-work, and neglect. For more than twenty years he had been earning a living for himself at the trade of engraving, which, though it was a highly-skilled and exceedingly exacting business was not, in those days, regarded as an art. It was not even as though the majority of the engravings which he executed were of his own design. Up to the time of his coming to Felpham he had in only four cases been commissioned to illustrate a volume with designs of his own, and in only one of these cases, the *Night Thoughts* of Edward Young, were the designs of any real importance; and even in this instance the payment he had received for the plates had been wretched, and had probably not exceeded a guinea apiece.

He had, on the other hand, already by this time produced the greater part of those extraordinary original works that he engraved on his own account, and by which now his fame is assured: *The Songs of Innocence and of Experience; The Book of Thel; The Marriage of Heaven and Hell; The Visions of the Daughters of Albion; America; Europe;* and the *Books of Urizen, Ahania* and *Los:* in fact, all of his major works in this form, with the exception of those two last vast scriptures, *Milton* and *Jerusalem*. But these were little known, and less regarded; and the paintings which he had executed and exhibited were neither numerous, nor considered important. That Hayley should have regarded him as being, primarily, a working engraver, a copyist of other men's works, was not, therefore, strange. After all, Blake himself made no bones about it; it was his livelihood.

Moreover, in 1800, Blake was no longer a young man, and had reached a bad patch in his career. Since his *Night Thoughts* designs had been completed in 1797, he had had few commissions for engravings, and they had been of a trivial sort, being plates to text-books on English or Roman History, to one on Gymnastics, and a few illustrations to the fourth edition of Dr. Darwin's *Botanic Garden*. These, with the addition of a small commission Flaxman had given him, represented the work of more than two years; and a man cannot live on that sort of thing. When Hayley's trifling commission for the three illustrations to the *Essay on Sculpture* came along, Blake was glad enough to avail himself of it.

Since 1794, Butts had been virtually Blake's only patron; and his house was rapidly becoming over-filled with the pictures he had bought. What Blake desperately needed in 1800 was another patron; and, in Flaxman's opinion, and in Blake's also, I think, Hayley was just the man for the part. In addition, Blake had now lived for seven years in Lambeth, which, though not at all like Lambeth is to-day, was still, not even then, the unspoilt country which he loved. The change to Sussex, which was welcome to Hayley because he was unhappy and desperately in need of society, was not less welcome, at the time, to Blake. All his letters of the period show how overjoyed he was by the removal.[6]

5

Few of the major incidents of English literature—and the transit of Blake to Felpham is such an incident—have been more uniformly misrepresented than this business of Blake's removal into Sussex. I do not only mean that the character of Hayley has been consistently written down, or the inference constantly drawn that he was a vain and foolish creature who, for his own ends, transported this man of great genius to his native village and there proceeded to harass, overwork, and, in the worse sense of the word, "patronize" him. All this, of course, has been said over and over again, and it is a charge with which I must deal. The point, however, that I am here concerned with is merely that of the actual mechanism of the transit, which is usually represented in a much simplified fashion, something after this style: Hayley, on Flaxman's recommendation, had employed Blake to work on his plates for the *Essay on Sculpture*, he had met him for the first time in this connection and had then impulsively carried him off to Felpham to assist in the preparation of the illustrations to the work upon which he was then starting, *The Life of Cowper*. Once secured, he had used Blake as his amanuensis and general factotum, and eventually had presumed so far in this direction that it had grown intolerable to Blake, who had, consequently, fled back indignantly to London.

Such a picture as this is quite untrue, and it is nearly as unfair to Blake as it is to Hayley. The best version of the facts which I have encountered is that given by Mr. Kenneth Povey, in an article contributed to the *Sussex County Magazine* of August, 1927; and the course of events that I am now going to describe is, very largely, summarised from this most lucid account.

In the first place, as this writer points out, it is quite absurd to make the suggestion that Hayley and Blake were total strangers to one another until they met over the matter of the engravings for the *Essay on Sculpture*. Flaxman was one of the oldest friends of both parties. He had met Hayley in 1783, and Blake some years earlier. He was, in addition, a great admirer of Blake's work both as draughtsman and as poet, and it is unbelievable that he should never have mentioned either of these aspects of his friend's genius to Hayley, who, as he knew, took a most lively interest in all the arts. Besides, we know that he did. When in 1783 he had financially assisted Blake to get his *Poetical Sketches* printed, one of the things he did to further the book's fortunes was to write to Hayley, telling him that he had left with their mutual friend, Dr. Long, a copy of it for transmission to Eartham. "The writings of a Mr. Blake you have heard me mention", he called it; and, furthermore, he proceeded to add that Blake had other qualities which deserved consideration: "I have before mentioned that Mr. Romney thinks his historical drawings rank with those of Michael Angelo. He is at present employed as an engraver, in which his encouragement is not extraordinary."

This letter demonstrates conclusively that the name of Blake was at least known to Hayley as early as sixteen years before the Felpham episode; and Mr. Povey proceeds to a conjecture that even this may not have been the first link between the two men. During the years from 1769 to 1774, Hayley was living at No. 5, Great Queen Street, at the very same time as Blake was serving his apprenticeship to Basire (from 1771 to 1778) at No. 31 in the same street. Basire was a print-seller, and Hayley was a collector of prints. There is no evidence that the two men met during this period; but it is, at any rate, extremely likely that they saw one another many times, without the least foreknowledge of the way in which, later, their destinies were to be linked.

Meanwhile, though there is no further record of contact after the despatch of the *Poetical Sketches* to Hayley, the probability that, from time to time, he heard from Flaxman of the performances of Blake (and *vice versa*) becomes almost a certainty when, in 1795, Thomas Alphonso entered upon his apprenticeship to the sculptor. Blake's relations with Flaxman at this period were cordial. We have already mentioned the occasion when, upon Flaxman's birthday, the boy and his master took tea with an unnamed person who lived on the other side of the river; and it is unbelievable that, during Tom's years in London, he should not, either at this time or some other, have met his master's eccentric though talented friend. It is unbelievable, I say, and for a very excellent reason; which is that the letter of April 1, 1800, which is the first we have of the correspondence between Blake and Hayley, is one that could not have been written to a total stranger with reference to a third party with whom he had not the least acquaintance. Blake, after all, for all his peculiarities, was a man perfectly capable of writing an impersonal business letter, when the occasion demanded it; but in this case what he wrote was very different. What did he say?

DEAR SIR,
With all possible Expedition, I send you a proof of my attempt to Express your & our Much Beloved's Countenance. Mr. Flaxman has seen it & approved of my now sending it to you for your remarks. Your Sorrows and your dear son's May Jesus and his Angels assuage & if it is consistent with his divine providence restore him to us & to his labours of Art & Science in this world. So prays a fellow sufferer & Your humble servant,[7]
WILLM. BLAKE.

"Surely," says Mr. Povey, in the article referred to, "this is an impossible letter for him to have written to a man totally unacquainted with his mode of expression, and if he did not know Thomas Hayley the words 'Our Much Beloved' are a lapse into almost incredible familiarity." I agree, absolutely.

Hayley's letter in reply to this, of April 17, which deals severely with the indeed not very satisfactory engraving, is largely taken up with technical considerations; but it ends, significantly enough for our purpose, with the words: "Accept our united benedictions & believe me dear Blake your very sincere friend."[8]

On May 2, Tom died; and within four days Blake was again writing to Hayley, this time a letter of condolence which is too familiar to need to be given here. It is the letter which contains his great phrase: "The ruins of Time build mansions in Eternity"; and this, once again, is not the letter of a man whose relations with the Hayleys were exclusively business ones. Tom is referred to as

261

"the departed angel", and Blake says that he feels Hayley's grief "with a brother's sympathy".

This is the last of Blake's letters that we have for some time, and for a very good reason: that the negotiations which now took place were verbal. Hayley, as we have seen, came to Kew after his son's funeral, and while he was in town he probably visited Blake to discuss the engravings to the *Essay* which he was now seeing through the press. These engravings never met with his entire approval, but apparently he thought none the worse of Blake for that, since it was during this July, at Felpham, that he presented the engraver with Tom's own copy of the *Triumphs of Temper*, with the inscription we have already quoted (p.129). The lines, even if they do not imply any particular comprehension on Hayley's part of the sort of man Blake was, do at least convey the sense that relations of a most cordial nature had been established.

And, in fact, we have independent evidence that this was so. On July 22, Hayley, who at that time was belabouring Lady Hesketh with letters on the Cowper project, included in a letter[9] to her sundry references to Blake, whom he calls "a most worthy, enthusiastic, affectionate engraver":

[He] has, (he said) attach'd himself so much to me that he has taken a cottage in this little marine village to pursue his art in various branches under my auspices, & as He has infinite Genius, with a most engaging simplicity of character, I hope He will execute many admirable things in this sequestered scene, with the aid of an excellent wife, to whom he has been married 17 years, & who shares his Labours & his Talents—

He has already made me most agreeable amends for the Mortification I suffered in seeing that *very unfaithful* representation of my dear child, which appears in the volume I had the Honour to send you—a portrait drawn from the medallion by an excellent artist, but in a most unfavorable season, when he was suffering from inflam'd eyes & too great a pressure of business! . . .

It is an interesting letter, and one which puts a rather different complexion upon the move to Felpham. Hayley had, when this letter was written, not yet been appointed the 'official' biographer of Cowper, though, of course, matters were already beginning to trend that way. And yet, Gilchrist and most other authorities make a great point of it that Blake was induced to come and live at Felpham, so that he might be conveniently at hand to engrave the illustrations for Cowper's *Life*. I believe this to be an oversimplification, for several reasons, the first of which is that the arrangement was made even before the *Life* was commenced, and therefore before any illustrations were needed. And the second is that it is ridiculous to suppose that anyone could, at any time, have thought that engraving the plates for this book would be a full-time job, necessitating Blake's undivided attention. The actual volumes, as we know, were far from being lavishly illustrated; but even if, in the initial stages of the project, Hayley had had a different intention, it would still be highly unreasonable to suppose that this work alone would have rendered imperative the total and protracted removal from London of William Blake and his retinue.

No; I think the move to Sussex can be ascribed to motives that were at once more simple and more complex. Blake, I believe, complained that times were hard; Hayley, as ever, sensed an occasion for the exercise of his customary benevolence, with which, as was so often the case with him, there was not unmixed a certain measure of self-interest (since he was lonely and in desperate need of society). He sang to Blake the praises of his beloved Felpham, sea-bathing and all; and told him that, if indeed he was weary of London, he thought he could provide him with enough work in that locality—between what he himself could give him, and what he could find for him among his friends—to enable him to make a living as good or even better than he was making in town. Flaxman, I apprehend, had told him that Blake's prospects were poor; and Blake, I fancy, confirmed this view. And so, in July, by which time Hayley had discovered that there was a vacant cottage in the village, Blake proceeded to Sussex to look over the premises, found them delightful, and forthwith rented them.

It was, I think, understood that Hayley would give him all the work he could; but at the same time Blake was a perfectly free agent. He rented the cottage himself, and his relationship with Hayley was one that was consonant with the entire independence of both parties.

Four days before their exodus took place, we find Blake writing, by the hand of his wife, to Mrs. Flaxman, to thank her and her husband for their services in the matter; and it is not the letter of a man who is displeased with his situation. It will, indeed, be recalled that, at the end of the letter, he drops into verse, saying:

> Away to Sweet Felpham, for Heaven is there;
> The Ladder of Angels descends thro' the air;
> On the Turret its spiral does softly descend,
> Thro' the village then winds, at My Cot it does end.
>
> You stand in the village & look up to heaven;
> The precious stones glitter on flights seventy seven;
> And My Brother is there, & My Friend & Thine
> Descend & ascend with the Bread & the Wine.
>
> The Bread of sweet Thought & the Wine of Delight
> Feeds the Village of Felpham by day & by night;
> And at his own door the bless'd Hermit does stand,
> Dispensing, Unceasing, to all the whole Land.

That, then, was the picture in Blake's mind as he set forth. Hayley was "the bless'd Hermit" who dispensed, unceasing, to all the whole land. The Hermit, no doubt, was enraptured. It seemed almost like his fraternal fellowship with Cowper, all over again.

CHAPTER XVIII

BLAKE AT FELPHAM (1800–1802)

I

AT THIS POINT A crux arises. This is a long book, and it is not ended yet. The greater part of the material I have used so far is virtually new, or has at any rate not been seen in print for over a hundred years. But rather different considerations apply to the documents in the case of William Blake, which in recent years have been printed over and over again. While some knowledge of them is essential to the picture I am trying to give, I do not propose to make exhaustive use of them here. They are readily accessible in Gilchrist's *Life*, or in the great Nonesuch edition of Blake, which should, at this stage, be consulted; so that, through them, the state of Blake's mind on his arrival at Felpham may be appreciated. On September 12, he sent Flaxman the lines which begin:

I bless thee, O Father of Heaven and Earth! that ever I saw Flaxman's face,

and which continue,

And now Flaxman hath given me Hayley, his friend, to be mine—such my lot upon Earth!

and, nine days later, after his arrival, he was writing to him again: "Mr. Hayley recieved us with his usual brotherly affection . . . Felpham is a sweet place for Study, because it is more Spiritual than London." All, indeed, was going very well.

Mr. Hayley was not only brotherly. He became almost immediately useful. The Blakes had arrived on September 18, and, upon the 22nd,[1] hardly giving them time to get settled into their new premises, Hayley, inspired by a sad story he had heard from Rose, indited the ballad of *Little Tom the Sailor*, the proceeds from the sale of which were destined for the relief of the Widow Spicer and her Orphans: the Widow Spicer being the bereaved mother of the aforesaid Little Tom. This work was forthwith handed over to Blake for illustration, and I see no reason to believe he was not paid in the usual way for the two designs which he provided, and also for the printing of the work, which was struck off in the form of a broadsheet (dated October 5th) from his own hand-press, which he had brought with him. Of this poem, Gilchrist remarks, with unusual fatuity, that "a tinge of Blake-like feeling seems to have passed for once into the smooth verse of the poet of Eartham".[1]

One can only say to this that, if it be true, the tinge of feeling passed remarkably quickly, since the two poets had had but four days together when it was composed.

This was an earnest of what was to be expected, and soon more was to come. By November, at the latest, Blake was busy upon another commission, and this time it was a sizeable one; and one which, though we do not know how he was paid for it, cannot have been unlucrative. What with the confusion contingent upon the death of Tom, Hayley had not proceeded far with the full embellishment of the Turret, and now, as the Cowper papers were coming to hand and he was anxiously pondering them, the idea struck him that his new friend might as well be profitably exercised upon some of these uncompleted decorations; and forthwith he gave him the job of painting for his unfinished library a most ambitious series of heads of the poets "accompanied by appropriate subsidiary compositions", and intended for the space above the frieze of that apartment. These heads were executed in tempera on canvas, so it was not necessary for them to be done *in situ*. Hayley, I imagine, told Blake what he wanted; gave him an appropriate engraving as a basis for his design; and let him get on with the work at home. And by so doing he provided the painter with an opportunity for creating some wonderfully fine compositions which have not yet received all the attention they deserve.

By an immense stroke of good fortune, these paintings, though now far from the place for which they were designed, are still together in one collection, and may be examined at the City Art Gallery of Manchester.[2] The credit for bringing them together once more, after they had been dispersed at the sale of Hayley's possessions, belongs to William Russell;[3] and, at the sale of his effects on December 5, 1884, the whole series was purchased by Messrs. Agnew for the very tempting figure of 119 guineas. A year later they were at Manchester.[4]

The canvasses range in width from 19″ to 41″, but their height is almost uniform, as was demanded by the exigencies of their situation, and does not exceed $16\frac{1}{2}$″. Having regard to the curious shape thus forced by circumstance upon the designs, they are, as decorative compositions, of quite extraordinary merit. In subject they are highly characteristic of Hayley's interests. Three are classical: Cicero, Homer and Demosthenes; and we shall see in a moment why Demosthenes was dragged into the scheme. Nine are English: Chaucer, Spenser, Shakespeare, Milton, Otway, Dryden, Pope, Cowper—and Thomas Hayley. And the remainder, with two exceptions, were those Italian and Spanish poets in whom Hayley, as one might say, had, since the days of the *Essay on Epic Poetry*, maintained a 'corner': Dante, Tasso, Camoens, and Ercilla. The two others were Voltaire, and, oddly but fashionably, Klopstock.

For the final identification of these subjects, Mr. Kenneth Povey, once again, is responsible.[5]

Now, as regards this somewhat arbitrary selection of designs, several interesting points have to be made. The first is, of course, what in the world was poor Tom Hayley doing in that gallery? The second, that, in the case of three of the compositions—the Demosthenes, the Tasso, and the Shakespeare—, Blake, acting of course on his patron's instructions, has introduced accessory designs which are either copies, or are based upon, drawings already referred to as having been executed by Tom himself. The design which accompanies the head of Demosthenes is a line for line copy of his picture of the Death of Demosthenes, which had already been engraved by Blake; while that accompanying Tasso shows Mary and the Two Angels at the tomb of Christ, which, if not a copy, is at least strongly reminiscent of Tom's drawing (now lost) of the same subject. And the Shakespeare is accompanied by a representation of Macbeth and the Witches, to which the same proviso applies.[4] To some extent, then, these pictures composed a sort of memorial to Thomas Alphonso.

For the rest, though the Heads vary in quality, some are very fine; and almost all are characteristically Blake-like, at least in the accessories. Otway was included because he was also a Sussex poet (there had been an Otway's Walk at Eartham); and Cowper was, naturally, a *sine quâ non*. The embellishments to his picture are interesting: on one side of the head is a small boy brandishing a book with true Blakeian abandon, in whom one would like to see an imaginary version of the youthful Thomas; and on the other side is a rather forlorn dog, who, though doubtless intended for Beau, is, doubtless also, not a bit like him. The Dante is a splendid drawing, and so is the Milton. It is not so very strange that, brought thus in close proximity to the most recent biographer of that poet, Blake's mind should so shortly have turned to that remarkable prophecy to which he gave the name of *Milton*, or that he should have visualised himself walking on the shore with the poet himself.

Most interesting of all, from our point of view, is the head of Thomas Hayley. His father had never approved of the engraving that Blake had done for the *Essay*, and here now was his chance to make amends. It is, perhaps, not a very prepossessing portrait, but it is, I think, a touching one; and Gilchrist is quite wrong when he says of it, with his usual bias against Hayley, that it is "encircled by cooing doves".[6] It is true that part of the composition which frames the head consists of a couple of doves, but they are formalised and structural, and there is nothing of that sentimentality about them which might be expected from his description. Moreover, there is no evidence that they are cooing!

Blake evidently enjoyed this commission. On November 26, when Hayley was away gathering Cowperian material, he wrote to report progress: "Absorbed by the poets Milton, Homer, Camoens, Ercilla, Ariosto, and Spenser, whose physiognomies have been my delightful study.... Time flies very fast and very merrily...."[7] Nor was this all. Hayley, with his usual officiousness (using the word in the same sense as Samuel Johnson used it when he called Levett 'officious, innocent, sincere'), had already introduced Blake to many of his friends among the neighbouring gentry: to Lord Egremont, to Lord Bathurst of Lavant, and to Miss Poole, the friend of Lord Sheffield, who about this time had settled in the neighbourhood. The Bathursts took drawing-lessons from Blake, and even offered him a salaried post as painter-in-ordinary to their family, which offer he fortunately did not accept. And both they and the other persons mentioned, as well as others unspecified, were, it seems, prevailed upon by Hayley to commission Blake to paint their portraits in miniature, a branch of art at which he had not yet, as far as we know, tried his hand.

Much commotion has been made about these miniatures by recent partizans of Blake, and still more about a "set of hand-screens" which one of Hayley's aristocratic friends (probably Lady Bathurst) asked him to paint for her, and which was the only commission, Blake himself said, that he ever refused. The implication seems to be that, while it was perfectly all right for Blake to drudge his life away executing other people's designs for such works as Euler's *Algebra*, or *The Elements of Medicine*, or even Mr. Wedgwood's trade catalogue, there was something intrinsically dreadful in his being asked to apply his genius to original portraiture. It is true that he did, for some reason, draw the line at the hand-screens, though even so I fancy it was more the way in which he was asked to do the job, than the job itself. For, after all, to execute an original design, even on a hand-screen, is surely no more degrading for an artist than engraving mathematical diagrams, or views of Mr. Wedgwood's tea-pots.

On May 10, 1801, Blake reported progress to his friend and patron, Butts,[8] to whom he wrote always in full sincerity: "Mr. Hayley acts like a Prince. I am at complete Ease, but wish to do my Duty, especially to you, who were the precursor of my present Fortune. I never will send you a Picture unworthy of my present proficiency. I soon shall send you several; my present engagements are in Miniature Painting. Miniature has become a Goddess in my Eyes, & my Friends in Sussex say that I Excel in the pursuit. I have a great many orders, & they Multiply."

Not much dissatisfaction there, one would think, particularly as, later on in the letter, he presses Mr. and Mrs. Butts to visit him that summer, saying that "Felpham ... is the sweetest spot on Earth". And this, it must be remembered, was not a first impression. He had now been resident in Sussex for eight months, and had endured the rigours of a rural winter.

Against this is the circumstance, to which the reader may give what force he chooses, that Hayley had been exceedingly busy. The *Life of Cowper* was rapidly taking shape. Hayley, when once he started, was a tremendous worker, and I doubt whether, during that first winter, Blake saw more of him than made an agreeable diversion. Certainly, there was nothing, as yet, to justify those later, devastating epigrams.

2

With Blake thus happily employed, and, with his reduced expenses, living, I suspect, much more comfortably than he had been able to do in London, we can now leave him for a time while we pursue Hayley's activities.

Cowper was the substance of his entire thought. He had even abandoned his intention of printing the devotional sonnets to the memory of Tom; and almost the whole of his time was taken up in writing long letters to Lady Hesketh, Rose, and Johnson, and in examining the vast piles of manuscript which they intermittently despatched to him.

In the autumn of 1800, he went to London, and it was upon this occasion that Blake wrote to him to report progress on the Heads; but soon he was home again, and endeavouring, with every artifice at his command, to satisfy the exacting demands of Lady Hesketh. On December 24 he wrote to her, evidently after a minor crisis in their affairs:

Let me hasten to meet you, my dear Lady Hesketh, as you profess to appear "with *the olive branch* in your hand". Your *pacific letter* has found me just returned to my marine cell, after an excursion, which infinite kindness from some old and some new friends had induced me to make of much longer continuance than I at first proposed. . . .

Send as much as you can send, both of prose and verse, to the care of our dear Rose, who will forward the papers to me. He has promised to visit my retirement by the 12th of next month; and I may possibly return with him to town, to glean a few more materials for a work which I certainly wish to render as perfect as I can. . . .

It was, he said in conclusion, a cordial satisfaction to him that he had been able to tranquillize the spirits of this truly good lady.

And, indeed, she was a lady who needed some tranquillizing. Some while later, for instance, the unfortunate Mr. Greatheed disclosed sundry events in Cowper's life which Lady Hesketh had wished to "shield from the Publick Eye", and this is what she wrote about him:[9] "Oh dear—can you Sir really suppose that I feel no enmity against the Man who has destroy'd my peace of mind for ever!— who has injured a whole family in its tenderest point!—has *cruelly* and *inhumanly* revealed Secrets disclosed to Him, under the sacred seal of Friendship! And broke ev'ry tye that binds man to man." It is proof of how, by this time, her trust in Hayley's discretion had grown that she could end all this by remarking: "In your hands, Sir, I know he [Cowper] will be safe."

Nevertheless, his task was not easy, and he must often have faltered. He did falter, and rather badly, in the January of 1801, when, upon the receipt of a present from that same Mr. Greatheed of a book of Missionary Voyages, he lapsed into the composition of a poem entitled *The Christian Navigator*, in cantos, the first of which, and also the last, I think, was completed by the end of February. It had a motto from Cicero, and, as was usual with his unfinished works, was "rather a favourite" of its author. Miss Poole had it read to her; so it is probable that William Blake did not escape either.

But the pull of conscience was fortunately strong. *The Christian Navigator* was abandoned, and the *Life of Cowper* set about in earnest, until March, when his health, he tells us, necessitated some relaxation and off he went to London. While there he heard of the death of yet another old friend, Aylward, the musician. For him he furnished the accustomed epitaph:

> Aylward adieu! My gentle antient friend!
> Regret and honour on thy grave attend:
> Harmonious skill thy rapid hand possess'd,
> And moral harmony enrich'd thy breast;
> For Heaven most largely to thy frame assign'd
> Benevolence, the music of the mind!
> Mild was the tenor of thy mortal scene,
> Thy death as easy as thy life serene.

But this by the way; since now all was for the service of Cowper. Rose was sent to call upon the formidable John Newton; Joseph Hill had to be seen, and of course Thurlow; and Mr. Greatheed was approached for information, and invited to Eartham. And with him the daring project of an interview with Lady Austen was canvassed. As early as September, 1800, Greatheed had run her to earth at 14, Charlotte Street, Portland Place, and had sent Hayley a lengthy and most interesting account of her;[10] and now through his good offices they met, and Hayley asked eagerly for a sight of the famous letter in which Cowper had broken off relations. Alas! she had burnt it. In the meantime, Lady Hesketh kept on badgering him to complete the book, and to keep it short; and Johnson was greatly exercised in mind about his new edition of the *Poems*. It was a scene of great activity.

In the Spring of 1801, Johnson came to Sussex, for the first time since the great visit of 1792, and brought with him Cowper's publisher, Johnson. Eartham was still empty, though a caretaker was installed who was instructed to provide the travellers with cold meat as they broke their journey there on the way down. Hayley confessed that, for his part, he was still too affected by his recollection of the scenes he had endured there to show them the house; but he asked his friend to do the honours on his behalf.

Through May, through June, July, the tale was the same: dates and documents, documents and dates. He depends, wrote Hayley, on Johnson's accuracy; he had seen Rose: still, however, an awful chasm yawned in the *Life* between 1770 and 1780. It was a chasm, for obvious reasons, not readily to be bridged.

In June, a stroke of good fortune befell him, and he acquired in Margaret Beke an admirable housekeeper, who greatly ameliorated the circumstances of his life. Her probity, he says, saved him from "the many ruinous depredations to which a solitary studious author is exposed".

By August, at last, traces of relaxation were to be observed. He was giving more of his attention to other matters, such as the projected memorial to be erected to Mrs. Unwin. The name of Joseph Seagrave, too, now for the first time appears, and calls for a little elucidation.

Seagrave was a printer of Chichester, and Hayley had now determined, despite considerable opposition on the part of Publisher Johnson, under whose imprint the *Life* was to be issued, that his book should be printed locally, by Seagrave's firm. I do not think this was for the sake of fostering local industry, but was rather because he thought it would be more convenient for him when it came to the matter of proof-reading. Seagrave was a good and honest man, though he had an impediment in his speech, and employed compositors who were in the habit of getting drunk. He must have done very well out of the printing of Hayley's most successful book, and they became fast friends. What Hayley thought of him may be indicated by a testimonial, dated February 17, 1805, which is to be seen in the British Museum:[11] "If you ever know Seagrave, you will certainly regard him with esteem and confidence, for there does not exist a man, in his line of Life, who has a more just and delicate sense of professional probity . . . most assuredly I shall never desert a Printer, who with a very clear and cultivated understanding, has a most upright and benevolent heart."

Later on, as we shall see, Seagrave's benevolent heart carried him into a sort of conditional immortality: he became one of the two sureties for William Blake on the occasion when he stood his trial for high treason.

3

Even Blake was at last coming back into the orbit of Hayley's activities. Presumably he had by now finished his Heads, and so Hayley felt it incumbent to provide him with further lucrative tasks.

This time his scheme resembled that which had been successful in the case of *Little Tom*. Hayley pondered the situation, and then, almost sooner than it takes to write the words, had composed a number of *Ballads founded on Anecdotes Relating to Animals*. All that remained was for Blake to illustrate them with suitable engravings and for Seagrave to print them as separate broadsheets. Then, while Hayley paid Seagrave for his part of the business, all profits accruing from the sales were to be Blake's. Hayley expected no return himself from the transaction; his compositions were a present to his friend the artist.

Consequently, on August 6, he was able to send Johnson the sensational tidings: "Our good Blake is *actually in labour with a young lion*. The new-born cub will probably kiss your hands in a week or two."

Now, a great deal of ridicule has been cast upon this project, and, while I should not for a moment claim that it was the sort of enterprise upon which the time of a William Blake could most profitably be spent, there are one or two misconceptions concerning it which it may be useful to clear up. The first and most important of these is that Hayley very clearly did not intend these truly infantine productions for the consumption of adults. His preface to the collected *Ballads*, published in book form in 1805, makes quite clear what his purpose was, and, as he expressed it with much greater brevity than was customary with him, I will print his preface entire:

> Three words of Horace may form an introduction to the following pages, the very words, which that amiable physician and poet, the late Dr. Cotton of St. Alban's, prefixed as a motto to his elegant and moral little volume of Visions in Verse:
>
> "VIRGINIBUS PUERISQUE CANTO."
>
> Or in plainer English prose:—This book is intended for young Readers.

Nothing, I apprehend, could be much clearer than that, and when it is understood I think we should be able to regard the *Ballads* in rather a different light, even if we still cannot but deplore that Blake's time should have been employed upon such trifles. Yet for this, too, there is a tolerably adequate reason, namely that Hayley was now so occupied with his *Life of Cowper* that he possessed insufficient time, even if he had possessed sufficient ability, to write anything more substantial. And, if he did not write anything for Blake to illustrate, no one else seemed disposed to oblige. It was the *Ballads* or nothing; and from Blake's point of view the *Ballads* were much better than nothing. *Little Tom* had even brought in a little money. It was always possible that the *Ballads*, professionally printed, might bring in more. That, at least, was the way Hayley's mind worked, and I can see no evidence that Blake played his part in the affair with any very peculiar travail of spirit.

Blake, at last, after nearly a year at Felpham, was engaged in the glorification of Cowper, though only by way of the illustrations to the now projected volume of the translations of Milton's Latin Poems which, to Hayley's bright fancy, had merely to be published to provide at once money sufficient to pay for a monument in Cowper's honour, to be set up "in the metropolis".

The scheme, however, fell through; no monument was erected; and it was not, in fact, until 1808 that the translations were published, and then the illustrations were not by Blake. As compensation for this disappointment, he was set to work on a series of plates to yet another edition of the *Triumphs of Temper*, from designs provided by Flaxman's sister, Maria; and, at last, by September, the great business of *The Life of Cowper* claimed him, and Hayley reports him "finishing very happily the plate of the Poet's mother". By October: "The warm-hearted indefatigable Blake works daily by my side, on the intended decorations of our biography. Engraving, of all human works, appears to require the largest portion of patience, and he happily possesses more of that inestimable virtue, than I ever saw united before to an imagination so lively and so prolific."

Hayley was overworking, with the inevitable result that his eyesight was affected. "I am often unwell;" he wrote to Johnson, "the natural consequence of much affliction; but, I thank Heaven, I have no very serious illness at present. . . ." And he added, with his usual flourish of trumpets, "If I die Rose would take over the biography."

He did not die, but he did, I am afraid, for a time rope in the indefatigable Blake as his amanuensis, in a fashion not altogether justifiable. On September 11, 1801, Blake wrote again to Butts:[12] "Time flies faster (as seems to me here) than in London. I labour incessantly & accomplish not one half of what I intend, because my Abstract folly hurries me often away while I am at work, carrying me over Mountains & Valleys, which are not Real, in a Land of Abstraction where Spectres of the Dead wander." Then comes a very typical and Blake-like passage, to be followed at last by a sober account of his more mundane labours: "I continue painting Miniatures & Improve more & more, as all my friends tell me; but my Principal labour at this time is Engraving Plates for Cowper's Life, a Work of Magnitude, which Mr. Hayley is now Labouring at with all his matchless industry, & which will be a most valuable acquisition to Literature, not only on account of Mr. Hayley's composition, but also as it will contain Letters of Cowper to his friends, Perhaps, or rather Certainly, the very best letters that ever were published."

Meanwhile Johnson was being difficult again. It was essential, Hayley thought, that they should meet to discuss progress; but Johnson had tiresomely taken a pupil, which rendered it impossible for him to come to Sussex. He countered by inviting Hayley to

Norfolk. But Hayley had always fought shy of Norfolk. He had, he said, "made an heroic resolution of not moving beyond a morning's ride from the turret, till I have completed my biographical work. My heart and soul are so full of those two dear affectionate angels, *Cowper and Tom*! that I seem to converse with them on my pillow before the dawn of day." And he added that, under their direct inspiration, he had, the other morning, composed some lines for the tomb of Mrs. Unwin, which really seem to me to have a good deal of quiet merit:

> Trusting in God, with all her heart and mind,
> This woman proved magnanimously kind;
> Endured affliction's desolating hail,
> And watch'd a Poet thro' misfortune's vale:
> Her spotless dust angelic guards defend,
> It is the dust of Unwin, Cowper's friend!
> That single title in itself is fame,
> For all, who read his verse, revere her name.

4

Winter was approaching once more, the second winter of Blake's sojourn at Felpham. It led to a surprising development which, if it is to be rightly understood, needs to be linked up with the fact that there was a strong streak of pedagogy in Hayley's make-up. He had instructed Eliza, as long as Eliza had consented to be instructed; he had educated Tom, as one might say, with his own hands; and he had played the schoolmaster with Henry Carwardine and Thomas Sockett and young George Wyndham. And so now, very likely at Blake's own request, we perceive him starting upon the staggering enterprise of teaching that mature student the Greek language.

It began with Johnson's new edition of Cowper's translation of the *Odyssey*, which had recently come to hand. Blake came every evening now, and together the pair of them collated the text with that of the first edition, and the Greek original. Blake, though he had had few educational advantages, had a natural flair for languages. Even in his old age he taught himself Italian sufficient to read Dante in the original. Yet for all that, it is an astonishing scene to ruminate upon; the library at Felpham during the winter of 1801–02, with the Romney portraits of Cowper and Charlotte Smith and Mme. de Genlis looking down upon them, and Lady Hamilton, too, as Sensibility—to say nothing of Blake's own recently completed Heads: and there, at the table, in the shadowed circle of the candlelight, William Blake and William Hayley, busily construing the *Odyssey*. It is, on the whole, a friendly spectacle.

Besides, as well as on their nightly sessions, during the daytime now Blake and Hayley were constantly together. Hayley, though he would have been the last to admit it, was recovering at length from the confusion into which the double catastrophe of Tom's and Cowper's deaths had plunged him. And he had also, at about this time, developed a new and pleasant routine excursion. Miss Poole of Lavant, who for some while has been hovering upon the margin of the picture, now at last moves up nearer its lighted centre.

Hayley, as will be remembered, met her first in 1794, when she came to Eartham with Lord Sheffield and his Maria. Presumably she was a friend of Maria's, since her family hailed from Chailey, which was near to Lord Sheffield's seat.[13] At some time that I have been unable to discover, Miss Poole's widowed step-mother had moved to Chichester, and Miss Poole herself had taken a house at Mid Lavant, a village some three miles north of that city. It had now become Hayley's custom to ride over twice weekly to visit Miss Poole, and, in the fashion of the time, to breakfast with her. The journey was a good ten miles each way, and the days chosen were always the same, Tuesdays and Fridays. Miss Poole was evidently a lady of literary interests, since Hayley was in the habit of reading his works aloud to her; and as she was a couple of years his junior, she was a companion sufficiently interesting to a lonely and romantic widower. Yet, despite this, Hayley did not always, by any means, make the journey alone. Blake, upon the pony Bruno, which had once belonged to Tom, and was now lent to him by Miss Poole, who had taken him over (I assume that it was the same Bruno, and not another pony of the same name), was now his constant companion; and, from the many references to her in Blake's letters after he had left Felpham, it is pretty clear that he, also, thought "the good Paulina" a most agreeable woman. Indeed, there was a period, to be referred to later, when the idea crossed his mind that he might do worse than go and live in Lavant himself.

Miss Poole's name was Henrietta, though it was always shortened to Harriet. The title "Paulina" was, it would seem, a sort of corruption of her surname, based upon the same romantic eighteenth century principle as caused Miss Seward to be known to her intimates as Julia. Her house, according to Gilchrist,[14] stood by the roadside, to the right, as you enter Mid Lavant from Chichester; and, if this be so, it is still standing, a solid, square red-brick building, with later Victorian additions. A gravel sweep leads up to the front-door, and, at the back, a small terraced garden commands a splendid prospect of the Lavant brook and the red roofs of the little village of East Lavant, beyond which rises up the bare line of the downs at Goodwood, and that famous hill which is known as The Trundle.

When I visited the place in 1949, it was derelict, and on the point of being converted into a country club. One wonders how many of the members of that club will ever give a thought to the scenes witnessed by the place almost a hundred and fifty years ago: of the arrival of Hayley on Hidalgo, and Blake on Bruno; of Miss Poole welcoming them with Hayley's favourite coffee; of his "seizing a pen", as he so frequently did upon these occasions, because, it seems, his proofs and letters were usually sent to him there on the days he was expected, so that he might receive them earlier than he would have done at Felpham.

Lavant was not the only place that Hayley visited with Blake. In October 1801, his old servant, William Metcalfe, now settled in a cottage on the Eartham estate, died; and Hayley and Blake were present at his death. It has been suggested that Blake's engraving for Blair's *Grave*, of the Death of the Good Old Man, owes something to this visit; and it is certain that Hayley once more came forward with an epitaph, which, as is the case of most of those that he wrote for his humbler friends, is not at all contemptible:

> To this plain grave, that Nature's hand will dress,
> That truth will honour, and affection bless,
> A kind old servant sunk; this stone may give
> His sweet and simple character to live:
> A hand to minister, a heart to feel,
> Good-natured diligence, and sprightly zeal,
> Metcalfe! were thine, on earth—in joy's bright sphere
> Now be it thine, these blessed words to hear—
> "Come, my good servant," from that Master's voice
> Who bids the living die, the dead rejoice.

It is gratifying to learn of the death of this old servant that, "Providence conducted his dissolution in a manner most merciful to his own feelings, and those of his affectionate master".

5

In January 1802, the elusive Johnson arrived again, and Hayley was able to cross-question him concerning Cowper's last days. Blake executed a portrait of Johnson which has now vanished. It is a pity, for Blake found him sympathetic, and said of him that he was "known by all his Friends as the most innocent forgetter of his own Interests". He also painted for him three panels to decorate a chimney-piece of his rectory at Yaxham: of *Olney Bridge*, of *Winter*, and of *Evening*. *Olney Bridge* has, unhappily, been destroyed; but the other two still exist, and are in the possession of the descendants of the man who commissioned them.[15]

By February, Johnson was back home again, and Hayley was writing to send him a title-page for his new edition of Cowper's *Homer*, with a Greek motto "which I and Blake, who is just become a Grecian, and literally learning the language, consider as a happy hit!" And he concluded his letter with the phrase: "The new Grecian greets you affectionately."

March saw the manuscript of the *Life of Cowper* in the hands of Seagrave; and Blake's four copper-plates to it were printed off. The whole job had taken just over a year, which was good going. Hayley was now able to turn his attention to other matters, and from March till the following December he was busy with his *Memoir* of his son, frequently breaking off to see the two volumes of his other *Life* through the press.

Nor was this all: the question of Cowper's monument at Dereham was becoming urgent, and a vast quantity of correspondence had to be entered into concerning it. Lady Hesketh had strong views on the subject. So had Hayley. As was natural, Flaxman had been pressed into service, and by the beginning of 1802 he had produced "some simply elegant sketches". Even with these Hayley was not quite satisfied, particularly with the shape of the lyre, which he "presumptuously" redesigned himself. And it did not stop at redesigning lyres: he himself, ignoring Flaxman's offering, "formed a device of *the Bible upright* supporting 'The Task', with a laurel leaf and *Palms*, such as I send you neatly copied by our kind Blake". Of this design both Blake and Miss Poole warmly approved; if Johnson and Lady Hesketh only did so too, all would be well.

But Lady Hesketh was indeed difficult. She wrote: "Indeed, dear Sir, the more I reflect on the Subject in agitation, the more I am convinced of the *very great impropriety* of such a monument as that on which you have set your heart!—Nothing can be more *degrading* to a Man of Genius and Talents than any endeavours (especially when made, too, by his own particular friends or Relations) to force him on the publick notice, by any means *distinct from his own* Talents and attainments! Let the Rich *Grocer*, or *Soap Boyler* who has acquired Hundreds of Thousands by his own Industry, shew the effects of *that industry* to the world! Let *him* try to lose his obscurity by a Sumptuous Monument, and let all the art of the Sculptor be employed in a Pompous display of those Riches on which he built his fame and which were *his only boast*—but suffer not our Modest—ingenious—all-excelling friend, whose merits when living courted the Shade, and who from early youth Cherished Retirement, as the great blessing of human life—let not *him* be surrounded with figures and Emblems, however beautiful in themselves, that are perfectly unappropriate to Him!"

Lady Hesketh's employment of italics is almost as terrifying as was Queen Victoria's. Nevertheless, Hayley, in the end, got his way, if indeed the foregoing letter does refer to his ultimate design, and not to some earlier and more grandiose one. There was, however, one adjustment needed. Instead of the Bible being made to support *The Task*, the positions of the volumes were reversed: a decorous modification for which we may hope the Revd. Johnson was responsible.

With this weighty matter off his mind, Hayley was once again in a position to turn his attention to the requirements of Blake, and this led soon to a revival of interest in the *Ballads* which, as we have seen, as long ago as August 1801 had been taking shape. Doubtless the illustrations to Cowper's *Life* had thrust this project to one side, since it was only now, in the June of 1802, that the first of the broadsheets was produced, with a frontispiece and two vignettes. It was *The Elephant*, and its price was half a crown.

By this time, however, the first rift in the good relations between Blake and Hayley was becoming apparent. As early as September 11, 1801, Blake had been complaining to Butts, though only that he was distressed by the rapid passage of time, which rendered it impossible for him to complete the work he wished most urgently to do. But now a second winter had passed, and in May both he and Mrs. Blake were ill. The cottage was damp, and during the winter Mrs. Blake had been stricken with ague and rheumatism. Perhaps also, at last, the essential imbecility of the *Ballads* project was becoming apparent to Blake; though one would never have guessed it from Hayley, who, that same May, wrote enthusiastically of him, "by my side, representing on copper an Adam, of his own, surrounded by animals, as a frontispiece"; and, again, in June: "Our alert Blake is preparing, *con spirito*, to launch his eagle, with a lively hope of seeing him superior to the elephant. . . . Our good Lady Hesketh has received and patronized his elephant with the most obliging benignity."

The allusion to "our good Lady Hesketh" was, in the circumstances, a charitable one, because we happen to have the other side of the picture; and I shall quote the correspondence with her on the subject of the Elephant in some detail, since not only is it not well known (indeed, I have not seen it in print before), but because it shows Hayley in relation to Blake in a light much more favourable than that in which he is generally represented.

On June 28, 1802, Hayley had written to her:[16] "Your extreme kindness, my dear Lady, to the group of Elephants [which he had recently sent her] . . . so endeared you to the Tribes of noble animals, that five imperial Eagles . . . hope in the course of next week to have the pleasure of perching in your presence."

On July 3, Lady Hesketh returned the following characteristic broadside:[16]

Dear Sir,

May I be *forgiven* if I say to *You*, that some, among the *very* few now here, who have any pretensions to *Taste*, find many defects in your friend's engravings?—I know you would be much better pleased that they should find fault with *You* than with Him whom you patronize. *Yet*,—if Mr. Blake is but new in the world, may it not be *in reality kinder*, to point out his failings, than to suffer him to think his performances faultless—surely it may, as it may stimulate his endeavours after Perfection!

Blake's chief critic, it appeared, was an artistic old gentleman of eighty-two, who had provided several hints which Lady Hesketh thought might prove useful to him.

Hayley, at Lavant, on July 6, seized a pen and wrote a speedy reply:[16] "Blake is in bed under care of perhaps the very best wife that ever mortal possessed, at least one that most admirably illustrates that expressive appellation *a Helpmate*."

It took more than this, however, to soften Lady Hesketh, and, on July 10, she returned to the attack,[16] this time on the subject of the Eagle, which had now reached her: "Will you not join with me," she wrote, "in the opinion that your ingenious friend pays little Respect of the 'Human Face Divine' . . . for certainly the Countenances of his women and children are nothing less than pleasing. . . . The faces of his babies are *not young*."

Hayley answered her on July 15, in a letter of much interest,[16] and one which should always be borne in mind when one is disposed to write facetiously on the subject of his relations with Blake:

> Pray suffer no mortal, my dear Lady, however you may give them *credit for refined taste in Art*, to *prejudice* you against the works of that too feeling artist, whose Designs met with so *little mercy* from your *Octogenaire admirable!* . . . [There is] great spirit and sentiment in the engravings of my friend. . . . Whatever the Merits, or the Failings, of my diligent and grateful artist may be, I know I shall interest your Heart and soul *in his Favour*, when I tell you, that he resembles our beloved Bard in the Tenderness of his Heart, and in the perilous powers of an Imagination utterly unfit to take due care of Himself. With admirable Faculties, his sensibility is so *dangerously acute*, that the common rough treatment which true genius often receives from *ordinary minds* in the commerce of the world, might not only wound Him *more than it should do*, but really reduce Him to the Incapacity of an Ideot, without the consolatory support of a considerate Friend—From these excesses of Feeling, and of irregular Health, (forever connected with such excesses) His productions must ever perhaps be *unequal*, but in all He does, however wild or hasty, a penetrating eye will discover true Genius, and if it were possible to keep his too apprehensive spirit for a Length of Time *unruffled* He would produce works of the pencil, almost as excellent and original, as those works of the pen, which flow'd from the dear poet, of whom He often reminds me—when his mind is darkened with any unpleasant *apprehension*— He reminds me of him also by being a most fervent Admirer of the Bible, and intimately acquainted with all its Beauties—I wish our beloved Bard had been as happy in a *Wife* for Heaven has bestow'd on this extraordinary mortal perhaps the only female on Earth who could have suited Him *exactly*—They have now been married more than 17 years and are as fond of each other, as if their Honey Moon were still shining— They live in a neat little cottage, which they both regard as the most delightful residence ever inhabited by a mortal; they have no servant:—

the good woman not only does all the work of the House, but she even makes the greater part of her Husband's dress, and assists him in *his Art*—she draws, she engraves, and sings delightfully, and is so truly the Half of her good man, that they seem animated by one soul, and that a soul of indefatigable Industry and Benevolence—it sometimes harries them both to labour *rather too much*, and I had some time ago the pain of seeing both confin'd to their Bed– I endeavour to be as kind as I can to two creatures so very interesting and meritorious, and indeed I consider it as a point of devotion to the two dear departed angels [Cowper and Tom] to be so, for I am confident I could gratify their spirits in nothing so much, as in befriending two wonderful Beings, whom they both, were they still on earth, and possess'd of Health, would peculiarly delight to befriend. . . .

It is a letter that does Hayley credit, and it is a pity Blake never knew of it. I think a good deal of the storm that was shortly to blow up might have been averted if he had understood that it was thus that Hayley regarded him—at least, when he was being subjected to outside attack. Even so, it is at the same time very probable that some, at least, of the growing irritation which Blake was soon to feel for his mentor may have been caused by the latter's well-meaning attempts to expound to him views such as those held by the *octogenaire admirable*, who did, in point of fact, represent pretty accurately the average level of the taste of his time.

Only two more *Ballads* were published as broadsheets: *The Lion*, in August; and *The Dog*, in September. They did not sell, and the series was discontinued. We shall encounter them later in another form.

6

As early as January 10, 1802, Blake had written to Butts:[17] "When I came down here, I was more sanguine than I am at present; but it was because I was ignorant of many things which have since occurred, & chiefly the unhealthiness of the place. Yet I do not repent of coming on a thousand accounts; & Mr. H., I doubt not, will do ultimately all that both he & I wish—that is, to lift me out of difficulty; but this is no easy matter to a man who, having Spiritual Enemies of such formidable magnitude, cannot expect to want natural hidden ones." He is, he adds, now working on the plates to illustrate the new edition of the *Triumphs of Temper*; and he continues, ominously enough: "if it was fit for me, I doubt not that I should be Employ'd in Greater things". And, further: "My unhappiness has arisen from a source which, if explor'd too narrowly, might hurt my pecuniary circumstances, As my dependence is on Engraving at present, & particularly on the Engravings I have in hand for Mr. H.: & I find on all hands great objections to my doing anything but the meer drudgery of business, & intimations that if I do not confine myself to this, I shall not live. . . . This from Johnson & Fuseli brought me down here, & this from Mr. H.

will bring me back again; for that I cannot live without doing my duty to lay up treasures in heaven is Certain & Determined, & to this I have long made up my mind, & why this should be made an objection to Me, while Drunkenness, Lewdness, Gluttony & even Idleness itself, does not hurt other men, let Satan himself explain." But the whole letter is a crucial one, and should be read in full if the approaching situation is to be understood.

It was, of course, perfectly true that Hayley regarded Blake, primarily, as an engraver. Even Fuseli, the one man of whom Blake never made injurious remarks, had, according to the foregoing, held the same opinion; and perhaps it was not greatly Hayley's fault if he did not realize that he was also much more. There is, I think, an interesting and an obscure question: the extent to which, at any time, Blake took Hayley into his confidence with regard to the projects which were really dear to his heart—his Prophetic Books, and his poems. "I am under the direction of Messengers from Heaven, Daily & Nightly," he had written to Butts. It is uncommonly doubtful if he made any such pronouncement to his Sussex patron. I believe that Hayley's letter to Lady Hesketh, quoted above, really gives as true a picture as possible of what Hayley thought of Blake at the time at which it was written. It was not, of course, a true picture, but it is hard to say how, upon the evidences Blake vouchsafed to him, he could have arrived at a truer. There are some people, and Blake was one of them, who never say more than they know their auditor will understand.

At the same time it is probable that Blake did show some of his original poems to Hayley, and if so it must have been *The Four Zoas*, which he had almost completed by the time he came to Felpham. With Hayley's background, and bearing in mind his own works, it is obvious enough what his reaction must have been. Indeed, the reaction of so staunch an admirer of Blake as William Michael Rossetti, as late as 1873, was not very different. "I must", he wrote,[18] "nevertheless avow that I think there was something in his mind not exactly sane. I apprehend that there are in the Prophetic Books many passages which show the author to have been possessed by ideas which he could not regulate or control—indeed, he himself proclaimed as much when he asserted that he wrote under immediate dictation, and without the exercise of any option of his own; and, what is far more symptomatic in the same direction, I think he every now and then 'boiled over' . . . into words which have no definable relevancy to anything that deserves to be called a thought or idea." And even the passionate partizanship of Swinburne confessed that the bewildering catalogues and genealogies in *Jerusalem*, and elsewhere, "seem at first invented only to strike any miserable reader with furious or lachrymose lunacy".

It was not until the nineties of the last century that a school arose, of which Ellis and Yeats were the harbingers, for which every word of the Prophetic Books was charged with the last extremity of esoteric meaning. This school remains with us, and this is not the place to discuss the soundness, or otherwise, of its doctrines. I will only remark, as mildly as possible, that a great many of the people who speak with the largest enthusiasm of Blake's Prophetic Books have, patently, never tried the experiment of reading them consecutively through. It is not an easy undertaking, and, for all the magnificent things in them, I doubt if anyone who (particularly as regards the two last, *Milton* and *Jerusalem*) formed of them an opinion not strikingly different from that expressed by W. M. Rossetti, would have any great need to feel ashamed of it.

This, however, is by the way, since what at the moment we are in pursuit of is not the real Blake, or the real Hayley, so much as the Blake who existed in Hayley's mind, and the Hayley who existed in Blake's. We have perhaps already given data enough to establish the nature of the former; and we must, therefore, see what can be done to elucidate the latter. For this two prime sources of evidence exist in, respectively, Blake's letters to Butts (and one very important one to his brother James), and his poem *Milton* which, from internal evidence, was composed, for the most part, at Felpham.

The references in his letters were, at first, guarded. On November 22, 1802, he apologized to Butts for his long delay in answering his last.[19] "I have been very unhappy," he said, "& could not think of troubling you about it, or any of my real Friends." Portrait-painting has been the trouble. But, "Tho' I have been very unhappy, I am so no longer. I am again Emerged into the light of Day ... I have travel'd thro' Perils & Darkness not unlike a Champion. I have Conquer'd, and shall still Go on Conquering. Nothing can withstand the fury of my Course among the Stars of God & in the Abysses of the Accuser." And, with this same letter, he enclosed those enigmatic verses that he had composed more than a year before, when he had been walking from Felpham to Lavant, and which contain that highly ambiguous couplet:

> Rememb'ring the Verses that Hayley sung
> When my heart knock'd against the root of my tongue.

As for *Milton*: well, what was Hayley to make of a man who, a couple of hundred yards from the chaste and classical walls of his Turret, was capable of seeing this kind of thing:

> The Spectre of Satan stood upon the roaring sea & beheld
> Milton within his sleeping Humanity; trembling & shudd'ring
> He stood upon the waves a Twenty-seven fold mighty Demon
> Gorgeous & beautiful; loud roll his thunders against Milton.
> Loud Satan thunder'd, loud & dark upon mild Felpham shore
> Not daring to touch one fibre he howl'd round upon the Sea?

Milton ultimately enunciates his creed, which, very naturally, is Blake's; and into it one can read just as much criticism as we please of the sort of thing that Hayley stood for:

> To bathe in the Waters of Life, to wash off the Not Human,
> I come in Self-annihilation & the grandeur of Inspiration,
> To cast off Rational Demonstration by Faith in the Saviour,
> To cast off the rotten rags of Memory by Inspiration,
> To cast off Bacon, Locke & Newton from Albion's covering,
> To take off his filthy garments & clothe him with Imagination,
> To cast aside from Poetry all that is not Inspiration,
> That it no longer shall dare to mock with the aspersion of Madness
> Cast on the Inspired by the tame high finisher of paltry Blots
> Indefinite, or paltry Rhymes, or paltry Harmonies,
> Who creeps into State Government like a catterpiller to destroy;
> To cast off the idiot Questioner who is always questioning
> But never capable of answering, who sits with a sly grin
> Silent plotting when to question, like a thief in a cave,
> Who publishes doubt & calls it knowledge, whose Science is Despair,
> Whose pretence to knowledge is Envy, whose whole Science is
> To destroy the wisdom of ages to gratify ravenous Envy
> That rages round him like a Wolf day & night without rest:
> He smiles with condescension, he talks of Benevolence & Virtue,
> And those who act with Benevolence & Virtue they murder time on time.
> These are the destroyers of Jerusalem....

And, further, he refers in a phrase cuttingly accurate to the school of poets to which Hayley belonged

> Who pretend to Poetry that they may destroy Imagination
> By imitation of Nature's Images drawn from Remembrance....

It is, indeed, not remarkable that the Felpham adventure should have ended in an imperfect sympathy between its two principals. What is much more remarkable is that it should have lasted without overt breach for so long. Blake was not given to suffering fools gladly, and, though it was of course to his financial interest to keep silent as long as he could, it is, I think, only fair to say that it was not until the end of January 1803, until, that is, he had been in Sussex nearly two years and a half, that the inner tension resulted in open explosion. The first undeniable sign of this was the very significant letter which, upon January 30, he despatched to his brother James, to say that he had decided to leave Felpham.

This letter we shall come to shortly, but, in the meantime, having just given a specimen of the work that Blake was even then composing, I feel I should, for contrast, also provide one of the work which Felpham was simultaneously producing by her "Eldest Son". It is not easy to do so briefly, for the *Ballads* are neither concise nor coherent. Perhaps the final stanza of *The Elephant* may serve, with its typically Hayleian moral:

> Ye, whom a friend's dark perils pain,
> When terrors most unnerve him,
> Learn from this Elephant to strain
> Your sinews to preserve him.

No wonder that, in after years, Blake was accustomed to say "the Visions were angry with me at Felpham!" It is an awe-inspiring thought that the author of *Milton* should have laid aside that prodigious scripture to peruse these productions, to make for them those designs which, in truth, are sometimes as queer as the verses they illustrate. Yet, for all that, Blake also called the *Ballads* "a beautiful little estate". After all, idiotic as they were, they had been written solely with the intention of benefiting him.

CHAPTER XIX

SUCCESS (1802-1804)

I

YET THE ODD THING was that, even now, while Hayley was producing these preposterous works, he stood upon the threshold of the greatest success of his life, the summit of his achievement.

The *Life of Cowper* was published at the beginning of 1803, and at once created a tremendous furore. Moreover, it deserved to; though not so much for the work Hayley had put into it, as for the wealth of Cowper's own letters which it contained. All along this had been his intention: that, as far as possible, Cowper should tell his own story. It was a fashion that had been set by Mason's *Life of Gray*; and Hayley, though he had been obliged to take considerable liberties with Cowper's text so as to satisfy the susceptibilities of Lady Hesketh, had, with this exception, carried his work out scrupulously.

He was unfortunate, I think. He had very nearly written a great biography. Indeed, I suppose his book would rank as such, if it had not speedily been superseded by fuller and better collections of the Letters. Even so, it is pleasant to know that, this time, he not only received his meed of applause, but also obtained a decidedly handsome financial reward. None of his earlier books had sold to anything like the same extent. When the project had been first mooted, he had said, "You will instantly give me credit for not wishing to derive any pecuniary advantage myself" from the work; and I think he spoke no less than the truth. Its success was, consequently, and he notes it himself, "a most gracious reward of Providence" and "a source of blessing". Though it is hard to believe nowadays, Horne Tooke, in a footnote to his *Memoirs*,[1] tells us that he had been assured that Mr. Hayley had received "the almost incredible sum of eleven thousand pounds" from its various editions.

Nor was it money alone. Encomiums came in from every hand. The legend of Cowper had been growing rapidly since his death; and his poetry had not yet reached the zenith of its popularity. Thurlow sent the author a warm letter of congratulation, so did the Bishop of Llandaff; while as for Lady Hesketh, she melted completely, and, when one of the earliest presentation copies reached her at Clifton on December 28, 1802, she acknowledged it in a letter in which her resources of italicising were extended to the full:

At four o'clock yesterday on my return from a half-hour's walk, I beheld on my table a square parcel, which my heart instantly told me, was *The Life of Cowper!*—*Hayley's Life of Cowper*! I surveyed it all round with fear and trembling; yet, with the most lively interest; but determined (whether *heroically or cowardly*, I know not by which name to call it) to defer opening it to some future time; when fortunately I discovered, that the paper was very wet, owing to something it had lain near in the coach. Of course, it was become necessary to strip it instantly; lest the precious contents should suffer: and having stripped it, was it in woman to do less than read the first volume quite through, only stopping to sleep? for as to dinner, it was impossible to eat any; neither could I have slept, had I not armed myself with ten drops of laudanum to tranquillize my agitated spirits. . . . I can go no further, till I have expressed to you some part of the admiration I feel on the Life. Its merit more than answered all the expectations I had formed. . . . You will not think I mean to flatter you, when I say that you have . . . executed it *con amore e con spirito*. . . . The elegance and animation of the style can only be equalled by the extreme tenderness and delicacy with which you touch on particular subjects, too affecting in their nature not to be seen with real pain by me, and which would indeed have been *insupportable*, had they been drawn by a rougher pencil.

It was a handsome tribute, coming whence it did, though it was succeeded by others of a less gratifying complexion. For Hayley, once he had tasted success, was quite unable to stop. Edition succeeded edition, each a little larger, each containing new matter; and eventually he put his foot in it badly by including a letter which, Lady Hesketh felt sure, would grievously upset King George III. But we anticipate; for the present all was sweetness and light, if we except one dissentient voice, that of the disgruntled Anna Seward, who on March 7, 1803, sent him an enormous letter saying all manner of disagreeable things about Cowper and about Hayley's high opinion of him. Hayley did not care. Anna Seward had passed out of his life. He did up with tape and with sealing-wax innumerable complimentary copies of his book and despatched them with letters and commendatory verses to all those for whose approbation he was especially ambitious. He even sent a copy to Pitt; and then, not wishing to seem partial, another to Pitt's old rival, Fox.

It is impossible to say now just what effect this uproarious success had upon him, after for so long being a comparative failure; but it is not, I think, without significance that it was upon the January 30th following the publication of his book that Blake despatched to his brother James, the letter to which reference has already been made:[2]

DEAR BROTHER,
    Your Letter mentioning Mr. Butts' account of my Ague surprized me because I have no Ague, but have had a Cold this Winter. You know that it is my way to make the best of everything. I never make myself nor

my friends uneasy if I can help it. My Wife has had Agues & Rheumatism almost ever since she has been here, but our time is almost out that we took the Cottage for. I did not mention our Sickness to you & should not to Mr. Butts but for a determination which we have lately made, namely To leave This Place, because I am now certain of what I have long doubted, Viz that H. is jealous as Stothard was & will be no further My friend than he is compell'd by circumstances. The truth is, As a Poet he is frightened at me & as a Painter his views & mine are opposite; he thinks to turn me into a Portrait Painter as he did Poor Romney, but this he nor all the devils in hell will never do. I must own that seeing H. like S., envious (& that he is I am now certain) made me very uneasy, but it is over & I now defy the worst & fear not while I am true to myself which I will be. This is the uneasiness I spoke of to Mr. Butts, but I did not tell him so plain & wish you to keep it a secret & to burn this letter because it speaks so plain. I told Mr. Butts that [I] did not wish to explain too much of the cause of our determination to leave Felpham because of pecuniary connexions between H. & me—Be not then uneasy on my account & tell my Sister not to be uneasy, for I am fully Employed & Well Paid. I have made it so much H's interest to employ me that he can no longer treat me with indifference & now it is in my power to stay or return or remove to any other place that I choose, because I am getting beforehand in money matters. The Profits arising from Publication are immense, & I now have it in my power to commence publication with many very formidable works, which I have finished & ready. A Book price half a guinea may be got out at the Expense of Ten Pounds & its almost certain profits are 500 G. I am only sorry that I did not know the methods of publishing years ago, & this is one of the numerous benefits I have obtained by coming here, for I should never have known the nature of Publication, unless I had known H. & his connexions & his method of managing. It now would be folly not to venture publishing. I am now engraving Six little plates for a little work [*Triumphs of Temper*] of Mr. H's, for which I am to have 10 Guineas each, & the certain profits of that work are a fortune such as would make me independent, supposing that I would substantiate such a one of my own & I mean to try many. But I again say as I said before, We are very Happy sitting at tea by a wood fire in our Cottage, the wind singing about our roof & the Sea roaring at a distance, but if sickness comes all is unpleasant. . . .

I ought to mention to you that our present idea is: To take a house in some village further from the Sea, perhaps Lavant, & in or near the road to London for the sake of convenience. I also ought to inform [you] that I read your letter to Mr. H. & that he is very afraid of losing me & also very afraid that my Friends in London should have a bad opinion of the reception he has given to me. My Wife has undertaken to Print the whole number of the Plates for Cowper's work, which she does to admiration, & being under my own eye the prints are as fine as the French prints & please everyone. In short I have got everything so under my thumb that it is more profitable that things should be as they are than any other way, tho' not so agreeable, because we wish naturally for friendship in preference to interest. . . .

[He encloses copies of the fourth Ballad, and adds:] These Ballads are likely to be Profitable, for we have Sold all that we have had time to print.

Evans the Bookseller in Pall Mall says they go off very well, & why should we repent of having done them? It is doing Nothing that is to be repented & not doing such things as these. . . .

I write in great haste & with a head full of botheration about various projected works & particularly a work now Proposed to the Public at the end of Cowper's Life, which will very likely be of great consequence. It is Cowper's Milton, the same that Fuseli's Milton Gallery was painted for, & if we succeed in our intentions the prints to this work will be very profitable to me and not only profitable, but honourable at anyrate. . . . These are works to be boasted of, & therefore I cannot feel depress'd, tho' I know that as far as Designing & Poetry are concern'd, I am envied in many quarters, but I will cram the dogs, for I know that the Public are my friends & love my works & will embrace them whenever they see them. My only Difficulty is to produce fast enough. . . .

I think the references in this crucial letter to the "immense Profits" arising from Publication speak for themselves; and so do the accounts of Blake's various commissions, and what he was paid for them by Hayley. For the rest, it does not seem very likely that, just at the height of his triumph, Hayley should have suddenly become jealous of Blake, or "frightened at" his prowess as a poet; while as for the imputation that Hayley had turned "poor Romney" into a Portrait Painter, the whole of the evidence, as we have seen, is just to the opposite effect. Romney painted portraits because it paid him to do so; it was Hayley who was always badgering him to cut loose from his portrait work, to execute those anomalous creations which he called "historical paintings". The imputation that he was trying to turn Blake into a portrait painter is, no doubt, juster. Hayley was trying to turn Blake in any direction which he thought likely to safeguard his livelihood. And, moreover, it must not be forgotten, in view of these strictures, that earlier, to Butts, in the previous January, Blake had made the quite contrary statement that what Hayley was trying to do to him was to keep him ground down to the mechanical routine of engraving.

So, though this letter represents very exactly what Blake, at the time, thought of Hayley, I do not feel that it can be taken altogether seriously as evidence as to Hayley's real state of mind. It is, among other things, as will be observed, a letter written in considerable agitation, due principally, I surmise, to the bad health that both Blake and his wife had lately been experiencing. At the same time, however, I am perfectly prepared to believe that the Hermit, at this juncture, while enjoying the first-fruits of a great success that came after nearly thirty years of relative failure, was a good deal above his normal self, and inclined, somewhat unduly, to pontificate.

For soon worse was to come. Blake's letter to Butts of April 25, 1803, spoke with certitude of his return to London, "with the full approbation of Mr. Hayley";[3] and, on July 6, in a letter to the same correspondent, his indignation against his mentor reached its

highest expression. After dilating a little on Hayley's latest project—
the monument to be erected to Cowper in Westminster Abbey or
St. Paul's, from the profits of his own *Milton*—he proceeded, with
no uncertain sound, to the attack:[4]

> As to Mr. H., I feel myself at liberty to say as follows upon this ticklish
> subject: I regard Fashion in Poetry as little as I do in Painting; So, if both
> Poets & Painters should alternately dislike (but I know the majority of
> them will not), I am not to regard it at all, but Mr. H. approves of My
> Designs as little as he does of my Poems, and I have been forced to insist
> on his leaving me in both to my Own Self Will; for I am determin'd to be
> no longer Pester'd with his Genteel Ignorance & Polite Disapprobation. I
> know myself both Poet & Painter, & it is not his affected Contempt that
> can move me to any thing but a more assiduous pursuit of both Arts. Indeed,
> by my late Firmness I have brought down his affected Loftiness, & he
> begins to think I have some Genius: As if Genius & Assurance were the
> same thing! but his imbecile attempts to depress Me only deserve laughter.
> I say thus much to you, knowing that you will not make a bad use of it.
> But it is a Fact too true That, if I had only depended on Mortal Things,
> both myself & my Wife must have been Lost. I shall leave every one in
> This Country astonish'd at my Patience & Forbearance of Injuries upon
> Injuries; & I do assure you that, if I could have return'd to London a
> Month after my arrival here, I should have done so, but I was commanded
> by my Spiritual friends to bear all, to be silent, & to go thro' all without
> murmuring, &, in fine, hope, till my three years should be almost accom-
> plish'd; at which time I was set at liberty to remonstrate against former
> conduct & to demand Justice & Truth; which I have done in so effectual
> a manner that my antagonist is silenc'd completely, & I have compell'd
> what should have been of freedom—My Just Right as an Artist & as a
> Man; & if any attempt should be made to refuse me this, I am inflexible
> & will relinquish Any engagement of Designing at all, unless altogether
> left to my own Judgment, As you, My dear Friend, have always left me. . . .

This now is a serious and explicit statement, and I think it contains the very essence of Blake's difficulties with his patron. If it had
been the last word, it would have left little more to be said. But
it was not the last word; was, indeed, little but the expression of a
mood that was of short continuance. I do not, by this, wish to imply
that Blake's strictures upon Hayley were unjust or ill-considered.
They were neither. It was simply that, running parallel with his
conviction that, so far as matters of art were concerned, the man,
by Blake's standards, was a fool, there was something else. This,
I believe, was the knowledge that, though his understanding was
limited, his heart was sound.

2

Besides the delicious accompaniments of successful authorship
that were now pouring in upon Hayley, new material was constantly

coming to hand which, quite clearly, was going to necessitate the publication of a third volume of his work. During 1802, what with his biographical labours and the composition, in spare moments, of the *Ballads*, he had had little time for relaxation; but now he was free to enjoy his triumph. Not quite free, however, since the *Life* of Thomas Alphonso, already commenced, made heavy demands on him. Moreover, at the end of November 1802, he had been shocked to read in the newspaper, at Lavant, of the death of Romney. Yet another biography, he told himself, that it was his bounden duty to write.

Rather oddly, from what Hayley has to say of him, Blake, whatever he might be writing to other people, remained ostensibly amenable. At the end of March, 1803, for example, Hayley read of the death of Klopstock, and at once took down that poet's *Messiah* from the shelf. He then "read Klopstock into English to Blake; and translated the opening of his third canto, where he speaks of his own death".

He was in greater danger than he knew. Blake had already formed his own opinion of Klopstock, and the lines in which he voices this are familiar:

> When Klopstock England defied,
> Uprose William Blake in his pride. . . .

Less familiar are those passages of the poem that are not commonly printed. Hayley could not, however, be expected to know this. Besides, he had recently started to take an interest in the German language, on learning that his *Life of Milton*, his *Old Maids*, and his *Triumphs of Temper* had been translated into that tongue.

In the June of 1803, an old chord sounded, when Flaxman's long-promised white marble memorial to Tom arrived at Eartham. Hayley thanked the sculptor with an extempore sonnet, and set about having the monument erected on the north side of the east window of Eartham Church, to balance the memorial to his mother that was on the other side.

They are there no longer, but have been removed by later hands to the comparative obscurity of the east wall of the tower, at the back of the nave.

The monument to Thomas Hayley had, according to a letter of Mrs. Flaxman's,[5] been promised to him by her, during his lifetime, while he was still in health: "Your Master's talents," she had said, "shall decorate your grave." Now Flaxman had kept his word. The memorial represents, within a vesica, the figure of an angel with a palm-branch in his lowered left hand, while the right hand raises above his head a chaplet of flowers. Over this a slab bears the inscription: "Be thou faithful unto Death and I will give thee a Crown of Life": while a lower tablet tells us that the figure is

"Sacred to the memory of Thomas Hayley, who having borne an agonising distemper with cheerful magnanimity, two years and four months, resign'd his pure spirit into the hands of his Redeemer, on the second of May 1800 in the 20th Year of his age. John Flaxman, Sculptor, dedicates this stone to the virtues & talents of his beloved scholar." Hayley's rhymed epitaph beneath this is not in his happiest vein. Almost simultaneously a further memory of the past was awakened: a legacy arrived from Romney, of the painting showing Flaxman modelling the bust of Hayley, which includes a portrait of Tom.

Small wonder then if, with all these reminders, and with the Cowper biography safely out of the way, Hayley should spend the greater part of the rest of the year in memorializing his son. It is an extraordinary reflection for us, as we read those often unendurably mawkish pages, that they should have been written by a man who must often have laid his pen aside to plunge directly into conversation with that singularly unsentimental being, William Blake.

The only respite that Hayley permitted himself from these melancholy exercises was to compose a "patriotic song" in the August of the year, and a "few rhymes of nocturnal devotion". Then, on September 1, he set himself to the entertainment of a new young friend, Edward Garrard Marsh of Oriel College, Oxford, who would not be worth much remark were it not for the fact that he has, rather like the nameless clergyman who innocently immortalized himself by asking Dr. Johnson: "Were not Dodd's sermons addressed to the passions?" attained a kind of precarious perpetuation in a phrase of William Blake's. "My much admired and respected Edward, the bard of Oxford," he wrote of him later, "whose verses still sound upon my ear like the distant approach of things mighty and magnificent, like the sound of harps which I hear before the Sun's rising, like the remembrance of Felpham's waves and of the glorious and far-beaming Turret."

After this magnificent tribute, it is an anticlimax to hear what Hayley has to say of young Mr. Marsh: "Edward began reading the first volume of my new biography [of Tom] with uncommon interest, and warmth of approbation. A singular comfort and delight to my heart! He read it admirably, aloud; and if his musical voice does not deceive me, the language is what I wished it to be."

Well, surely it cannot have been this reading that resembled the distant approach of things mighty and magnificent, or the sound of harps; surely Edward Marsh must also have read some compositions of his own! Inspired by the belief that such strains would be well worth the hearing, the redoubtable Mr. Kenneth Povey set out upon Edward Marsh's track to find the forgotten harmonies, and this, very briefly, is what he unearthed.[6]

Marsh was a clergyman, born at Salisbury, the son of a solicitor who came into money and eventually, in 1787, settled at Chichester. When Blake met him he was about twenty years old, and, in the following year, he obtained a fellowship at Oriel; and, two years later, won a university prize for an essay on the not inappropriate subject of "Posthumous Fame". He was ordained in 1807, and held various country livings until, in 1820, he became curate of St. John's, Hampstead Road, London. In 1841 he was vicar of Aylesford in Kent; and, in 1862, he died. In 1837 he published a volume of Two Hundred and Ten Psalms and Hymns Adapted to Seventy Tunes. Seventy of the hymns were of his own composition, and a sample verse of one of them runs:

> Though unsteady our behaviour,
> Though our footsteps always err,
> Still in Heav'n we have a saviour,
> Still a heavenly comforter.

It would be interesting, indeed, to know what it was that he read to Blake which created so memorable an impression. The unpublished works of the Revd. Edward Garrard Marsh must, however, I am afraid, remain one of the unsolved mysteries of literature. It is odd to think that perhaps, after all, it was a case of *vox et praeterea nihil*.

3

Now at last, with the new volume of Cowper's *Life* in the press, and Tom's *Memoirs* drafted out, Hayley's restless mind turned to other fields. About the middle of December 1803 he started his *Life of Romney*. As he himself says, in an ecstasy of self-approbation: "The chief occupation and delight of Hayley seems to have consisted in zealous and constant endeavours to serve his friends, while they lived, and to celebrate their talents and virtues after their decease." It was largely true; but it was a pity that he could trust no one else to make the observation for him.

Meanwhile, in August 1803, a new and splendid occasion had arisen for zealous endeavours to serve one of his living friends. It was in this month that Blake's famous brush with the villainous ex-Sergeant Schofield occurred, and, in a letter of August 16, Blake sent Mr. Butts a full account of the fracas. Since this letter may be seen in Gilchrist and a dozen other places, I do not include it here, but will introduce the story by a less familiar account of the business, namely that which Hayley sent to Lady Hesketh. "I perceive (he wrote) by your striking intimation that you have heard some extraordinary incidents relating to poor Blake, incorrectly if not malevolently reported. You wonder that I should continue to befriend Him; but I must be a despicable mortal in my own opinion, if I utterly renounced a very industrious tho not a very successful artist, who, while his zeal in my service induced him to work peaceably in this village, was involved (by residing here) in as vexatious, & unjust a persecution as an innocent well-meaning creature could possibly fall into. The fact simply was, that a brutal quarrelsome soldier (a degraded sargent) intruded into the garden of Blake's cottage, and refused to quit it. Blake who has courage, agility, and strength, seized the abusive intruder & pushed him (over several paces of ground) to the door of his quarters. The vindictive soldier, provoked to frenzy, swore he would have the artist hanged, and actually engaged a comrade to swear also, in league with himself, that Blake had uttered the most horrible seditious expressions. . . ." There is more of this letter, to which we shall return after we have sorted out what actually happened.[7]

It was upon August 12, 1803, that Blake first encountered John Schofield, a private in Captain Leathes's troop of the First Dragoons, and became involved in a dispute with him. How it started we do not know, but it is pretty clear that, in the course of it, Blake expressed the sensible though untimely opinion that, if Bonaparte should ever succeed in effecting a landing in England, he would be the master of Europe, and that every Englishman would then have to choose between having his throat cut or joining the French. More recent experience of invasion-threats have rendered our present generation susceptible to such obvious truisms as this; but Schofield was a man of low intelligence, and full of patriotic sentiment; so that he took grave exception to Blake's academic observations, and, like Mr. Midshipman Easy, he argued the point. Blake was, it seems, of the Blue Water school of thought; he believed in the Navy; and Schofield, as a soldier, could hardly be expected to agree with him. Consequently, the talk ran high; and, in the course of it, Blake probably made use of some highly tactless expressions, such as, "Bonaparte doesn't care a damn for the King of England", or, "Damn your talk about King and Country!" Schofield, on the strength of these observations, being a naturally stupid man, concluded that Blake had said: "Damn the King", and at once went off to report the matter to his captain.

Captain Leathes was not much impressed; but he did not think it expedient to damp Schofield's patriotic ardour, so he sent him to see Hayley, who, as a leading inhabitant of Felpham, he probably supposed to be a magistrate; and he told him that, after thus reporting the matter, he was to go and let the Blakes know he had done so.

Schofield, however, before seeing Hayley, went to Blake's cottage with a message for William, the ostler at the *Fox*, who was digging Blake's garden for him. His message was to the effect that he should be unable to help William as he had promised, and it is possible that he embarked on this errand with the worthy intention of seeing

Blake once more, and trying to make peace with him before matters went any further. But, unfortunately, Blake saw him in his garden, and at once came out. Schofield made an offensive remark, and Blake ordered him off the premises. When Schofield disregarded this, Blake lost his temper, and, though he was a little man only five foot six in height, he sprang at the soldier and, seizing him by the elbows, bundled him through the gate, and frog-marched him some fifty or sixty yards down the road to his billet at the *Fox*.

While this remarkable feat of arms was taking place, Schofield very naturally struggled, and did his best to hit Blake; and all the while he was cursing and swearing sufficiently loudly to bring the neighbours to their doors. Mrs. Blake came out, and so did Mrs. Haynes, the wife of the miller, next door; and they, together with William, who had relinquished his spade, followed in the wake of the procession to the door of the *Fox*. There they met several other persons, Mrs. Grinder, the wife of the innkeeper, and Private Cock, a crony of Schofield's, among them. Mr. Grinder himself emerged from his tap-room to see what the matter was, and persuaded the outraged Schofield to go inside. Once he was safely out of Blake's hands, Schofield began to threaten William, saying he would knock his eyes out if he refused to accompany him at once to Chichester, to swear an information that he had heard Blake use seditious expressions; and, moreover, he told Mrs. Grinder that Blake's house ought to be searched forthwith for treasonable documents. Was he not, said Schofield, a military painter? Doubtless the word he wanted was "miniature"; but that was quite near enough for Schofield.

And now the fat was in the fire. Schofield had been publicly humiliated, and by such a little man too; and he went about everywhere swearing that he would be revenged, and that he would see his assailant hanged; and two or three days later, off he went to Chichester to lay his information to the effect that, upon three separate occasions, he had heard Blake say: "Damn the King!"

So that we may know precisely the sort of thing Blake was up against, I here append Schofield's Sworn Statement:[8]

The Information and Complaint of John Schofield, a Private Soldier in His Majesty's First Regiment of Dragoons, taken upon his Oath, this 15th Day of August, before me, One of His Majesty's Justices of the Peace, in and for the County aforesaid.

Who saith, that on the twelfth Day of this instant August, at the Parish of Felpham, in the County aforesaid, one — Blake, a Miniature Painter, and now residing in the said Parish of Felpham, did utter the following seditious expressions, viz., that we (meaning the People of England) were like a Parcel of Children, that they would play with themselves till they got scalded and burnt, that the French Knew our Strength very well, and if Bonaparte should come he would be Master of Europe in an Hour's Time, that England might depend upon it, that when he set his Foot on English Ground that every Englishman would have his choice whether to have his Throat cut, or to join the French, and that he was a strong Man, and would certainly begin to cut Throats, and the strongest Man must conquer—that he damned the King of England—his country, and his subjects, that his Soldiers were all bound for Slaves, and all the Poor People in general—that his wife then came up, and said to him, this is nothing to you at present, but that the King of England would run himself so far into the Fire, that he might get himself out again, and altho' she was but a Woman, she would fight as long as she had a drop of blood in her— to which the said — Blake said, My Dear, you would not fight against France—she replyed no, I would for Bonaparte as long as I am able—that the said — Blake, then addressing himself to this Informant, said, tho' you are one of the King's Subjects, I have told what I have said before greater people than you, and that this Informant was sent by his Captain to Esquire Hayley to hear what he had to say, and to go and tell them—that his Wife then told her said Husband to turn this Informant out of the garden —that this Informant thereupon turned round to go peaceably out, when the said — Blake pushed this Deponent out of the Garden, into the Road down which he followed this Informant, and twice took this Informant by the Collar, without this Informant's making any Resistance and at the same Time the said Blake damned the King, and said the Soldiers were all Slaves.

JOHN SCHOFIELD.

In ordinary times, no doubt, the magistrates would have made short work of such a farrago, but these were not ordinary times, and the fear of invasion, and of what we have now learnt to call Fifth Columnists, was in all men's minds, and particularly in the minds of the county magistrates who knew that, anyhow, painters were pretty bad lots, and that any friend of that peculiar Mr. Hayley was certain to possess strongly Whiggish principles. And so they issued a warrant, and the next morning Blake appeared before them. He took William the ostler with him, to swear that no word of sedition had passed his lips; but Schofield also, by this time, had his witness. He brought his friend, Private Cock, who cheerfully testified that he had heard Blake damn the King at the very door of the inn. The word of a mere painter and a mere ostler had little weight in face of this testimony from two gallant soldiers, and Blake was committed to the Quarter Sessions, and released on bail, in two sureties of £100 on behalf of himself and Hayley, and one of £50 from Seagrave.

The next West Sussex Sessions were held at Petworth on October 4, in the present Town Hall, no doubt; and bills of indictment were duly presented against Blake for using seditious words, and for assault. By this time the seditious words had become more clearly defined: Schofield and Cock had had time to think what they were. The Grand Jury returned a true bill, Blake pleaded not guilty and entered into recognizances for his appearance at the next sessions; since it was then the practice to prefer the indictment at one sessions, and to try the case at the next.

Meanwhile, what was Hayley about? Well, he was very much upset by the whole business, and very much exercised to assist his friend in every way he could. Already by August 16, when Blake wrote his account of the affray to Butts,[9] we can see that Hayley's evident concern had had a most salutary effect upon Blake's rapidly waning opinion of him. "Dear Sir (he wrote), This [meaning the trouble] perhaps was suffer'd to Clear up some Doubts, & to give opportunity to those whom I doubted to clear themselves of all imputation. If a Man offends me ignorantly & not designedly, surely I ought to consider him with favour & affection. Perhaps the Simplicity of myself is the origin of all offences committed against me. If I have found this, I shall have learned a most valuable thing, well worth three years' perseverance. . . .

"Give me your advice in my perilous adventure; burn what I have peevishly written about any friend. I have been very much degraded & injuriously treated; but if it all arise from my own fault, I ought to blame myself. . . ." In other words, he was now veering round to the point of view which he was to hold pretty consistently for at least another couple of years, that Hayley meant well, and, provided he was stood up to, could do him no harm, and certainly intended him none. "If a Man offend me ignorantly and not designedly, surely I ought to consider him with favour and affection." That was how he saw Hayley now; and that, I believe, is how we best can see him.

And now, though it had not been necessary for Blake to be legally represented at Petworth, it was manifestly important to secure for him, without delay, the best advice. Hayley set to work. There was no doubt of the man to employ. Hayley always employed his friends, and he had a friend for every purpose. Rose, obviously, was the man for the job; and, for the enlightenment of Rose, Blake now prepared a very comprehensive memorandum, which is entitled "In Refutation of 'The Information and Complaint of John Scholfield, A Private Soldier' ". As this largely recapitulates matters already described, it need not be given here. It may be found in its entirety in the Nonesuch *Blake*.

With this to guide him, Rose set to work; and Blake, whose lease for the cottage had, in any event, run out in September, packed up his goods and left Felpham for No. 17, South Molton Street. He had intended to go in any case, and if, as is probable, his lease was for an exact period of years, I do not think that the trouble with the soldier expedited his departure. By the end of September he was in London, and, upon October 7, he sent a letter to Hayley which shews very clearly that he had been deeply touched by the other's kindness to him in his present disagreeable situation. It may, by the way, be necessary at this point to say that the disagreeableness of his situation need not be exaggerated: he was not, for instance, on trial for his life. Even so, the position was unpleasant enough, and the havoc it played in his mind may readily be seen by anyone who reads in his future prophetic utterances the references to "Skofeld" and "Kox" and the other demons of the piece. For this reason, Hayley's genuine kindness was grateful and comforting to him. This is part of what he wrote on October 7:[10]

> Your generous & tender solicitude about your devoted rebel makes it absolutely necessary that he should trouble you with an account of his safe arrival, which will excuse his begging the favor of a few lines to inform him how you escaped the contagion of the Court of Justice—I fear that you have & must suffer more on my account than I shall ever be worth— Arrived safe in London, my wife in very poor health, still I resolve not to lose hope of seeing better days.
> Art in London flourishes. Engravers in particular are wanted. . . . Other Engravers are courted. I suppose that I must go a Courting, which I shall do awkwardly; in the meantime I lose no moment to complete Romney to satisfaction. . . .

There is a good deal more, and it is a most friendly letter; moreover, the reference to Romney is interesting. Though his life at Felpham was at an end, the business ties between patron and protégé had not parted. There was still work to be done on the *Cowper*, and, now that Hayley was embarked upon the Romney project, there is no doubt that he promised Blake work on this book too; and Blake, for his part, set off for London with a whole list of commissions to execute for Hayley in this connection.

But that is of the future, and what now concerns us is the impending trial, which was due for hearing in Chichester on January 11, 1804. Hayley, in his usual fashion, contrived to meet with a misfortune just before the event. He was thrown from his horse, and cut his head rather badly. His own version of the affair is a piece of that detailed prose which he reserved for the description of his personal calamities: "In the opening of the year 1804, Hayley had a narrow escape of life, from one of the most dangerous accidents to which life can be exposed; a strong horse falling under him in a gallop, threw him forward with such vehemence, that his head pitching perpendicularly on a very large flint fixed in the road, made his faithful attendant, a very feeling servant, apprehend that his master must be killed on the spot. He spoke to the bleeding figure on the ground without expecting an answer; but Hayley soon cheered the honest fellow, by exclaiming, 'No! my good Walwyn, I am not stunned; but to tell you the truth, I feel as if my neck was broken: however, you shall see I can mount my horse, and as it will not be right to alarm our friends at Lavant with this bloody visage, we will ride home together.' The life of Hayley was preserved by a petty circumstance, which he was fond of relating, as an example of the gracious guardianship of Providence, which he, on all occasions delighted to contemplate and acknowledge. It happened, when he was going to set forth on his ride, his excellent domestic, Margaret Beke, observed that he had an old hat on his head; and requested him to change it for a new one sent home on the preceding evening. The new hat proved a helmet of preservation. It was remarkably thick and strong; so that, although it was completely cut through by the flint, it so far guarded the wearer, that his skull was not wounded, and his blood flowed only from an unimportant gash on his forehead. . . . His intimate medical friend Guy was summoned [and] the poet said to him very cheerfully, 'My dear *Machaon*, you must patch me up very speedily; for, living or dying, I must make a public appearance within a few days at the trial of our friend Blake.' "

Guy's patching-up was completely successful, and, in the company of Rose and Mr. and Mrs. Blake, Hayley duly put in his appearance at the Chichester Guildhall upon the fateful day.

This Guildhall, which still stands in what is now known as Priory Park in Chichester, had been the choir of the old monastery church of the Grey Friars. It is a tall, cold, Early English building which, like a ship, rides the level greensward hard by the pitch where county cricketers now disport themselves. To-day it is gaunt and empty; though at the time of which I am writing it was naturally equipped with all the panoplies proper to a court of justice. In the same park, and a little way off, there also stands, with apparent irrelevance to our story, a large stone figure of Neptune. It is not, as it happens, totally irrelevant: since an inscription upon its base tells us that, starting its career upon the Conduit in South Street, Chichester, it was then purchased by Dr. William Guy, and stood for many years on the vault in the cathedral in which he was buried. "The pupil of John Hunter, and the friend of Hayley and Flaxman," says the inscription. It might have added that Romney painted him, that he was the doctor of Thomas Alphonso, and the first man ever to hear of the great project of Hayley's "Heavenly Vision".

4

To return: the case against Blake was a frivolous one and should never have been brought; would not have been proceeded with in normal times. The Duke of Richmond, however, was on the bench; and the Duke, who was a Tory, did not like Hayley, who was not. Rose was an able advocate, and handled his defence pretty well. It is at this point that we can resume Hayley's interrupted letter to Lady Hesketh:

> Our dear Rose made an eloquent speech in the cause of the poor artist entangled in the snare of these perjured wretches, but it was not the eloquence of an advocate, that saved the innocent man on his Trial; & Heaven seem'd

to show in a striking manner, that He was to owe his security to different defenders: for our beloved Barrister, who had caught his fatal cold in the evening of the preceding day, felt the faculties of his admirable Head desert him, before He concluded, & failed to reply (as he otherwise would have done) to the art and malevolence of the opposite counsel. Yet his client was safe, for Providence had graciously raised for him a little host of honest & friendly rustic witnesses, particularly one benevolent clear-headed woman, the wife of a Miller's servant, whose garden adjoined Blake's, & who, by her shrewd remarks, clearly proved several impossibilities in the false accusation.

Under the rules of evidence then obtaining, neither Blake nor his wife could be called to testify, so that the whole case rested largely on these witnesses. Rose's defence was of the simplest: he denied that the words complained of had been uttered, and he made great play with Schofield's indifferent reputation, since he had been reduced to the ranks for drunkenness. Moreover, neither of the soldiers stood up at all well to cross-examination. Much the best witness for either side was the miller's wife, Mrs. Haynes, who made the profound rural observation that, when two people quarrelled, they were invariably at pains to inform the bystanders just what they were quarrelling about, and that, upon the day in question, Schofield had said not a word about sedition. For those who are interested further, there is an excellent account of the proceedings in Gilchrist; here it is sufficient to say that, despite considerable bias on the part of the Duke of Richmond, Blake was eventually acquitted on both charges. Hayley, of course, had, among other witnesses, testified to his friend's placid and gentle disposition.

It is pleasant to end the story by saying that the verdict, "in defiance of all decency" as the local press relates, was received with tumultous rejoicing. It must have been the sole occasion in his life that William Blake was favoured with popular applause.

When all was over, it was late in the evening. Hayley was in a state of great relief and delight. Miss Poole, who had been dangerously ill, had not been able to attend the proceedings, and was anxiously awaiting the result. And so the whole party journeyed very cheerfully to Lavant, where they were entertained to supper. It must have been a happy evening: the shadow which had been hanging over Blake, and which obviously had worried him very much, was dispelled; and Hayley's kindness and genuine solicitude had done much to amend the strained relations between the two men; while as for Miss Poole, everyone, it seemed, loved her. There was but one circumstance to diminish their joy. During the course of his final speech as we have seen, Rose, never a strong man, had been taken ill, and so could not share their triumph. No doubt the Guildhall had been wretchedly cold on that January day. Poor Rose! what had been Blake's deliverance proved to be his doom.

His cold turned to galloping consumption. Before the end of the year he was dead, leaving a wife and numerous children to form the target of yet further of Hayley's benevolences.

He was only in his thirty-eighth year. He had first visited Cowper as a lad of twenty, in 1786. Cowper had loved him and given him his friendship. Everyone had loved Rose, even Lady Hesketh, who called him "a friendly little being . . . delicate . . . and amiable".[11] Hayley loved him so well that, in the later editions of his *Life of Cowper*, he inserted gratuitously a lengthy and curiously featureless encomium of him, which dealt principally with his courageous and edifying last days. He had played a considerable part in the editing of Gibbon's posthumous works; and, when he died, Blake, who was not ungrateful for the service he had rendered him, wrote: "Farewell, Sweet Rose, thou has got before me into the Celestial City. I also have but a few more Mountains to pass: for I hear the bells ring & the trumpets sound to welcome thy arrival among Cowper's Glorified Band of Spirits of Just Men made Perfect."[12]

5

Cowper, though dead, lived on. Shortly before the trial of Blake, Lady Hesketh, inspired by the success of *The Life*, made an exhaustive search of her archives, and sent Hayley a further "cargo of manuscript", which this time contained a treasure: the holograph of a hitherto unknown composition, that quite considerable poem, *Yardley Oak*. Hayley was entranced. This was the sort of thing he had been praying for. On January 1, 1804, he wrote excitedly to Johnson: "Where is Yardley? Hasten to tell me all you can."

Johnson replied, giving the requisite information, and, on January 18, Hayley wrote again to thank him, and saying that Cowper's poem will make the oak in question "not less precious than the mulberry-tree planted by Shakespeare. I shall write, therefore, to our friend Greatheed, and beg him to get up a large lump from the roots of the said ruined oak, which our ingenious friend Weller shall make into nice little boxes, for the toilette of the fair."

Doubtless, since Hayley was a man of his word, the ingenious Weller (upon whose possible descendants I dare not speculate, save to say that Dorking is on the road to Sussex) duly contrived these boxes, and, oak being a durable substance, doubtless also some of them are still in existence, unknown, unhonoured. Hayley printed the poem in full in his next edition of the *Life*, together with every other piece of Cowper's unpublished verse he could lay hands on. Since these included *The Castaway*, I think we may say that here, too, he deserves honourable mention for his services to what he would, assuredly, have called The Muse. It should not, after all, be forgotten that even that austere man, Sainte-Beuve, deemed *Yardley Oak* to be a great poem.

Now Blake had gone from Felpham, was life for Hayley a little lonely? The Turret was as full as ever of literary activity: the new volume of Cowper's *Life* was in process of publication, and Hayley was still vigorously writing occasional verse: to Marsh, to Lady Donegall, and to that singular youth, J. Romney Robinson, a son of one of Romney's pupils, who had, in the December of 1803, while still of the tender age of ten years and eight months, produced an *Elegy on the Death of George Romney Esq.* of which Hayley thought so well that he included it in his *Life of Romney*. Beside these lucubrations, Hayley also this spring produced a "serious song" on the health of the King, entitled *The Loyal Prayer*, which the Chichester organist obligingly set to music; and the whole thing was then performed, and highly applauded, "in the Queen's palace". Inspired by this success, he next turned his attentions to a poem on Music which eventually grew into that most curious performance, *The Triumphs of Music*, of which we shall have something to say later. With these works, and the *Life of Romney*, the time passed like a flash. It almost seemed that he was managing very well without Blake.

Yet, for all this, the correspondence between him and what might be called his London agent in the matter of Romney continued unabated. Blake was most obliging. He pursued all manner of hares which Hayley set running as he delved among the materials of his new biography. Indeed, in the whole of the correspondence of this time, there are singularly few signs of that contempt and dislike with which Blake is popularly supposed (on the strength of those epigrams) to have regarded Hayley since at least the end of 1802. It is perfectly true, of course, that, as a man of business, he still regarded the Bard of Sussex as a source from which further commissions might flow; but, even so, it must be admitted that his letters from the time of the trial to the end of the succeeding year are to a quite uncommon degree more friendly than purely business considerations would have seemed to demand. I think that a great deal of the bitterness which Blake had undoubtedly felt towards his patron, prior to the incident of the soldier, had been cancelled out by Hayley's generous response to that event; and that, at last, he had adopted the line of taking him as he was, and not expecting him to be otherwise. Besides, he was in daily proximity with him no longer, and that made it easier to regard with a certain nostalgic pleasure his days at Felpham, which had, after all (as his earlier letters show), often been decidedly agreeable.

For one thing, at any rate, we must give Hayley full credit. He was an inveterate hoarder of letters, and, in the case of Blake, this propensity has done posterity good service. So far as I know, only eighty-nine letters of William Blake's are still in existence, and of these no less than thirty-six are addressed to Hayley. Furthermore, of the remainder, fourteen of them—to Butts, to Flaxman, and to James Blake—were written while he was at Felpham, and would not have been written if Hayley had not conveyed him into Sussex. When we reflect that these fifty letters would not have existed but for Hayley, I think we may say that, even as in the case of Cowper, posterity is more in his debt than it realizes.

Meanwhile, what of the correspondence between Felpham and South Molton Street? On January 14, Blake, returned from his trial, wrote at once to give Hayley a tip or two concerning his deplorable aptitude for falling off his horse:[13] "I write immediately on my arrival," he said, "not merely to inform you that in a conversation with an old soldier, who came in the coach with me, I learned that no one, not even the most expert horseman, ought ever to mount a trooper's horse. They are taught so many tricks, such as stopping short, falling down on their knees, running sideways, and in various and innumerable ways endeavouring to throw the rider, that it is a miracle if a stranger escape with his life. . . . I therefore, as it is my duty, beg and entreat you never to mount that wretched horse again, nor again trust to one who has been so educated."—"Pray, my dear sir," he says later, "favour me with a line concerning your health; how you have escaped the double blow both from the wretched horse and from your innocent humble servant, whose heart and soul are more and more drawn out towards you, Felpham and its kind inhabitants. . . . Gratitude is Heaven itself; there could be no Heaven without gratitude; I feel it and I know it. I thank God and man for it, and above all, you, my dear friend and benefactor, in the Lord."

It is a handsome tribute, the aftermath of the trial, no doubt; but surely with something in it more than a lively desire for future favours.

6

But, while we are upon the subject: this question of Hayley's horsemanship! Though lame, he was, it seems, an accomplished rider, which makes it all the more odd that he should come to grief quite so frequently as he did. There was, however, very good reason for it. Johnson, in his account of him, recalls that Hayley was never seen abroad without an umbrella, which in fine weather he used as a parasol, to shield his eyes. "He even," adds Johnson, "rode with it on horseback; a very awkward operation, considering the high-spirited animals that composed his stud, and the constitutional malady in his hip-joint, which, in addition to his weight . . . and his never riding without military spurs, reduced his danger of falling almost to a certainty, when he opened his umbrella without due precaution."

Military spurs, an open umbrella, high-spirited troop-horses! No wonder he took a toss sometimes! The resemblance to the White Knight, which has been noted earlier, seems enhanced. Nevertheless, Johnson assures us "he was a stranger to fear in equestrian matters", and so he "always mounted his horse again, as soon as it could be caught". And then follow two unforgettable pictures. Johnson was once "riding gently by his side, on the stony beach of Bognor, when the wind suddenly reversing his umbrella, as he unfolded it, his horse, with a single but desperate plunge, pitched him on his head in an instant. Providentially he received no hurt, and some fishermen being at hand, the plunging steed was stopped at a gate, and being once more subjected to his rider, took him home in safety." The other occasion was even more dramatic: Hayley, riding upon the Downs, was tossed into the air at the precise instant that "an interesting friend, whom they had just left, being apprehensive of what would happen, was anxiously viewing him from her window through a telescope". For topographical reasons, I like to think that the interesting friend was Miss Poole, and that the scene of this remarkable concatenation of events was Lavant; but I am not dogmatic about it.

As Johnson most rightly says, Hayley's determination in his equestrian vagaries was "a source of considerable anxiety to his friends", so much so that they besought him to cease to imperil his life, and to give up riding. It is pleasant to relate that he took no notice of them, but continued these exercises until a few years before his death.

To return. Most of Blake's letters of the early part of 1804 relate to his researches into Romney's business, or to the plates he had been executing for the new volume of the *Cowper*. He is "sincerely affectionate", and seldom fails to enquire after Miss Poole's now improving health. On April 7, yet a further testimonial came to hand.[14] "Literature", Blake wrote, "is your child. She calls for your assistance! You, who never refuse to assist any, how remote so ever, will certainly hear her voice." Literature, incidentally, at this juncture, was up to her old trick of trying to get somebody to start a review.

Our old acquaintance Mr. Walker of the Eidouranion, turned up in May, Blake having paid him a visit to see Romney's picture of Lear and Cordelia, "five feet by four", which that fortunate and ingenious gentleman had purchased from "a broker's shop" for the reasonable sum of five shillings.[15] Likewise he had been to see poor Rose, whom he thought a little better. Hayley had sent him a copy of his *Loyal Prayer*, and Blake very kindly remarked of it: "It is one of the prettiest things I ever read." And Mrs. Blake still had rheumatism.

On May 28 came a touch of the old nostalgia, whether real or assumed, for Felpham. "Engravers, Painters, Statuaries, Printers, Poets," Blake wrote, "we are not in a field of battle but in a City of Assassinations. This makes your lot truly enviable, and the country is not only more beautiful on account of its expanded meadows, but also on account of its benevolent minds."[16]

Perhaps, one feels, by force of contrast, Hayley was beginning to appear not so bad a fellow after all; besides, it is clear from the correspondence that he was still paying Blake tangible sums of money for the work he was doing for him. A letter of September 28 refers specifically to "the favour of Ten Pounds" required to complete a Plate.[17]

By October, Mrs. Blake's rheumatism was yielding at last—to Electricity; and Hayley in the meantime had published his lamentable *Triumphs of Music*, and had sent Blake a copy. On December 18, Blake dealt boldly with this offering: "Your beautiful and elegant daughter *Venusea* [the heroine of the poem] grows in our estimation on a second and third perusal"; and he ended his letter[18] in this very happy strain:

> My wife joins me in wishing you a merry Christmas. Remembering our happy Christmas at lovely Felpham, our spirits seem still to hover round our sweet cottage and round the beautiful Turret. I have said *seem*, but am persuaded that distance is nothing but a phantasy. We are often sitting by our cottage fire, and often we think we hear your voice calling at the gate. Surely these things are real and eternal in our eternal mind, and can never pass away. My wife continues well, thanks to Mr. Birch's Electrical Magic, which she has discontinued these three months.

The correspondence of the early part of 1805 relates to a new matter: the projected publication of the *Ballads* in one volume, again for Blake's benefit. And then, on April 25, comes an ominous passage:[19] "The idea of seeing an engraving of Cowper by the hand of Caroline Watson is, I assure you, a pleasing one to me. It will be highly gratifying to see another copy by another hand, and not only gratifying, but improving, which is much better." What had happened? Well, we shall come to that in a moment, when we have dealt with the few remaining letters of the correspondence. It is clear, I think, from his most urbane reference to Caroline Watson, that Blake did not, at the time, see the full significance of the tidings Hayley had just broken to him; and, since he did not do so, we will not do so either, but will wait till the moment, not very far off, when he did.

In May, there came an allusion to a matter that is familiar to these pages: "Reading in the Bible of the Eyes of the Almighty," wrote Blake, "I could not help putting up a petition for yours."[20] And, on November 27, the first news of Cromek's commission for the designs for Blair's *Grave* led him to say, rather surprisingly in the circumstances, "I now have reason more than ever to lament your

Distance from London, as that alone has prevented our Consulting you in our Progress".[20] He went on to report of the *Ballads* volume, which had been published that June: "I hear them approved by the best, that is, the most serious people, & if any others are displeased it is also an argument of their being Successful as well as Right, of which I have no Doubt; for what is Good must succeed first or last. . . ." An astonishing observation indeed!

The tale is almost told. On December 11, 1805, Blake wrote to Hayley his last letter, the last, at any rate, that has survived. It is not in Gilchrist, so I shall give it in full:[21]

DEAR SIR,
　　I cannot omit to Return you my Sincere & Grateful Acknowledgements for the kind Reception you have given my New Projected Work. [*The Grave*.] It bids fair to set me above the difficulties I have hitherto encountered. But my Fate has been so uncommon that I expect Nothing. I was alive and in health and with the same Talents I now have all the time of Boydells, Machlins Bowyers & other Great Works. I was known to them and was look'd upon by them as Incapable of Employment in those Works it may turn out so again notwithstanding appearances I am prepared for it, but at the same time sincerely Grateful to Those whose Kindness & Good opinion has supported me thro' all hitherto. You Dear Sir are one who has my Particular Gratitude, having conducted me thro' Three that would have been the Darkest Years that ever Mortal Sufferd, which were rendered thro your means a Mild and Pleasant Slumber. I speak of Spiritual Things. Not of Natural. Of Things known only to Myself and to Spirits Good and Evil but Not known to Men on Earth. It is the passage thro these Three Years that has brought me into my Present State and *I know* that if I had not been with You I must have Perish'd. Those Dangers are now passed and I can see them beneath my feet. It will not be long before I shall be able to present the full history of my Spiritual Sufferings to the dwellers upon Earth and of the Spiritual Victories obtained for me by my Friends. Excuse this Effusion of the Spirit from One who cares little for this World which passes away, whose happiness is Secure in Jesus our Lord, and who looks for suffering till the time of complete deliverance. In the meanwhile I am kept Happy as I used to be because I throw Myself and all that I have on our Saviours Divine Providence. O what Wonders are the Children of Men! Would to God that they would consider it,—that they would consider their Spiritual Life regardless of that faint Shadow called Natural Life and that they would Promote Each other's Spiritual labours, Each according to its Rank, & that they would know that Receiving a Phophet [sic] as a Prophet is a Duty which If omitted is more Severely Avenged than Every Sin and Wickedness beside. It is the Greatest of Crimes to Depress True Art and Science. I know that those who are dead from the Earth & who mocked and Despised the Meekness of True Art (and such I find have been the situation of our Beautiful Affectionate Ballads), I know that such Mockers are Most Severely Punished in Eternity. I know it for I see it & dare not help. The Mocker of Art is the Mocker of Jesus. Let us go on Dear Sir following his Cross let us take it up daily, Persisting in Spiritual Labours & the Use of that

Talent which it is Death to Bury and of that Spirit to which we are called.

Pray Present My Sincerest Thanks to our Good Paulina whose kindness to Me shall receive recompense in the Presence of Jesus. Present also my Thanks to the generous Seagrave In whose debt I have been too long but perceive that I shall be able to settle with him soon what is between us. I have delivered to Mr. Sanders the 3 works of Romney as Mrs. Lambert to me you wished to have them a very few touches will finish the Shipwreck those few I have added upon a Proof before I parted with the Picture. It is a Print that I feel proud of on a New inspection. Wishing you and all All [sic] Friends in Sussex a Merry & Happy Christmas

I remain Ever Your
Affectionate
WILL. BLAKE AND
HIS WIFE CATHERINE BLAKE.

The rest, so far as we know, is silence; and that, in view of the tone of the foregoing letters, and especially of the last of them, is singular. For, at length, Blake was writing to Hayley with very nearly as much freedom (and obscurity) as he for years had been writing to Butts. It was true, alas, that "our Beautiful Affectionate Ballads" had proved an utter failure, but there is no suggestion that he deemed this to be due to any fault of Hayley's. What happened next is mere matter for conjecture.

All that I think is certain is that the supersession of Blake's version of the Cowper portrait by that of Caroline Watson, which he had, at the first onset, appeared to take with such genial nonchalance, may well have proved the earliest source of discord. No artist likes to have his work supplanted; and even if, as in this case, the fault was not Hayley's, Blake could hardly have been expected to know it. Lady Hesketh had been at the root of the trouble. She had never liked Romney's picture, which she thought, quite rightly, evinced signs of derangement; and she had always insisted that her cousin's calamity should be concealed as much as possible. For this reason, Blake had been instructed, at the very outset, to tone down his engraving. And now, the more she regarded it, the more sure Lady Hesketh felt that he had not toned it down enough. She agitated, and Caroline Watson was called in; who succeeded in making Cowper look almost entirely sane. Lady Hesketh was delighted, and Hayley was acquiescent. The 1805 edition was published without any of Blake's engravings at all.

And, moreover, this was only the thin end of the wedge. As we have seen, Blake had busied himself valiantly in getting material for the *Life of Romney*, but the publication of the book was long delayed, and, when at last it appeared, in 1809, only one of his designs was used, the *Sketch of a Shipwreck*, to which reference has been made in the preceding letter. The remaining plates were given to Caroline Watson, to Raimbach, and to William Haines (who also got later, for his pains, a nasty epigram). It is useless to blame

Hayley, though I think he broke faith with Blake: Caroline Watson was an admirable artist, and the softer style of her stipple-engravings was, in many ways, more suited than Blake's to the kind of book Hayley was making.

There may have been another reason. On December 17, 1805, Flaxman wrote to Hayley:[22] "When you have occasion to write to Mr. Blake pray inquire if he has sufficient time to spare from his present undertaking to engrave my drawings of Hero and Leander, and the orphan family, if he has not I shall look out for another engraver, I would rather this question should be proposed by you than me because I would not have either his good nature or convenience strained to look after my designs."

This letter is proof positive that, so far as Flaxman was concerned, there was no evidence, in December 1805, of strained relations between Hayley and Blake. On the contrary, or Flaxman would not have suggested that his enquiry would come better from Hayley, than directly. There is, on the other hand, some slight evidence here that Blake was starting to be busy again. It would, at any rate, be pleasant to think that Hayley did not break his word, and that it was Blake's concentration on *The Grave* which prevented him from doing more than he did for the *Life of Romney*. But this, I am afraid, is merely conjecture.

What is not conjecture is that, when *The Grave* came out in 1808, with Blake's designs executed (through Cromek's treachery) by Schiavonetti, the list of subscribers to it comprised the names of William Hayley Esq.; William Guy Esq.; Mrs. Harriet Poole; Mr. Seagrave, Printer; and Richard Vernon Sadleir. His Sussex friends had not forgotten him. Nor, though I do not suggest that Hayley had anything to do with their subscribing, had some other minor characters in our story: Mrs. Udney (of Teddington); and—Lady Hamilton of Merton.

7

We have now pursued the matter of Blake so far that we had better follow it to the end, remembering that this is a life of Hayley and not of Blake, and that all we are in search of is a reason for the revulsion of feeling which resulted in Blake's bitter epigrams, and also, perhaps, in that ambiguous figure in *Jerusalem*, called Hyle, in whom some commentators have thought to discern the lineaments of Hayley.

Hyle, in sober fact, does not do anything very terrible, and is by no means so desperate a fellow as our old friends, Skofeld or Kox, or that Hand who is conjectured to be the Robert Hunt that, in *The Examiner*, attacked Blake's Exhibition of 1809. "Hyle" (for example) "dwelt in Winchester, comprehending Hants, Dorset, Devon, Cornwall", and

> ... on East Moor in rocky Derbyshire rav'd to the Moon
> For Gwendolen; she took up in bitter tears his anguish'd heart
> That, apparent to all in Eternity, glows like the Sun in the breast:
> She hid it in his ribs & back; she hid his tongue with teeth.

It is true that Hayley might well have raved to the moon for Gwendolen; but, later on, Hyle "is become an infant Love!", and, still later, "a winding Worm" beneath the daughters of Albion; which is very confusing. I do not think it is altogether fair to bring in *Jerusalem* as evidence, save perhaps for those great words of Los:

> It is easier to forgive an Enemy than to forgive a Friend.
> The man who permits you to injure him deserves your vengeance:
> He also will recieve it. . . .

The epigrams, however, are quite another story; and I have set them at the start of this book as evidence of the difficulties anyone at this time of the day must fairly and squarely face who tries to make of William Hayley a reasonably sympathetic figure.

The misfortunes which befell Blake after leaving Felpham are common ground: there was the swindling behaviour of Cromek over the designs for *The Grave*; there was the disastrous failure of his Public Exhibition of 1809; and there were the savage attacks of *The Examiner*. Worse than all, Blake was not now getting commissions. His record for 1808–09 in the field of engraving is a blank, save for the one plate that came out in the *Life of Romney*; and that had been done years earlier. It is, indeed, difficult to know what he lived on after the money he received for *The Grave* was gone (and this in any case amounted only to twenty guineas for a dozen of the most superbly imaginative designs ever made). And he was no longer a young man. In 1809 he was fifty-two, and, after a life-time of hard work, and at the very zenith of his powers, poorer than he had ever been. Is it a wonder, then, that he was bitter, or that perhaps at times he thought Hayley should have done more for him, or even suspected that his present neglect was in some way directly attributable to the shortcomings—nay, the machinations—of the only patron (except the ever-faithful Butts) he had ever enjoyed?

I stress all this because I think that the epigrams which he now wrote in his little manuscript-book (usually known as the *Rossetti M.S.*) are things which, in their way—and for all their brilliance—are as uncharacteristic of Blake's true, though past, relationship with Hayley, as they are unjust to Hayley.

The history of this volume is curious enough in all conscience. It was bought in 1847[23] by Dante Gabriel Rossetti for ten shillings from one Palmer, an attendant in the antique gallery of the British Museum, who had had it direct from Mrs. Blake. It is a book of rough notes, though containing some things of the very finest, notably *The Everlasting Gospel*, and it was obviously never intended by Blake for publication. Those who have examined the volume assure us that on unimpeachable internal evidence the vituperative epigrams against Hayley and Flaxman (for Flaxman, who, unlike Hayley, remained Blake's good friend to the day of his death, comes in here for nearly as much abuse) were all written during the period 1807–10,[24] when the various catastrophes, detailed above, had persuaded Blake that he was the victim of a conspiracy; when, in short, in the modern jargon, he was suffering from a modified form of persecution-mania.

This matter of the dates is, naturally, all-important, because it would be an entirely different story if it could be shown that the epigrams were contemporary with his stay at Felpham. To this supposition, however, the general tone of his letters (save for those at the beginning of 1803 which we have cited) gives little confirmation. I think we are obliged to take the dates as given.

What follows? Well: first and foremost that the most violent of Blake's strictures against Hayley were due to a series of calamities for which Hayley was not responsible, even if Blake thought he was. His complaints in the letters of 1803 are grave enough, heaven knows, and genuine enough: they were felt at the time, and they were, I apprehend, largely forgiven and forgotten a few months later when Hayley comported himself with so much solicitude in the unhappy business of the soldier. From that time until the last letter of December 11, 1805—a letter which Ellis & Yeats in their book call, oddly enough, "the high-water mark of Blake's friendship with Hayley"—matters were on a much easier footing. And it follows, I think, that if Blake was able to maintain friendly and even affectionate relations with Hayley during the time he was actually in contact with him, then it is nonsense to suggest that at least two years (and possibly as much as five years), after that friendship was, so far as we can now tell, terminated, he was on worse terms with him than ever before, *through Hayley's own fault*. Of course Hayley had often got on his nerves, and of course in his darker hours Blake had remembered those occasions and had brooded over them; but nevertheless I think it is true that these highly injurious (and often highly amusing) lines were written primarily because Blake had himself been grievously hurt, and was lashing about him at all and sundry, not caring in the least whether the attacks he made were just or otherwise.

Besides, the most deadly epigram of all is also the one which, in its total lack of credibility, reveals the greatest depth of unbalance. It is that which says:

> To forgive enemies Hayley does pretend,
> Who never in his life forgave a friend,
> And when he could not act upon my wife
> Hired a villain to bereave my life.

This, if it means anything, means presumably that Schofield was hired by Hayley to get Blake into trouble with the forces of the Law. Having gone somewhat exhaustively through what really happened, I find it difficult to believe that even Blake managed to persuade himself that this was true. If he did, it can make no difference to our view of Hayley, because it is obviously absurd. But it is not even as if the line were original: "Hired a villain to bereave my life" comes from Blake's own poem, *Fair Elenor*, which was printed in 1783 with the *Poetical Sketches*; and I cannot help thinking that, if anyone had told him, as he idly scribbled down the quatrain in his little book, that in years to come scholars would spend an immense deal of valuable time trying to find out just what he meant by it, he would have been seized with strong amazement. As for "acting upon his wife": well, Hayley was no angel where women were concerned, but where, in heaven's name, in all the documents, is there a single shred of other evidence in support of this assertion? There is, on the other hand, notably in Hayley's letters to Lady Hesketh, pretty strong evidence that he regarded the Blakes as an ideally happy couple, with whose felicity it would have been not only imprudent but also unprofitable to meddle.

I am afraid that, the matter not being susceptible to mathematical proof, we must leave it there; assuming, if we choose to do so, that when Blake wrote this and the other epigrams he did so under the conviction that Hayley had entered into the general conspiracy to ruin him, of which he saw manifest proofs on every hand; and for which a certain temporary coolness on the part of Flaxman is now the only evidence that is apparent. Flaxman, of course, was an older friend of Hayley than Blake was; and, if Flaxman had turned against him for the time, it is not unlikely that he carried Hayley with him. That Blake was injured and unhappy we know well enough. In this same manuscript book, under the date Tuesday, January 20, 1807, he wrote: "Between two and seven in the evening. Despair." It is a sombre phrase; and we know no more than that.

The rupture when it came was Hayley's fault in so far as he ceased to employ Blake, and preferred other engravers. Blake did not forgive him this; and when, for other reasons, bitterness had overflowed his soul, he remembered all his old injuries which at the time had seemed tolerable because of Hayley's fundamental amiability, and because he was a patron.

> Thus, Hayley on his toilette seeing the soap,
> Cries, "Homer is very much improv'd by Pope,"

he wrote. It is wickedly clever; it is most revealing: yet it overlooks the fact that all he knew about Homer he derived from the first and only man who had taken the trouble to teach him Greek. And so he had his revenge, and has set Hayley in an everlasting pillory—which, unhappily, in many respects, fits him like a glove.

Yet for all that, I think it was a pity. Blake was not a fundamentally vindictive man. "Burn this letter because it speaks so plain," he wrote to his brother James; and again, to Butts, "burn what I have peevishly written about any friend". I think he would have been sorry to know that his peevishness must now stand for ever revealed in the cold light of day. It was, I feel, better when he remembered Hayley with that half-affectionate contempt with which the man who bears the heavy burden of genius regards the lighter-loaded traveller who has none: when he remembered him as Felpham Billy, who rode out every morn, Horseback with Death, over the fields of corn.

At the last, surely, the fever burned itself out, and he saw his old patron as he really was: a man like another, conditioned by his own nature and his own limitations, and bound with every man else on his long road to Eternity. And then he wrote what was perhaps a final, and though an arrogant, a justly arrogant, conclusion to the whole matter:

> Was I angry with Hayley who us'd me so ill,
> Or can I be angry with Felpham's old mill?

That, he thought, was the last word. Posterity has not agreed. It has forgotten, perhaps, that however dearly Blake had to pay for what Hayley did for him, Hayley did, at least, do something for him. Not many did as much.

CHAPTER XX

THE SOLITARY HERMIT (1804-1809)

I

IT IS A DESCENT, after these weighty considerations, to the social and literary jog-trot of the Turret. But it must be made. The great figure of William Blake has taken us a long way off our road; and, I fear, after the alarums and excursions we have been chronicling, the events to which we now turn may seem trivial. Hayley had touched the heart of English letters in his relations with Cowper and Blake; and of English painting in his friendship with Romney; but now the first and the last of the trio were dead, and the other estranged. It was the time of lesser men. And Hayley, too, was long past such prime as he had ever enjoyed. In 1804 he stood on the verge of sixty.

The beginning of the year saw him engaged in a characteristic activity. Romney had left him a small sum of money in his will, and he decided to spend it upon "a little Memorial that will bring him every day at a certain hour most agreeably to my tender Recollection". The Memorial was to take the form of a dozen coffee-cups, of the most elegant china, painted, "after a fancy of my own" by Lady Donegall's sister. "I would have," he stipulated, "a wreath of flowers, only the red Fusia & the black lotus mixed alternately & running round the top of the Cup—under the Flowers as a central ornament a Golden Pallet & pencils—& at the bottom the name Romney formed of large letters made of diminutive flowers in such a manner as to extend round the lower part of the Cup." It was a charming conception, and we only hope that Lady Donegall's sister rose to the occasion.

Upon December 1 of this same year, his new long poem, *The Triumphs of Music*, was issued by Seagrave. "Is not the Hermit a bold fellow," the author wrote to Johnson, "to be producing long poems on love and music, on the verge of threescore? As he blends some devotion with love, he trusts the old ladies will forgive him; and as to the young ones, dear creatures, they are generally indulgent to a poet, who, whatever his age may be, has a lively sense of their charms."

He was a bold fellow, indeed. It was much the worst poem he had written, and even he realized that he had composed it a great deal too hurriedly, the last canto, for instance, having been completed within the space of a couple of days. Miss Poole, loyal as ever, predicted that it would "gradually become a favourite work", while the author himself considered that the allusions which it contained to the feelings and fate of his son made it "a fascinating performance". But I am afraid no one agreed with them. Byron's verdict has been given; and even Anna Seward, her veneration for Hayley frayed at last beyond repair by his indefatigable partizanship of Cowper, really let herself go on the subject, and to no less a person than Walter Scott; to whom, on April 17, 1805, she despatched what is, I fear, an entirely adequate criticism[1] of the poem:

> Mr. Hayley has sent me his last publication. . . . Ah! I could well have excused the present, since I cannot flatter, and am sorry to mortify. . . .
> This strange composition is a chaos of ludicrous absurdities, on which scarcely one ray of genius gleams. The versification is hard and jirking; the epithets generally inappropriate, and inconsistent with each other; the metaphors ridiculous—witness one taken from the toes to illustrate kissing:
>
> > Intoxicated friendship made a trip,
> > He touch'd, in blind temerity, her lip.
>
> From this mass an apparition of a mother, and no mother, two purses, an old maiden aunt, and a parrot at prayers, pop up their heads, challenging reverence, admiration, and applause. Possibly this quiz of a poem may obtain sale and circulation among the methodists, on account of its eternal hymns and praying sonnets, which, like the tenets of that insane sect, caricature the fair face of genuine religion. . . .

Blake's very tolerant comments on the poem of *Venusea*, as he called it, have been given. The work was a total failure.

Yet despite this, Hayley's ebullient spirits remained undaunted. He was as ready as ever to give counsel to others. In the November of 1804 he even branched out in a new direction, and sent Johnson, who was contemplating building a house, a quantity of suggestions on the laying out of his estate: "If you have a good sloping piece of ground near the spot where you mean to place your house, I would advice you to make three . . . lines of plantation upon it, either semicircular, or shaped like the segments of a large circle. The line of plantation nearest the house, should be of bearing almond trees; the second, of standard cherries, of various sorts; the third, and broadest, of various apples, and quinces. Contrive so that the bloom of all these trees may be visible from the windows of your own library, which I advise you not to make on the ground floor, but upstairs . . . with windows to the East, to encourage you in the salutary habit of cheerful early morning study." Admirable advice, and that of a true poet, one would say; moreover, it was based upon Hayley's own practice, since his library, both at Eartham and at Felpham, had been upstairs—though only in the latter case had he been able to follow his own theory, and have it facing east.

At the end of 1804, poor Rose, who had been growing worse, and had migrated to Ramsgate in the hope of deriving benefit from the sea-air, died. His end, according to Hayley's version of it, had been much comforted by Paley, and was as edifying as that of Addison. What is, I find, a great deal more touching is the circumstance that, a few hours before his departure, he "desired to see a little sweetmeat distributed to his children as an expression of kindness from him".

He left a widow and "four helpless boys", and Hayley was once again busy with schemes to promote the welfare of the destitute. He wrote the inevitable epitaph; and then, the plan for erecting a monument to Cowper out of the proceeds of his *Milton* not having gone very satisfactorily, though the subscription list, at six guineas a time, was a formidable one, he then and there coolly proposed that the moneys already thus collected should be diverted to the benefit of that son of Rose's who had been Cowper's god-child. Such subscribers as did not agree to this were to ask for their money back, but it is not recorded, I think, that any did.

Much shaken by this loss, Hayley at the beginning of 1805 was, for him, singularly idle. All he did was to sketch the exordium of yet another poem, to be entitled, this time, *The Triumphs of Friendship*. He added, rather surprisingly in the circumstances, that the friendship which he proposed to celebrate was that of a young lady. But it came to nothing; his grief at Rose's premature end had afflicted him too much to extol friendship, or anything else.

In June, Johnson came to Felpham once more, bringing from his apparently inexhaustible store fresh Cowper papers for the new edition; and Romney's brother came too. But the *Life of Cowper* diverted Hayley's attention from the *Life of Romney*, to such an extent indeed that, throughout the summer, he remained at Felpham working upon it, and only indulged himself in one brief excursion to Southampton, where he contemplated with satisfaction the green old age of his remarkable friend, Mr. Sadleir, and brought home with him Miss Poole, who had been having medical treatment there.

By September the new volumes were out, and Lady Hesketh, as has been mentioned, was lashing herself into a frenzy over his indiscreet inclusion of some new material that was unwelcome to the eye of the Court. She wrote to Hayley from Weymouth on September 12: "By the insertion of the cruel letter in question, the King has been deprived of the amusement he would have received from the third volume. The Princess told me it was necessary to tell him the letters were not worth reading . . . Judge how much this hurts me!"

Hayley, who regarded the matter as one of principle, replied with what he himself calls "tenderness and fortitude", the very next day. He said that Lady Hesketh's letter had both grieved and astonished him:

But you must allow your old faithful Hermit to present to you his genuine sentiments upon it, with that perfect frankness and sincerity which form the essence of his character. . . .

As to cancelling any public sentiments of Cowper that may have been misrepresented, I would sooner be beheaded instantly than so servilely forsake what I deem my sacred duty to a dear, blameless, buried friend.

A heated correspondence followed, in the course of which Lady Hesketh's eyesight gave way. Hayley sympathized with her in her "ocular calamity", and said that he fervently prayed she would soon be rewarded "by all the exquisite delights of recovered vision". His inflexible attitude to Royal susceptibilities is given added point by a letter which came to him from Flaxman on December 1.[2] Trafalgar had been fought and Nelson had fallen, and already the proposal for a national monument was being canvassed. Flaxman was naturally after the commission, and had requested Hayley to give him a "testimony". "I thank you", he wrote, "with all my heart for the winged speed with which you sent me the testimony . . . and for the still greater and more friendly exertions used to reach the king on my behalf, this in you is a characteristic virtue, that an act of common kindness being required, becomes by your act an effort of the most friendly zeal." And, what renders the whole thing more piquant, it seems pretty certain that Hayley's "friendly exertions" with the King were directed through the channel of Lady Hesketh, who was *persona grata* at Court!

The beginning of 1806 brought to Felpham again Mr. Marsh, who exhorted Hayley to proceed with his much delayed *Life of Romney*; and, at about the same time, Hayley forwarded to the Secretary of the Board of Ordnance some complimentary stanzas to thank that gentleman for a favourable report he had made, concerning the advantages which Ireland had derived from the activities of Captain Godfrey, who was then holding an appointment under that Board in that country. Hayley himself remarks that the "perusal of this honourable eulogy was one of the most lively gratifications he ever received", and that it had brought tears to his eyes. The first time, in all human probability, that a report of the Secretary of the Board of Ordnance on the work of a subordinate had had so striking a result, or had received metrical recognition.

1806 passed, but still the *Life of Romney* did not get on. Hayley was tired and solitary. He had been working very hard, in his fashion, ever since the deaths of Tom and Cowper; and now he was stale. Caroline Watson is almost the only recorded visitor this summer, and she stayed in Felpham for several weeks—though not, I think, for reasons of propriety, at the Turret—to work upon the illustrations to the *Romney*. However, there were always epitaphs. This year brought yet another couple to memorialize: Charlotte Smith, and the Revd. Alexander Hay, whose "copious and respectable" *History of Chichester* Hayley had presented to Blake.

1807 was a little livelier. In the first place, after many years of trying, Hayley was able at last to do something for Captain Godfrey. This came about in a curious fashion. Early that year Hayley received a present from no less a personage than Lord Holland. It was the latter's *Life of Lope de Vega*, and enclosed with it was a very polite letter saying that his Lordship had been induced to learn the Spanish tongue by what Hayley had written, in his *Essay on Epic Poetry*, concerning the poet Ercilla. Hayley replied at once, and in his letter informed Lord Holland that his worthy relative coveted the post of Ordnance Store-keeper at Purfleet. It is pleasant to relate that, just for a change, his application was successful. Lord Holland responded "with a graceful celerity of beneficence" that the job was Godfrey's.

Alas that we should have so few Triumphs of Friendship in this vein to record! I rather think the most extraordinary flight of the kind in which Hayley ever indulged was that which caused him to apply, on the ominous date of April 1, 1805, to his ever increasingly eminent acquaintance, Huskisson, for the situation of a Tide-waiter for Mrs. Rose's brother; which appointment was, obscurely, supposed to benefit Rose's orphans. It was odd that he should for so long have retained his faith in Huskisson's willingness to oblige. As early as 1796 he had applied to him, without success, for assistance to some person unspecified;[3] and, as recently as May 1804, he had tried, also unsuccessfully, to get him to help Godfrey; and yet again, in the December of the same year, young Meyer. The application on Godfrey's behalf had been turned down by Mrs. Huskisson, as her husband had been too busy to reply; but when the case of Mrs. Rose's brother came to hand, Huskisson felt, one concludes, that it was high time a stop were put to all such nonsense, and his reply, made in his own hand, was a classic of its kind: "The situation of a *Tide Waiter* in the scale of official Rank is so very much below that of a *landing Waiter* as to render the removal highly improper in itself, and (however respectable the Individual may be in this instance) galling to the Feelings of the latter Class, as well as destructive, in the opinion of the Board of those lines of distinction, which, for the public purposes, it is desirable should be maintained."[3]

January 1807 brought news of the death of Lady Hesketh. The relationship had been a long, though never an entirely easy, one. Lady Hesketh was not only an ardent Tory but she was also extremely pious; and, though she undoubtedly valued Hayley for the great services he had done her cousin, I fear that his playful epistolary style must often have disturbed her. What, for instance, could she have made of the letter which he had sent to her on April 4, 1802?[4]—"Pray, Madam (said a good sensible girl of our post office, to the Lady whom I ride to visit every Tuesday morning [Miss Poole]), pray, Madam, if it is not impertinent, may I ask you if Mr. Hayley is not going to be married to a Lady Hesketh?— Indeed I am *pretty sure He is*, because I have lately forwarded so many letters from Him to that Lady, and I heartily hope she is *handsome, rich and good*." It was only Hayley's sportive touch; but, to employ another of his favourite words, one cannot help feeling that Lady Hesketh was, as a general thing, more given to the aweful than the sportive.

Moreover, she had not at all approved of Blake. Perhaps she thought that, after having been privileged to know her cousin, Hayley should never have befriended anybody else. At any rate, she flatly refused to let Blake paint her portrait, and said she would rather pay five guineas instead.[5] This had grieved Hayley. He wished ardently to be surrounded by the portraits of all his friends, and, only a day or two after the good lady's death, he was writing to Johnson at Bath and begging him to find out if there were no likeness of her in existence which he might have.

Lady Hesketh had bequeathed to him all Cowper's writings that related to Milton, and Hayley now determined he would edit them, for the benefit of Johnson. Nor was this the only benevolence he intended towards Johnson: he also decided to acquire for him ecclesiastical preferment. It was a difficult undertaking. Johnson was one of those easy-going fellows who seem unable to help themselves. "Dear Tantalus of Cathedrals!" Hayley wrote to him in March, 1807, "Wading in a wide sea, with ecclesiastical cushions floating around thee, yet wanting power to squat thyself comfortably down on any one of them. . . . Who knows but thy old friend, the Hermit, may yet be enabled to hoist thee up, and give thee a nice neat toss into some pleasant prebendal stall." But somehow it never came off; and Johnson lived and died a simple parish clergyman. He had apparently not, as they now say, got what it takes. And shortly he was about to complicate matters still further by getting married, and producing an ever-increasing family.

Yet though Hayley failed in this, he had one success to record in 1807: on October 22 he completed his *Life of Romney*, upon which he had been engaged, on and off, for nearly four years.

Felpham this year had been solitary. Raimbach, the engraver, had visited him[6] to discuss some of the Romney plates; and so had Hurdis's sisters. But their visit had been on business, too, since they were preparing their brother's collected works for publication, and wished for Hayley's advice on the matter. He had done what he could: he had recommended them to Johnson, the publisher; and he had exhorted Johnson, the clergyman, to get for them all the subscribers—at a guinea a head—that he could find.

He was out of sorts. He had been ill in the spring, and had dosed himself with blisters and sudorifics; and now at last he thought he had earned a holiday. It was only a short one. In the late autumn he went once more to visit Mr. Sadleir at Southampton; and this time he took with him for company his printer, Seagrave.

No sooner was he back than a note out of the remote past sounded. In November his earliest love, Fanny Page of Watergate, died; and on November 23 she was buried at Yapton. She had, Hayley assures us, "passed many years of rural beneficence, as the wife of Mr. Thomas, Member of Parliament for the city of Chichester". On the day of the funeral, her old lover locked himself away in the Turret and composed, not only the inescapable epitaph, but some stanzas as well. In the epitaph he spoke of

> Thy tender virtues, to all ranks endear'd,
> The high respected, and the low revered,

but in the stanzas he really let himself go, as the following sample makes clear:

> Gentlest of women! in our youth,
> I deem'd our destinies combined,
> And bless'd my promised wife;
> But delicately proud, my love,
> To shield thee from an angry sire,
> Released thee from thy word.

It will be noticed that, upon this occasion, the Bard's emotions were so strong that he neglected to cast them into rhyme, which was wholly unusual. Doubtless he reflected that day how very different his life would have been if it had been Fanny rather than Eliza that he had married. And very likely it would.

2

And indeed there seems no doubt that at this time, after more than ten years of widowerhood, Hayley's thoughts were turning again to the potential joys of matrimony. He was lonely; the biographical tasks he had set himself were almost done; and he was approaching his grand climacteric. Besides, Johnson was married now, apparently very happily, and had brought his young bride, Maria,* to the Turret, in May, for what one presumes was the honeymoon.

There were yet other signs. After a brief visit from William Meyer, who had been working as secretary to the British resident in Corfu, a most ominous event seems to have occurred. It can hardly be told better than in Hayley's own portentous phrases. He was, he tells us, now inspired to "indulge his fancy in various poetical compositions, and some in which his heart and his imagination were so singularly interested, that they almost hurried him

* Maria Dorothea Livius (1788–1864).

into a serious passion for a lady, whom he never beheld." She was a widow, related to one of his female correspondents; and the husband she had lost had been a soldier and a poet. "The Hermit's poetry had the happy effect of soothing her troubled spirit"; and this had so gratified him that, "a sight of her would probably have inspired him with a presumptuous passion". The only difficulty was that "they resided at different extremities of the island, and destiny determined that they should not meet".

It is plain that, when a man reaches this state of mind, something is likely to happen to him before long; and something did, quite shortly, as we shall see.

But before we reach the logical outcome of all this, there are a few minor matters to chronicle. The first of these was the death, in July 1808, of the admirable Seagrave. "Perhaps," Hayley adds, very curiously, as he recalls the departure of this friend, "perhaps the poet [i.e. himself] felt his sudden decease the more keenly, as he had accidentally omitted to impart to him the commencement of a new poem on a subject peculiarly interesting to his liberal mind." This poem was called *The Stanzas of an English Friend to the Patriots of Spain*; and at the end of the year it was printed in London, and issued anonymously. Alas! once more the public utterly neglected it.

In August, however, a much pleasanter event occurred, and the Hermit's cell was for the first, and indeed the last, time honoured by the presence of a royal visitor. On the 26th of that month, the Princess Charlotte (then aged twelve), together with her governess and Lord and Lady Dudley, took tea at the Turret. The poet was "highly pleased with the graceful manners of his young extraordinary guest", and expressed his "cordial wishes for the prosperity of her maturer life" in verses which, he tells us, "his unwillingness to be suspected of a propensity to flatter the great", prevented him from giving either to the princess or her attendants. Perhaps it was just as well, seeing what her "maturer life" amounted to.

3

It was also in August, 1808, that Hayley first became embroiled with the rather sinister figure of William Hersee, of Coldwaltham in Sussex, and, like himself, a poet. Since the story of his relations with Hersee[7] gives a sort of type-pattern of Hayley's patronal activities, and of his genuine kindness too, it is perhaps allowable to deal with it here in some little detail.

The eighteenth century and the early years of the nineteenth were notable for, among other things, a little cluster of self-educated poets. One of them, Burns, was also a great poet; but the majority, such as Bloomfield, or Miss Seward's Peak Minstrel, or Hannah More's lyrical milkwoman, Mrs. Yearsley, were interesting—and were, indeed, taken up—not because they wrote good verse, but because it was remarkable that people in their station of life should write verse at all. Hersee was of this class. The son of a wheelwright and small farmer, he had learnt to read at the village school, and at the age of seven was already working as a shepherd-boy on the Downs. By 1808 he was twenty-two years of age, and had travelled about somewhat, first to Reigate and later to Portsea. In Reigate he may have worked for a printer, and in this way have acquired literary leanings. At any rate, by August, 1808, he had somehow contrived to compile a little volume of verse, and, as he had already secured Hayley's name as a subscriber to it, he took it upon himself to write to the veteran poet and ask if he might dedicate the book to him. This was no novelty to Hayley. Many years before he had been the dedicatee of Charlotte Smith's book of sonnets; and, in 1787, Miss Elizabeth Sophia Tomlins had most handsomely addressed to him in a long rhymed utterance her novel, *The Victim of Fancy*. He at once accepted the dedication; and Hersee, encouraged by this, wrote again, told him that he had no means of livelihood but his pen, and begged his help in obtaining a situation.

Wherefore, on October 24, 1808, on the receipt of his complimentary copies of Hersee's book, Hayley sent him the following very sensible letter:[8]

SIR,
    I yesterday received 3 Copies of the little Book which you have done me the Honour of dedicating to me tho I most sincerely recommended to you for a Patron those worthy of your praise & better situated to render you service—Your poems & your letter have raised in me various Emotions of pleasure & of pain—pleasure from the simplicity nature & pathos in your poetry; & pain from hearing that a young man whose Feelings appear to me so strong & so tender has such difficulties to struggle against & to use your own words no means of procuring Subsistence but by his Pen—a very precarious Assistant as I know by long experience of my own & of others with whose literary Hopes & Disappointments I have been familiar.

I should esteem myself fortunate if Time & Chance shall afford me any opportunity of recommending you to a Situation that might secure a certain and decent maintenance for the tender Objects of your delight & your Anxiety but I must be so sincere with you as to add that however I may hope I have very little reason to expect such an Opportunity.

I will not however forget to seek for it by the best Means in my power—& I entreat you to accept the Trifle of 3 Chichester Notes of £1 which I have sealed up directed to you & sent to the care of Mr. Mason Printer in Chichester to be left till called for. Pray receive this as a proof of the very limited powers & the benevolent inclination of
                    Your obliged & sincere Wellwisher
                              W. HAYLEY.

Despite the not very optimistic tone of this missive, Hayley was better than his word, for he once more approached (after so many and such vigorous rebuffs!) his old acquaintance Huskisson, who now held the important office of Secretary of the Treasury. Huskisson said he would see Hersee at Eartham during the Christmas holidays; and Hersee called on him, and proceeded thence to Felpham for a first visit to his patron. Hayley at once set him to work, on the strength of his previous connection with the printing trade, on seeing through the press yet another edition of the *Life of Cowper*; which was now, since the death of Seagrave, being produced by the other Chichester printer, Mason.

Nothing having, on the face of it, come of his interview with Huskisson, Hersee eventually, on March 13, 1809, wrote again to Hayley, asking him if he could "recommend him to a friend" who would lend his father a hundred and fifty pounds on a mortgage, and who could, moreover, let him have fifty pounds of it immediately.

To this Hayley replied in terms which elicited from Hersee vociferous praises of his generosity; but at the same time he said he was obliged to go to London, and told Hersee he had better get in touch with his solicitor. Hersee, who knew far better than to go anywhere near a solicitor with his proposition, did nothing further; and there for the while the matter must rest while we pursue the other theme which runs parallel with it.

4

The month of October, 1808, says Hayley, with a measure of reticence unusual to him, "brought some new unexpected female guests to the hermitage . . . who gave new complexion to his retired life"; and then he drops the matter and goes on to tell us of yet another of his autumnal visits to the cheerful patriarch of Southampton. This time his companion was young Meyer. The travellers set out on October 4; called upon the Marquis of Lansdowne who showed them the costly and fanciful works of architecture upon which he was at that time engaged, in rebuilding the now-destroyed castle at Southampton; and were back again at Felpham by October 6. But, on the day of their setting-out, Hayley's diary had contained the following "remarkable expression": "Read Homer, and translated his brief prayer for a wife." With which entry he elects to finish the penultimate Book of his *Memoirs*.

The reason soon becomes plain. The new and unexpected female guests at the hermitage were brought there by an old "ecclesiastical acquaintance" of his, and their names were Mary and Harriet Welford (or Wellford, as it is sometimes spelt). They were the daughters of an aged retired merchant who lived at Blackheath.

The ladies were young. The countenance and the musical talents of the elder sister, Mary, made a strong impression on the susceptible

Hayley. He had at last discharged the whole of what he called his sacred duties to the dead (for even *Romney* was in proof); and he felt old age approaching. It was expedient, he thought, to provide against that dreariness of heart which is apt to throw a gloom round the solitary recluse in the autumn and winter of his life. Besides, he was beginning to believe in his star; for all his other failures, the *Life of Cowper* had been a great success; and it now seemed to him that destiny might yet be disposed to conduct to his cell "some compassionate fair one, fond of books and retirement, who would be willing to enliven, with the songs of tenderness, the solitude of a poetical hermit".

Mary Welford, he imagined, was just such a one. He told her so; and, to his great delight, she was inclined to agree with him. Negotiations were at once set on foot regarding a marriage-settlement; and it is in this connection that we catch our last glimpse of Huskisson.[9] Hayley requested him to be a Trustee to the Settlement, together with old Mr. Welford; and Huskisson replied, with characteristic ungraciousness and by his wife's hand, that he did not desire to assume such a responsibility, unless he were assured that it involved no duties whatsoever. Because of this, he said, he would only accept if a third and working Trustee were appointed.

What Hayley said to that I do not know, nor does it matter. The Settlement was quickly drawn up, and the wedding took place, in London, on March 28, 1809. "It was," poor Hayley observed, "an event attended with much exultation and delight."

5

The event delighted others beside Hayley. Notably William Hersee, whose memorials we are now in a position to resume.[7]

When he learnt that his patron's sudden journey to London had been occasioned by his getting married for the second time, he at once proclaimed his intention of producing a nuptial ode, and, in the meantime, filled up his paper with a few raptures suited to the occasion: "Oh! what state can be so happy, so delightful," he wrote, "as conjugal felicity! My Fancy will often bring before me the sweet little Picture of Mr. & Mrs. H. by the Study fireside, enjoying domestic and literary Conversation!" And, instantly turning his mind to the business in hand, he composed and sent off in the course of the next post or so a set of verses entitled *On the Marriage of a Friend*, which earned for him the title of Poet Laureate of the Turret.

Better still, it soon turned out that Huskisson had not, after all, on this occasion been supine. He had actually managed to find Hersee a post—a clerkship in the Excise Office, at the salary of eighty-four pounds a year. Hersee paid a farewell visit of thanks to the Turret, and went off, with his family, to take up his abode in lodgings at Pentonville.

Thence, within a week of starting work, he was writing to Hayley, saying that his job was an extremely easy one, but that he feared he might have to wait years for a rise in salary; could nothing further be done with Huskisson? And, also, would Hayley be so kind as to stand surety for him in the sum of five hundred pounds? Hayley agreed to do so, and, into the bargain, drew up a general scheme for the improvement of Hersee's mind.

Thereafter ensued a brisk interchange of letters. Hersee's employment apparently left him plenty of time both for correspondence and for literary work. He met the poet Bloomfield, whose origins had been similar to his own; he proposed a new and enlarged edition of his works; and he wrote a further poem about the battle of Talavera, which had recently taken place. Upon this production, however, Hayley laid what he called "a friendly embargo". Still, at frequent intervals, huge parcels of manuscript arrived for correction at the Turret; and the Christmas package contained, in addition, a demand for ten or fifteen pounds to help Hersee pay his income-tax. "It should," he wrote with ineffable insolence, "be with great pleasure repaid out of the £500 (Burns raised so much at Edinburgh) which may be the *Produce of my Poems*." Meanwhile Hayley did all he could to help, and, when the new volume of Hersee's works, *Poems, Rural and Domestic*, came out in 1810, dedicated to Mrs. Huskisson, many of the subscribers to it had been secured by his exertions.

The poems, valueless as they were, sold tolerably well, and soon the intrepid Hersee was proposing that he should augment his income by opening a bookshop. Apparently it was common form in the Excise Office in those days for a man to work at two jobs at once. Most of his fellow-clerks, he told Hayley, did so; many of them being, like Mr. Micawber, in the coal-trade. For this purpose he besought a loan from his patron of three or four hundred pounds. This egregious appeal was dated August 11, 1810, and it apparently proved a little too much even for Hayley (who after all had already done quite a lot for him), since there now comes a gap of six years in the correspondence, during which time, however, Hersee managed to produce a couple more topical poems in his Talavera vein, one on the Fall of Badajoz, the other on the Battle of Vittoria. The last of these, which was adorned by a dedication to the Prince Regent himself, was published under the imprint of Hersee & Cooper. In some clever fashion, he had succeeded in entering the publishing business while still maintaining his employment under the Inland Revenue.

And there for the while we may leave him, as we turn back to the fortunes of the newly-married Hayley. He will reappear later.

CHAPTER XXI

WILLIAM AND MARIA OF THE TURRET
(1809-1817)

I

HAYLEY AT THE TIME of his second marriage was in his sixty-fourth year; and his bride was twenty-eight.[1] It was the sort of age at which, in those days, young ladies were apt to grow desperate and bestow themselves upon elderly poets.

Not much is known of the circumstances of the marriage. Hayley himself tells us little, merely remarking that "like the usual steps of poets in the world it was rather one of hasty affection than of deliberate prudence"; and, unfortunately for us, that assiduous collector of matrimonial gossip, Anna Seward, had at last died, just three days before her old friend's wedding.

This is indeed the least well-documented period of Hayley's life. His day as a literary man was nearly over. It had lasted a long time, and its end was inglorious. His *Life of Romney*, published a few months after his marriage, was a disastrous failure. It was not to be wondered at. It is a huge and cumbrous quarto, and Romney, in contradistinction to Cowper, was no hand at letter-writing. The text is, consequently, almost all Hayley's own. And again, Cowper's *Milton*, in 1810, in "four neat pocket volumes" intended for the emolument of Johnson, did no better. There is little doubt that Hayley's vanity in his new role of husband led him to publish all that he could at this time, because once more, and undeterred by previous calamities, in 1811 he brought out another book—the last to be produced in his lifetime—consisting of three of his early plays that had not before been printed. They met with no better luck, for though, as he says, they had been "honoured with the most fervent and sincere applause from his literary friends, Gibbon and General Burgoyne", they did not interest the public. There was a last flourish: "Hayley," he tells us, "only smiled . . . and said, 'If I have lost my popularity, it is the more incumbent on me to shew my friends that the cheerfulness of my spirit is built on a much nobler foundation than the precarious breath of popular applause.'" He was determined to the end to Triumph over Temper.

As for the part which the new Mrs. Hayley played in these exercitations, we can but dimly surmise. There is a letter in the British Museum in her handwriting, which exhibits a quite hideous regularity. She had evidently been well brought up and efficiently educated. There is little doubt that, to begin with, she participated in all her husband's activities. Indeed, it is difficult to imagine how anyone actually living with Hayley could escape doing so. On February 7, 1810, for instance, he wrote to Johnson: "Your friends of the Turret are very diligent in your service; as my dear Maria and I are revising together a proof sheet with the conclusion of *Paradise Lost*." And, earlier, he signed a letter to the same correspondent in his customary playful manner:

GULIELMUS ET MARIA,
of the Turret.

There is another brief glimpse into these happy days. George Engleheart, miniature-painter to King George III, had been a friend of Meyer, and near neighbour to him at Kew. He had, he says,[2] been introduced to Hayley by Meyer as long before as 1783, though I fancy that in this Engleheart's memory may have been a little at fault. But that is by the way, because what is certain is that, in 1809, Engleheart painted miniatures of Hayley and the new Mrs. Hayley. Thereafter all is plain sailing: Engleheart visited Felpham; drew a couple of admirable sketches of the Turret in its unspoilt condition; and received from Hayley many of those poetical tributes which, especially in his later years, he was liable to bestow upon his friends at the slightest provocation.

Engleheart's visits to Felpham seem to have coincided chiefly with the brief period of the second Mrs. Hayley's reign, and it is consequently of rather melancholy interest that he should have received from her, in March 1811, a large sort of printed card,[2] almost like an illuminated address, which, assuming the matter of it was of her own composition rather than that of her husband, would seem to suggest that she had temporarily assimilated to a nicety the latter's way of expressing himself. This card accompanied a present, and I deduce that this present was, at least partially, composed of human hair, since the address reads as follows:

To
Our beloved ENGLEHEART of Hertford Street,
with a little Gage d'Amitié from his Friend
Maria of the Turret
March 1811.
Three Weird Sisters join'd their Hair
And in their Spells have blest
A Trinket, form'd with magic care
To guard thy friendly Breast:
Dear Painter! if their triple prayer
Has influence above,
Safe from all pains, thy heart will wear
This Amulet of LOVE.

Quite like a Royal Warrant! Evidently in March 1811 all was still well with William and Maria of the Turret. And so it was in August that same year, as a most unexpected witness testifies. On the 31st of that month, we find none other than William Godwin sending to his wife a most vivid account[3] of a flying visit which he had paid the Hermit the day before.

> MY BEST LOVE, (he wrote from Chichester) . . . I have passed few pleasanter days in my life than I passed yesterday. . . . Finding that there was no means of public conveyance, I resolved to walk to Felpham (between seven and eight miles.) The weather was very hot (the literary hermit insisted on receiving me at noon), yet, to my astonishment, I was not at all fatigued. The literary hermit I dismiss in one word—I do not like him. His wife, however, seems a pleasant, unaffected, animated girl (he swears he himself is only sixty-five); and his house is quite a toy. He has erected a turret on the top, with a corridor over that, for the sake of the prospect, and to this corridor he climbs at least once every day by a ladder, which can only be descended by crawling backwards, and which, being on the top of the house in the open air, looked to me frightful, but I escaped without breaking either my neck or my leg. Pictures, drawings, splendid books, and splendid bindings adorn every room in the house, everything that cannot be consumed or worn out. He does not go out of his little domain, prison in that sense, I should call it, four times in a year, and he told me that he made it a rule never to invite anybody to dinner. His bookseller (with whom I have been negociating) [presumably Mason] tells me he was in the habit of dining with him every Sunday, but with a Chichester shopkeeper he could dispense with display. Thus he has everything for the eye, and nothing for the heart. Damn him.
>
> I say this in the sobriety of my deliberate judgment, and without a spice of resentment, for the moment I quitted his baby-house my happiness began. I went to Bognor, I inhaled the life-giving breezes of the sea. . . .

But, apart from these oblique, even alarming, evidences, there is little enough to go on as to the happenings at the Turret during 1809 to 1812. The principal reason for this is that Hayley elected to wind up his *Memoirs* with the occasion of his second marriage, saying as he did so, "as this curious history, though adhering inviolable to truth, has in many parts of it a romantic air, the writer is inclined to close it as the most agreeable romances are apt to terminate with a wedding. . . . Notwithstanding the disproportion of their respective ages, the adventurous couple seemed as happy for a considerable time as any mortals could expect to be." And that was all he did say, and Johnson, who resumes the narrative where he leaves it off, though only by the slovenly method of reprinting a selection of the letters he had received from Hayley, is not much help either. Johnson was determined to be discreet. The only letters he gives us of the period between 1809 and 1812, are those which deal with the thoroughly reliable subject of Cowper.

One of these is sufficiently characteristic of Hayley's mode of thought to be included. The matter under discussion was the edition of Milton; and Hayley had proposed that the frontispiece of the book should show the heads of Milton and Cowper "elegantly united" in one composition. Johnson accordingly instructed an artist to make such a design, and despatched the sketch to Felpham, with the result that, on February 7, 1810, Hayley was in full eruption, and gushing forth improvements:

> What negligent idle rogues are you, and your painter. . . . Cannot your artist devise any neat and graceful mode of uniting the portraits of Milton and Cowper in one plate? Surely it may be done, either as busts, or as medallions. In the latter case, he might sketch an eagle, holding in his beak a ribband, or ring, from which may descend a medallion of Milton, and a dove, as its companion, with a similar image of Cowper. Or, if you prefer their busts, they may be placed on terms, or pilasters, forming the entrance to a bower, in which, at a distance, you should discover the Muse Urania in a pensive attitude, with her harp, and a Bible: the figure of the Muse much smaller than the features of the busts. . . . Or he may draw two neat altars, inscribed to *Piety*, in the shady recesses of a garden, placing the bust of Milton on one, and that of Cowper on the other; the first near a *Cedar*, or *Palm*; the second, near a *Cypress*.

Evidently, there was no shadow of doubt in Hayley's mind as to the way in which these things were done; and, further, he suggested that, if Johnson's artist could not rise to the occasion, then it would be as well for him to apply to Smirke or to Stothard. Blake, it may be noticed, is not mentioned.

Then, however, we come to a blank wall. Johnson's discretion gives us no further letters until 1813; and before then, in the spring or early summer of 1812, Mrs. Hayley II had followed the example of her predecessor, and had left her husband. The break must, I fancy, have come quite suddenly, since, as late as February 26, Hayley was still cheerfully subscribing himself to the Flaxmans as "your Friends in the Turret";[4] whereas in a letter of April 10 (for which unfortunately no year is given), Mrs. Flaxman refers to his "domestic misfortunes", and says, "we are all *heartily sorry*".[5]

The causes for the separation are obscure. Hayley was a man of curious habits, and his persistent desire for seclusion may very well have got as much on the second Mrs. Hayley's nerves as it had upon those of Eliza. It is not, in any case, I fear, in his relations with women that Hayley shows to best advantage. Except for Miss Poole, he never had a woman-friend who did not in the end, like Anna Seward, turn on him. I doubt if the trouble this time, as in the case of Eliza, was monetary. His expenses were now much reduced, and the success of his *Life of Cowper* had strengthened his finances. In addition, he had by now, with an ingenuity which to-day seems beyond belief, contrived to secure for himself, during the last twelve years of his life—that is, from 1808—a very considerable annuity (and from the astute Henry Colburn, too!), as the price of his *Memoirs* which he had sold for posthumous publication. He had thus become, as Southey remarks,[6] "perhaps the only person who ever dealt with his posthumous reputation as a post-obit, and converted it into a present income". Hayley may have been a man "of incoherent transactions", as Southey so happily calls him; but I cannot think that there was anything particularly "incoherent" about this brilliant stroke of business!

Mark Antony Lower, in his *Worthies of Sussex*,[7] is the only authority I have come across that provides any tangible reason for the second Mrs. Hayley's evanishment. He says that the cause of it was "groundless jealousy" on her part; but adds, rather contrarily, that he has before him a letter which states that Hayley "kept her so closely confined to the house, and indeed treated her so unkindly, that her brothers came down and took her away". This statement, which is anonymous and unsupported, must be taken for what it is worth; for I suggest that it does not seem in keeping with the general character of Hayley as we have learnt to know it. What is, I think, a good deal more to the point is the story which Cary tells of his visit to Felpham in 1818. He says he did not learn the reason for the separation, but that Hayley ruefully showed him some gaps in his library, and said they had been made by proceedings in Doctors' Commons.

Whatever the rights and wrongs of the business, there is, however, no doubt that Hayley was deeply wounded, or that he believed, as do most husbands in his situation, that the fault was by no means all on his side. The fact that he never endeavoured to explain it, and never, with his customary loquacity, wrote a lengthy justification of himself, reveals just how deep the hurt went.

There is but one more thing to be said about this miserable business, and that is well prefaced by a further remark of Lower's, who writes:[7] "Hayley does not appear to have left a favourable impression at Felpham." That may well be true, for one has still only to survey his lofty walls to understand what any villager of the present time would have to say of a man who immured himself in such a fashion. They would say now, as they doubtless said then, that he was up to no good, or he would not require such a deal of privacy. Besides, he was a writer, which was odd and unnatural, and he entertained other people, still more odd and unnatural, such as engravers and painters. It was true that the carriages of the gentry stood at times outside his gates; but they were not the local gentry. Dr. Cyril Jackson, for instance, the famous Dean of Christ Church, Oxford, and tutor to the Prince Regent, who had retired to Felpham in his old age, was distinctly cool, and never called; and, though Hayley's latter years were singularly devout and included a full quota of family prayers, he did not go to church, because of his eyes, so I do not suppose the Vicar called either.

And so, gradually, a legend was built up in Felpham that, behind the strong walls of the Turret, some sort of ogre was to be found; and I daresay that, to this tradition of ogreishness, was added the fact that he had once been friendly with a queer fellow named Blake, who had got himself into trouble with the authorities. Out of all this was evolved, at last, the myth that Hayley had had two wives at once, and had treated both with an equal severity. The second he had kept habitually chained to an elm-tree in his garden. Moreover, if you didn't believe it, you had only to go up to Turret House and see the manacles for yourself!

And so, until a comparatively recent date, you could. E. Sage, in an article contributed to *Memorials of Old Sussex* in 1909, assures us that it was only the then owner of the Turret who had buried these incriminating objects in his garden. I suppose he grew tired of people asking to see them.

It is a great pity. I should have liked to know what they really were.

Tradition, however, dies hard. When in the summer of 1949 I was looking at Hayley's grave in the church at Felpham, I met the present incumbent, and we exchanged a few words on the subject of his erstwhile parishioner. He knew all about the manacles. Indeed, he seemed rather taken aback that I thought the story an improbable one.

Is it improbable? You have as much evidence as I.

2

From his first arrival at Felpham up to the time of the separation, Hayley's seclusion within the Turret had been complete. He was shy of strangers, and disliked any intrusion upon his privacy. Marriage had made no difference to him in this respect. Johnson has an amusing anecdote illustrating what a business it was to penetrate the defences with which he surrounded himself. He had come to visit Hayley, and, upon applying at the great gateway, had found a woman at the lodge who did not know him. She partly opened the wicket, but showed no signs of being willing to admit him. "Sir, Mr. Hayley sees no strangers," she said. Johnson ignored her and passed inside the gate, whereupon she seized hold of the tails of his coat. Hayley, it seemed, had forgotten to tell her he was expecting a guest, and her instructions were inviolable. Fortunately, however, just as the incident appeared likely to develop into a brawl, Hayley, who had heard the bell, went and peered through the Venetian blinds, which, because of the weakness of his eyes, he kept drawn all day. He observed the fracas that was taking place at his gate, and at once precipitated himself down the stairs, and on to the front porch, crying aloud: "Johnny! Johnny! Let him in!"

That was how it had been while the biographies were in the making; but now all that was over, and the failure of his second marriage had altered things too. He was lonely and unhappy, and he sought the society he had previously shunned. It was natural enough, poor man: the defection of yet another wife must have been a great shock to him. And besides, it was hardly pleasant for an individual whose favourite word was benevolence, and whose ruling principle throughout life had been to perform as many humane actions as possible, to find himself suddenly charged with inhumanity. That he was so charged, and that he knew he was, is made all too clear by a pathetic document in the British Museum: a Valentine which he sent, on February 13, 1814, to Mrs. Flaxman.[8] This begins:

> Sweetheart! May Bard of sixty-nine
> Presume to be your Valentine?

And it proceeds to thank her, in words that, behind their flippancy, expose clearly enough what he was really feeling, for being

> Still partial to your antient Bard!
> Who (tho base Slander is at Work
> To wound Him with a treacherous Dirk,
> And with the Lies of guileful vanity
> Accuses Him of Inhumanity.)

And so, henceforth, he grew quite sociable again. All the local families called upon him, and few strangers of distinction now went holidaying at Bognor without going to pay their respects. There was a sprinkling of the old regulars left, too: Johnson, of course; and Sargent, who regularly came over every autumn; and the Miss Godfreys, the daughters of the gallant Captain, who helped to enliven his winters. Miss Poole, also, went to Bognor each summer, so that she might be near him; though a severe fall which she had in 1816 latterly rather curtailed her activities.

It is a pathetic list to set against the distinguished society he had enjoyed in his prime, and it is pleasant to know that soon one will be able to add to it another name, in its own day at any rate, a good deal more illustrious: that of Amelia Opie.

Before we turn to Mrs. Opie, however, there are one or two minor matters to be tidied up; and the first of these is the question of how Hayley was now employing his pen. For well over five-and-thirty years he had been an indefatigable man of letters, and the fact that, after 1811, he did not publish again, by no means implies that he had ceased to write. On the contrary, the stream of verse flowed much as before: improving poems to each new addition to Johnson's family; complimentary addresses to his friends; and letters—endless letters, some of them still seeking advancement for such out-of-the-way people as the friends of his friends. And still Cowper obsessed him. It seems probable, indeed, that, at the beginning of 1814, he had actually completed a new work upon this subject, since he wrote to Johnson, saying: "You will see, when you next visit my cell . . . what posthumous works of my own, relating to our dear bard, I have prepared for *your emolument*, whenever I depart. . . ." And, again, two years later, he wrote in much the same strain to Miss Poole. But it is to be feared that such works, if completed, are now lost for ever.

Finally, and as a small corrective to the view earlier expressed that Hayley was regarded in somewhat askance fashion by the inhabitants of Felpham, there is the circumstance that, about 1814, a society known as the Amicable Club was founded in the village, to which each year, for the remainder of his life, Hayley furnished a Patriotic Song that was printed and circulated among the members. The Amicable Club was, further, with its own band of music and colours flying, graciously permitted, upon its annual feast-day, to parade through the grounds of the Turret, presumably chanting the song of the year.

In 1814, the great day was May 31, and the chant composed for the occasion started:

> Ye shores of blest England! Heaven's favourite isle!
> On the face of Old Ocean continue to smile!
> For in this happy scene every Briton may boast,
> Now glory's pure sunshine illumines our coast.
> A time we have known when an insolent sound
> Of threaten'd invasion re-echoed around;
> But fearless Britannia her standard unfurl'd,
> And a lesson of fortitude gave to the world.

It was natural to be cheerful, for the first Peace of Paris had been signed only the day before, and Bonaparte was safe on Elba; and yet so jolly does it all seem that one cannot help feeling a little dubious about the tradition of distrust previously referred to. And the same may be said of the performance on the Whit Tuesday of 1817, when a further composition was rendered by "the little musical cherubs" of the village. Thus:

> With the pleasures, that Providence loves to bestow,
> There wisely is blended some portion of woe;
> For bounty would injure, if always profuse:
> Sweet (as Shakespeare has said) is adversity's use.

There were eight stanzas like this, the moral of which would seem to be the unexceptionable one that

> 'Tis the glory of Britons to succour each other.

Hayley certainly did not seem at this time to be totally excluded from the delights of living in a rural community; and one rather concludes that if, to begin with, they had been a little doubtful about him, the rude fathers of the hamlet had, at long last, taken him to their bosoms.

3

These delightful exercises must, however, no longer deflect us from the consideration of Mrs. Opie,[9] who, though her reputation is faded now, must nevertheless rank as the last of Hayley's friends in their own day accounted eminent.

The comparatively youthful widow of the painter John Opie, whom she had contrived, through sheer strength of will, to have buried in St. Paul's Cathedral, this redoubtable lady was, in 1812, one of Britain's leading novelists. Her novels were didactic and improving, her poetry almost exclusively lachrymose: one of her later collections, for instance, being entitled *Lays for the Dead*. In the year 1812, however, her principal production had been a novel called *Temper, or Domestic Scenes*; and, in this, since her theme was not dissimilar from that with which, years before, Hayley had made his greatest hit, she introduced a graceful reference to her predecessor's work in the same field. "The author of that interesting poem 'The Triumphs of Temper' ", Mrs. Castlemain says, "is of your opinion, Mr. Egerton, with regard to the importance of good temper, for he says:

> VIRTUE's an ingot of Peruvian gold,
> SENSE the bright ore Potosi's mines unfold;
> But TEMPER's image must their use create,
> And give these precious metals sterling weight."

"I thank you, Madam", replies Mr. Egerton, "for reminding me of my coincidence in opinion with the author of that poem; but I should wonder if any one, who thinks at all, were to deny the truth of this sentiment."

This compliment (for such he took it to be) came to Hayley's notice when he was preparing yet another edition of his poem, which Mrs. Opie herself calls the twelfth, though I think it was really the fourteenth; and he took immediate steps to return it. His Serena had been addicted to reading herself to sleep, and her choice of books, which, in each edition since 1781, had varied with the taste of the times, was once again revised, and, in the new version, the relevant passage was made to read:

> Still in the novels of the bolder sex
> She oft regretted many coarse defects.
> To guard enamour'd innocence from harms
> By moral picture, of pathetic charms,

> With delicate address, scarce known to men,
> She deem'd the glory of the female pen:
> And with this glory, in her fond esteem,
> Her friend, the graceful Opie, shone supreme.

Having thus repaid his debt, Hayley instructed his publisher to send a copy of the revised edition to Mrs. Opie, who was a total stranger to him; and he soon received from her a most gushing acknowledgement, dated Norwich, January 23, 1813, part of which has already been cited in the section in which *The Triumphs of Temper* is discussed. Her letter continued: "Every succeeding year has confirmed the judgment of my childhood, & my youth relative to this immortal work; & tho I am well acquainted with *all* your writings, & feel for them the admiration which they deserve, still, owing perhaps to many affectionate, & grateful associations, 'The Triumphs of Temper' retains the *first* place in my regard, & I read it through every year."

Hayley replied instantly,[10] in a manner which he deemed suited to a lady who was not only a professional moralist but was also one who knew all about his matrimonial difficulties, both as they had been ventilated in the recently published *Letters* of Anna Seward, and by his recent separation:

DEAR THOUGH UNSEEN AMELIA,

Your Kind & very graceful Letter is a Cordial to my Heart—It has had the blessed Effect to turn my Thoughts from many galling Troubles to most soothing Sensations of Gratitude & of encreasing Regard for an Authoress of a most delicate & energetic Mind: In reading your Prose & your Rhyme I had been induced to wish, tho' not to expect that our Sentiments of reciprocal literary Esteem might gradually ripen into confidential Friendship.

We have both experienced I believe "mighty Joy and Mighty Woe". Some of the afflictions that I have suffered you have described with exquisite Pathos

> "The Parent's woe,
> When forc'd a darling Offspring to forgo,
> Ordain'd to follow to the silent Grave
> The Child, whose Virtues glowing Transport gave;
> To hear that precious Child's expiring Groan,
> Whose filial Fondness should have sooth'd his own."

Years of devotional Contemplation & Study reconciled me to that Heart-rending Decree of Heaven—Sorrows of a very different Nature have succeeded—But there can be no trials of Patience & Fortitude in which the Courage of a Man should desert Him while He has reason to hope for the Protection of Heaven & while He feels the cheering Sympathy of compassionate Friendship—The Afflictions of the tender & amiable Amelia have been tempered I trust by the Kindness of Providence as "the Wind is tempered to the shorn Lamb"—It would be a high Gratification to me to be informed by your own Hand that you are now as free from oppressive troubles of every Kind as I most heartily wish you to be & I confess from an interested Motive namely that your admirable Faculties may continue to exercise & unfold themselves in new Volumes which will interest improve & delight the Heart like your Novel entitled *Temper*—What I attempted in a sportive Poem you accomplished in serious & more instructive Prose

> Your Mind may Treachery never vex
> Nor Malice on your Merits trample
> Long may you guide your lovely Sex
> Both by your Precepts and Example

You, dear Amelia, are still in the Prime of Life & I may justly exhort you to fresh literary Exertions but it may be doubted if instead of hazarding such perilous Suggestions to a veteran in his 68th Year [which she had done, at the end of her letter] you should not rather advise Him to discard all earthly Ambition & only prepare Himself for a peaceful Exit—However we may decide this Question & whether the Concerns of this World or of the next may attract his Thoughts you will equally be secure of his Benedictions as He most cordially wishes you happy both here & hereafter & is most sincerely & fervently

Your Friend & Admirer
WILLIAM HAYLEY.

P.S. I am such a confirmed Hermit that I very seldom rove out of my own Cell & little Garden in this pleasant *Marine Village*—I shall therefore pray that my good Stars may in some propitious Season lead you to our Sussex Coast that I may have the Gratification of giving you a personal Benediction before I vanish from the Earth—

Mrs. Opie, understandably enough, took fright at this epistle. Hayley's reputation was ambiguous, and, though the lady, at forty-four, was quite old enough to look after herself, her position was complicated by the fact that she was now moving in the very precise Quaker circle of the Gurneys of Earlham,* which made her feel that to receive the personal benediction of even so elderly a gentleman as Hayley might gravely prejudice her reputation, especially in the eyes of Joseph John Gurney who, she hoped, took a rather special interest in it.

And so, though highly gratified, she made no reply for nearly thirteen months to his offer of friendship; and it was not until February, 1814, that Hayley heard from her again. Her reply was guarded. She very ingeniously explained her silence by saying that she had been waiting until she could truthfully answer one of the questions he had asked her (namely, the hope he had expressed that she was "free from oppressive troubles of every Kind"), and could tell him: "Yes, dear Sir, I *am* happy." She had, she added, hoped to spend part of the previous summer at Brighton, and to have visited him from there; but her plans had gone awry. Nevertheless,

---

* For some sidelights upon which, see Mr. Percy Lubbock's beautiful book, *Earlham*.

he had not been absent from her thoughts, and, as earnest of this, she enclosed for him a little netted purse of her own making, similar in design, no doubt, to that which Becky Sharp, at about the same time, was constructing for the captivation of Jos Sedley. She ended by apologizing for her long silence, and hoped he would write again soon.

Hayley wasted no time. He replied the following day, saying that her delightful packet had made ample amends for the mortification he had experienced at not hearing from her; and he renewed his invitation. "I long," he wrote, "to converse with you on many Topics of Literature & to convince you that your personal Happiness & literary Renown are objects that truly Interest the Heart of your very sincere and affectionate Friend"; and he enclosed, just to show what he was still capable of, a few stanzas addressed to the purse:

> Ye silken Threads like vital Flame
> Sweet is the Glow that you impart
> Coming from Her most skilled to frame
> Pure Tokens of a triendly Heart,

and so on, for three more verses, with variant readings.

Even Mrs. Opie's recent Quaker affiliations were unable to resist this blandishment. Besides, she hoped, I think, to inspire a spark of jealousy in the sober breast of Joseph John Gurney, who disapproved strongly of the "sickly, mawkish, romantic verse" that was soon filling the now frequent letters of her new friend and admirer. Moreover, for some reason, she had got it into her head that Hayley was hoping to persuade her to write his Memoirs for him, which, when reported to young Mr. Gurney, upset him immensely. He was even more put out when Amelia reported to him, somewhat coarsely, that her cousin, Tom Alderson, had suggested that Hayley's reputation was such that he might be likely to try to "interfere with her person".[11]

Eventually she decided to risk it; she accepted Hayley's invitation, and arranged to visit Felpham in August, and to stay at the Turret, which was thought uncommonly daring of her. On July 27, 1814, her host despatched her final dispositions:

> Well Thou dear Humourist without Humour It shall be all according to thy own Word & if Truth & Cordiality of Welcome are sufficient to delight Thee Thou shalt be delighted at Felpham although it must be thy Lot to find thy Host a Cripple on Crutches—but whatever years and afflictions may have taken from me I still retain I thank Heaven a warm Heart & a cheerful Spirit that will regard it both as a Duty & a Delight to render your beneficent Visit to your old Hermit's Cell as agreable [sic] to yrself as the sincerest Friendship & paternal Interest in the Compositions of my poetical Daughter can render it.
>
> Many thanks for your kind & sprightly Rhyme—an Intercourse of

private friendly familiar Verse is to my Fancy a tie as sacred as the having broken Bread together among the Arabians so treat me as you may you are secure from incurring my Enmity—There is but one thing for which I am likely to scold you & that is for running away from my Hermitage much sooner than I wish to let you depart—I begin therefore thus early to implore you that you will contrive to indulge me with as much of yr Society as you can—The Hermit's usual Hour of Dinner is four oclock

> But guide his Time while yet his Time endures
> And regulate his Hours since all are yours

There's Gallantry for you from an honest *Diable boiteux* of 69 who altho He gives Himself so wicked a Title is not less anxious for the welfare of your body & your Soul than your beloved filial Quaker to whom rivals as we are in the Sublimest of Passions Evangelic Love I send my Benediction.

> So Heaven preserve & send you happily
> to your faithful & affectionate Hermit.

Early in August, Mrs. Opie arrived, and found that her hostess was one of the Miss Godfreys. She thought her host charming, and very distinguished. He was tall and portly, with a commanding air and carriage more suited to a military officer than to a hermit. His white upstanding hair continued in small side-whiskers down his now heavy cheeks, and his eyes, under thick and highly-arched brows, were bright and large, though with something of an ingratiating expression in them which sometimes inspired mistrust. He was lame, and walked with a stick; and in his other hand he habitually bore the large umbrella with which he was accustomed to protect his eyes from the sun or the wind. His riding and swimming days were over now, but his mind was alert as ever, and his conversation was vivacious, ceaseless, and most amusing. His temper, too, was extremely equable; and, what is even more extraordinary in an author, he was most lavish in the praise of his now more successful competitors. His principal failing was an irrepressible obstinacy, to which, in conjunction with his extreme lack of judgment, most of his misfortunes in life, both matrimonial and literary, might be attributed. Amelia thought him fascinating.

He received her in his first-floor library, which ran the entire length of the house. This exceedingly handsome room was crowded with busts, statues and pictures, all of which had a history, and had, for the most part, been commissioned by himself from the hands of Romney, Flaxman, Blake and Wright of Derby; and, in addition to these treasures, it also housed his splendid collection of books and prints, and the very finest pieces of his Chinese porcelain.

Hardly less remarkable than her host or the appointments of his house was the routine to which Mrs. Opie was subjected during her stay at the Turret. "Nothing," she records, "could exceed the regularity and temperance of Mr. Hayley's habits. We did not breakfast till a little before eight, out of compliment to me, I believe; but, as he always rose at six, he breakfasted at half past seven when he was alone; as soon as he returned from his usual walk in the garden. . . . During breakfast, at which he drank cocoa only, he always read; and while I was with him, he read aloud to me. We then adjourned to his sitting-room, the upper library, and he read to me, or I to him, till coffee was served in the dining-room, which was, I think, at eleven o'clock. That repast over, we walked in the garden, and then returned to our books; or I sang to him till it was time for us to dress for dinner; with him a very temperate meal. He drank water only at dinner, and took coffee instead of wine after it. The coffee was served up with cream and fruit in the upper library. After dinner I read to him, or he read to me, till it was near tea-time, when we again walked in the garden, and on our return to the house, cocoa was served for him, and tea for me. After tea I read aloud or sang to him, till nine o'clock, when the servants came in to prayers, which were manuscript compositions, or compilations of his own; which . . . he read in a very impressive manner. He then conversed for half an hour or I sang one or two of Handel's songs to him, or a hymn of his own; and then we retired for the night. . . .

"With the single exception of a drive to Chichester, and to Lavant, where we spent a day with Mrs. Poole, and of having one or two friends to tea three times, there was no *variety* in the life which I have above described, during the whole month I passed with Mr. Hayley; and, I believe, the years that followed, to the time of his death, were as little varied. . . ."

To this comprehensive description, it may be added that, in the matter of early rising, Hayley had, for many years, been an inveterate offender. He was frequently to be found walking in his garden, even in winter and when the ground was covered with snow, with a lantern in his hand, long before sunrise; and sometimes, on these occasions, he would greatly alarm those of his guests who happened to be sleeping on the ground-floor by throwing up their bedroom windows, in what appeared to be the middle of the night, so as to give them "the benefit of the morning air".

Under this tranquil regimen, Mrs. Opie found plenty of time to write to her other friend, Joseph Gurney; and she told him that she had been quite mistaken in fancying Hayley had wanted her to write his Memoirs, for the simple reason that he had already written them himself. What, on the other hand, he did require of her was that she should do for him what he had done for so many others—compose his epitaph. "*I am here alone*," she wrote, savouring all the delicious naughtiness of it, "tête-á-tête with Mr. H." To her it was the acme of innocent literary enjoyment, though she was aware that to others it might seem different: "*I* feel and see no harm in a woman like me being alone with a lame man of sixty-nine, and upwards, but . . . I should be *quizzed* and dear me'd! and wondered at, and probably censured, till I was at least vexed, if not angered."[11]

One wonders why. The scene is one of the strictest propriety. When the day permitted of secular music, she sang to her host songs of her own composition, notably one called *The Poor Hindoo*, a touching ditty which began: "Well, ah well, my reindeer knew, The path that only leads to you." What a Hindoo was doing in the vicinity of a reindeer, Mrs. Opie alone knew. On the other hand, on the occasions when a more solemn music was required, she would render "a hymn of Handel's", a choice of which even Miss Seward would have approved.

As for the frequent readings, they were chiefly from modern publications or Hayley's own unpublished manuscripts; such trifles as a "well-written Epistle to a Socinian friend on the errors of his belief": while the conversation was carried on in the best vein of sentimental friendship. Hayley called his guest "Serena" and "carissima figlia", and she called him "caro padre", and all was as sprightly as possible. Indeed, one fears that sometimes it was even a little excessively sprightly, since Amelia, in the letter of thanks which she wrote after her departure, felt obliged to address her host in an improving strain: "The only drawback on the pleasure of my recollections is, that I profited so little by the means of improvement in many things which my association with you afforded me, & that the *flippancy* enduced [sic] by my great animal spirits led me to play the fool, & talk nonsense when your more sobered feelings would have led *you* to rational employments, & intellectual pursuits."

Well, perhaps Hayley had had almost enough of rational employments and intellectual pursuits by now, and it is pleasant to think of him being, for a short while, led away from them by the "animal spirits" of his charming guest. He confided in her, too; and told her something at least of his troubles with his second wife, which caused her to form the opinion, so customary in sympathetic females who lend their ears to husbands that discuss their matrimonial disasters, that he was "more sinned against than sinning".

On her return to Norwich, she sent him a gold watch-chain, and a silk gown of lilac and black, his favourite combination, for the housekeeper; and Hayley responded with some fervent verses.

Mrs. Opie's reply to these reveals just how far the friendship had progressed by reason of their meeting: all now is arch and daughterly in the extreme:

> And so ye hermit becomes *no* hermit as soon as I leave him! you were certainly *acting a part* while I was with you—O-fye!—Thanks for ye lines on ye chain—but I aspire to binding you in a better chain than a golden one—Your lines composed on yr pillow, I read, with pleasure, at Earlham,

337

& a copy was eagerly demanded. . . . I must tell you that my poor father is gone *raving mad* about yr Milton! "It is ye most beautiful life that ever was written!" and you are so clever! and so *candid*, & so every thing! Doubt not, but I am pleased to hear one of my papa's, speak thus of ye other.

She was not yet a Quaker, but, when in the following year she repeated her visit, the prolongation of her acquaintance with Joseph John Gurney caused her to regard her host in a rather less indulgent light. On the first visit she had written of him, "he would excite religious tenderness even in sceptical minds"; but, in 1815, to Joseph John at any rate, the tune was changed: "He takes the Lord's name in vain, *incessantly, profanely* . . . he loves to dwell on loose images and till frightened by my *thunder* face, will read exceptional passages from books."

Still, despite the exceptional passages from books, the second visit passed off nearly as well as the first had done. She noticed that this time Hayley had grown more gregarious, more eager to welcome such distinguished holiday-makers as she could introduce to him; though he defended himself with the playful suggestion that, if there were many more of them, she had better make a business of it, and "show him at a shilling a head". All the same, she thought he was failing; his infirmities made him unable to bear the motion of a carriage, and he rarely quitted his own grounds. Perhaps she deemed him near his end, because, this time, she even ventured to take him to task a little, and to harangue him upon past weaknesses. She wrote to Joseph John, and told him about it:[11] "Have I persuaded Mr. H. to see himself in his *true colours*?" she enquired. "For some time after I came I judged from what he occasionally said, that he was humbly kissing the rod for very flagrant conduct past. . . . But the very day before I received your letter, I heard him talk as usual. . . . Oh, how shocked I felt! for I found he still defended to his conscience, his having thought proper as he had no child by his wife, to have one by his servant—his wife being privy to the connexion—I was silent—as I always am—though I flatter myself it was a silence that speaks and reproves."

Yet, notwithstanding this distressing interlude, she enjoyed her visit. Captain Godfrey was at the Turret too, this time, and perhaps it was he who encouraged Hayley in his exceptionally unregenerate behaviour. It was, at any rate, to this exclusively masculine audience that Mrs. Opie read the manuscript of her new novel, *Valentine's Eve*; and they both told her they were delighted with it. Indeed, when she carelessly left the manuscript behind on her departure, it was posted back to her accompanied by some verses in which Hayley expressed his approval in terms so immoderate that Amelia could not forbear showing them to the Gurneys, who thought poorly of her novel because the heroine of it is carried off by the villain to a house of ill-fame, though not of course to the detriment of her chastity. The name of this heroine was Catherine, and part of Hayley's salute to her is worth quoting, if only for the reference (in the seventh to the tenth lines) to his own solitary excursion into the realms of prose fiction. The remarkable metaphor therein contained, it will be noted is drawn, as Canon Chasuble would say, from Hayley's own favourite Electricity:

> Thy Catherine follows Thee—How just her Claim
> To share, and to encrease, Amelia's Fame!
> Thou, on whose Fictions Truth and Nature smil'd!
> Thou, whom I fondly call'd "my Fancy's Child!"
> In every Scene, inventive Powers inspire,
> Thou hast surpassed thy visionary Sire.
> The Task I boldly tried (my mental Hope
> When young Ambition had a heavenly Scope)
> From Fiction's Urn Faith's Current to produce,
> And of Romances make rel'gious Use:
> In that nice Task, where coarser Spirit fails,
> Thy purer Genius gloriously prevails. . . .

Amelia was extremely upset about the Gurneys's verdict, and wrote to Hayley: "Indeed I was almost distracted . . . intimate friends abusing me for my impurity and immorality! Well—I could however lift up my torn soul with confidence to my *creator*, that my motives were not only *pure* but *good*." But it was no use; the Gurneys continued to think houses of ill-fame a topic unsuited to the pen of a female author, and, when the desperate Amelia told them that both Captain Godfrey and Mr. Hayley had thought highly of her book, they only responded that their tastes must be very low.

But now, unhappily, it was not only the Gurneys that had fallen foul of Mrs. Opie. The business of Hayley's second wife was still not satisfactorily concluded, and, in the November following her second visit, we find Amelia writing sympathetically to her host, saying: "And so you are really now preparing all your forces against your malignant foes—I shall feel quite *anxious*, till this teazing business is at an end—& the damage you are to sustain in property, *ascertained & ended*." Evidently the trouble at Doctors' Commons had come to a head; and Mrs. Opie was quite unable to restrain her curiosity. She wrote point-blank, asking Hayley for more information on the subject, but he refused to give her any, reminding her that she left her letters lying about, and that she had herself told him that she knew her maid read all her correspondence. She protested; it was quite untrue; she burnt all letters as soon as she had read them, or, if not, she locked them up. It had been entirely different at the Turret, because there she had had nothing, but her trunk, that would lock. Hayley was distracted by the legal proceedings, and irritated by her exigence. He replied coldly, in the third person; and Mrs. Opie, relinquishing her usual form of address, *Caro amico e padre mio*, converted him into *My dear Sir*. The wrangle continued for some time, but was finally made up; upon which Mrs. Opie promptly transferred her rancour to the plaintiff in the suit. By the following February, she was able to inform her "dear, kind friend, & *pa*" that his last letter had greatly relieved her mind in one respect, "though it made me *shudder* in another, as it conveyed to me such a picture of *female enormity*, & such a *dereliction* of all that a wife should be—for no sister could so have *written* to a sister who felt her duty properly—*Surely*, if these beings knew you *had* such a letter, they would be *afraid* of having it . . . produced". Mrs. Opie was not the only one, apparently, who left letters lying about.

Nevertheless, these asperities had left their mark. All was no longer as it had once been; and in 1816 Mrs. Opie did not pay her customary visit, but, describing herself as Hayley's "false-hearted *figlia*",[10] went to Scotland instead. But in the following year Joseph John Gurney married another, and the unhappy Amelia sped once again to Felpham for consolation. It is pleasant to know that upon this occasion all was ostensibly as before; Hayley was "the paternal hermit", she his *carissima figlia*; and, on her return home, she sent him her portrait, as requested, so that he might add it to his gallery of friends; while he, in return, despatched to her, with the usual poem, his picture of Virgil's Tomb, by Wright of Derby, which he had intended to bequeath her as a legacy.[12] More than this, she gave him this time a solemn assurance, for which he had asked: that she would visit him on his death-bed.

She did her best. He was very ill in 1819, and she posted down in great alarm to see him. But instead of dying he got better; and when he did die, she was not there.

4

Meanwhile we have been neglecting the ever faithful Johnson, whose record of these years, however, pales before the animated account of Mrs. Opie. He was a much-busied man, greatly exercised in raising a family; and besides, unlike the lady, he had now known Hayley a long time. The novelty had worn off.

But still, punctually, the letters sped from Felpham; and, in June 1815, Johnson himself came once more to the Turret, still to discuss the inexhaustible Cowper. Hayley had little company to show him on this occasion. He had, however, recently received a very kind letter from Hannah More, and he bade Johnson send her forthwith his new Cowperian volume, as he believed it would "gratify the angelic spirit of our dear sainted bard" that she should have it.

Again, in March, 1816, he was instructing Johnson to peruse "the excellent Amelia's" new novel, so that he might thereby be better fitted to instil into the hearts of his children the cordial lessons of simple, genuine Christianity. What the Gurneys would have had to say to this, I cannot imagine; for the excellent Amelia's new novel was *Valentine's Eve*.

On August 28, 1816, he wrote in a less hortatory strain: "I can perfectly sympathize in all your connubial delights, although my own destiny, in the most important lottery of life, has proved so deplorable a contrast to yours." And enclosed were a couple of epitaphs on the recently deceased, on the Bishop of Llandaff and on William Meyer's sister, Caroline.

This, indeed, was a busy year for epitaphs, since, before it was over, he had also commemorated Cowper's faithful attendant, Margaret Perowne, and Johnson's little daughter. And then, suddenly, there comes a most touching line, which in itself epitomizes all the pathetic interest which the old and feeble take in the affairs of those who are still young enough to be really living: "Continue," he wrote, "to give me enlivening accounts of your pleasures, and your studies."

5

With 1816, another old friend suddenly reappears: the ineffable Hersee.[13] Some time this year he paid a visit to Hayley, at which a reconciliation was, no doubt, effected; since he was soon back at his old tricks. He had a friend, he wrote, a Mr. Brown, an artist who urgently needed help. Would Hayley oblige? Hayley would; and, rather neatly killing two birds with one stone, assisted Mr. Brown by placing under him as pupil another protégé of his, an orphan, his godson, William Gregory.

Apparently this arrangement suited Hersee to perfection, since, by Brown's agreeing to take Gregory under his wing, for payment, he conceived he had placed Hayley under a heavy obligation. The opportunity was too good to miss; and so, on December 10, he wrote peremptorily requesting a loan of two hundred pounds.

But, in the meantime, the arrangement with Brown had broken down; and so Hayley, full as ever of hope and trust, was seized with the bright idea of transferring Gregory to Hersee's care, to learn from him the mysteries of the printing-trade, in which he was now, according to his own account, flourishing. By the following December, 1817, Hersee reported that business was booming, and that he was printing and also editing a new weekly journal, supported by the Government and designed to oppose the prevalent spirit of unrest. It was good for a certain two hundred a year profit, he assured his patron, only he must have a loan of a hundred straight away. If only Hayley would do that for him, then he would take over young Gregory entirely and treat him as his son. Hayley duly provided the hundred pounds; and the new journal, *The White*

Dwarf; or General Miscellany of Political, Moral, and Entertaining Essays, dropped dead, as is the way of such enterprises, in three months.

After this collapse, Hersee's prospects were, of course, better than ever; only unfortunately it was essential for him to have thirty pounds without delay. Hayley, this time, drew the line, so the ingenious Hersee sent him instead the proofs of a book which he had just concocted, called *Specimens of Poems,* and pointed out that, with a preface by William Hayley Esq., it could not fail to prove a little gold-mine. But still Hayley refused to grasp the fortune that was offered him. He was old and he was ill, and he had now put up with Hersee for ten years.

Hersee, however, like all professional borrowers, was not thin-skinned. On February 20, 1819, he propounded a further little loan of three hundred pounds, to be repaid in annual instalments of one hundred. Hayley, who had previously asked him for an exact statement of his financial position (which had naturally encouraged him very much), now forgot that he had done so, and roundly reproached him for his rapacity. This was too much for Hersee, who, with a certain sublimity of effrontery, wrote back: "With an aching heart, I feel convinced that your *Memory* begins very much to decline. I weep over this conviction. I anxiously pray for your long continuance in health; and may heaven forgive me for the pain which I have so unintentionally given to my best friend on earth!"

There were no further letters. Even Hayley could endure no more. Yet, all things considered, he had been very good to Hersee, who, except for the fact that he was a self-made man, had never done the least thing to justify his continuous extortions.

It is instructive to know that Hersee continued to flourish long after his earliest patron and "best friend on earth" was in the grave. By 1831 he was editor of *The Warwick & Warwickshire Advertiser & Leamington Gazette*; and when, on August 6, 1854, he died at Warwick, he did so "much respected by a numerous circle of relations and friends", having begotten during his earthly pilgrimage at least ten children.

CHAPTER XXII

"THE LAND UNKNOWN" (1817-1820)

I

NOTHING IS LEFT NOW but the merest scraps: dregs of a long life drawing to its close. Hayley was seventy-two, and almost all his contemporaries were gone.

Mostly they are poetical scraps: the old faculty of rhyming, the first to come, was also the last to leave him. Not that he regarded it without suspicion. Early in 1817, a Mr. Davies wrote requesting an opinion on his poetry, and Hayley replied:[1] "I consider a Love and a Talent for Poetry as the most delightful and the most dangerous of mental endowments—That Heaven may graciously direct you to escape the Dangers, and to enjoy the Delights arising from a Gift so momentous, shall be the hearty wish of your obliged." And, on October 13 of the same year, he wrote to Johnson: "I hope you all continue to cultivate music, for the sake of your little singing cherubini. I will transcribe for you a recent song." He did so, and it was rather a pretty one:

>Of all the gifts the heavens dispense,
>Or nature can impart,
>Be ours that charm to every sense,
>True gaiety of heart!
>
>Ever a cheerful hope maintain,
>Be fortune kind or coy!
>For hope alleviates every pain,
>And heightens every joy.

In 1818 he saw an old friend once more, whom he had not met for nearly a quarter of a century. Cary was staying at Littlehampton, and he went over to Felpham several times to chat with the old poet about Spanish and Italian literature, and to be entertained by stories of Hayley's two unfortunate marriages, and of his rather frigid relations with Dr. Cyril Jackson, who had been the head of Cary's former college. And touching indeed is the picture that he gives us, of the aged bard standing before Romney's portrait of Cowper, and saying, with a sigh: "There is our idol!"[2]

It was in this year, too, that Hayley wrote *A Veteran's Adieu to his Harp*, in which he plaintively observed:

>Of years what a number has now pass'd away,
>Since my country was kind to my juvenile lay!

and concluded, not too unwisely, that,

> From inditing too late pensive age should abstain,
> Lest he satiate the world with the dregs of his brain;
> Truth kindly has taught us, in prose and in song,
> The danger of singing and preaching too long.

Even so, throughout 1819 he did not fail to keep his epitaph-book up to date with several new entries. They were to be, with one exception, his last verses.

For seven or eight years now he had suffered from a painful disorder of the kidneys, which was, in 1818, complicated by the fact that his doctor decided he was growing dropsical; for which complaint he was rather strangely ordered to drink one glass of port-wine after dinner. Already by the summer of 1819, he was beginning to make preparations for his departure by anticipating the bequests he had made in his Will; so that, as he said, he might have the pleasure of seeing his gifts received by the persons for whom they were intended. His last recorded letter to Johnson deals with such an event: the presentation to him of a portrait of Mrs. Unwin.

In June, 1817, he had made his Will,[3] though it was to be fortified by four additional codicils, the last of which was added only a few months before his death. It was a comprehensive document: his servants were not forgotten, nor were the poor of Felpham. Captain Godfrey was his principal heir, and he was also an executor, together with Philip Courtenay, his legal adviser, and N. B. Engleheart, son of his old friend the painter, and a proctor of Doctors' Commons. Each executor received a legacy of fifty guineas; and Engleheart, who had conducted the case against his second wife, obtained special mention for his "friendship, zeal and liberality" as "my defender in the Commons", and the additional bequest of "my well bound copy of Macklin's bible and my picture of Sensibility by Romney".

Indeed, much the most interesting part of this testament is that which deals with the disposition of the famous pictures; for Hayley had gone to great pains to see that they should be appropriately bestowed. Johnson, in addition to the portrait of Mrs. Unwin, was to receive the Romney head of Cowper; and that of Charlotte Smith, which had been painted at the same time, was to go to her children, first to her daughter, and then to her son. The ungrateful John Romney was bequeathed the portrait of his father; and Mrs. Opie's picture, by her husband, was to go first to Miss Poole, and then to Amelia's favourite cousin, Tom Alderson. Godfrey was to have the family portraits; Courtenay, the lawyer, those of Mme. Genlis by Romney, and of Dr. Warner by Thomas Alphonso; and Dr. Guy, the head by Romney that was called "A study for the Miranda in *The Tempest*". Nor was Sargent forgotten; he was to have Wright's picture of Horace's Villa, and Thornton's portrait;

and the Cathedral Church of Chichester the paintings of Eliza's father and mother, with the injunction that they should be "suspended in the vestibule of the library of the Cathedral, which served me in my youthful days as my study". Most magnanimous of all, Hersee, who had been included in the 1817 document as receiving "my portrait of Mr. Brown the artist with William Gregory by his side . . . with a copy of posthumous publications", was, despite the final breach of 1819, left to the enjoyment of his bequest, though at least two of the codicils are of a later date than that of the rupture.

In conclusion, the library was to be sold to provide an annuity for his housekeeper, Margaret Beke; while a second annuity was provided for his godson, Gregory.

It was time to think of these things. In the September of 1819 he had an apoplectic fit; and everyone thought all was over. Mrs. Opie, true to her promise, dashed down to Bognor, fearing she would be too late. But the attack was not so severe as had been thought. He rallied, and, by the end of the week, she was able to return to London. During this time, however, local anxiety grew to fever pitch; to such an extent, indeed, that the assistants at Binstead's circulating-library in Bognor were obliged to take a leaf out of the book of Royalty, and post up a daily bulletin outside their premises.

But Hayley, for all his life-long complaints of ill-health, was a strong man. By October, he was sufficiently well again to write a letter of congratulation to Cary,[4] who had just sent him a copy of the new edition of his now completed translation of Dante. There is a good deal of fitness in the fact that this—his last letter that we shall quote—should also be one that celebrates, and in no ungenerous terms, the achievement of the man who had trodden to its very end the path Hayley himself had indicated more than thirty-seven years earlier.

MY DEAR ADMIRABLE DANTE REDIVIVUS! (he wrote on October 5.)

My best thanks have been long due to you for a delightful Present—the new Edition of the divine old Bard, whom you have naturalized most happily. . . .

I have been assailed by two of the most formidable enemies of the human frame, and have been almost demolished by a fit of apoplexy, and a fit of the stone. The blow from the former was so violent, that my physician despaired of my revival; but, by the mercy of Heaven, I am so far revived, that I can again enjoy a social and literary intercourse with my Friends; and even dabble again in Rhimes—but as I suspect that my Rhimes, like the Homilies of Gil Blas' Archbishop, may savour of apoplexy I think it right to keep them in utter privacy—otherwise I should be eager to celebrate your Felicity in having converted the old Italian Bard into an English

Classick—your Book is a glorious acquisition to the Literature of our Country, and will, I hope, produce to you all the Honour and emolument that it so richly deserves.

Having accomplished your arduous Enterprize so happily, I wish you may be tempted to devote your Pen to some grand original Project of your own Imagination, for the Honour of our Country—at my age it is Time to exclaim "claudite jam rivos"*—but you are in the Prime of Life, and in the full vigour of rare poetical Power, to which I heartily wish long, honourable, and most felicitous Exertion, being most truly

my dear Brother of Parnassus,
Your sincere old Friend
and admirer,
W. Hayley.

2

The rest is, very largely, piety. I do not, for a moment, suggest that Hayley did not make an exemplary end; but, even had he not done so, the good Johnson was so fearful of his reputation (the friend of the Infidel Gibbon, the victim of double matrimonial misfortune!) that he would certainly have provided him with one in the *Memoirs*. Besides, those who were with him most at the last were the Sargents, father and son, and the latter was a clergyman and, as we have seen, a Simeonite. Hayley's end, under these auspices, was edifying to the last degree: he exhibited extreme fortitude under excruciating torments, he read volumes of sermons, he took the sacrament, and his last recorded words were a pious ejaculation.

He did not have an easy death. That part of the description of the final scenes which relates to his resignation under his sufferings may be implicitly believed, for what killed him was a very large stone in the bladder. His death was brought on by a fall which shifted the stone; and, while his doctors were arguing whether there were any such obstruction or not, he, true to the last to his propensity for knowing best, settled the matter by saying he was certain there was; since he could feel it. The day before he died, he "expressed a strong hope that God was, in mercy, about to put a period to his sufferings".[5] That, if he used, as I like to think he did, those precise words, was his last characteristic utterance.

No: let it rather be his last but one. All his long life through, Hayley had poured forth verse in enormous quantities. It is only fitting that his final word should be in verse. Some brief while before his death, he saw the swallows gathering together on his turret to make ready, once again, for their autumn departure; and yet once again, and for the last time, he seized his pen and wrote ten short lines which as much resemble true poetry as any he ever produced:

* "Claudite jam rivos, sat prata biberunt." *Virgil*.

> Ye gentle birds, that perch aloof,
> And smooth your pinions on my roof,
> Preparing for departure hence,
> Ere winter's angry threats commence;
> Like you, my soul would smooth her plume
> For longer flights beyond the tomb.
>
> "May God, by whom is seen and heard
> Departing man and wandering bird,
> In mercy mark us for his own,
> And guide us to the land unknown."

He died on November 12, 1820, three days after his seventy-fifth birthday; and nine days later he was buried in the vault of his old friend and schoolfellow, Robert Steele, the Recorder of Chichester, in the parish church of Felpham. The position of this vault is now marked by a small marble stone, lettered R.S., let into the paving.

Hayley, who had written so many epitaphs for others, now required the same service for himself. On the north wall of the chancel of Felpham Church, upon a plain square slab (for there were to be no Flaxman angels for him who had negotiated so many for other people) he is described simply, as was—more or less—his own wish, as

THE FRIEND & BIOGRAPHER OF COWPER.

It is a modest designation for a man who had, himself, written so much; and even so it is a little less modest than the request he had made in his Will, and which his executors disregarded, that the phrase should read: "The friend and biographer of William Cowper, the Poet." Moreover, the quotation which follows, somewhat garbled from the twenty-ninth chapter of the Book of Job, is also unexpected:

> When the ear heard *him*, then it blessed *him* . . . because *he* delivered the poor that cried, and the fatherless, and him that had none to help him.

After that comes thirty lines from the chaste pen of Amelia Opie; which dilate at considerable length upon his benevolences, and with considerable brevity upon his literary accomplishments. I doubt if Hayley would have thought much of them. He would, I am confident, have made a far better job of it himself.

And how he would have enjoyed doing it!

CHAPTER XXIII

THE AFTER-RECORD

I

Such is the story of Hayley's life. All that remains is to conduct a brief survey of his posthumous reputation. It is a sorry tale, and one in which everything was handled about as badly as it could have been. In the first place, less than three years after he had, as he himself would undoubtedly have phrased it, "sunk into the grave", the good-humoured, and, I am afraid, rather chuckle-headed Johnson deposited upon his memory that vast and indigestible slab of miscellaneous reading-matter: The *Memoirs of the Life and Writings of William Hayley, Esq.*

It is unfair to blame Johnson. Hayley had compiled this mammoth work himself, and had left Johnson, as his literary executor, full instructions as to the manner of its publication. Indeed, I am sure Johnson did his best. The book as Hayley had left it was wildly indiscreet, especially on the subject of his rupture with Fanny Page, and the anonymous letters which brought it about. This part was too much for Johnson, and so he deleted the passages in question. It is a pity that he did not (for Hayley's sake, if not for ours) deal similarly with some of the many pages in which the author had endeavoured to justify his relations with Eliza; for nowhere does Hayley's unfortunate propensity to point out the excellence of his conduct and intentions rise to such heights as in the passages which deal with this topic.

Even the physical appearance of his *Memoirs* is intimidating: two vast tomes of 484 and 728 pages respectively; and they are pages of no mean size, though the margins are wide and the print excellent. Nor, when we turn from the physical aspects of the book to its contents, is the situation much eased. Hayley, for some reason best known to himself, had elected to write his story in the third person; and, what was worse, had done it in such a coy and tentative way that it really seems likely that, at one time, he had contemplated the notion of pretending it had been written by somebody else. Events are stated with hesitancy, or are inferred from other events. A very favourite gambit is to introduce a statement of fact, which he must have known to be true, with some such disingenuous phrase as "it seems probable", or "Hayley could never perfectly ascertain". "By this useless artifice of style," as Southey very sensibly observes in his review of the book,[1] "one charm of autobiography is destroyed:

the truth remains; but the stamp which should authenticate it is wanting."

Moreover, by the time he had completed it, Hayley had lost all sense of proportion. In conjunction with matter of much interest, the merest trifles were laboriously set out at enormous length; while the style of the whole thing, as may be seen from the extracts I have quoted, is, to say the least, leisurely. Anna Seward, as early as 1790,[2] had some acute things to say on the subject of Hayley's prose style, in a few observations which she made upon his novel, *The Young Widow*: "The author (she wrote) is so much of a mannerist that every different personage of the novel writes and speaks in precisely the same style—a style loaded with epithets, and in everlasting recurrence—'the dear, delightful, dainty widow';—'the lively, interesting, enchanting Seymour' . . . 'the muscular, luxuriant, glowing Caroline.' In short, scarce a name is mentioned through the work, without three epithets prefixed—which all the characters bestow, as if by compact, upon each other." And she adds, crushingly, that one of the characters—Seymour—is referred to, even in his coffin, as "the enchanting Seymour". This, coming from Miss Seward, who was not herself unaddicted to the employment of adjectives, shows that Hayley, as a stylist, was, even so early, pretty far gone.

It is a pity. There are, as I have tried to show, good things and amusing things in these *Memoirs*; and sometimes, indeed, when he was able to get off his high horse, Hayley could write naturally and well. But there it is. A book which, had it been a quarter the length, might still be being read with pleasure, was firmly, and by his own hand, deposited upon his memory: an intimidating pyramid of print which, by its bulk, scared away all but the hardiest, and, by its tone, repelled even those that had the courage to take it up.

The *Gentleman's Magazine* reviewed it, in the June of 1823, in the most non-committal fashion, saying, in conclusion, "we doubt not the work will be considered as an acquisition to our stores of National Biography and Literary History".

Two voices alone, more generous, were raised in its favour; and one was Southey's. Southey was given the volumes to review for the *Quarterly*. On May 26, 1824, he wrote to his friend, Henry Taylor:[3] "I am reviewing Hayley's *Memoirs*. Hayley has been worried as schoolboys worry a cat. I am treating him as a man deserves to be treated who was in his time, by popular election, king of the English poets, who was, moreover, a gentleman and a scholar, and a most kind-hearted and generous man, in whose life there is something to blame, more to admire, and most of all to commiserate. My first introduction to Spanish literature I owe to his notes; I owe him, therefore, some gratitude."

Southey had never, so far as I know, met Hayley, but there was a bond of sympathy between them. For one thing, there was their mutual interest in Spanish; for another, Anna Seward had been one of the earliest patrons of Southey's muse. And so he duly wrote his notice, and a very fine and full one it was. He did not minimise Hayley's faults either as a poet or as a man. He quite brilliantly summarised his life-story as it was given in the *Memoirs*; and he wrote kindly, and I fancy truthfully, of the influence which Hayley had exerted on the course of English letters by his studies in the Romance languages. He made no attempt to resuscitate his reputation as a poet. It would, he said, be useless to try to "revive that which in the course of time and nature is defunct". His approach was different. "To slay the slain," he said, "were a work of useless severity, even if the memory of a gentleman and a scholar were not entitled to respect from all who have any pretensions themselves to either of those characters." And, in conclusion, he summed up the whole matter generously and justly by saying, "The judgment of that reader must be strangely warped by a censorious disposition who does not agree with me in admiring Hayley as a truly generous, and gentle-hearted man."

He sent his completed notice to Gifford, and that potentate was so enraged by its lenient tone, that he deferred its insertion for nearly a year. It did not appear until the March of 1825.

Meanwhile, in the November of 1824, Hayley's old friend Cary had, in the *London Magazine*, paid a similarly judicious tribute. His verdict was not unlike Southey's. Hayley had been, he said, too much extolled at the beginning of his poetical course, and undeservedly neglected or ridiculed at the close of it; and he added something else, from his own personal knowledge of the man, that was true and just: "In one respect he is deserving of most honourable notice. During the course of a long literary life, I doubt whether he was ever provoked to use a single word of asperity or sarcasm towards any of his contemporaries."

Well, it was an uncommon trait in a literary man; and, as will be shown in a moment, his moderation in this respect did not preserve his memory from either asperities or sarcasms from the pens or the tongues of his successors. Some kindly references by Samuel Rogers, in his *Table Talk*, is almost the only exception to this. Never was there a case in which virtue had, most manifestly, to be its own reward.

2

For that was the end of the posthumous praise. In 1830, the Revd. John Romney let loose upon the world his *Memoirs of the Life and Works of George Romney*. In this he did his best to whitewash the rather ambiguous reputation of his father, and also to—as one might say—blackwash that of his father's biographer and lifelong friend. For years Hayley's *Life of Romney* had rankled in the mind of Romney's son, and now he felt that at last, by the publication of his own unfortunate *Memoirs*, the author of it had delivered himself, bound, into his hands.

There was, for instance, the matter of Romney's extraordinary treatment of his wife. Hayley had handled it tactfully enough, heaven knows, but not half tactfully enough for the Revd. John Romney; and so, with a glee that was highly unparsonic, he was now able to write:

> Mr. Hayley, however, with a feeling that ill accords with friendship, has insinuated that Mr. Romney, in thus withdrawing from his family, was acting upon a plan of preconceived and deliberate abandonment. This is so manifest a calumny that it is almost unnecessary to confute it. . . . Romney had resolution to forego the endearments of domestic life for the noble purpose of providing for the future welfare of his family. . . . If Mr. Hayley had had any gratitude in his heart, or delicacy in his nature, he would have shewn more tenderness for the memory of his deceased friend; but how could delicacy, or feeling, be expected from a man who has blazoned his own dishonour!

And, in short, he charged Hayley with having been responsible for all his father's shortcomings, matrimonial and otherwise. With crocodilian tears, he added:

> It is an invidious task to disturb the repose of the dead, and I have no inclination to animadvert upon the character of Mr. Hayley further than as it comes in contact with the life of Mr. Romney. He, however, by writing his own Memoirs, and leaving them for posthumous publication, may in truth be said to have perpetrated that unholy deed himself, and to have set an example for the justification of others. Mr. Hayley's friendship was grounded on selfishness, and the means by which he maintained it was flattery. By this art he acquired a great ascendancy over the mind of Mr. Romney, and knew well how to avail himself of it for selfish purposes. He was able, also, by a canting kind of hypocrisy, to confound the distinctions between vice and virtue, and to give a colouring to conduct, that might, and probably did mislead Mr. Romney on some occasions. . . . By having intimated an intention of writing Mr. Romney's life, he made him extremely afraid of doing any thing that might give offence. There was a wrongheadedness in the general conduct of Mr. Hayley, arising from the influence of powerful passions, that disqualified him from being a judicious and prudent adviser; yet he was always interfering in the affairs of Mr. Romney, and volunteering his advice: and I have too much reason to believe, that whatever errors the latter may have committed, they were mainly owing to the counsel, or instigation of Mr. Hayley.

I do not think it worth while to refute these charges in detail. All sense, and all reason, and all that I have earlier written concerning the relations between Hayley and Romney, demonstrate their malicious falsity. Besides, the Revd. John Romney had had eleven years in which, after the publication of Hayley's biography, he could have made them to his face. He had not done so; he had preferred to wait until he could not be answered.

Still more, it was not Hayley alone that was dead by 1830. Flaxman had died in 1826, and Miss Poole and Blake in the following year. Of those who had been Hayley's literary associates, only Johnson, and Cary, and Mrs. Opie, were still living; and they were all too young to know the rights of the matter. The attack, so far as I know, went unchallenged. That is why I have taken the trouble to refer to it here.

3

And now there came a long silence. As early as 1833, Tom Hood, writing under the style of John Dryden Grubb, in his *Comic Annual* for that year, provides a facetious pairing of poets' names—"Chaucer and Cottle, Spenser and Hayley, Milton and Pratt, Pope and Pye, Byron and Batterbee"—which demonstrates with great clarity the depths to which Hayley's reputation had already sunk.

One by one, the figures of our story drop away: Huskisson in 1830; Johnson in 1833; Cary in 1844; and Mrs. Opie in 1853. Hersee's death has already been recorded, and so has that of Edward, the Bard of Oxford, who outlived them all; but we may perhaps spare a moment to regard the astonishing career of that promising young man, Thomas Sockett.[4] We have already followed his steps *via* Eartham, *via* Sheffield Place, to Petworth and the patronage of Lord Egremont. From that point he never looked back. As tutor to the Wyndham children he gave every satisfaction, and in 1806 he was despatched to Exeter College, Oxford. Livings thereafter showered upon him. When he died on March 17, 1859, he held no fewer than three of them at once, with a total yearly income of £1,755; and the most important was that of Petworth itself. The monument that was erected to him in the church of that place, at the charge of his (and Hayley's) old pupil, George Wyndham, commemorates him as "a scholar, a sincere friend, of a most benevolent disposition, and an honest man".

There, at any rate, was a man who owed all that he had become to the amiable, if muddled, activities of William Hayley; and we can only hope that he was duly grateful.

4

In 1863, when even the Bard of Oxford was dead, Alexander Gilchrist's masterpiece, *The Life of Blake*, appeared. It was only just in time, for Blake was rapidly receding into the shadows.

From Hayley's point of view the book was by no means an unmixed blessing. Gilchrist tried hard to be fair to him; was, for the most part, fair: but he was a man with a considerable sense of humour, and he found himself quite unable to resist the comic possibilities which are so obviously latent in the relationship between his hero and Hayley. One cannot blame him. It would not have been human to resist the temptation: there *is* something irresistibly comic in the close juxtaposition of these two men who were about as different from one another as it is possible for two members of the same species to be. But, unfortunately for Hayley, in order to make perfect his design, Gilchrist decided to cast him as a foil to Blake, as a sort of ludicrous Sancho Panza to the spiritual Quixote whose portrait he was drawing; and, in so doing, I believe he threw the real figure of the man something out of perspective, and falsified somewhat the relationship which I have tried, in earlier pages, to reconstruct.

Hayley, of course, in relation to Blake, was a comic figure; and Gilchrist, as he composed his picture along these lines, naturally did nothing to minimise his comic possibilities. But it was not the whole truth. He failed, for instance, to make it at all clear that, when the two first met, Hayley had by no means recovered from the crushing impact of the double loss of Tom and Cowper; and he did not, likewise, give a true picture of the complicated financial distresses which, at the time, still afflicted Blake's patron. He gave us instead, and very amusingly, a simplified figure of a wealthy dilettante, pompous and self-satisfied. This was an undue simplification, though, in the main, it must be insisted that his version was not unkindly. That was left for others who built upon the foundations he had laid, and who, carried away by their admiration of Blake, and by Blake's scarifying epigrams, did not take the trouble to read carefully what he had written:[5]

> Hayley the valued friend of Gibbon in one generation, of Cowper in the next, whose reputation, like many another reputation then and since, was for a time in excess of his literary deservings, has since been, even from a literary point of view, just as disproportionately despised—sneered at with excess of rigour. By Allan Cunningham he is never mentioned, in connection with Blake or Romney, but to be injuriously spoken of, and the worst construction put upon his motives. This he does, swayed by the gratuitous assertions of Romney's too acrimonious son. . . .
>
> As a poet, Hayley was no worse, if little better, than his compeers; Cowper and Burns standing, of course, apart. One must judge him not as a literary man, but as a literary country gentleman; an amateur, whose words flowed a thousand times faster than his thoughts. His *Life of Cowper* was one of the earliest and best examples in that modern school of biography wherein authentic letters form the basis and the hero draws his own portrait. . . .
>
> If Hayley was always romancing, as it were, which his position in life allowed; always living in a fool's paradise of ever-dispelled, ever-renewed self-deceptions about the commonest trifles; seeing all men and things

athwart a fog of amiability; it was not in the main a worse world than common, and sometimes it was a useful life to others. The pension his bustling energy obtained for Cowper outweighs many an absurdity and inanity. He was surely an endurable specimen, for variety's sake, among corn-law and game-preserving squires. A sincere, if conventional love of literature, independence of the great world, and indifference to worldly distinctions, are, after all, not criminal foibles. Pertinacious, wrong-headed, and often foolish in his actions; weakly greedy of applause, as ready to lavish it; prone to exaggeration of word or thought; without reticence: he was also an agreeable companion, really kind-hearted and generous; though vanity mixed itself with all he did; for ever going out of his way to befriend someone, to set in motion some well-intended, ill-considered scheme. For Blake, let us remember, to the hermit's honour, Hayley continued to entertain unfeigned respect. And the self-tutored wilful visionary must have been a startling phenomenon to so conventional a mind. During the artist's residence at Felpham his literary friend was constantly on the alert to advance his fortunes.

This, besides being acute, is not unhandsome; and if it had been left at that, no reasonable man could have taken exception to the picture.

But it was not left at that. Five years after the publication of Gilchrist's book, the brilliant if erratic pen of Algernon Charles Swinburne entered the fray, with his *William Blake, a Critical Essay*. This study, just and over-just as it was to Blake, bore uncommonly hard on the wretched Hayley; and especially hard when one reflects that for Swinburne's devastating strictures there was really no further evidence than what had already been set down in temperate fairness by Gilchrist. Swinburne, however, was a partizan; he liked white to be white, and black to be black; and he was also a master of the art of invective. No one who has a feeling for vigorous English can fail to relish such an image as: "While a grazing public straightened its bovine neck and steadied its flickering eyelids to look up between whiles, with the day's damp fodder drooping half-chewed from its relaxed jaw, at some dim sick planet of the Mason system, there was a poet, alive if obscure, who had eyes to behold"; or would wish to dispute the felicity of such a phrase as "the rancid flavour of rotten dance-roses and mouldy musk" to describe the trifling poesies of Tom Moore.

Yet, for all this, it was only now that the chorus of detraction against the unhappy Hayley, which has not ceased to the present day to swell ever louder, was at last in full cry; as we find the biting pen of the ferocious little poet etching such memorable, if highly misleading, pictures as the following:

Hayley was ready enough to cage and exhibit among the flock of tame geese which composed his troop of swans this bird of foreign feather; and until the eagle's beak and claws came into play under sharp provocation, the Felpham coop and farmyard were duly dignified by his presence and behaviour as "a tame villatic fowl". The master bantam-cock of the hen-roost in person fluttered and cackled round him with assiduous if perplexed patronage. . . . Let a compassionate amateur of human poultry imagine what confusion must by this time have been reigning in the poor hen-roost and dove-cote of Eartham! [which should, of course, read Felpham.]

And, finally, commenting upon the couplet which Blake wrote on Hayley's birth, Swinburne administers what he conceives to be the *coup de grâce*:

> With this couplet tied to his tail, the ghost of Hayley may perhaps run further than his own strength of wind or speed of foot would naturally have carried him: with this hook in his nose, he may be led by "his good Blake" some way towards the temple of memory.

Well, so it began, and so it has continued. The partizans of William Blake are a curious race. They appear to think that, because Hayley was an infinitely lesser man than their hero, and because, at times, he certainly got very much on their hero's nerves, they are, in some peculiar fashion, elevating Blake's stature by depressing that of Hayley. They forget, I think, that, for all his shortcomings, he was in some respects as good a friend as Blake ever had, and they forget also that, by representing him as a mean and stupid fool, they are, at the same time, misrepresenting Blake and rejecting all the evidence which shows quite clearly that, for long periods, he got on very well with Hayley, and even relished his society.

It is needless to multiply instances. The same adjectives, with monotonous iteration, tramp their way across the countless pages which, of late years, have been written by the hagiographers of William Blake: for Hayley they are—"feeble, bustling, self-satisfied, sentimental, insensitive"; while Blake is "tethered and tied" by an "irksome patronage". Miss Mona Wilson goes so far as to say that Hayley treated Blake "little better than a hired companion". Perhaps the most surprising creation I have come across in this kind is that of one M. Jourdain,[6] who, helping herself to a phrase of Horace Walpole's, remarks that "Hayley was a good-natured, harmless little soul, more like a silver penny than a genius".

There I must leave it, since the criticism touches a sublimity of meaninglessness. Hayley himself certainly never laid claim to being a genius, and I have yet to hear of anyone who has done so on his behalf.

To-day, of course, when he leaves the protecting shadow of Blake, his situation is desperate. It is indeed ironical that it should have been Blake, whom he regarded with affection but without much comprehension (as I think his letter to Lady Hesketh of July 15, 1802, previously quoted, makes clear), who, in the end, should prove both his salvation and his undoing. Blake is a very great man; of the greatest; but that, just now, is by the way, since here the last word is not with Blake. That is the prerogative of another, not much regarded now, but still in his own right a great man and a great writer. It is Cowper's: who, in life, accepted Hayley's friendship with delight, and, in death, owes much of his celebrity to the exertions of his friend. This, alone and unsupported, is proof enough, and more than enough, that Hayley was by no means the zany he is now represented.

The wheel comes full circle. Twice, as we have seen, Hayley "endeavoured to serve his friend". Yet a third time he served him well when he rendered his letters and his unpublished poems safe for posterity. Now it is Cowper's turn. Their reputations are too closely intertwined for them to be separated; and Hayley cannot be destroyed until Cowper is destroyed. That will not be to-morrow.

Hayley, I think, would have been well content that the last word of his *Life* should be the name of Cowper.

Woodbury, 1949–51.

LIST OF THE PRINCIPAL SOURCES

(*The most important items are starred*)

I. Hayley's own Works

*Poems and plays. London, T. Cadell, 1785. 6v., 8o.

A philosophical, historical, and moral essay on old maids. By a friend to the sisterhood. London, T. Cadell, 1785. 3v., 8o. [Anonymous]

*The life, and posthumous writings, of William Cowper, Esqr. A new and enlarged edition. Chichester, printed by J. Seagrave, for J. Johnson, London, 1806. 4v., 8o.

Ballads, by William Hayley, Esq. founded on anecdotes relating to animals, with prints, designed and engraved by William Blake. Chichester, printed by J. Seagrave, for Richard Phillips, London, 1805. 8o.

*The life of George Romney, Esq. Chichester, printed by W. Mason, for T. Payne, London, 1809. 4o.

*Memoirs of the life and writings of William Hayley, Esq. the friend and biographer of Cowper, written by himself. With extracts from his private correspondence and unpublished poetry. And memoirs of his son Thomas Alphonso Hayley, the young sculptor. Edited by John Johnson, LL.D. London, H. Colburn, 1823. 2v., 4o.

II. Other Sources

Note. Reference is made in the Notes hereafter by the catch-words printed in italics before each title. The place of publication is London unless otherwise stated. Unpublished items marked †.

†*B.M.* British Museum, Additional Manuscripts, as under:
  29300X [Hayley's recommendation of Seagrave]
  *30803A, B [Lady Hesketh's correspondence with Hayley]
  *30805 [Letters to and from Hayley (Cowper, Romney, Hersee, Mrs. Opie, et al.)]
  34887 [Hayley's correspondence with Lord Sheffield over the Gibbon Papers]
  38734 [Huskisson's correspondence with Hayley]
  *38887 ['Two Memorials of Hayley's Endeavours to serve His friend Cowper']
  39168 [Hayley's letter to Pitt]
  *39673 [Correspondence between Hayley and Cowper]
  39780-1-9 [Correspondence with Flaxman]

Brightwell. Memorials of the life of Amelia Opie, by Cecilia Lucy Brightwell. 2nd ed. Norwich, 1854.

*Cary. Lives of the English poets, from Johnson to Kirke White, designed as a continuation of Johnson's Lives. By the late Rev. Henry Francis Cary. 1846.

Cecil. The Stricken Deer. By Lord David Cecil. 1929. [Biography of William Cowper.]

Chapman. Jane Austen: facts and problems. By R. W. Chapman. Oxford, 1948.

Coleridge. The complete poetical works of Samuel Taylor Coleridge. Edited by Ernest Hartley Coleridge. 2v., Oxford, 1912.

**Cornhill, 1913*. How Cowper got his pension. By H. Rowlands S. Coldicott. (Cornhill Magazine, new series, vol. 34, pp. 493–507.)

**Cornhill, 1914*. Siste, viator! Choice epitaphs from the pen of William Hayley. By H. Rowlands S. Coldicott. (Ibid., vol. 37, pp. 399–409.)

Dally, 1828. Bognor, Arundel and Littlehampton guide. [By R. Dally.] Chichester, 1828.

Dally, 1831. The Chichester guide. By Richard Dally. Chichester, 1831.

Dowden. Essays modern and Elizabethan. By Edward Dowden. 1910. [Pp. 151–180: Cowper and William Hayley.]

Ellis & Yeats. The works of William Blake, poetic, symbolic, and critical: Edited by E. J. Ellis and W. B. Yeats. 3v., 1893.

Engleheart. George Engleheart, 1750–1829, miniature painter to George III. By George C. Williamson and Henry L. D. Engleheart. 1902.

Farington. The Farington diary. By Joseph Farington, R.A. Edited by James Greig. Vol. 1, 2. 1922–3.

†*Fitzwilliam*. Manuscript copy of Hayley's will, in Fitzwilliam Museum, Cambridge.

G.M. The Gentleman's Magazine; especially Hayley's obituary, vol. 90, part 2, 1820, pp. 469–70, and review of his Memoirs, vol. 93, part 1, 1823, pp. 538–9.

Gibbon. The miscellaneous works of Edward Gibbon, Esq. With memoirs of his life and writings, composed by himself. [Edited by] John, Lord Sheffield. A new edition. 5v., 1814.

*Gilchrist. Life of William Blake. By Alexander Gilchrist. 1942. [Reprint of 2nd edition, vol. 1, edited by Ruthven Todd.]

Godwin. William Godwin: his friends and contemporaries. By C. Kegan Paul. 2v., 1876.

Guide, 1859. The visitors' guide to Bognor and its vicinity. Bognor, 1859.

Hunt. The autobiography of Leigh Hunt. With an introduction by Edmund Blunden. 1928.

*_John Romney_. Memoirs of the life and works of George Romney. By the Rev. John Romney, B.D. 1830.

Johnsonian Miscellanies. Johnsonian miscellanies. Arranged and edited by George Birkbeck Hill. 2v., Oxford, 1897. [Vol. 2, pp. 419–22: Anecdotes by Mrs. Rose.]

*_Keynes_. Poetry and prose of William Blake. Edited by Geoffrey Keynes. Nonesuch Press, 1927.

King. The translator of Dante: the life, work and friendships of Henry Francis Cary (1772–1844). By R. W. King. 1925.

Lockhart. Memoirs of the life of Sir Walter Scott, Bart. [By J. G. Lockhart.] 7v., Edinburgh, London, 1837–8.

*_Lower_. The worthies of Sussex. By Mark Antony Lower. Lewes, 1865.

Lucas. A Swan and her friends. By E. V. Lucas. 1907. [Biography of Anna Seward.]

Macaulay. [Macaulay's article on William Pitt the Younger in Encyclopaedia Britannica, 8th ed., 1859, many times reprinted.]

Maxwell. George Romney. By Sir Herbert Maxwell. 1902.

Memorials. Memorials of old Sussex, edited by Percy D. Mundy. 1909. [Hayley and Blake at Felpham, by E. Sage; Literary associations, by M. Jourdain.]

Menzies-Wilson & Lloyd. Amelia: the tale of a plain friend. By Jacobine Menzies-Wilson and Helen Lloyd. 1937. [Biography of Amelia Opie.]

_N. & Q., 1921_. A letter of William Hayley [to William Hersee]. (Contributed by C. W. Clark Durant.) (Notes & Queries, 12th series, vol. 9, pp. 167–8.)

_N. & Q., 1926_. Blake's 'Heads of the poets', by K. Povey. (Notes & Queries, vol. 151, pp. 57–8.)

†_Olney_. Letter from Hayley to Thomas Cadell, April 12, 1793, in Cowper Museum, Olney.

*_Quarterly_. [Review of Hayley's Memoirs, by Robert Southey.] (Quarterly Review, vol. 31, 1825, pp. 263–311.)

Redgrave. A century of British painters. By R. and S. Redgrave. New edition. 1947.

Review of English Studies. Vol. 10, 1934, pp. 417–427: Cowper and Lady Austen, by Kenneth Povey.

—— Vol. 15, 1939, pp. 392–400: The banishment of Lady Austen, by Kenneth Povey.

Rossetti. The poetical works of William Blake, lyrical and miscellaneous. Edited, with a prefatory memoir, by William Michael Rossetti. (Aldine Edition.) 1874.

*_S.C.M. Blake_. William Blake in Sussex. By Kenneth Povey. (Sussex County Magazine, vol. 1, Eastbourne, 1927, pp. 385–90.)

S.C.M. Flaxman. John Flaxman's monuments in Sussex churches. By Kenneth Povey. (ibid., vol. 2, 1928, pp. 102–7.)

S.C.M. Hersee. The poet of Coldwaltham. By Kenneth Povey. (ibid., vol. 1, 1927, pp. 481–4.)

S.C.M. Marsh. Blake and "the bard of Oxford". [Signed K.P., i.e. K. Povey.] (ibid., vol. 1, 1927, p. 391.)

S.C.M. Opie. Amelia and the Hermit. By Kenneth Povey. (ibid., vol. 3, 1929, pp. 37–44.)

S.C.M. Sockett. The rise of Thomas Sockett. By Kenneth Povey. (ibid., vol. 2, 1928, pp. 38–40.)

S.C.M. Trial. The case of Rex v Blake. By Kenneth Povey. (ibid., vol. 3, 1929, pp. 314–7.)

Sampson. The poetical works of William Blake. Edited by John Sampson. Oxford University Press, 1913.

Scott's Letter-Books. The private Letter-Books of Sir Walter Scott. Edited by Wilfred Partington. 1930.

Scott's Post-Bag. Sir Walter's post-bag: more stories and side-lights from his unpublished Letter-Books. Written & selected by Wilfred Partington. 1932.

Seward: Letters. Letters of Anna Seward: written between the years 1784 and 1807. 6v., Edinburgh, 1811.

Seward: Poems. The poetical works of Anna Seward; with extracts from her literary correspondence. Edited by Walter Scott, Esq. 3v., Edinburgh, 1810.

Sitwell. Narrative pictures. By Sacheverell Sitwell. 1937.

Southey's Cowper. The works of William Cowper, Esq. Comprising his poems, correspondence, and translations. With a life of the author, by the editor, Robert Southey, Esq. 15v., 1835–7.

Southey's Letters. Letters of Robert Southey. [Edited] by M. H. Fitzgerald. 1912.

Swinburne. William Blake: a critical essay. By Algernon Charles Swinburne. 1868.

Symons. The romantic movement in English poetry. By Arthur Symons. 1909.

T.L.S. "The Lady of Lavant", by K. Povey. (Times Literary Supplement, 1926, p. 782.) [Miss Poole.]

Teedon. The diary of Samuel Teedon. Edited by Thomas Wright of Olney. 1902.

Tooke. Memoirs of John Horne Tooke. By Alexander Stephens. 2v., 1813.

Walpole. The letters of Horace Walpole. Edited by Mrs. Paget Toynbee. 19v., Oxford, 1903–25.

Ward & Roberts. Romney: a biographical and critical essay with a catalogue raisonné of his works. By Humphry Ward and W. Roberts. 2v., 1904.

Wilson. The life of William Blake. By Mona Wilson. 1932.

NOTES

Chapter I
1. *Southey's Letters* p57.
2. *Scott's Letter-Books.*

Chapter II
1. *Lower.*
2. *B.M.Add* 39673.
3. *Quarterly.*
4. *G.M.* Jan. 1763.

Chapter III
1. *Dally, 1831.*

Chapter IV
1. *Maxwell* p72.
2. *Farington* VI, p259.

Chapter V
1. *Scott's Post-Bag.*
2. *Farington* VI, p259.
3. *European Magazine*, v32, p359.
4. *Scott's Letter-Books.*
5. *Seward: Poems.*
6. *Gibbon*, letter July 3, 1782.
7. *Seward: Letters.*

Chapter VI
1. *B.M. Add* 39780, f33.
2. *Johnsonian Miscellanies.*
3. *Gibbon.*
4. *Seward: Letters.*
5. *Coleridge* p1139.
6. *Autobiography of Sir S. Egerton Brydges*, v2, p286.

Chapter VII
1. *Farington*, VI, p255.*n.*
2. *John Romney.*
3. *Maxwell* p92.
4. *Ibid.* p132.
5. *Ibid.* p129.

Chapter VIII
1. *Wilson.*
2. *Seward: Letters.*
3. See *Le Voyage du jeune Anacharsis* by J. J. Barthelemy, pubd. 1788.
4. *Lockhart* v2, p277.

Chapter IX
1. *Hunt* pp.271–2.
2. *Cary.*
3. *Cornhill, 1914.*
4. *Quarterly.*
5. *B.M. Add* 39673.
6. *B.M. Add* 30805.
7. *Gilchrist* p125.
8. *Farington* v2.
9. *Seward: Letters.*
10. In the shop of **Mr. H. Day,** Dorchester.
11. *Autobiography of Sir S. Egerton Brydges*, VI, p129.
12. *Chapman.*

Chapter X

1. *Seward: Letters.* 2. *John Romney.*
3. *B.M.Add* 38734.

Chapter XI

1. *B.M.Add* 39673. 2. *Teedon.*
3. *B.M.Add* 38887. 4. *John Romney.*

Chapter XII

1. *B.M.Add* 39673. 2. *B.M.Add* 38734.
3. *B.M.Add* 39168, f76–8. 4. *B.M.Add* 30805.
5. Now in the Olney Museum. 6. *Sitwell.*
7. *Gibbon,* letter Nov. 5, 1793. 8. *B.M.Add* 38887.
9. *Chapman.*

Chapter XIII

1. *Seward: Letters.* 2. *B.M.Add* 34887, v14.
3. *S.C.M.Sockett.* 4. *Cary.*

Chapter XIV

1. *Seward: Letters.* 2. *B.M.Add* 30805.
3. *B.M.Add* 39780.

Chapter XV

1. *B.M.Add* 38887. 2. See *Southey's Cowper,* v3, pp.212–14.

Chapter XVI

1. *B.M.Add* 38734. 2. *B.M.Add* 39780.
3. *Keynes.*

Chapter XVII

1. *Seward: Letters.* 2. *B.M.Add* 30803A.
3. *Gilchrist* p129. 4. *Dally, 1828.*
5. *Gilchrist* p125. 6. *Gilchrist, passim.*
7. *Keynes.* 8. *Wilson.*
9. *B.M.Add* 30803A.

Chapter XVIII

1. *Gilchrist* p133. 2. *Ibid.* p379.
3. *Ibid.* p141. 4. Information supplied by the Manchester City Art Gallery.
5. *N. & Q. 1926,* v151, pp.57–8. 6. *Gilchrist* p140.
7. *Ibid.* p141. 8. *Ibid.* p142.
9. *B.M.Add* 30803A. 10. *Review of English Studies,* v10, 1934.
11. *B.M.Add* 29300X, f139. 12. *Gilchrist* pp.145–6.
13. *T.L.S. 1926,* p782. 14. *Gilchrist* p173.

15. *Ibid.* p379.
16. *B.M.Add* 30803A.
17. *Gilchrist* pp.149–50.
18. *Rossetti* p.lxxxviii.
19. *Gilchrist* pp.156–7.

Chapter XIX

1. *Tooke* v2, p498.
2. *Keynes.*
3. *Gilchrist* p161.
4. *Ibid.* pp.164–5.
5. *B.M.Add* 39780.
6. *S.C.M.Marsh.*
7. *S.C.M.Trial.*
8. *Wilson.*
9. *Gilchrist* pp.166–9.
10. *Keynes.*
11. *B.M.Add* 38887.
12. *Gilchrist* p193.
13. *Ibid.* p174.
14. *Ibid.* p182.
15. *Ibid.* p184.
16. *Ibid.* p187.
17. *Ibid.* p189.
18. *Ibid.* pp.192–3.
19. *Ibid.* pp.194–5.
20. *Keynes.*
21. *Ellis & Yeats* p172.
22. *B.M.Add* 39780, f95.
23. *Sampson* p.xxxiii.
24. *Sampson* p.xxxiv, and p209.

Chapter XX

1. *Seward: Letters.*
2. *B.M.Add* 39780.
3. *B.M.Add* 38734.
4. *B.M.Add* 30803A.
5. *Wilson.*
6. *B.M.Add* 39780.
7. *S.C.M. Hersee.*
8. *N. & Q.1921*, v9, pp.167–8.
9. *B.M.Add* 38734.

Chapter XXI

1. Information from parish register, Southborough, Kent.
2. *Engleheart.*
3. *Godwin*, v2, pp.188–9.
4. *B.M.Add* 39780.
5. *B.M.Add* 30805.
6. *Quarterly.*
7. *Lower* p266.
8. *B.M.Add* 39780.
9. *S.C.M.Opie.*
10. *B.M.Add* 30805.
11. *Menzies-Wilson & Lloyd.*
12. *Brightwell.*
13. *S.C.M.Hersee.*

Chapter XXII

1. Letter formerly with Mr. Kenneth Povey.
2. *King.*
3. *Fitzwilliam.*
4. *Cary, King.*
5. *Cary.*

Chapter XXIII

1. *Quarterly.*
2. *Seward: Letters.*
3. *Southey's Letters* p377.
4. *S.C.M.Sockett.*
5. *Gilchrist* pp.135–6.
6. *Memorials.*

INDEX

Note.—In this index "H." is used as an abbreviation for William Hayley, "TH." for Thomas Alphonso Hayley, and "E." for Eartham. Hayley's writings are listed together, after his name.

Adamo of Andreini, 162, 165
Aiton, William, curator of Kew Gardens, 122-3, 185, 206, 245
Althorp, 174-5
Anonymous letter-writers, 40, 134-5, 348
Araucana, The, of Ercilla, 124
Arcadia, The, of Sir Philip Sidney, 32
Ariosto, 122, 130
Ashburnham, Sir William, Bishop of Chichester, 41-2
Austen, Jane, 135, 178
Austen, Lady, 146, 253, 255, 269
Austin, Dr., 96, 140, 152, 171
Autobiography of Edward Gibbon, 83, 187-8
Aylward, Theodore, musician, 45, 269

BAGE, ROBERT, NOVELIST, 210
Bailey, John, farmer, 119-20
Ball, Elizabeth (Mrs. William Hayley I), 35, 39, 129, 131; courted by H., 40-1; marries, 41; signs of temperament, 44, 91; marriage a failure, 61; character, 62-66; alleged circumstances of birth, 65; fortune, 66; visits Bath, 66-7, 69, 72; translates *Essays on Friendship and Old Age,* 68; music-lessons, 69; attempted separation, 91; at Eartham, 101; separated, 109-11; attempts to return, 117, 162; restive, 142; pays tribute to H., 164; revolts, 185; returns to London, 186, 196; publishes *The Triumph of Acquaintance over Friendship,* 186; final rupture with H., 193, 195; dies, 228; epitaph, 230
 Letters to H. quoted: 41, 72, 73, 74, 109, 142-3, 163-4
— Margaret, her mother, 35, 41, 65, 88, 345
— the Very Revd. Thomas, Dean of Chichester, 35, 41, 44, 65, 88, 345
— monument in Chichester Cathedral, 78
Barlow, Joel, American poet, 144
Barnard's Inn, 105, 108
Barnet, *The Mitre,* 161
Bath, 47, 59, 66, 69, 72, 316
Bath Easton vase, the, 66-7, 72
Batty, Dr. "physician of insanity," 65
Beadon, Dr., Bishop of Gloucester, 221, 222
Beau, spaniel, 161, 166, 266; stuffed, 208
Bedlam, 198
Beke, Margaret, H.'s housekeeper, 270, 297, 337, 345
Bentinck Street (Gibbon's house), 81, 82

Beridge, Dr. and Mrs., of Derby, 37, 38-9, 41, 46, 47, 53, 69, 91-2, 109
Betts, W.A.B., 114
— Miss, mother of TH., 61, 65-6, 77, 93, 104, 338
— Sarah, 30, 32, 49, 50, 61, 74, 87, 104, 143; on Gibbon, 67, 108; painted by Romney, 143; epitaph, 122
Biographers, H. on, 231
Blake, Catherine, 254, 262, 278-9, 286, 293, 294, 302-3, 307
Blake, William, 18, 22, 56, 198, 241, 247, 252, 257-8, 270, 276, 316, 326, 352, 352-6; *Triumphs of Temper* inscribed for, 129, 262; first meeting with TH.?, 197, 261; portrait of TH., 248; visits Felpham, 253-4; settles there, 254; his condition in 1800, 258-9, 263; mechanics of his removal, 259-60, 263; earlier relations with H., 260-1; mood on arrival, 260-1; *Little Tom the Sailor,* 264; Heads of the Poets, 265-6; miniature painting, 267; H.'s *Ballads,* 271, 277; *Life of Cowper,* 272, 276, 296; *Triumphs of Temper,* 272, 279, 286; learns Greek, 273, 275-6, 309; visits Miss Poole, 274-5; meets Johnson, 275; paints panels for Yaxham Rectory, 275; Designs for Blair's *Grave,* 275, 303-4, 306, 307; ill-health, 277, 279, 285-7; relations with H., 277, 279-83; opinion of H., 281-2, 287-8, 295, 300, 308-10; opinion of *Ballads,* 286-7, 304; resolved to leave Felpham, 286; H.'s "genteel ignorance", 288; on Klopstock, 289; on Edward Marsh, 290; affray with Schofield, 291-6; leaves Felpham, 295; response to H's. solicitude, 295-6; *Life of Romney,* 296, 300, 302, 305; trial in Chichester, 297-8; on Samuel Rose, 299; on gratitude, 301; on *Triumphs on Music,* 303; on Caroline Watson's engraving of Cowper, 303, 305; last letter to H., 304-5; 308; H. ceases to use his work, 305, 307; *The Examiner* attacks, 306, 307; his bitterness, 308-10
 Letters quoted: to James Blake, 285-7; to Butts, 267, 272, 277, 279-80, 281, 287-8, 295; to Flaxman, 264; to Mrs. Flaxman, 263; to H., 261, 262, 267, 296, 301, 302, 303, 304-5
 Works: Epigrams on H., 18-19, 307-10, 353, 355; *Jerusalem,* 306-7; *Milton,* 281-2; *Poetical Sketches,* 260-1, 309
 Opinions of Blake: Flaxman's, 260; Hayley's, 262, 278-9, 280; Lady Hesketh's, 316; Romney's, 260; W. M. Rossetti's, 280
Bloomfield, Robert, 318, 322
Bognor, 255, 329, 345
Boltby, Mr., animal painter, 210

365

Bonaparte, Napoleon, 238, 256, 292, 293-4, 330
Boswell, James, 21-2, 68, 71, 72
Boydell, Alderman, 101, 144, 145, 304
Brighton, 81, 138, 164, 233, 333
Bristol, 27, 47
Brotherton, Mr., H.'s drawing-master, 36
Brown, Mr., artist, 341, 345
Bruno, pony ridden by Blake, 175, 274-5
Buckingham Street, Fitzroy Square (Flaxman's house), 192
Bunce, Samuel (Palladio), architect, 200, 203, 204, 205, 208, 209, 211, 212-13, 215, 227, 231, 232, 238, 244, 245, 246, 248
Burke, Edmund, 140, 171
Butts, Thomas, senr., 259, 291
Byron, Lord, 122; on H., 19, 312

CADELL, THOMAS, PUBLISHER, 82, 87, 89, 107, 136, 172
Canterbury, Archbishop of, 115-16
Cape St. Vincent, battle of, 211; effect on H., 212
Carter, Mrs. Elizabeth, 135
Carwardine, Henry, 94, 120, 140
— Revd. Thomas, 94, 107, 120, 137, 138, 159
Cary, Revd. Henry Francis, 72, 113, 114, 124, 125, 327, 343, 345, 352; at Eartham, 189; on H., 350; on H's. tragedies, 128
Castle Street, Cavendish Square (Romney's house), 56
Charlotte, Princess, visits H., 318
Chichester, 24, 35
— All Saint's Church, H. christened at, 25
— Cathedral, H. married in, 41
— Deanery, 25, 40
— Guildhall, 297
— Priory Park, Dr. Guy's monument in, 297
— The Pallant, 26
Cipriani, Giovanni, artist, 46
Clarke, Revd. James Stanier, 177-8, 226
Clyfford, H's. college-friend, 37, 52-3, 102, 119
Cock, Pte., First Dragoons, 293-4
Cocking, Mr., of Kendal, 232
Colburn, Henry, publisher, 7, 327
Coleridge, Samuel Taylor, 20, 21, 22, 85
Collins, William, cenotaph in Chichester Cathedral, 79, 197, 235
Colman, George, the elder, 44, 89, 103
Constantinople, 24, 26, 105
Cook, Capt. James, 46, 69
Cotton, Dr., of St. Alban's, 58, 271
Courtenay, Mrs. Catherine, 125, 158, 165, 184
Covent Garden Theatre, 102, 118-19
Cowper, General, 161, 167
Cowper, William, 19, 22, 33, 37, 58, 125-6, 144, 265, 266, 340, 353, 356; his condition in 1792, 146; at Weston, 150; his finances, 152-3; portrait by Abbott, 160; "hunted by spiritual hounds", 161; journey to Eartham, 161-2; at Eartham, 51, 52, 157, 162; painted by Romney, 164; described by H., 165; return to Weston, 167; sonnet to Romney, 168; laudanum, 173; collapse, 181, 183; pensioned, 181; to Norfolk, 189; false hopes, 201, 207; letter to H., 217; H's. "Vision", 218; his reaction, 219; the letters, 221-3; his diary, 224; death, 248

His translations of Milton, 272; monument at Dereham, 276; reception of H's. *Life*, 284; discovery of *Yardley Oak*, 299; *The Castaway*, 299; lost memorials, 330
Letters quoted: to Mrs. Courtenay, 51; to Greatheed, 162; to H., 147, 154, 156-7, 160-1, 168, 172. 217; to Lady Hesketh, 146-7, 151, 152, 166; to Hurdis, 166; to Johnson, 150
Opinions of Cowper: Blake's, 272; Romney's, 165; Anna Seward's, 71
Works: *Homer*, 146, 173, 175, 176, 202, 224, 247, 273, 275; *Milton*, 146, 148, 165, 287, 313, 316, 323, 324, 326
Cunningham, Allan, 353

DANDELION, FARM OF, NR. MARGATE, 45
Dante, 124, 130, 189, 265, 266, 273, 345
Darwin, Dr. Erasmus, 22, 69, 70, 111, 156, 259; his *Botanic Garden*, 112; Anna Seward on this, 71
David, J. Louis, 138
Decline and Fall of the Roman Empire, 58, 67, 83, 107, 108
Derby, 47, 69, 111; Mrs. Hayley I at, 186
Derby archers, 142-3
Detroit, fort of, 47
Devonshire, Duchess of, 82, 226
Doctors' Commons, proceedings in, 327, 339-40, 344
Dodsley, publisher, 69, 87
Donegall, Marchioness of, and her sister, Maria, 227, 237, 311
Drury Lane Theatre, 118-19
Duncton, Sussex, 162

Eartham, by Percy Lubbock, 333n.
Earl's Colne, Essex, 120
Eartham, Christmas festivities at, 119
— *George Inn*, 51, 204
— House, purchased, 26; rendered habitable, 48; to-day, 51-2; new library, 78, 312; project of letting, 200, 227, 242-3, 254; sold, 255
— riding-house at, 52, 97, 105
— St. Margaret's Church, 27, 51; monument to TH. in, 289-90
— summer-house at, 52, 202
Edinburgh, 38-9
Egremont, Edward O'Brien Wyndham, 3rd Earl of, 79, 94-5, 177, 196, 205, 206, 209, 210, 267
Eidouranion, The, 110
Electrical machines, 87, 96, 151-2, 156-7, 162, 165, 303
Engleheart, George, painter, 324
— N.B., lawyer, 344
Ercilla, 124, 265, 315
Erskine, Thomas (later first Baron), 194
Eton, 33-4

FAGG, SIR ROBERT, 26
Felpham, 44, 142, 231, 253-4, 255-8; Blake on, 263, 267, 281, 303; its opinion of H., 327, 330-1

Felpham—*continued*.
— Amicable Club of, 330
— blacksmith, epitaph on, 123
— Church, 347
— *Fox Inn*, 257
— Marine Turret, 200, 204, 206, 211, 254, 255; rustic arcade, 209, 214; outer walls, 211, 256, 327; foundation-stone laid, 212-13; lay-out of library, 214-15; other details, 215, 216, 312, 325, 335; "Druidical seat", 227; to-day, 256-7
Fido, TH.'s spaniel, 197, 204, 206
Flaxman, John, R.A., 20, 51, 65, 78-9, 136, 191-2, 199, 209, 210, 227, 232, 235, 297, 308, 309, 326, 352; at Eartham, 78, 197; on Eartham, 79; in Rome, 79, 109; returns, 190; takes TH. as apprentice, 191-2; meets Blake, 191, 260; TH.'s opinion of him, 196; Collins's cenotaph, 197; Mary Lushington's monument, 236, 243; his views on TH., 226, on Blake, 260, on Mrs. Lushington, 237; medallion of TH., 248; TH.'s death mask, 250; Cowper's monument, 276; monument to TH., 289-90; seeks "testimony" from H., 314
    Letters quoted: to H, 192, 226, 235, 236, 306, 314; to TH., 243-4
— Maria, his sister, 272
— Mrs. Nancy (Anna), his wife, 192, 196, 206, 209, 289, 326, 329
Ford Abbey, near Crewkerne, 47
Fox, Charles James, 285
Fuseli, Henry, R.A., 101, 144, 279-80; his Milton Gallery, 243, 287

GARRICK, DAVID, 43
Genlis, Comtesse de, 125, 138, 143, 199, 238, 273, 344
George III, King, 110, 156, 210, 285, 300, 313
German translations of H's. works, 289
Gibbon, Edward, 20, 22, 31, 58, 60, 76, 79-83, 94, 107-8, 133, 136, 173, 177, 323; his schooldays, 29; at Bath, 66; loses his post, 74; read to by H., 105-7; his views on H's. works, 76, 81, 82, 105; at Althorp, 174; death, 179; last words, 182; religious beliefs, 183; epitaph, 183
    His posthumous papers, 183, 187-8; H's. opinion of his conversation, 173, his philosophy, 188, his history, 210 (*see also* Betts, Sarah).
Gibraltar, the Rock of, 102-3
Gifford, William, 121, 350
Gilchrist's, Alexander, *Life of William Blake*, 19, 254n., 262, 264, 266, 274, 291, 298, 352-4
Glasgow, 39
Glover, "Leonidas", 72
Godfrey, Capt. John, H's. cousin, 208, 213, 232-3, 244, 248, 314, 315, 338, 344
— Misses, his daughters, 329, 335
Godwin, William, at the Turret, 325
Gooch, Dr., Bishop of Ely, 28
Gordon Riots, The, 60
Governess, The French, 137, 139-40
Gower, Lord (later Marquis of Stafford), 137, 138, 169
Great Queen Street, Lincoln's Inn Fields (H's. house), 38, 43, 110, 260

Greatheed, Revd. Samuel, 146, 150, 184, 268-9, 299; letter quoted, 183-4
Greene, Miss Matilda, 232
Gregory, William, H's. godson, 341, 345
Greuze, Jean-Baptiste, 138
Grinder, Mr., Blake's landlord, 257, 293
Gurneys of Earlham, the, 333, 334, 336, 338-9, 340, 341
Guy, Dr. William, of Chichester, 86, 87, 197, 200, 213, 217, 231, 240, 243, 246, 247, 248, 297, 306, 344; his appearance, 204

HAINES, WILLIAM, ARTIST, 305
Hales, Revd. Stephen, 32-3
Hali, son-in-law of Mahomet, 24
Hamilton, Lady, 97-100, 306; poses for "Sensibility", 97-8; letter to Romney on Serena, 99-100, 129
— Sir William, 98, 100
Hammond, Harry, parish clerk, 116, 122
Handel, 72, 336, 337
Harlowe, Sarah, H's. paternal grandmother, 25
Harris, Mr. (later Lord Malmesbury), 45
— Mr., manager of Covent Garden, 102-3, 118
Harry, affectionate valet, 111, 127-8, 142
Hastings, Mrs. Warren, 102
Hawkins, Mr., Grecian traveller, 243, 245
Hayley, Mary, H's. mother, *see* Yates, Mary.
— Mrs., I, *see* Ball, Elizabeth.
— Mrs., II, *see* Welford, Mary.
— Thomas, H's. brother, 25, 27, 29, 35
— Thomas, H's. father, 25, 26-7; Southey on, 27
— Thomas, H's. grandfather, Dean of Chichester, 24-5
— Thomas Alphonso, "The Young Sculptor", 51, 52, 268; born, 61; infancy, 73-4; childhood, 92-4; destined for medical career, 96, 137; visits London, 110; writes a play, 110; helps with epitaphs, 120; keeps family books, 142; visits Derby, 142; sees corpse and dances with countess, 143; criticizes Cowper's *Homer*, 173; at school, 175; wishes to hunt, 175, 189; painting-lessons from Wright, 172, 175; consoles Cowper, 185; plays flute, 185; visits Kew, 185; apprenticed to Flaxman, 191-216 *passim*; his studies, 196, 198; drinks tea with Blake?, 197, 261; model for Collins's monument, 197; does medallion of Romney, 197, bust of Minerva, 197, 198, 202, 205; meets Wilkes, 198; paints "Mary and the Two Angels", 198; illness, 199, 203, 213-16; returns to Eartham, 200; has curvature of the spine, 200; visits Wilton and Stonehenge, 204; returns to London, 204; skates, 206; a scene at Flaxman's, 209; his views on animal-painters, 210; offers to fight the French, 211; Druid's head, 212, 216; lays foundation-stone of Turret, 212; models Bunce, 213; his views on riches, 216; ordered home, 216; returns to work, 227; collapse, 232; moves to Felpham, 231, into the Turret, 232; loses use of his legs, 233; remains "suave", 234; alone in the Turret, 235; sufferings, 239; returns to Eartham, 240; draws "Death of Demosthenes", 241, 247, 266; draws Romney fencing, 244; has *Essay on Sculpture* read to him, 246; exhibits fortitude, 246-8; corrects

Hayley, Thomas Alphonso—*continued*.
H's. proofs, 247; models in wax, 247; opium, 248; dies, 248; his character, 249; head painted by Blake, 265, 266; Flaxman's monument, 290 Letters quoted: to H., 209, 210, 211, 238, 239; to Mrs. Hayley, 110, 143; to Mrs. Meyer, 239-40

— William, of Bridgnorth, 24
— William, Dean of Chichester, H's. great-uncle, 24
— William, ancestry, 24; arms, 24; birth, 25; christening, 25; early vicissitudes, 28-9; early education, 29; illness, 30; effects of this, 31-2; addiction to poetry, 32; at Eton, 33-4; interest in theatre, 34; Trinity Hall, 35, 36-7; Frances Page, 35-6, 39-40; first publication, 36; interest in Romance languages, 37, 124-5, 189, 315, 343, 349-50; in painting, 36-7; enters Middle Temple, 37; writing for the theatre, 38, 43-4, 86; tour of Scotland, 38; courting Eliza Ball, 40-1; marries, 41; life in London, 43-8; writing poetry, 44-5, 57-60; ophthalmic afflictions, 46, 74, 86, 117, 148, 303, 328; holiday excursions, 46-8; return to Eartham, 48-9; death of his mother, 49-50; painted by Romney, 53; involved in Gordon Riots, 60; becomes a father, 61; health, 68, 101; money troubles, 69, 74-5, 92, 136, 227, 244, 353; visits Anna Seward, 69; helps Charlotte Smith, 84, 172; transfers his copyrights to Cadell, 87; advises Wright of Derby, 88, Romney, 98, 173-4, 206, his son, 201; his plays produced, 89, 118-19; rising from his horse, 90, 296, 302; "connubial infelicity", 91-2, 101; inception of the Shakespeare Gallery, 101; "The Magical Opera", 102-3; Barnard's Inn, 105; reads to Gibbon, 106; separates from his wife, 109; final meeting with Anna Seward, 111-14; addresses the Archbishop of Canterbury, 115; declines laureateship, 120; discussion of his earlier works, 121-35; lines on himself, 128; earnings, 136; in Paris, 136-9; meets Huskisson, 141-2; purchases cottage at Felpham, 142; his Hebrew valet, 149; at Weston Underwood, 150-4; wins Cowper's confidence, 151-4; Cowper's Pension, 153-81 *passim*; interview with Thurlow, 156; prepares for Cowper's visit, 159-60; remonstrates with Eliza, 162-3; presents his portrait to Cowper, 167; writes to Pitt, 169; Gibbon at Eartham, 173; second journey to Weston, 174; at Althorp, 175; working with Cowper, 175-6; interviews Pitt, 178-9; third visit to Weston, 184; at Sheffield Place, 187; working on Gibbon's papers, 187; takes TH. to Flaxman, 192; final break with Eliza, 195; Collins's epitaph, 197; schemes for Meyer and Rose, 205-7, for Godfrey, 208-9, 213; purchases substitute in the cavalry, 210-11; begins building the Turret, 212; his "Heavenly Vision", 217-25; death of his wife, 228-30; composes funeral sermon, 228; comments on the event, 229; writes her epitaph, 229-30; endeavours to console Mrs. Lushington, 235-8; bestows Eartham on TH., 241-2; in London, 242-3; in despair, 246; notes to the poem on sculpture, 247; death of Cowper, 248; death of TH., 248; another funeral sermon, 250; at Kew, 250; writing biography, 253-5; his condition in 1800, 258; Blake comes to Felpham, 259-63; writes *Little Tom* for him, 264; commissions the Heads, 265; at work on *Life of Cowper*, 268-70; on the *Ballads*, 271, 277; teaches Blake Greek, 273; breakfasts with Miss Poole, 274; designs Cowper's monument, 276; defends Blake from Lady Hesketh, 277-9; reception of *Life of Cowper*, 284-5; his relations with Blake, 289; TH's. monument, 289; stands bail for Blake, 294; procures Rose for his defence, 295; gives evidence at his trial, 298; supersedes him as engraver, 305-6; working in the Turret, 313; new thoughts on matrimony, 317, 320; royal visit, 318; second marriage, 321, 323, 325; second separation, 326-7; his finances, 326; secures advance on his *Memoirs*, 327; grows sociable, 329; final writings, 329; Mrs. Opie's visits, 331-40; old age, 134, 343; last illness, 344-5, 346; his Will, 344-5; death, 346-7; epitaph, 347; Gilchrist's character of him, 353-4; posthumous reputation, 17, 19, 348-56

Characteristics: his abstemiousness, 116, 149, 189, 209, 336; ambiguous reputation, 90, 132, 328, 329, 330-1, 335, 338; appearance, 335; benevolence, 22, 189, 201, 205, 207-8, 208-9, 210, 313, 314, 315, 316, 323, 347, 352; capacity for work, 268, 276, for self-justification, 65, 111, 348, for combining good deeds with personal advantage, 235, 263; disingenuousness, 182; early rising, 203, 205, 217, 336; hopefulness, 201, 216, 219, 244, 248, 321; hospitality, 52, 54, 173; impracticality, 104, 225, 272, 327; independence, 95, 189; intensity, 186, 318; liability to pontificate, 287, to prophesy his end, 119, 163, 192, 272; literary style, 7, 348-9; love of seclusion, 328; modesty, 149; obstinacy, 137, 335; partizanship, 124, 207-8, passion for liberty, 44, 74, 120, 215; patience, 103, 221; pertinacity, 159, 179, 219, 314; political and religious views, 82, 120, 137, 140, 182, 188, 213, 221, 294, 297, 346; religious activities, 46, 189, 327-8, 336; resemblance to cats, 117; resilience, 251, 274; self-complacency, 90, 108, 250, 291, 323; sensibility, 21, 179, 184, 194, 270, 275; taciturnity, alleged, 75; truthfulness, 7; unaccountableness, 151, 224; views on marriage, 42, 196

The biographer, 23, 252, 255, 291, 299, 321, 347; collector of portraits, 316; designer, 200, 206, 214, 276, 326; economist, 116, 142; epitaph-writer, 23, 122-3, 241, 344; scholar, 175, 198, 204; horseman, 296, 301-2, 335; landscape gardener, 312; medical man, 95-6, 116, 143, 214; painter, 37, 47; patron, 22-3, 210, 259, 271, 283, 302, 303, 318-20, 321-2, 341-2; pedagogue, 93, 94-5, 273; sea bather, 96, 166, 167, 197, 205, 227, 232, 233, 335; student of Persian, 47

Letters quoted: to the Archbishop of Canterbury, 115; to Cadell, 172; to Cary, 345-6; to Cowper, 144, 148-9, 154, 156, 167, 168-9, 173, 218; to Flaxman, 207; to Gibbon, 60; to Mrs. Hayley I, 40, 67, 69, 72, 73, 74, 75, 84, 117-18, 142, 157, 163, 164, 165, 184, 185, 187, 192, 193, 195; to TH., 199, 210, 211, 212,

Hayley, William—*continued*.
214, 215, 216, 217, 228-9, 237; to Hersee, 319;
to Lady Hesketh, 220, 221, 225, 252, 262, 268,
277-9, 291-2, 297-8, 314, 315-6; to John
Johnson, 247, 252, 255, 271, 272, 273, 275-6,
276, 277, 284, 299, 311, 312, 316, 324, 326, 330,
341, 343, 344; to Melmoth, 59; to Mrs. Opie,
332-3, 334-5; to Pitt, 170, 177, 180-1; to
Romney, 53-4, 150; to Rose, 184, 220; to
Sadlier, 91-2; to Walter Scott, 64; to Lord
Sheffield, 188, 189; to Lord Thurlow, 158, 176
Principal literary works:
   Epistle on Painting, 57, 58, 123-4
   Epistle to Admiral Keppel, 58
   Elegy to the Bishop of London, 58
   Elegy on Mr. Thornton, 58-9
   Essay on History, 58, 60, 123-4
   Ode to Philanthropy, 60, 123-4
   The Triumphs of Temper, 29, 53, 60, 66, 67, 68, 73, 82, 123-4, 129-32, 243, 331-2
   Essay on Epic Poetry, 57, 69, 73, 75, 123-4, 265, 315
   Plays for a Private Theatre, 86, 88; *Lord Russel*, 89, 127; *Marcella*, 103, 118-19, 127; *The Happy Prescription*, 127; *The Mausoleum*, 127-8; *The Two Connoisseurs*, 82, 89, 127-8
   Poems and Plays, 88, 132, 135; *Ode to the Countess de Genlis*, 125; *to Wright of Derby*, 125; *Receipt for a Tragedy*, 126-7; *Sonnets*, 83, 125,
   Essay on Old Maids, 89-90, 104, 132-5
   Dialogues comparing the styles of Johnson and Chesterfield, 105
   Stanzas for Gibbon's birthday, 107-8
   Centenary Ode on the Glorious Revolution, 108
   The Young Widow, or the History of Cornelia Sedley, 114-15, 132, 349
   Eulogies of Howard, a Vision, 115
   Eudora, 119
   Life of Milton, 144, 145, 165, 168, 173, 174, 182, 338
   The National Advocates, 194
   Elegy on Sir William Jones, 194
   Essay on Sculpture, 194, 198, 206, 209, 213, 231, 232, 233, 240-1, 245, 246, 249, 251-2
   Little Tom the Sailor, 264
   Life of Cowper, 18, 19-20, 151, 252-4, 268, 269-70, 276, 284-5, 288-9, 299, 300, 313, 320, 326, 353
   Ballads founded on Anecdotes relating to Animals, 271, 277, 303
   Triumphs of Music, 300, 303, 311-12
   Stanzas of an English Friend to the Patriots of Spain, 318
   Life of Romney, 291, 300, 313, 314, 316, 321, 323, 351;
   Plays, 323
   Memoirs, 7, 18, 202, 327, 334, 336, 348-9, 351
   Memoirs of TH., 245, 252-3, 276, 289, 290
   Principal projected or unpublished works:
   The Expulsion of the Rod, 33
   The Afflicted Father, 43
   Epic Poem on Magna Charta, 44, 57-9
   Epistle to the King of Poland, 45
   Epistle by the Inca of Quito, 57
   The Trial of the Rock, 103
   Les préjugés abolis, ou l'Anglois juste envers les François, 140

   Two Memorials of Hayley's Endeavours to serve His friend Cowper, 155, 217
   The Art of Choosing a Wife, 198
   Prose work on a naval topic, 212
   Poem on a new constitution for France, 213-14
   The Christian Navigator, 269
   The Loyal Prayer, 300, 302
   The Triumphs of Friendship, 313
   Stanzas to the Secretary of the Board of Ordnance, 314
Haymarket Theatre, 89-90, 103
Haynes, Mrs., miller's wife, 293, 298
Heberden, Dr., 30-1
Heron, Fanny, of Portsmouth, 77
Hersee, William, poet, 318-20, 321-2, 341-2, 345
Hesketh, Lady, 146, 154, 189, 219, 220-5, 252-3, 268, 269, 276, 277, 284-5, 299, 305, 313, 314, 315, 316
   Letters quoted: to H., 219, 220, 221, 223, 224, 268-9, 276, 277-8, 285, 313; to Johnson, 219, 221, 224
Hidalgo, H.'s charger, 197, 206, 275
Hill, Joseph, 153, 269
Hodges, William, R.A., artist and banker, 172-3
Holland, Lord, 124, 315
Holroyd, Maria, 187-8; on Sockett, 188-9
Hood, Tom, 352
Hotham, Sir Richard, hatter, 172, 231, 255
Howard, Henry, R.A., 209, 243, 244, 248
Howard, John, philanthropist, 32, 60, 104-5, 110, 115; projected statue for, 104
Howell, —, H.'s protégé, 77, 82, 87; drowned, 107; Anna Seward on this, 112
Humphry, Ozias, R.A., 56, 130
Hunt, James Henry Leigh, on H., 121
Hunter, Dr. John, 90, 297
Hunter, Prebendary, Dr. Johnson's schoolmaster, 80
Hurdis, Revd. James, poet, 166 *and n.*
Huskisson, William, 141-2, 169-71, 233, 255, 315, 320, 321, 352
"Hyle", 306-7

ILIFFE, ELIZABETH (MRS. WYNDHAM), 95, 209
Irwin, Eyles, poet and humorist, 240
Isola, —, Italian teacher of languages, 36-7

JACKSON, DR. CYRIL, DEAN OF CHRIST CHURCH, OXFORD, 327, 343
Johnson, Revd. John, 7, 146, 160, 161, 174, 217-24, 252-3, 269-70, 272, 275, 276-7, 301-2, 316, 317, 323, 325, 328-9, 340-1, 346, 348, 352; Blake's opinion of, 275; torpidity of, 221, 252, 316
   Letters quoted: to H., 219, 221, 222, 223
— Joseph, publisher, 144, 145, 269, 270, 279, 316
— Dr. Samuel, 21, 30, 105, 128, 226, 267, 290; on *The Triumphs of Temper*, 80; Anna Seward's opinion of, 71, 72; H.'s opinion of, 80
Jones, Lady, widow of Sir William Jones, 194
Joseph, Romney's man-servant, 178-9

KANGAROOS, 210
Kemble, John Philip, 118-19
Kenyon, Lord, Chief Justice, 156, 220, 221, 222, 223, 224

Keppel, Admiral, 58
Kew, Surrey, 103, 114, 185, 201, 206, 210, 214, 250, 324
Kingston-on-Thames, 161, 193; *The Sun Inn*, 167
Kingston Grammar School, 29
Klefekerus, author of *Bibliotheca Eruditorum Praecocium*, 94
Klopstock, F. G., 265, 289
Kneller, Sir Godfrey, 38
"Kox", 296, 306

LA FAYETTE, MARQUIS DE, 214
Lamb, Charles, 31, 113, 132
Lansdowne, Marquis of, 320
Latham, Dr., 214, 216, 228, 238
Leathes, Capt., First Dragoons, 292
Lewisham Church, 236, 237
Lichfield, 69, 72; its effect on H., 73
Lister, Thomas, 72
Long, Dr., surgeon, 53, 68, 102, 201, 212, 228, 238, 239, 243, 260
Long, Mr. Secretary, of the Treasury, 169-71
Longford Castle, nr. Salisbury, 204
Lowth, Dr., Bishop of London, 58
Lushington, Mrs. Paulina, 235-8
Lyme Regis, 47

Madoc, Southey's yearly profits from, 72
Man of Feeling, The, by Henry Mackenzie, 20
Manchester City Art Gallery, 265
Manning, Cardinal, 83
Mansel, Dr., Bishop of Bristol, 70
Marmontel, J. F., 57
Marsh, Revd. Edward Garrard, 290-1, 314
Mason, Chichester printer, 320, 325
— Revd. William, 57, 354; letter to H., 75; meets H., 89; H's. tributes to, 89, 128
"Medical knowledge, uncertainty of", 200, 228, 231, 232, 233, 243
Melmoth, William, poet, 59-60, 66
Metcalfe, William, H's. servant, 275
Meyer, Jeremiah, R.A., miniaturist, 36-7, 40, 46, 53, 102, 103, 105, 107, 114, 324; monument in Kew Church, 103
— Mrs. and family, 103, 114, 185, 201, 202, 204, 232, 233-4, 250, 341
— William, 198, 201, 202, 205, 208, 227, 246, 250, 315, 317, 320
Mid Lavant, Sussex, 274, 286, 298, 302
Middle Temple, 37
Miller, Margaret, H's. maternal grandmother, 27
Millman Place, 2, Bedford Row, scene of Mrs. Hayley I's death, 229
Milton, John, 162, 266
Mine, The, by John Sargent, the elder, 83-4
Miss in her Teens (comedy), 110
More, Hannah, 67-8, 318, 340
Morrison, Capt., adherent of the Great Mogul, 47
Mulberry-tree, planted by H., 235, 257
Mundy, Francis Noel, "bard of Needwood Forest", 71, 91

NELSON, Lord, 233-4, 314
Newton, Revd. John, 146, 255, 269

Newton, William, the Peak Minstrel, 71, 85, 318
Nicol, George, bookseller, 101, 144, 182
Night Thoughts, Young's, 17, 21, 258, 259
Nile, battle of the, 233-4
North, Lord, 82

Octogenaire admirable, Lady Hesketh's, 278, 279
Opie, Mrs. Amelia, 22, 329, 331-40, 341, 344, 345, 347, 352; letters to H., 129, 332, 333, 337-8, 339, 340
Orleans, Duke of, and family, 138-9
Ossian, 21, 71
Otway, Thomas, 265, 266

PAGE, FRANCES, H's. FIRST LOVE, 35-6, 39-40, 41, 317
Pamela (Anne Stéphanie Caroline Sims), 138, 143, 199
Parr, Dr., 71, 183
Paul III, Emperor of Russia, 240
Payne, Roger, bookbinder, 34
— Thomas, the elder, bookseller, 199-200, 212; epitaph, 122
Pembrokeshire, French landing in, 211 *and n*.
Pension, Cowper's, 153-81 *passim*, 185
Perowne, Margaret, Cowper's attendant, 223, 341
Petworth, 95, 173, 198, 204, 206, 209, 216, 226, 352; Sessions at, 294
Pitt, William, the younger, 47-8, 120, 155, 169, 176-7, 178-9, 180-1, 285; Macaulay on, 171
Pocock, Isaac, Romney's disciple, 235, 241
Poole, Harriet, 187-8, 267, 269, 274-5, 276, 298, 302, 305, 306, 311, 313, 326, 329, 330, 336, 344, 352
Porteous, Dr. Beilby, Bishop of London, 221, 222
Portsmouth, 190
Povey, Kenneth, 260, 266, 290
Prince Regent, The, 36, 322, 327

RAIMBACH, ABRAHAM, ENGRAVER, 305, 316
Read, Catherine, artist, 33
Resolution, The, Captain Cook's ship, 46
Richmond, Duke of, 226, 297, 298
Ripley, Surrey, 161
Roberts, Dr., of Eton, 34, 36, 107
Roberts, Sam, Cowper's servant, 161, 223
Robertson, William, historian, on H., 81
Robespierre, Maximilien, 21
Robinson, J. Romney, infant prodigy, 300
Rogers, Samuel, 350
Roland, Madame, *Memoirs* of, 199
Romney, Colonel, 313
— George, 20, 37; first meeting with H., 53; invited to Eartham, 53-4; his early career, 55-6; relations with his family, 55-6, 351; character, 56; H's. influence on him, 55-7, 287, 351; meets Anna Seward, 76; at Eartham, 78, 105, 108, 116, 173, 190, 202-3, 226; paints Gibbon, 82, studies of Serena, 97; his finances, 97; Lady Hamilton, 97-100; Shakespeare Gallery, 101-2, 145; low-spirited or ill, 105, 107, 108, 139, 190, 201, 226; paints Anna Seward, 112; visits France, 137-9; paints TH.

Romney, George—*continued*
as Robin Goodfellow, 143, 230; meets Cowper, 164; his portrait of Cowper, 164, 168, 189, 305, 343, 344; paints Charlotte Smith, 165, 199, 344; paints Egremont family, 197, 204; taken to Mr. Udney's, 201; paints "The Four Friends", 202, self-portrait, 203, 344; "Flaxman modelling the bust of H.", 203, 290, Dr. Guy, 204; visits Wilton and Stonehenge, 204; his opinion of H., 207-8; at inception of the Felpham villa, 212; paints "Tobit and Tobias", 226; his spleen, 227; his valediction of Eartham, 227; retires to the North, 232; invited to Felpham, 232; at Brighton, 233; last visit to Eartham, 241; draws H., and self-portrait in spectacles, 241; final return to North, 244, 289; his "Lear and Cordelia", 302; H's. memorial to him, 311; H's. *Life of*, 98, 291, 316, 323
Letters quoted: to H., 173, 174, 191, 197, 201, 227; to John Romney, 138, 165
— Revd. John, 353; on Lady Hamilton, 97; on H., 202-3, 350-2
Rose, Mrs., and family, 80, 299, 313, 315
— Samuel, 146, 147, 161, 167, 175, 180, 187, 189, 194-5, 198, 220, 232, 243, 269, 270, 272; his gout, 205; defends clergyman, 241; visits Cowper in Norfolk, 244; defends Blake, 295, 297-8; falls ill, 298, 302; dies, 299, 313
Rossetti, Dante Gabriel, 307
— William Michael, 280
Russell, Philadelphia, H's. first schoolmistress, 29
Russell, William, 265

SADLEIR, RICHARD VERNON, OF SOUTHAMPTON, 86, 89, 306, 313, 317, 320
Sainte-Beuve, on *Yardley Oak*, 300
Salisbury, 204
Sargent, John, the elder, poet, 83, 197, 206, 329, 344, 346
— Revd. John, the younger, 83, 346
Saville, Revd. John, Vicar-choral of Lichfield Cathedral, 70, 71, 72, 76
Schofield, John, ex-sergeant First Dragoons, 291-5, 298; his statement in the case of Blake, 293-4
Scott, Sir Walter, 20, 62, 64, 86, 130, 312; on Anna Seward, 113
Seagrave, Joseph, printer, 270, 271, 276, 294, 305, 306, 311, 317, 318
Sense and Sensibility, 135
Seward, Anna, 22, 350; her character, 70-2; meets H., 69; her feeling for him, 71, 113, 187, 326; described by him, 69; visits Eartham, 76; laments her departure, 77; H's. second visit to Lichfield, 111-14; on his *Life of Cowper*, 285; her *Letters*, 7, 332; quoted, 71-2, 77, 112, 113-14, 187; on H's. works, 72, 112; his *Old Maids*, 90; his *Triumphs of Temper*, 130; his *Life of Milton*, 182; his *Triumphs of Music*, 312; his misfortunes, 112-13, 251; his resilience, 251; his style, 349; on Mrs. Hayley I, 63-4, 186, 196; on Southey, 71, 72; on Sargent's *Mine*, 84; on Charlotte Smith, 85; on French governesses, 137; dies, 323

Works: *Elegy on Captain Cook*, 69; *Epistle to H.*, 73; *Letters, see above*; *Louisa*, 111
Shakespeare Gallery, The, 101, 145, 197
Sheffield, Lord, 81, 106, 173, 183, 187-9, 192; his sister, 66
Siddons, Mrs., 72
"Skofeld", 296, 306
Smirke, Robert, R.A., 326
Smith, Adam, his remarks on sculpture, 200
— Mrs. Charlotte, 84-6, 114-15, 163, 199, 314, 319; meets Cowper and Romney, 164-5; in deep waters, 171-2
Sockett, Thomas, 52, 94, 95, 152, 157, 162; with Lord Sheffield, 188, 196; with Lord Egremont, 352
Southampton, 313, 317, 320
Southey, Robert, 20, 21, 22; on H., 20, 124, 327, 350; on his *Memoirs*, 348, 349-50
Spencer, Lord, 174, 177, 179, 180-1, 194
Stanislaus, King of Poland, 45
Steele, Robert, Recorder of Chichester, 347
Steevens, George, 29, 44
Stonehenge, 204, 212, 216
Stothard, Thomas, R.A., 197, 238, 326
Swedenborg, Emanuel, 78
Swinburne, Algernon Charles, his *Essay on Blake*, 19, 280, 354-5

TASSONI, ALESSANDRO, 122, 130
Teddington, Middlesex, 32, 201
Thelassie, or Thalassie, French model, 100
Thornton, John, H's. college-friend, 37, 41, 45, 52, 53, 58, 344; *Elegy* on, 58-9
Thurlow, Lord, 107, 108-9, 153-4, 155, 158-9, 176, 221, 226, 269, 284; his spleen, 227
Tomlins, Elizabeth Sophia, 319
Tooke, John Horne, 194, 284
Trafalgar, battle of, 314
Trinity Hall, Cambridge, 35, 36-8
Trumbal, Sir William, Ambassador in Constantinople, 24

UDNEY, MR. AND MRS. OF TEDDINGTON, 201, 306
Unwin, Mrs., 52, 96, 126, 146, 161, 176; her second stroke, 150; electrical treatment, 152; her fortune, 153; dies, 207; memorial to, 270; epitaph, 273; her portrait, 344
Upmarden, Sussex, 35

Village Curate, The, by James Hurdis, 166 *and n.*

WALKER, ADAM, SCIENTIST, 110 *and n.*, 199, 302
Walpole, Horace, on H's. poetry, 80-1
Warner, Dr. John, 104, 116, 137, 138, 140, 144, 205, 242, 247, 344
Warton, Dr. Joseph, 86, 89, 93, 204, 243
Watson, Caroline, engraver, 202, 303, 305, 306, 314
Watson, Dr. Richard, Bishop of Llandaff, 199, 205, 213, 222-3, 284, 341

Welford, Mary (Mrs. William Hayley II), 320-1, 323-4, 326-7
West, Benjamin, P.R.A., 37, 107
Wickham, Hants., 86, 204
Wilberforce, Samuel, Bishop of Winchester, 83
— William, 220, 221
Wilkes, John, 198
William, ostler at the *Fox*, Felpham, 292-4
Wilton House, 204, 216
Windsor, 107, 201
Wooddeson, Richard, master of Kingston School, 29

Wright, Joseph, A.R.A., of Derby, 47, 53, 69, 88, 110*n*., 172, 175, 227, 258, 340, 344
Wyndham, George (later first Baron Leconfield), 94-5, 199, 207, 215, 352; his heroism, 215

Yardley Oak, 299-300
Yates, Colonel, 25, 27
Yates, Mary (Mrs. Thomas Hayley), H's. mother, 25, 27-8, 49-50, 218; on H's. marriage, 41; epitaph, 50
Yearsley, Mrs., the Bristol milk-woman, 71, 318